I & II PETER AND JUDE

THE NEW TESTAMENT LIBRARY
Current and Forthcoming Titles

Editorial Advisory Board

C. CLIFTON BLACK
M. EUGENE BORING
JOHN T. CARROLL

COMMENTARY SERIES

MATTHEW. BY R. ALAN CULPEPPER, MCAFEE SCHOOL OF THEOLOGY, MERCER UNIVERSITY
MARK. BY M. EUGENE BORING, BRITE DIVINITY SCHOOL, TEXAS CHRISTIAN UNIVERSITY
LUKE. BY JOHN T. CARROLL, UNION PRESBYTERIAN SEMINARY
JOHN. BY MARIANNE MEYE THOMPSON, FULLER THEOLOGICAL SEMINARY
ACTS. BY CARL R. HOLLADAY, CANDLER SCHOOL OF THEOLOGY, EMORY UNIVERSITY
ROMANS. BY BEVERLY ROBERTS GAVENTA, PRINCETON THEOLOGICAL SEMINARY
I CORINTHIANS. BY ALEXANDRA R. BROWN, WASHINGTON & LEE UNIVERSITY
II CORINTHIANS. BY FRANK J. MATERA, THE CATHOLIC UNIVERSITY OF AMERICA
GALATIANS. BY MARTINUS C. DE BOER, VU UNIVERSITY AMSTERDAM
EPHESIANS. BY STEPHEN E. FOWL, LOYOLA COLLEGE
PHILIPPIANS AND PHILEMON. BY CHARLES B. COUSAR, COLUMBIA THEOLOGICAL SEMINARY
COLOSSIANS. BY JERRY L. SUMNEY, LEXINGTON THEOLOGICAL SEMINARY
I & II THESSALONIANS. BY SUSAN EASTMAN, DUKE DIVINITY SCHOOL
I & II TIMOTHY AND TITUS. BY RAYMOND F. COLLINS, THE CATHOLIC UNIVERSITY OF AMERICA
HEBREWS. BY LUKE TIMOTHY JOHNSON, CANDLER SCHOOL OF THEOLOGY, EMORY UNIVERSITY
JAMES. BY REINHARD FELDMEIER, UNIVERSITY OF GÖTTINGEN
I & II PETER AND JUDE. BY LEWIS R. DONELSON, AUSTIN PRESBYTERIAN THEOLOGICAL SEMINARY
I, II, & III JOHN. BY JUDITH M. LIEU, UNIVERSITY OF CAMBRIDGE
REVELATION. BY BRIAN K. BLOUNT, UNION PRESBYTERIAN SEMINARY

CLASSICS

HISTORY AND THEOLOGY IN THE FOURTH GOSPEL. BY J. LOUIS MARTYN, UNION THEOLOGICAL SEMINARY, NEW YORK
IMAGES OF THE CHURCH IN THE NEW TESTAMENT. BY PAUL S. MINEAR, YALE DIVINITY SCHOOL
PAUL AND THE ANATOMY OF APOSTOLIC AUTHORITY. BY JOHN HOWARD SCHÜTZ, UNIVERSITY OF NORTH CAROLINA, CHAPEL HILL
THEOLOGY AND ETHICS IN PAUL. BY VICTOR PAUL FURNISH, PERKINS SCHOOL OF THEOLOGY, SOUTHERN METHODIST UNIVERSITY
THE WORD IN THIS WORLD: ESSAYS IN NEW TESTAMENT EXEGESIS AND THEOLOGY. BY PAUL W. MEYER, PRINCETON THEOLOGICAL SEMINARY

GENERAL STUDIES

THE LAW AND THE PROPHETS BEAR WITNESS: THE OLD TESTAMENT IN THE NEW. BY J. ROSS WAGNER, PRINCETON THEOLOGICAL SEMINARY
METHODS FOR NEW TESTAMENT STUDY. BY A. K. M. ADAM, UNIVERSITY OF GLASGOW
NEW TESTAMENT BACKGROUNDS. BY CARL R. HOLLADAY, CANDLER SCHOOL OF THEOLOGY, EMORY UNIVERSITY

Lewis R. Donelson

I & II Peter and Jude
A Commentary

WESTMINSTER
JOHN KNOX PRESS
LOUISVILLE · KENTUCKY

© 2010 Lewis R. Donelson

2013 paperback edition
Originally published in hardback in the United States
by Westminster John Knox Press in 2010
Louisville, Kentucky

13 14 15 16 17 18 19 20 21 22—10 9 8 7 6 5 4 3 2 1

All rights reserved. No part of this book may be reproduced or transmitted in any form or by any means, electronic or mechanical, including photocopying, recording, or by any information storage or retrieval system, without permission in writing from the publisher. For information, address Westminster John Knox Press, 100 Witherspoon Street, Louisville, Kentucky 40202-1396. Or contact us online at www.wjkbooks.com.

Except as otherwise indicated, Scripture outside 1–2 Peter and Jude is from the New Revised Standard Version Bible, copyright © 1989 by the National Council of the Churches of Christ in the United States of America, used by permission, with all rights reserved.

Book design by Jennifer K. Cox

Library of Congress Cataloging-in-Publication Data
Donelson, Lewis R., 1949–
 I & II Peter and Jude : a commentary / Lewis R. Donelson.
   p. cm.— (The New Testament Library)
 Includes bibliographical references and index.
 ISBN 978-0-664-22138-6 (alk. paper)
 1. Bible. N.T. Peter—Commentaries.   2. Bible. N.T. Jude—Commentaries.
I. Title.   II. Title: First and Second Peter and Jude.
 BS2795.53.D66   2010
 227'.9077—dc22
                                                                                2010003668
ISBN 978-0-664-23980-0 (paperback)

∞ The paper used in this publication meets the minimum requirements
of the American National Standard for Information Sciences—Permanence
of Paper for Printed Library Materials, ANSI Z39.48-1992.

CONTENTS

Preface	ix
Abbreviations	xi
Bibliography	xv
Introduction to 1 Peter, 2 Peter, and Jude	1

The First Letter of Peter

Introduction to 1 Peter		7
The Recipients of 1 Peter		9
Persecution		11
Date		14
Authorship		15
Literary Structure		17
Outline		19
Theology		19
Text and Translation		23
1:1–2	**Epistolary Prescript**	25
1:3–12	**Opening Blessing**	28
1:13–2:10	**The Holy Life**	39
1:13–21	Call to Holiness	39
1:22–25	Love and the Word	50
2:1–3	Milk of the Lord	55
2:4–10	The Living Stone	58
2:11–4:6	**Life as Aliens and Sojourners**	67
2:11–12	Call to Beautiful Deeds among the Gentiles	67
2:13–17	Submission to the Authority of the Gentiles	70
2:18–25	Submission of Servants to Masters	77

3:1–7	Submission by Wives and Honoring by Husbands	87
3:8–12	Exhortation and Blessing for All	95
3:13–17	Suffering While Doing Good	101
3:18–22	Christ as Model of Suffering and Victory	107
	Excursus: The Tradition of Enoch and the Fallen Angels	116
4:1–6	Separation from the Gentile Life	117
4:7–5:11	**The End Is Near**	**126**
4:7–11	Love within the Community	126
4:12–19	Suffering as Judgment	131
5:1–5	Elders and Their Flocks	140
5:6–11	Concluding Call to Suffering	147
5:12–14	**Epistolary Postscript**	**153**

The Letter of Jude

Introduction to Jude		**161**
Authorship		161
The Opponents		163
Date and Setting		164
Literary Structure		165
Canonical Status		167
Text and Translation		167
1–2	**Opening Salutation**	**169**
3–4	**Statement of Purpose and Opening Accusation**	**172**
5–16	**Condemnation of the Impious**	**177**
5–7	Three Examples of Divine Punishment	177
8–13	The Naming of the Impious	181
	Excursus: Michael and the Body of Moses	184
14–16	Enoch's Prophecy of Judgment	189
17–23	**Appeals to the Beloved**	**192**
17–19	The Prophecy of the Apostles	192
20–23	Appeal for Mercy	196
24–25	**Concluding Doxology**	**201**

The Second Letter of Peter

Introduction to 2 Peter — 207
   Relationship to Jude — 207
   Authorship and Date — 208
   The False Teachers and Mockers — 209
   Literary Structure — 210
   Theology — 211
   Text and Translation — 212

1:1–2	Opening Salutation	213
1:3–11	Exordium	216
1:12–15	Testamentary Reminder	224
1:16–21	Apostolic and Prophetic Witnesses	228
2:1–22	**False Teachers and Their Punishment**	**236**
2:1–3	The Prediction of False Teachers	236
2:4–10a	Examples of God's Judgment	240
2:10b–16	The Immorality of the False Teachers	248
2:17–22	The Slavery of the False Teachers	255
3:1–13	**The Promise of His Coming**	**263**
3:1–7	The Coming of Mockers	263
3:8–13	God's Patience	271
3:14–18	**Final Exhortation and Doxology**	**280**

Index of Ancient Sources — 287

Index of Subjects — 297

PREFACE

A rich, diverse, and ancient conversation awaits anyone who writes a biblical commentary. Many people through the centuries have read, pondered, and discussed these texts. Perhaps the primary task of any commentary is simply to share with others a few moments of this wonderful conversation about the Bible. Thus my first note of gratitude belongs to all those who have read, studied, and written about 1 Peter, 2 Peter, and Jude. This commentary arises out of those many voices and hopes only to join the discussion.

I am grateful to the editors of the New Testament Library and the editors of Westminster John Knox Press. Throughout this process, every encounter has been productive and every person helpful. In particular, I want to thank C. Clifton Black, who is, in my opinion, the perfect editor for this series and for a somewhat obstinate author like me. Whatever good quality this commentary might have owes much to him. Thanks also to my colleagues at Austin Presbyterian Theological Seminary for their institutional and personal support. It is in conversation with students that we teachers often learn what we think. Such is the case here. I want to thank the many students who worked through these texts with me and helped me find these readings. Finally, particular thanks should go to Lisa Straus, Stephanie Cripps, and Megan Dosher, all of whom helped enormously in the final editing of this commentary.

ABBREVIATIONS

AB	Anchor Bible
ABD	*The Anchor Bible Dictionary*
ACNT	Augsburg Commentaries on the New Testament
AnBib	Analecta biblica
ANRW	*Aufstieg und Niedergang der römischen Welt*
ANTC	Abingdon New Testament Commentaries
AsSeign	*Assemblées du Seigneur*
AUSS	*Andrews University Seminary Studies*
BBET	Beiträge zur biblischen Exegese und Theologie
BBR	*Bulletin for Biblical Research*
BDAG	A Greek-English Lexicon of the New Testament and Other Early Christian Literature
BECNT	Baker Exegetical Commentary on the New Testament
BETL	Bibliotheca ephemeridum theologicarum lovaniensium
Bib	*Biblica*
BibInt	*Biblical Interpretation*
BTB	*Biblical Theology Bulletin*
BZ	*Biblische Zeitschrift*
CBQ	*Catholic Biblical Quarterly*
CNT	Commentaire du Nouveau Testament
ConBNT	Coniectanea biblica: New Testament Series
CTJ	*Calvin Theological Journal*
Did	*Didaskalia*
EKKNT	Evangelisch-katholischer Kommentar zum Neuen Testament
EstBíb	*Estudios bíblicos*
ExpTim	*Expository Times*
HNT	Handbuch zum Neuen Testament
HNTC	Harper's New Testament Commentaries
HTKNT	Herders theologischer Kommentar zum Neuen Testament
IBS	*Irish Biblical Studies*
ICC	International Critical Commentary
Int	*Interpretation*

JBL	*Journal of Biblical Literature*
JETS	*Journal of the Evangelical Theological Society*
JSNT	*Journal for the Study of the New Testament*
JSNTSup	Journal for the Study of the New Testament: Supplement Series
JSOTSup	Journal for the Study of the Old Testament: Supplement Series
JSPSup	Journal for the Study of the Pseudepigrapha: Supplement Series
JTS	*Journal of Theological Studies*
KEK	Kritisch-Exegetischer Kommentar über das Neue Testament
LXX	Septuagint
MT	Masoretic Text
NA^{27}	*Novum Testamentum Graece*, Nestle-Aland, 27th ed.
NABPR	National Association of Baptist Professors of Religion
NCB	New Century Bible
Neot	*Neotestamentica*
NIB	*The New Interpreter's Bible*
NIBC	New International Bible Commentary
NICNT	New International Commentary on the New Testament
NovT	*Novum Testamentum*
NovTSup	Novum Testamentum Supplements
NRSV	New Revised Standard Version
NT	New Testament
NTM	New Testament Message
NTS	*New Testament Studies*
OT	Old Testament
PNTC	Pillar New Testament Commentary
ResQ	*Restoration Quarterly*
RevExp	*Review and Expositor*
RTP	*Revue de théologie et de philosophie*
SB	Sources bibliques
SBLAcBib	Society of Biblical Literature Academia Biblica
SBLDS	Society of Biblical Literature Dissertation Series
SBLMS	Society of Biblical Literature Monograph Series
SecCent	*Second Century*
SNTSMS	Society for New Testament Studies Monograph Series
SP	Sacra pagina
TBT	*The Bible Today*
TDNT	Theological Dictionary of the New Testament
TJ	*Trinity Journal*
TNTC	Tyndale New Testament Commentaries
TynBul	*Tyndale Bulletin*

UBS⁴	*The Greek New Testament*, United Bible Societies, 4th ed.
USQR	*Union Seminary Quarterly Review*
VSpir	*Vie spirituelle*
WBC	Word Biblical Commentary
WTJ	*Westminster Theological Journal*
WUNT	Wissenschaftliche Untersuchungen zum Neuen Testament
ZNW	*Zeitschrift für die neutestamentliche Wissenschaft und die Kunde der älteren Kirche*

BIBLIOGRAPHY

Commentaries on 1 Peter

Achtemeier, Paul J. *1 Peter*. Hermeneia. Minneapolis: Fortress, 1996.
Beare, Francis Wright. *The First Epistle of Peter: The Greek Text with Introduction and Notes*. 3rd ed. Oxford: Blackwell, 1970 [1st ed., 1947; 2nd ed., 1958].
Best, Ernest. *1 Peter*. NCB. London: Oliphants; Grand Rapids: Eerdmans, 1971.
Boring, M. Eugene. *1 Peter*. ANTC. Nashville: Abingdon, 1999.
Brox, Norbert. *Der erste Petrusbrief*. 2nd ed. EKKNT 21. Zurich: Benziger; Neukirchen-Vluyn: Neukirchner Verlag, 1986 [1st ed., 1976].
Calvin, John. *Commentaries on the Catholic Epistles*. 1551. Ed. and trans. J. Owen. Calvin's Commentaries 22. Grand Rapids: Baker, 1979.
Craddock, Fred B. *First and Second Peter and Jude*. Westminster Bible Companion. Louisville, Ky.: Westminster John Knox, 1995.
Dalton, William J. "The First Epistle of Peter." Pages 903–8 in *The New Jerome Biblical Commentary*. Edited by Raymond E. Brown, Joseph A. Fitzmyer, and Roland E. Murphy. Englewood Cliffs, N.J.: Prentice-Hall, 1990.
Davids, Peter H. *The First Epistle of Peter*. NICNT. Grand Rapids: Eerdmans, 1990.
Elliott, John H. *I–II Peter/Jude*. ACNT. Minneapolis: Augsburg, 1982.
———. *1 Peter*. AB 37B. New York: Doubleday, 2000.
Feldmeier, Reinhard. *The First Letter of Peter: A Commentary on the Greek Text*. Translated by Peter H. Davids. Waco, Tex.: Baylor University Press, 2008.
Fitzmyer, Joseph A. "The First Epistle of Peter." Pages 362–68 in vol. 2 of *The New Jerome Biblical Commentary*. Edited by Raymond E. Brown, Joseph A. Fitzmyer, and Roland E. Murphy. Englewood Cliffs, N.J.: Prentice Hall, 1968.
Garland, David E. "1 Peter." Pages 229–319 in *NIB* 12, *Hebrews, James, 1 & 2 Peter, 1, 2, and 3 John, Jude, Revelation*. Nashville: Abingdon, 1998.
Goppelt, Leonhard. *A Commentary on 1 Peter*. Edited by Ferdinand Hahn. Translated and augmented by John E. Alsup. Grand Rapids: Eerdmans, 1993.
Green, Joel B. *1 Peter*. The Two Horizons New Testament Commentary. Grand Rapids: Eerdmans, 2007.

Hillyer, Norman. *1 and 2 Peter, Jude*. NIBC. Peabody, Mass.: Hendrickson, 1992.
Jobes, Karen H. *1 Peter*. BECNT. Grand Rapids: Baker Academic, 2005.
Kelly, J. N. D. *The Epistles of Peter and of Jude*. HNTC. New York: Harper & Row, 1969.
Krodel, Gerhard. "1 Peter." Pages 42–83, 146–47 in *The General Letters: Hebrews, James, 1–2 Peter, Jude, 1–3 John*. Rev. ed. Proclamation Commentaries. Minneapolis: Fortress, 1995.
Michaels, J. Ramsey. *1 Peter*. WBC 49. Waco, Tex.: Word, 1988.
Perkins, Pheme. *First and Second Peter, James, and Jude*. Interpretation. Louisville, Ky.: John Knox, 1995.
Selwyn, Edward Gordon. *The First Epistle of St. Peter: The Greek Text with Introduction, Notes, and Essays*. 2nd ed. London: Macmillan; New York: St. Martin's, 1947 [1st ed., 1946].
Senior, Donald P. *1 & 2 Peter*. NTM 20. Wilmington: Michael Glazier, 1980.
———. *1 Peter*. SP 15. Collegeville, Minn.: Liturgical Press, 2003.
Spicq, Ceslas. *Les Épîtres de Saint Pierre*. SB 4. Paris: Gabalda, 1966.
Windisch, Hans. *Die katholischen Briefe*. HNT 4.2. Tübingen: J. C. B. Mohr (Paul Siebeck), 1911.

Other Studies on 1 Peter

Achtemeier, Paul J. "Suffering Servant and Suffering Christ in 1 Peter." Pages 176–88 in *The Future of Christology*. Edited by Abraham J. Malherbe and Wayne A. Meeks. New York: Crossroad, 1993.
Agnew, F. H. "1 Peter 1:2: An Alternative Translation." *CBQ* 45 (1968): 68–73.
Applegate, J. K. "The Coelect Woman of 1 Peter." *NTS* 32 (1992): 587–604.
Balch, David L. "Early Christian Criticism of Patriarchal Authority: 1 Peter 2:11–3:12." *USQR* 39 (1984): 161–73.
———. *Let Wives Be Submissive: The Domestic Code in 1 Peter*. SBLMS 26. Chico, Calif.: Scholars Press, 1981.
Balch, David L., and Carolyn Osiek. *Families in the New Testament World: Households and House Churches*. Family, Religion, and Culture. Louisville, Ky.: Westminster John Knox, 1997.
Bammel, Ernst. "The Commands in 1 Pet. ii. 17." *NTS* 11 (1964–65): 268–81.
Bauckham, Richard J. "Spirits in Prison." *ABD* 6 (1992): 177–78.
Bechtler, Stephen R. *Following in His Steps: Suffering, Community, and Christology in 1 Peter*. SBLDS 162. Atlanta: Scholars, 1998.
Best, Ernest. "1 Peter II 4–10: A Reconsideration." *NovT* 11 (1969): 270–93.
Black, C. Clifton. *Mark: Images of an Apostolic Interpreter*. Personalities of the New Testament Series. 1994. Repr., Minneapolis: Augsburg Fortress, 2001.

Blazen, I. T. "Suffering and Cessation from Sin according to 1 Peter 4:1." *AUSS* 21 (1983): 27–50.
Boismard, Marie-Émile. "La typologie baptismale dans la première épître de Saint Pierre." *VSpir* 94 (1956): 339–52.
Borchert, Gerald L. "The Conduct of Christians in the Face of the 'Fiery Ordeal' (1 Pet. 4:12–5:11)." *RevExp* 79 (1982): 451–62.
Brown, Raymond E., Karl P. Donfried, and John Reumann. *Peter in the New Testament: A Collaborative Assessment by Protestant and Roman Catholic Scholars*. New York: Paulist Press, 1973.
Brox, Norbert. *Falsche Verfasserangaben: Zur Erklärung der frühchristlichen Pseudepigraphie*. Stuttgarter Bibelstudien 79. Edited by Herbert Haag et al. Stuttgart: Katholisches Bibelwerk, 1975.
Cook, J. D. "1 Peter iii.20: An Unnecessary Problem." *JTS* 31 (1980): 72–78.
Cross, Frank Leslie. *I Peter: A Paschal Liturgy*. London: Mowbray, 1954.
Dalton, William J. *Christ's Proclamation to the Spirits: A Study of I Peter 3:18–4:6*. 2nd, rev. ed. AnBib 23. Rome: Pontifical Biblical Institute, 1989.
———. "The Interpretation of 1 Peter 3,19 and 4,6: Light from 2 Peter." *Bib* 60 (1979): 547–55.
Danker, Fredrick W. "1 Peter 1:14–2:17—A Consolatory Pericope." *ZNW* 58 (1967): 95–102.
Dupont-Roc, Roselyne. "Le jeu des prépositions en 1 Pierre 1,1–12: De l'espérance finale à la joie dans les épreuves présentes." *EstBíb* 53 (1995): 201–12.
Elliott, John H. "Disgraced yet Graced: The Gospel according to 1 Peter in the Key of Honor and Shame." *BTB* 25 (1995): 166–78.
———. *The Elect and the Holy: An Exegetical Examination of 1 Peter 2:4–10 and the Phrase* βασίλειον ἱεράτευμα. NovTSup 12. Leiden: Brill, 1966.
———. "1 Peter, Its Situation and Strategy. A Discussion with David Balch." In *Perspectives on First Peter*. Edited by Charles H. Talbert. NABPR Special Study Series 9. Macon, Ga.: Mercer University Press, 1986.
———. *A Home for the Homeless: A Sociological Exegesis of I Peter, Its Situation and Strategy*. Philadelphia: Fortress, 1981.
———. "Ministry and Church Order in the New Testament: A Traditio-Historical Analysis (1 Pt 5,1–5 and parallels)." *CBQ* 32 (1970): 367–91.
———. "Salutation and Exhortation to Christian Behavior on the Basis of God's Blessings (1 Pet 1:1–2:10)." *RevExp* 79 (1982): 415–25.
———. "Silvanus and Mark in 1 Peter and Acts." In *Wort in der Zeit*. Edited by Karl H. Rengstorf. Leiden: Brill, 1980.
Feinberg, John. "1 Peter 3:18–20, Ancient Mythology, and the Intermediate State." *WTJ* 48 (1986): 303–36.
Feldmeier, Reinhard. *Die Christen als Fremde: Die Metapher der Fremde in der antiken Welt, im Urchristentum und im 1. Petrusbrief*. WUNT 64. Tübingen: J. C. B. Mohr (Paul Siebeck), 1992.

Ferguson, Everett. *Baptism in the Early Church: History, Theology, and Liturgy in the First Five Centuries*. Grand Rapids: Eerdmans, 2009.

Francis, James. "'Like Newborn Babes'—The Image of the Child in 1 Peter 2:2–3." Pages 111–17 in vol. 2 of *Studia biblica 1978: Sixth International Congress on Biblical Studies, Oxford, 3–7 April 1978*. Edited by E. A. Livingstone. JSNTSup 3. Sheffield: JSOT Press, 1980.

Gross, C. D. "Are the Wives of 1 Peter 3.7 Christians?" *JSNT* 35 (1989): 89–96.

Grudem, Wayne A. "Christ Preaching through Noah: 1 Peter 3:19–20 in the Light of Dominant Themes in Jewish Literature." *TJ* 7 (1986): 89–96.

Hanson, Anthony T. "Salvation Proclaimed, I: 1 Peter 3:18–22." *ExpTim* 93 (1981–82): 100–112.

Hellerman, Joseph H. *The Ancient Church as Family*. Minneapolis: Fortress, 2001.

Hemer, Colin J. "The Address of 1 Peter." *ExpTim* (1982): 239–43.

Hill, David. "On Suffering and Baptism in 1 Peter." *NovT* 18 (1976): 181–89.

———. "'To Offer Spiritual Sacrifices . . .' (1 Peter 2:5): Liturgical Formulations and Christian Paraenesis in 1 Peter." *JSNT* 16 (1982): 45–63.

Hillyer, Norman. "'Rock-Stone' Imagery in 1 Peter." *TynBul* 22 (1971): 58–81.

Horrell, David G. "The Product of a Petrine Circle? A Reassessment of the Origin and Character of 1 Peter." *JSNT* 86 (2002): 29–60.

Jobes, Karen H. "The Syntax of 1 Peter: Just How Good Is the Greek?" *BBR* 13, no. 2 (2003): 159–73.

Johnson, D. E. "Fire in God's House: Imagery from Malachi 3 in Peter's Theology of Suffering (1 Pet 4:12–19)." *JETS* 29 (1986): 285–94.

Kendall, Daniel. "The Literary and Theological Functions of 1 Peter 1:3–12." Pages 103–20 in *Perspectives on First Peter*. Edited by Charles H. Talbert. Macon, Ga.: Mercer University Press, 1986.

———. "On Christian Hope: 1 Peter 1:3–9." *Int* 41 (1987): 66–71.

Kiley, Mark. "Like Sara: The Tale of Terror behind 1 Peter 3:6." *JBL* 105 (1987): 689–92.

Kline, Leslie L. "Ethics for the Endtime: An Exegesis of 1 Pt. 4:7–11." *ResQ* 7 (1963): 113–23.

Koenig, John. "Hospitality." *ABD* 3 (1992): 299–301.

Légasse, Simon. "La soumission aux authorités d'après 1 Pierre 2. 13–17: Version spécifique d'une parénese traditionelle." *NTS* 34 (1988) : 378–96.

Manns, Frédéric. "La morale domestique de 1 P." *Did* 30 (2000): 3–27.

Martin, Troy W. *Metaphor and Composition in 1 Peter*. SBLDS 131. Atlanta: Scholars Press, 1992.

———. "The Present Indicative in the Eschatological Statements of 1 Pet 1, 6, 8." *JBL* 111 (1992): 307–12.

———. "The TestAbr and the Background of 1 Pet 3,6." *ZNW* 90 (1999): 139–46.

McCartney, D. "*Logikos* in 1 Peter 2:2." *ZNW* 82 (1991): 352–59.
Michaels, J. Ramsey. "Eschatology in 1 Peter iii.17." *NTS* 13 (1966–67): 394–401.
Minear, Paul S. "The House of Living Stones: A Study of 1 Peter 2:4–12." *Ecumenical Review* 34 (1982): 238–48.
Omanson, Roger. "Suffering for Righteousness' Sake (1 Pet 3:13–4:11)." *Rev-Exp* 79 (1982): 439–50.
Osborne, T. P. "Guide Lines for Christian Suffering: A Source-Critical and Theological Study of 1 Peter 2,21–25." *Bib* 64 (1983): 381–408.
Ostmeyer, Karl-Heinrich. *Taufe und Typos: Elemente und Theologie der Tauftypologien in 1. Korinther 10 und 1. Petrus 3*. WUNT, 2nd ser., 118. Tübingen: J. C. B. Mohr (Paul Siebeck), 2000.
Patterson, D. K. "Roles in Marriage: A Study in Submission—1 Peter 3:1–7." *Theological Educator* 13 (1982): 70–79.
Perdelwitz, Emil Richard. *Die Mysterienreligion und das Problem des I. Petrusbriefes: Ein literarischer und religionsgeschichtlicher Versuch*. Religionsversuche und Vorarbeiten 11.3. Giessen: Alfred Töpelmann, 1911.
Perkins, Pheme. *Peter: Apostle for the Whole Church*. Columbia: University of South Carolina Press, 1994.
Pilch, John J. "'Visiting Strangers' and 'Resident Aliens.'" *TBT* 29 (1991): 357–61.
Piper, John. "Hope as the Motivation for Love: I Peter 3:9–12." *NTS* 26 (1980): 212–31.
———. *"Love Your Enemies": Jesus' Love Command in the Synoptic Gospels and in the Early Christian Paraenesis; A History of the Tradition and Interpretation of Its Uses*. SNTSMS 38. Cambridge: Cambridge University Press, 1979.
Prasad, Jacob. *Foundations of the Christian Way of Life, according to 1 Peter 1,13–25: An Exegetico-Theological Study*. AnBib 146. Rome: Pontifical Biblical Institute, 2000.
Reichert, Angelika. *Eine urchristliche praeparatio ad martyrium: Studien zur Komposition, Traditionsgeschichte und Theologie des 1. Petrusbriefes*. BBET 22. Frankfurt: Peter Lang, 1989.
Richards, E. Randolph. "Silvanus Was Not Peter's Secretary: Theological Bias in Interpreting *dia Silouanou . . . egrapsa* in I Peter 5:12." *JETS* 43 (2000): 417–32.
Schertz, Mary H. "Nonretaliation and the Haustafeln in 1 Peter." Pages 258–86 in *The Love of Enemy and Nonretaliation in the New Testament*. Edited by Willard H. Swartley. Louisville, Ky.: Westminster/John Knox, 1992.
Scholer, David M. "Woman's Adornment: Some Historical and Hermeneutical Observations on the New Testament Passages 1 Tim 2:9–10 and 1 Pet 3:3–4." *Daughters of Sarah* 6 (1980): 3–6.

Senior, Donald P. "The Conduct of Christians in the World (1 Pet 2:11–3:12)." *RevExp* 79 (1982): 427–38.
Snodgrass, K. R. "I Peter ii.1–10: Its Formation and Literary Affinities." *NTS* 24 (1977–78): 97–106.
Soards, Marion L. "1 Peter, 2 Peter, and Jude as Evidence for a Petrine School." Pages 3827–49 in *ANRW* 2.25.5. Edited by Wolfgang Haase and Hildegard Temporini. Berlin: de Gruyter, 1988.
Speyer, Wolfgang. *Die literarische Fälschung in heidnischen und christlichen Altertum: Ein Versuch ihrer Deutung*. Handbuch der klassischen Altertumswissenschaft part 2. Munich: C. H. Beck, 1971.
Spicq, Ceslas. "L'Épître de Pierre: Prière, charité, justice . . . et fin des Temps (1 Pierre 4:7–11)." *AsSeign* 50 (1966): 15–29.
Stevick, Daniel B. "A Matter of Taste: 1 Peter 2:3." *Review for Religious* 47 (1988): 707–17.
Talbert, Charles H. "The Critique of Paganism in I Peter 1:18." Pages 129–42 in *Neotestamentica et Semitica: Studies in Honour of Matthew Black*. Edited by E. Earle Ellis and Max Wilcox. Edinburgh: T&T Clark, 1969.
———. "The Educational Value of Suffering in 1 Peter." Pages 42–57 in *Learning through Suffering: The Educational Value of Suffering in the New Testament and in Its Milieu*. Collegeville, Minn.: Liturgical Press, 1991.
Villiers, J. L. de. "Joy in Suffering in 1 Peter." *Neot* 9 (1975): 64–86.
Warden, D. "The Prophets of 1 Peter 1:10–12." *ResQ* 31 (1989): 1–12.
Winter, Bruce W. "The Public Honouring of Christian Benefactors: Romans 13.3–4 and 1 Peter 2.14–15." *JSNT* 34 (1988): 87–103.
Zerbe, Gordan M. "Non-retaliation in 1 Peter: A Pragmatic or a Christological Ethic?" Pages 270–88 in *Non-retaliation in Early Jewish and New Testament Texts: Ethical Themes in Social Contexts*. JSPSup 13. Sheffield: JSOT Press, 1993.

Commentaries on Jude and 2 Peter

Bauckham, Richard J. *Jude, 2 Peter*. WBC 50. Waco, Tex.: Word, 1983.
Bigg, Charles. *A Critical and Exegetical Commentary on the Epistles of St. Peter and St. Jude*. 2d ed. ICC. Edinburgh: T&T Clark, 1902.
Davids, Peter H. *The Letters of 2 Peter and Jude*. PNTC. Grand Rapids: Eerdmans, 2006.
Elliott, John H. *I–II Peter, Jude*. ACNT. Minneapolis: Augsburg, 1982.
Fuchs, Eric, and Pierre Reymond. *La deuxième épître de saint Pierre. L'Épitre de Saint Jude*. CNT 13b. Neuchâtel: Delachaux & Niestlé, 1980.
Green, Gene L. *Jude and 2 Peter*. BECNT. Grand Rapids: Baker Academic, 2008.
Green, Michael. *The Second Epistle of Peter and the General Epistle of Jude*. TNTC. Grand Rapids: Eerdmans, 1968.

Grundmann, Walter. *Der Brief des Judas und der zweite Brief des Petrus.* Berlin: Evangelische Verlagsanstalt, 1974.
Harrington, Daniel J., S.J. *Jude and 2 Peter.* SP 15. Collegeville, Minn.: Liturgical Press, 2003.
Kelly, J. N. D. *A Commentary on the Epistles of Peter and of Jude.* HNTC. New York and Evanston, Ill.: Harper, 1969.
Kraftchick, Steven J. *Jude, 2 Peter.* ANTC. Nashville: Abingdon, 2002.
Mayor, Joseph B. *The Epistle of St Jude and the Second Epistle of Peter.* London: Macmillan, 1907.
Neyrey, Jerome H. *2 Peter, Jude.* AB 37C. New York: Doubleday, 1993.
Paulsen, Henning. *Der zweite Petrusbrief und der Judasbrief.* KEK 12.2. Göttingen: Vandenhoeck & Ruprecht, 1992.
Reicke, Bo. *The Epistles of James, Peter, and Jude.* AB 37. New York: Doubleday, 1964.
Schelkle, Karl H. *Die Petrusbriefe, der Judasbrief.* HTKNT 13.2. Freiburg: Herder, 1961.
Senior, Donald. *1 and 2 Peter.* NTM 20. Wilmington, Del.: Michael Glazier, 1980.
Vögtle, Anton. *Der Judasbrief, der 2. Petrusbrief.* EKKNT 22. Neukirchen-Vluyn: Neukirchener Verlag, 1994.

Other Studies on Jude and 2 Peter

Cothenet, Edouard. "La tradition selon Jude et 2 Pierre." *NTS* 35 (1989): 407–20.
Desjardins, Michael. "The Portrayal of the Dissidents in 2 Peter and Jude: Does It Tell Us More about the 'Godly' than the 'Ungodly'?" *JSNT* 30 (1987): 89–102.
Gerdmar, Anders. *Rethinking the Judaism-Hellenism Dichotomy: A Historiographical Case Study of Second Peter and Jude.* ConBNT 36. Stockholm: Almqvist & Wiksell, 2001.
Karris, Robert J. "The Background and Significance of the Polemic of the Pastoral Epistles." *JBL* 92 (1973): 549–64.
Knight, Jonathan M. *2 Peter, Jude.* Sheffield NT Guides. Sheffield: Sheffield Academic Press, 1995.
Watson, Duane F. *Invention, Arrangement, and Style: Rhetorical Criticism of Jude and 2 Peter.* SBLDS 104. Atlanta: Scholars Press, 1988.

Other Studies on Jude

Bauckham, Richard J. *Jude and the Relatives of Jesus in the Early Church.* Edinburgh: T&T Clark, 1990.

———. "The Letter of Jude: An Account of Research." Pages 3791–3826 in *ANRW* 2.25.5. Edited by Wolfgang Haase and Hildegard Temporini. Berlin: de Gruyter, 1988.

Birdsall, J. Neville. "The Text of Jude in $\mathfrak{P}^{72}$." *JTS* 14 (1963): 394–99.

Charles, J. Daryl. "Jude's Use of Pseudepigraphical Source-Material as Part of a Literary Strategy." *NTS* 37 (1991): 130–45.

———. "Literary Artifice in the Epistle of Jude." *ZNW* 82 (1991): 106–24.

———. *Literary Strategy in the Epistle of Jude*. Scranton, Pa.: University of Scranton Press, 1993.

———. "'Those' and 'These': The Use of the Old Testament in the Epistle of Jude." *JSNT* 38 (1990): 109–24.

Eybers, I. H. "Aspects of the Background of the Letter of Jude." *Neot* 9 (1975): 133–23.

Gunther, John J. "The Alexandrian Epistle of Jude." *NTS* 30 (1984): 549–62.

Joubert, Stephen J. "Facing the Past: Transtextual Relationships and Historical Understanding in the Letter of Jude." *BZ* 42 (1998): 56–70.

———. "Language, Ideology and the Social Context of the Letter of Jude." *Neot* 24 (1990): 335–49.

———. "Persuasion in the Letter of Jude." *JSNT* 58 (1995): 75–87.

Klijn, Albertus K. J. "Jude 5–7." Pages 137–44 in *The New Testament Age: Essays in Honor of Bo Reicke*. Edited by W. C. Weinrich. Macon, Ga.: Mercer University Press, 1984.

Landon, Charles. *A Text-Critical Study of the Epistle of Jude*. JSOTSup 135. Sheffield: Sheffield Academic Press, 1996.

Osburn, Carroll D. "The Christological Use of *1 Enoch* 1.9 in Jude 14–15." *NTS* 23 (1977): 334–41.

Rowston, Douglas J. "The Most Neglected Book in the New Testament." *NTS* 21 (1975): 554–63.

Sellin, Gerhard. "Die Häretiker des Judasbrief." *ZNW* 77 (1986): 206–25.

Thurén, Lauri. "Hey Jude! Asking for the Original Situation and Message of a Catholic Epistle." *NTS* 43 (1997): 451–65.

Webb, Robert L. "The Eschatology of the Epistle of Jude and Its Rhetorical and Social Functions." *BBR* 6 (1996): 139–51.

Wendland, Ernest R. "A Comparative Study of 'Rhetorical Criticism,' Ancient and Modern: With Special Reference to the Larger Structure and Function of the Epistle of Jude." *Neot* 28 (1994): 193–228.

Wisse, Frederick. "The Epistle of Jude in the History of Heresiology." Pages 133–43 in *Essays on the Nag Hammadi Texts*. Edited by Martin Krause. Leiden: Brill, 1972.

Wolthuis, Thomas. "Jude and Jewish Traditions." *CTJ* 22 (1987): 21–41.

Other Studies on 2 Peter

Adams, Edward. "Where Is the Promise of His Coming? The Complaint of the Scoffers in 2 Peter 3.4." *NTS* 51 (2005): 106–22.

Bauckham, Richard J. "2 Peter: An Account of Research." Pages 3713–3752 in *ANRW* 2.25.5. Edited by Wolfgang Haase and Hildegard Temporini. Berlin: de Gruyter, 1988.

Callan, Terrance. "The Christology of the Second Letter of Peter." *Bib* 82 (2001): 253–63.

———. "The Soteriology of the Second Letter of Peter." *Bib* 82 (2001): 549–59.

Cavallin, Hans C. C. "The False Teachers of 2 Pt as Pseudo-prophets." *NovT* 21 (1979): 263–70.

Charles, J. Daryl. "The Function of Moral Typology in 2 Peter." Pages 331–43 in *Character and Scripture*. Edited by William P. Brown. Grand Rapids: Eerdmans, 2002.

Dschulnigg, Peter. "Der theologische Ort des Zweiten Petrusbriefes." *BZ* 33 (1989): 161–77.

Farkasfalvy, Dennis. "The Ecclesial Setting of Pseudepigraphy in Second Peter and Its Role in the Formation of the Canon." *SecCent* 5 (1985–86): 3–29.

Fornberg, Tord. *An Early Church in a Pluralistic Society: A Study of 2 Peter*. ConBNT 9. Lund: Gleerup, 1977.

Gilmour, Michael J. *The Significance of Parallels between 2 Peter and Other Early Christian Literature*. SBLAcBib 10. Atlanta: Society of Biblical Literature, 2002.

Green, E. M. B. *2 Peter Reconsidered*. London: Tyndale, 1960.

Kraus, Thomas. *Sprache, Stil und historischer Ort des zweiten Petrusbreifes*. WUNT 2.136. Tübingen: J. C. B. Mohr (Paul Siebeck), 2001.

Kruger, Michael J. "The Authenticity of 2 Peter." *JETS* 42 (1999): 645–71.

Meier, Sam. "2 Peter 3:3–7—An Early Jewish and Christian Response to Eschatological Skepticism." *BZ* 32(1988): 255–57.

Miller, Troy A. "Dogs, Adulterers, and the Way of Balaam: The Forms and Socio-Rhetorical Function of the Polemical Rhetoric in 2 Peter." *IBS* 22 (2000): 123–44, 182–91.

Neyrey, Jerome H. "The Form and Background of the Polemic in 2 Peter." *JBL* 99 (1980): 407–31.

Snyder, John. "A 2 Peter Bibliography." *JETS* 22 (1979): 265–67.

Wall, Robert W. "The Canonical Function of 2 Peter." *BibInt* 9 (2001): 64–81.

INTRODUCTION TO 1 PETER, 2 PETER, AND JUDE

The letters of 1 Peter, 2 Peter, and Jude have traditionally been grouped together. They share a certain formal relationship. Both 1 Peter and 2 Peter have the name Peter as author. Jude and 2 Peter share a direct literary relationship, with 2 Peter taking over much of Jude. Beyond this formal relationship, the three letters have typically been seen as coming from similar situations in early Christian history and out of similar theological traditions.

Since this commentary adopts the position that the apostle Peter did not write either 1 Peter or 2 Peter and that Jude, the brother of Jesus, did not write Jude, all three letters are placed within the postapostolic period of Christian history. The intense christological debates of the third and fourth centuries, with their indebtedness to Greek philosophy, are not anticipated in any of these letters. In fact, there is no hint even of the gnostic debates of the late second century. These letters come from a time in Christian history about which we know little. They precede the explosion of documents that begins in the late second century and increases in the third and fourth. Thus they represent rare voices from a crucial time in the history of Christianity.

The picture of early Christianity suggested by these letters is a fascinating one. The debates with Judaism that dominate Paul and the Gospels seem to be of little concern. These are communities embedded in the Roman world and thinking about their place in that world. Nevertheless, the way they think about the Roman world is through a rich and diverse combination of readings of the Old Testament and more specifically Christian traditions. All three of these letters display a complex and creative relationship to the Old Testament. Traditional Jewish images, the stories of Israel, and the oracles of the prophets provide the core theological language of the letters. These stories are read and their images employed in a variety of ways. None of the letters follows a consistent interpretive pattern, such as topology or prophecy and fulfillment. The syntax of these letters interweaves the syntax of the OT in patterns that defy categorizations. It is as though all three authors think in the syntax of the OT.

All three letters also rely upon a rich and diverse Christian tradition. In some ways, these letters stand mostly in the traditions and language of the

Pauline Letters and the Synoptic Gospels. But they are not limited to that. First Peter seems to echo, one way or another, almost every other book in the NT. The echoes in 2 Peter, while not quite as numerous as 1 Peter, range over most of the NT. Since Jude makes its arguments mostly through a series of readings and images from the OT, it does not display this same indebtedness to Christian traditions. The traditions that feed these letters come largely in the form of moral categories and christological doctrines. In the Christian communities of the letters, there seems to have existed a fluid set of traditions, which focused upon the story and example of Jesus and upon the details of the ethical life. The fluidity of these traditions speaks against the notion of discrete theological trajectories. There is no suggestion of the existence of distinctive Pauline, Matthean, Johannine, or even Petrine configurations. These letters draw a picture of Christian thought in which everything is flowing into everything else. Christians appear to be reading not only throughout the OT but also throughout the corpus that came to be the NT, arranging those readings into their own theologies.

These Christians are also in conflict. The immediate occasion for 1 Peter is conflict with Roman neighbors. The Christians of 1 Peter have in some ways rejected significant parts of their former lives. This rejection has drawn abuse from their Roman friends. Thus 1 Peter gives one of the earliest glimpses of what will become an intense debate in early Christianity. The question of what it means to be Christian, what it means to be Roman, and what it means to be a Roman Christian or Christian Roman will occupy much of Christian thought for several hundred years. In 1 Peter, it is clear that there is both a yes and a no to the Roman world. Early shadows of third- and fourth-century persecution of the Christians by the Romans have already fallen upon the Christians of 1 Peter. However, the post-Constantinian claim that Christians make the best Romans is foreshadowed here as well.

The Christians in Jude and 2 Peter are in conflict as well. However, they are in conflict with one another, not with their Roman neighbors. The danger comes from inside the community, not from the outside. Jude and 2 Peter are mostly attacks on other Christians. As we shall see, the grounds and purposes of these attacks are difficult to reconstruct. It is hard to tell what occasioned the bitter polemic that dominates these letters. Nonetheless, it is clear that conflict with other Christians can be nearly as harsh, although rarely as lethal, as conflict with non-Christians. In this way, these two letters belong on an endless trajectory of internal Christian debate. They anticipate not only the strident debates between the so-called orthodox and heretics that dominate much of Christian theology in the Roman era, but also the controversies within Christian communities throughout history.

The sketchy and incomplete portrait of early Christianity drawn by these letters is fascinating. Christianity, it seems, exists as an intersection of readings of the OT, stories and traditions about Jesus, and the demands of living in the Roman world and the still-emerging church. The commentaries that follow will show that each letter gathers those forces in its own way. Viewed collectively, these documents portray communities deep in conflict, both with outsiders and with insiders. However, the letters also portray communities full of enormous theological resources and theological creativity.

THE FIRST LETTER OF PETER

INTRODUCTION TO 1 PETER

The very first word of 1 Peter has proved to be the most controversial word in the letter. The letter begins with a standard letter opening: "Peter, an apostle of Jesus Christ, to the elect . . ." For most of Christian history, the authorship of this letter by the apostle Peter was accepted by readers. The classic tendency to read biblical sentences less in the context of their given document and more in the context of the whole of Christian thought meant that affirming authorship by Peter had little impact on how the letter was read. The rise of historical criticism has, of course, changed this pattern of reading.[1] Modern readers want to place biblical documents in their original historical context. They assume that texts are written by historical people in particular historical contexts. One aspect of a good reading requires re-creating, as much as possible, the moment of origin of a text. Thus a good reading must recount the character and intentions of the author. This shift in reading strategy is not only well documented, but the complications that ensued are also rather infamous.[2] In order to read 1 Peter, the story of the apostle Peter had to be connected to the origin and theology of the letter. However, combining a portrait of the apostle Peter with the text of this letter has proved to be difficult. This is not a text that historians would have expected the apostle Peter to write.

The difficulties of maintaining authorship by Peter are numerous.[3] Perhaps the most formidable problem is the character and quality of the Greek. Though

---

1. Among the many accounts of the rise of historical criticism, a good place to start is Robert Morgan with John Barton, *Biblical Interpretation* (Oxford Bible Series; Oxford: Oxford University Press, 1988).

2. Summaries of the debate over historical criticism can be found in Steven L. McKenzie and Stephen R. Haynes, eds., *To Each Its Own Meaning: An Introduction to Biblical Criticisms and Their Application* (rev. and expanded ed.; Louisville, Ky.: Westminster John Knox Press, 1999); and George Aichele et al., eds., *The Postmodern Bible: The Bible and Culture Collective* (New Haven, Conn.: Yale University Press, 1995). For a discussion more focused on the problems of the role of the author, see Stephen D. Moore, *Literary Criticism and the Gospels: The Theoretical Challenge* (New Haven, Conn.: Yale University Press, 1989).

3. For more detailed discussion of the question of authorship and for all the introductory issues, see Elliott, *1 Peter*, 3–152, esp. 118–30; and Achtemeier 1–75. For a different analysis, which supports Petrine authorship, see Jobes, *1 Peter*, 1–57.

this Greek is not as sophisticated as what second- and third-century Christians will write, it is far beyond what most historians imagine a fisherman from Galilee, no matter how bright, would have written. It is too complex and shows little Semitic influence. Faced with this problem, some readers have suggested that Silvanus, who is mentioned in 5:12, was responsible for the Greek, while Peter was responsible for the ideas. Peter is thereby maintained as author even as his role is reduced. Most readers have found this solution dubious at best.

There are other difficulties with Petrine authorship. While 1 Peter cites and echoes many OT texts, it typically relies on the Greek version, not the Hebrew. There are only a few allusions to the life and ministry of Jesus in 1 Peter. Apart from the reference to the author being a "witness of the sufferings of Christ" (1:11), a few echoes of Jesus' sayings, and the example of Jesus' suffering, 1 Peter does its Christology on a cosmic level. There is no interest in Israel, no interest in the law or covenant. The OT is read almost exclusively through the lens of Christology. There seems to be no controversy over the status of the law. The social and historical context that is assumed by the letter fits awkwardly with the life of Peter. The kind of persecution that 1 Peter projects fits much better in the time after Peter's death. The occasional and localized enmity between Christians who were once Gentiles and their Gentile neighbors that this letter describes coheres wonderfully with the end of the first century and awkwardly with its middle. Furthermore, the apostle Paul insists that Peter's ministry was to Jews (Gal 2:8). This letter seems to be written predominantly to former Gentiles. All of this is seen as problematic for the historical Peter.

These problems have led many readers to conclude that the apostle Peter did not write 1 Peter. In some ways, such a conclusion is not surprising. Early Christian literature is filled with pseudepigrapha. Within the first few centuries, about a hundred Christian documents known to historians have a false name affixed as author. The apostle Peter is attached as author or source to a whole series of early Christian documents of which only 1 Peter has any real possibility of coming from the apostle himself (e.g., 1 Peter, 2 Peter, *Letter of Peter to Philip, Acts of Peter, Slavonic Acts of Peter, Acts of Peter and Andrew, Acts of Peter and Paul, Apocalypse of Peter, Gospel of Peter*). Thus there is nothing historically improbable in 1 Peter's not being written by Peter. Though this decision eliminates the problem of fitting this letter into the life of Peter, it creates other problems. Early Christian pseudepigrapha are so diverse in their character that almost nothing about the origin or reception of a document can be concluded from the simple fact of its being pseudepigraphical. Deciding that Peter did not write 1 Peter is not the same thing as deciding who wrote it, when it was written, how it was received, or why it was attributed to Peter. Once the letter is cut loose from the anchor of Peter's life, it floats into early Christian history without a determinative context.

The Recipients of 1 Peter

If the face and situation of the author is unknown, then the next place to look for a historical anchor is in the situation of the recipients of the letter. First Peter actually provides a good deal of data about its recipients and their situation. Most of them, perhaps even all of them, were Gentile. According to 4:2–4, the source of their persecution lies in their rejection of their former Gentile way of life. There is no hint, in this passage or anywhere in the letter, that this problem of abuse by Gentile neighbors is confined to a particular segment of the community. The terms used throughout 1 Peter in describing their former lives seem more fitting to Gentile lives than Jewish. They lived in ignorance (1:14); their ancestral way of life was "futile" (1:18); they were "not a people" (2:10).

Some readers, however, detect arguments in 1 Peter that assume Jewish traditions. In typical Jewish style, non-Christians are called "Gentiles" (*ethnē*, 2:12; 4:3). The letter assumes extensive knowledge of the OT. The only people referred to by name who are not part of the occasion of the letter are Sarah and Abraham (3:6). Its theological terminology is filled with OT imagery. If these are Gentiles, they have been extensively schooled in the OT. In fact, the rhetoric of 1 Peter does not have to argue on behalf of the relevance of the OT and its imagery. It assumes both its relevance and familiarity. However, apart from the use of the term "Gentile," 1 Peter addresses none of the usual tensions between Jews and Gentiles in the Roman world. There is, for instance, no problem with the law or any of its requirements. The classic Jewish imagery has all been transformed and reconfigured by the Christian experience. Election is now election in Christ. Holiness is now to live as Christ lived. Thus, if there are Jews in this community, the rhetoric of the letter subsumes their peculiar history to that of the Gentile Christians in their midst. Not only does the rhetoric of 1 Peter assume knowledge of the OT; it also assumes knowledge of the story of Jesus and of a rather diverse Christian tradition. First Peter is best seen as written to Gentile Christians who have immersed themselves both in the OT and in the peculiarities of Christian thought.

They were probably rural. The letter was sent to "the elect sojourners of the dispersion in Pontus, Galatia, Cappadocia, Asia, and Bithynia." Within the rhetoric of pseudepigraphical letters, these places may simply be literary fictions, with the letter having no real connection to these places. It is more likely that these names identify the original home of the letter. Geographical terminology in the Roman world was notoriously imprecise. However, in this case each of the terms designates a Roman province. Pontus and Bithynia were officially one province but were often divided in common usage. The sequence of these names has led to the suggestion that the carrier of the original letter traveled in this order. Starting in Pontus and ending in Bithynia, this imagined letter carrier would traverse most of Asia Minor (modern Turkey) north of the Taurus Mountains. Except for the province of Asia, these regions were primarily rural. Furthermore, these areas were less influenced by Greco-Roman culture than was most of the Roman world. This was a culturally, religiously, and politically diverse environment. This means that it is impossible to be precise about the social norms of the pre-Christian Gentile lives of the letter's recipients.

If the letter gives any hints about the social rank of the recipients, it would be that they were primarily of lower rank. Though it has proved to be difficult to use modern terminology of class when speaking of the Roman world, it is clear that social rank was crucial to a person's identity. In the adaptation of the Greco-Roman household code in 2:15–3:7, it is the persons in the subordinate position who are the focus of the exhortation. The primary address is to household servants and women. There is no address to any masters of these servants, and husbands warrant only a quick note. Although it is possible that these people are addressed because servants and wives embody the subordination ideal better than masters and husbands, it is more likely that the weight of the argument reflects the social profile of the community. This was a community of servants, not of masters. Some readers have suggested that the admonition to elders in 5:1–4 is striking in its avoidance of the title "overseer" (*episkopos*), even while using the verb (5:2). The title "overseer" was typically used for a person in a public office who was of higher social rank than the people in this community. "Elder" is a term of honor within the community that does not carry echoes of social status in the public arena. Perhaps it is only Jesus who can be termed "overseer" (2:25).

The final bit of evidence is more difficult to evaluate. In 1:1 the recipients are called "sojourners" (*parepidēmoi*). In 2:11 they are exhorted as "aliens" (*paroikoi*) and "sojourners" (*parepidēmoi*) to abstain from desires of the flesh. The terms *parepidēmos* and *paroikos* have sparked debate among readers because both terms can have technical meanings about a person's legal residential status. The term *parepidēmoi* generally refers to people living in exile away from their home city. The term *paroikoi* refers to people with the legal status of resident aliens. Both terms designate people who are living in a city yet without full rights of a normal citizen of that city. These terms should be distinguished from the general term "stranger" (*xenos*), which refers primarily to personal familiarity and not legal status. The question is whether these terms in 1 Peter are literal or metaphorical.[4] It is perhaps significant that in non-Christian literature these terms are almost always technical. This leads some readers to suggest that 1 Peter uses these terms in the normal technical way and that all, or nearly all, of the Christian readers of this letter are people who are not full citizens of the cities in which they live. This lower legal status

---

4. Compare, e.g., Victor P. Furnish, "Elect Sojourners in Christ: An Approach to the Theology of 1 Peter," *Perkins Journal* 28 (1975): 1–11; and Elliott, *1 Peter*, 476–83.

contributed to the alienation and hostility between them and Gentile neighbors who were full citizens.

Most readers of 1 Peter find such a narrow social profile of the recipients to be unlikely. It is also difficult to know how those terms functioned in the largely rural context of the letter. Furthermore, the argument of 4:1–4 assumes that these Christians were once regarded as indistinguishable from the Gentiles around them. They seem to have had full social status before becoming Christian. Thus most readers see these terms as metaphorical. The rejection of the Gentile life has placed these Christians in a compromised social position that can be compared to that of sojourners and aliens. This does not mean that the terms are spiritual in the sense that these Christians are now alienated from all life on earth. The terms retain their social echoes. They are alienated from a certain pattern of social life, not from all social life. Both terms suggest a social and legal vulnerability that permits the kind of abuse from neighbors that they seem to have endured. Part of the texture of suffering is a sense of lost social status that the terms *parepidēmos* and *paroikos* effectively evoke.

Persecution

There are references to suffering and abuse in 1:6–7; 2:12, 20–23; 3:6, 9, 13–18; 4:1–4, 12–19; and 5:8–10. Most of these references offer no hint about what instigated the abuse or the character of the abuse. The only clear statement of the cause of this abuse is in 4:2–4, where the Gentiles are surprised because these Christians "no longer run with them in the same pouring out of wastefulness, and thus they slander." In 4:14 the readers of the letter are pronounced blessed if they "are abused in the name of Christ." In 4:16 they are admonished to "glorify God" if they suffer "as a Christian." This suffering in the name of Christ or as a Christian is distinguished from suffering "as a murderer or thief or evildoer or as a mischief-maker" (4:15). In 3:15 is a hint of the possibility of suffering in being asked "for an account of the hope that is in you." The dominant image is that abuse is caused by good behavior (3:16; 4:2–4, 14, 16). Christian behavior seems to inspire abuse from neighbors. However, this same behavior is ultimately recognized by these Gentile neighbors as being good behavior and may even convert them (2:12, 15; 3:1–2, 16).

In none of these references is there any real hint about the character of the abuse. The usual terms for persecution (*diōkō* and *diōgmos*) do not occur in 1 Peter. Instead, there is a range of terms that suggest verbal shaming: "abuse" (*loidoreō, antiloidoreō*, 2:23), "slander" (*katalaleō*, 2:12; 3:16; *blasphēmeō*, 4:4), "disparage" (*epēreazō*, 3:16), and "insult" (*oneidizō*, 4:14). It is impossible to reconstruct the precise context of this abuse or the social force of this verbal shaming from such a list of terms. Whatever the form of this public shaming, in a society built upon social status, such abuse could have been powerful.

These inconclusive allusions to persecution make it difficult to connect 1 Peter in a definitive way to the larger story of early Christian persecution.[5] Nevertheless, some boundaries can be suggested. The well-known correspondence (ca. 111–112 C.E.) from Pliny the Younger to the emperor Trajan (98–117 C.E.), who had sent Pliny to organize the province of Bithynia, includes an inquiry to the emperor as to the propriety of Pliny's procedures for the questioning and punishment of Christians. Pliny's portrayal of the situation creates an interesting contrast to that of 1 Peter. Pliny thought the Christians were mostly harmless, although he noted that their superstition was encouraging neglect of temples and festivals. The imagery of 1 Pet 4:2–4 implies similar behavior on the part of Christians. Christian avoidance of the life of Gentile vices almost certainly included avoiding temples and festivals. Beyond this one overlap, everything else seems quite different. Pliny asks the emperor if bearing the name "Christian" is a crime in itself, or if Christians should only be punished for other crimes. He reports that his practice thus far has been to execute Christians who three times confess the name, more for their obstinacy than anything else. If these Christians appealed to the usual gods, cursed Christ, and offered sacrifice to Trajan's image, Pliny released them. Trajan responds that no searches should be made for Christians and that no anonymous accusations should be heard. However, refusal to recant should lead to punishment. None of this seems to have much to do with the situation of 1 Peter. The contrast is, in fact, instructive. The kind of official attention to the legal status of Christians that existed in Bithynia during Trajan's reign was not in place in Bithynia when 1 Peter was written.

Though it is difficult to trace in any detail the story of Christian persecution in the first century, the general shape of the story suggests that the reign of the emperor Domitian (81–96 C.E.) provides the most likely context for 1 Peter. The infamous burning of Christians by the emperor Nero in 64 C.E. seems to have been confined to the city of Rome (Tacitus, *Ann.* 15.44). In fact, Nero's persecution appears to have inspired sympathy for Christians rather than antipathy. Even though there is no evidence of persecution of Christians being ordered by the Roman emperor until the third century, Domitian in the latter part of his reign organized a period of enormous violence against anyone perceived as dangerous to the empire or the person of emperor. Domitian not only killed or banished his personal enemies; he also banished philosophers and suppressed the collegia. Roman authorities were famously tolerant of diverse and even deviant religions, but they were equally intolerant of political gatherings. Their fear of political gatherings clashed with the constant formation of social groups (collegia) in the empire. These collegia were formed by all kinds of people for

---

5. W. H. C. Frend, *Martyrdom and Persecution in the Early Church* (Oxford: Blackwell, 1965; repr., Grand Rapids: Baker, 1981).

all kinds of purposes, the most common being artisan groups and burial societies. Most of the groups posed no threat to the political order. However, some did. Gatherings of people with common interests and concerns often drift into the area of politics. The political aspirations of some of these collegia resulted in the authorities' suspicion of and the suppression of all collegia. Whenever an emperor became concerned about social order, an automatic first step would be the banning of collegia.

It is possible that the Christian communities in 1 Peter were caught up in a general suppression of collegia, but there is no evidence in the letter to suggest such. It is also not clear whether Domitian specifically targeted Christians. There is, however, strong evidence from Christian sources that Christian persecution first occurred on a widespread basis during his reign. Whether Domitian focused on Christians or not, Christians were being persecuted in the late 80s and 90s. In one way, the pattern of persecution implied in 1 Peter coheres with the general pattern of persecution prior to the third century. Persecution was not instigated by the authorities but by concerned neighbors. Such was probably the case during the reign of Domitian. There was no imperial edict against Christians, but the violence of Domitian's reign created a volatile context for social deviations. It is neighbors in 1 Peter, encouraged by the paranoia of the times, who instigated the persecution.

The language of "in the name of Christ" (4:14) and "as a Christian" (4:16) raises the possibility of the name itself already being illegal. By the second century, the charge of simply being a Christian was a serious matter in itself, even if different emperors took different attitudes toward Christianity, and each governor of each province enforced rules in different ways. However, before the second century it is not clear whether the name "Christian" in itself would draw official attention. Furthermore, the lack of any hint of official participation in the abuse of the Christians in 1 Peter suggests that the name is not yet the key issue. Persecution in 1 Peter does not seem to include formal charges.

The best guess about persecution in 1 Peter is that it arose from Christian refusal to participate in the usual social and religious practices of the Roman world. This refusal inspired suspicion and animosity from neighbors. These neighbors verbally abused their former friends. It is not possible to reconstruct what was said or where it was said. This abuse produced what was considered to be "suffering" within the community. Such suffering was at least social, involving loss of social rank. It may also have been economic. It is significant that 1 Peter describes suffering that, on the one hand, is instigated by neighbors and not by authorities, but, on the other hand, has spread throughout northern Asia Minor. The persecution in 1 Peter is not an isolated occurrence. This suggests that animosity against Christians is growing throughout the empire. This fits nicely with the paranoia and violence of the reign of Domitian.

Date

The first incontrovertible citation of 1 Peter is from Irenaeus (ca. 180 C.E.). Polycarp, bishop of Smyrna, in his *Letter to the Philippians* (ca. 140), also probably cites 1 Peter (Polycarp, *Phil.* 1.3; 8.1) . The real question is whether *1 Clement* (ca. 96) cites 1 Peter. While there is no direct quote, the letters share so many unusual terms and phrases that many readers conclude that *1 Clement* knew 1 Peter (e.g., *1 Clem.* 7.6; 9.3–4; 21.7; 49.5). If *1 Clement* did not know 1 Peter directly, then both letters participated to a remarkable degree in a particular Christian tradition. The uncertainty of the Clementine citations means that external evidence provides no clear data for determining the latest possible date for the letter, although *1 Clement* reinforces the possibility of the era of Domitian.

External evidence also provides little help in determining the earliest possible date. Of the many attempts to find citations within 1 Peter of other NT texts, the only ones that have much credence are those that detect citations of Acts, Ephesians, or Romans. Readers have long noted the similarities between 1 Peter and the speeches of Acts (e.g., 1 Pet 1:10–12 and Acts 2:14–20; 1 Pet 1:21; 3:22 and Acts 2:32–36; 1 Pet 1:17 and Acts 2:39; 10:34). Readers have also noted the numerous agreements in terminology and phraseology between 1 Peter and Ephesians (e.g., 1 Pet 1:3 and Eph 1:3; 1 Pet 1:3–5 and Eph 1:18; 1 Pet 1:10–12 and Eph 3:5; 1 Pet 1:14 and Eph 2:2–3; 1 Pet 2:4–6 and Eph 2:20–22; 1 Pet 3:22 and Eph 1:20–22). However, most readers find no conclusive evidence of direct citations. The overlap probably comes from a shared participation in a common Christian tradition. There are some intriguing connections between 1 Peter and Romans (e.g., 1 Pet 1:14 and Rom 12:2; 1 Pet 2:6–8 and Rom 9:32–33; 1 Pet 2:13–17 and Rom 13:1–7; 1 Pet 3:8–9 and Rom 12:16–17; 1 Pet 4:10–11 and Rom 12:6). None of these is a direct quotation, but the number and extent of similarities between the texts suggest that 1 Peter could well have known Romans. Of course, since Romans was written somewhere between 55 and 58 C.E., 1 Peter's possible knowledge of Romans does little to assist in dating.

Thus the dating of 1 Peter depends upon the rather uncertain and subjective process of fitting its thought and situation into the most likely historical context. There are three common arguments suggesting the 80s and 90s as the most likely date. First, as shown above, the portrayal of persecution in 1 Peter suggests the reign of Domitian (81–96). Pliny's letters draw a picture of persecution during the reign of Trajan (98–117) that implies a more developed official process than existed in the time of 1 Peter. Pliny, writing ca. 111–112, asserts that some of the Christians he interviewed had actually renounced their faith about twenty years earlier. Their renunciation would have been at the height of the Domitian turmoil. Second, it is difficult to imagine the spread of Christianity into the rural areas of northern Asia Minor before the 80s, which 1 Peter assumes. Unless our reconstruction of the growth of Christianity is considerably inaccurate, then 1 Peter needs to be no earlier than 80 C.E. In fact, a date in the 90s would make even more sense. Third, 1 Peter cites a Christian tradition that fits best with the late first century. First Peter shares a general Christian terminology with Acts, Ephesians, and *1 Clement*, all of which belong, more or less, to this period. All of this means that the best guess for the date of 1 Peter is between 85 and 95 C.E.

Authorship

Once the possibility of pseudonymity is raised, the question of authorship becomes difficult to answer. Pseudepigraphical letters in early Christianity emerged from many different contexts and with many different purposes. A decision that a letter is pseudepigraphical does not indicate anything definite about the motives of the author or the reaction of the readers. Some letters appear to have been designed to deceive readers about authorship.[6] When letters were recognized as pseudepigraphical, they were routinely denied authority by Christian communities. Greek philosophical schools were in the habit of writing documents under the name of the founder of the school. Such documents were recognized as pseudepigraphical but were accorded authority by the communities. It is possible that some early Christian documents were of this kind, although it is difficult to name any document that is irrefutably so.

All of this means that the setting of a Christian pseudepigraphical letter cannot be determined by comparisons with other such letters. The setting of each letter must be determined on its own. First Peter offers a quite plausible scenario. The apostle Peter writes a circular letter from Rome that is to be carried by Silvanus to Christian communities throughout the area of western and northern Asia Minor. However, if Peter is not the author, the question becomes What pieces of this projected context reflect the real origins of the letter? There are many possibilities.

Some readers see 1 Peter as a real letter written from Rome under the name of Peter. It was penned either by members of the Petrine school in Rome or by an unknown person with loyalties to Peter. Some of these readers suggest further that reference to Silvanus as the carrier of the letter actually signals the authorship of the letter by Silvanus. However, most readers who see the letter as a real letter conclude that Silvanus would have been a very unlikely author. In any case, if the letter was actually carried by Silvanus, then it is likely that

---

6. For the most complete surveys of ancient pseudepigraphy, see Speyer, *Die literarische Fälschung*, vol. 1, pt. 2; and Norbert Brox, *Falsche Verfasserangaben: Zur Erklärung der frühchristlichen Pseudepigraphie* (ed. Herberg Haag et al.; Stuttgarter Bibelstudien 79; Stuttgart: Katholisches Bibelwerk, 1975).

the naming of Peter as author would have been an act of humility on the part of the author(s) and would have been recognized as such by the Christians in Asia Minor. Readers who want to date the letter late in the first century typically find it unlikely that Silvanus actually delivered the letter. If Silvanus was not the carrier, his naming becomes part of the apostolic fiction, and the letter would have been carried by an unknown and unnamed member of the Petrine school. All of this is possible, although we know little about the character of these so-called schools. There is no conversation in early Christian literature about the existence of schools that were dedicated to apostolic figures and that wrote in their names. The historical reality of such schools is inferred from the existence of so many pseudepigraphical letters.

It is much simpler to see the publication of the letter as a moment in the manuscript tradition of early Christianity. Most historians assume that pseudepigraphical letters were not written under the pretense of their being the original autographs. It is hard to imagine the pretense of producing an old parchment with proper handwriting, along with the fabrication of a story of its discovery. There would be no need for such. Christians in Asia Minor in the late first century were not reading the original autographs of Paul's Letters. It is much simpler to write the letter as a copy, perhaps adding it to a scroll or codex of other Christian documents. Of course, if 1 Peter emerged in such a fashion, then every piece of the claimed origin of the letter could be a fiction. Most readers, however, seek an explanation for Peter in Rome being named as the author and for persecuted Christians in Pontus, Galatia, Cappadocia, Asia, and Bithynia being named as the recipients.

The easy part of this puzzle is the destination. If the letter was supposedly sent to these communities in Asia Minor, then its first appearance would likely have been in this area. Thus the real purpose of the letter would coincide with its explicitly stated purpose. The letter was written to encourage Christians in this area who were in the midst of persecution. In fact, it could well have been written by a member of one of these communities.

If the letter emerged within persecuted communities in Asia Minor, the role of the apostle Peter and the city of Rome needs explanation. Many readers see the ascription to Peter and Rome as evidence of a connection between the writer and Petrine traditions or even a Petrine school in Rome. However, there is little in 1 Peter that sounds much like the Peter we encounter elsewhere in the canon. The difficulty in imagining how the historical Peter could have articulated the theology of 1 Peter holds for a Petrine school as well. If this letter was authored by a group of Christians whose primary theological allegiance was to the apostle Peter, then either historians have a quite inaccurate image of Peter, or the school has moved far from its founder. Thus the simplest conclusion is that Peter and Rome are evoked because this personality and that city have authority in these communities. Peter and Rome represent reliable apostolic tradition. Peter's martyrdom, which is not mentioned in the letter and in the fiction of the letter could not be, may even play a silent role. The apostle Peter, who himself was martyred, is the ideal person to encourage faithfulness in the midst of persecution.

Though an origin in Asia Minor from the hand of a member of those communities, who evokes the authority of Peter and Rome, is perhaps the simplest explanation for the origin of 1 Peter, the truth is that such a scenario is little more than an educated guess. There are many possible scenarios for the origin of this letter. It is even possible that it came from the hand of Peter himself, although that seems unlikely.[7] Uncertainty over authorship and provenance suggests a certain modesty in reading strategy. Rather than having a theory of authorship direct the reading of the text, it is better to focus upon the syntax of the letter while keeping the historical context fluid.

Literary Structure

Beyond the debate over authorship, the other most persistent debate among readers of 1 Peter is over its literary structure. The letter is difficult to outline. It does not follow the familiar structure of a Pauline letter, with its formal shifts from theological argument to exhortation. Yet the letter displays classic rhetorical strategies that suggest care in composition. It has a rather traditional prescript (1:1–2) and postscript (5:12–14). It opens with the usual blessing (1:3–12) and closes with a typical summary (5:6–11). The letter is filled with numerous rhetorical devices common to ancient rhetoric. These range, for example, from a tendency to gather synonyms (1:8, 10; 2:25; 3:4) or even words of similar sound (1:4, 19; 3:18) to a fondness for parallelisms (2:14, 22–23; 3:18; 4:6, 11; 5:2–3). The author of 1 Peter employs a rich and diverse rhetorical style. The letter also divides itself into explicit and obvious pericopes. Almost all commentaries on 1 Peter divide the letter into the same passages. The only real debate is whether 5:5b goes best with what precedes or what follows. Nevertheless, the literary logic of 1 Peter is difficult to track. The individual passages do not display an obvious argumentative logic. The distinct passages in 1 Peter do not so much make arguments as gather images and exhortations around a set of themes. The force of these passages does not lie in the logic of the argument but in the cumulative power of the gathering. The connection between passages is also difficult to track. There does not seem to be a narrative logic that connects one passage to the next. The passages connect to one another more by a building up and intertwining of images and imperatives and less by a sequencing of argument.

---

7. For recent defenses of Petrine authorship see Hillyer 1–9; and Jobes, *1 Peter*, 5–19.

The narrative disorder of 1 Peter has led many readers to question its literary unity. The debate has turned upon two arguments. First, some readers have argued that the shift in tone between 4:11 and 4:12 indicates a radical literary break that can best be explained by the presence of two different sources. The doxology in 4:11 concludes one source. The address "beloved" in 4:12 introduces another source. This theory of sources was reinforced by an argument that the situation of the community with regard to the character of persecution was different in the two parts of the letter. Second, some readers also have argued that the first part of the letter from 1:3–4:11 was originally a baptismal homily. They have proposed that the presence of baptismal imagery (e.g., 1:3; 2:2; 3:21), along with the various exhortations to the holy life (see esp. 1:15), fits the model of a baptismal homily or even pieces of a baptismal liturgy. Although these theories have taken many variations, the usual model is that 1 Peter is composed of a baptismal homily (1:3–4:11) to which has been added an eclectic gathering of exhortations (4:12–5:11). However, few readers hold to such theories anymore. Upon closer examination, most readers have concluded not only that Peter has no more baptismal imagery than many other NT letters, but also that there is no compelling evidence of a historical or literary break at 4:12. Thus almost all readers of 1 Peter now see the letter as a unified piece.

All of this means that the most readers of 1 Peter see the letter as loosely organized at best. Even if no formal argumentative structure that has been proposed has proved to be persuasive, the letter does appear to have recognizable sections and transitions. In addition to the usual epistolary openings and closings, the body of the letter shifts from passage to passage in an ordered way. The rhetoric of 1 Peter works by way of repetition and accumulation, with the various passages reinforcing one another. For example, there is not just one analysis of suffering in the letter but several. While images of suffering are scattered throughout the letter, suffering is the central image in 1:6–7; 2:18–23; 3:9, 13–18; 4:1–4, 12–19; 5:8–10. Each of these passages in some ways stands on its own. There is no explicit connection among them. Nevertheless, together they build a richer image and fuller account of the character of suffering and the communities' expected response.

First Peter reads as a gathering of passages and images that build upon one another. Each passage echoes other passages. Each image intertwines with other images. This rhetorical interconnectedness means that manufacturing an outline of the letter seems either beside the point or misleading. Most outlines of 1 Peter are effectively identical. They differ mostly by the number of sections they impose upon the letter. For instance, some readers divide the body of the letter into three sections (1:13–2:10; 2:11–4:11; 4:12–5:11); some into six (1:3–2:10; 2:11–12; 2:13–3:12; 3:13–4:6; 4:7–11; 4:12–5:11); and some avoid sections altogether. In terms of how the letter is read, there is little at stake in these differences. No matter how the letter is divided, each section is interconnected with the others.

Outline

1:1–2 Epistolary Prescript
1:3–12 Opening Blessing
1:13–2:10 The Holy Life
    1:13–21 Call to Holiness
    1:22–25 Love and the Word
    2:1–3 Milk of the Lord
    2:4–10 The Living Stone
2:11–4:6 Life as Aliens and Sojourners
    2:11–12 Call to Beautiful Deeds among the Gentiles
    2:13–17 Submission to the Authority of the Gentiles
    2:18–25 Submission of Servants to Masters
    3:1–7 Submission by Wives and Honoring by Husbands
    3:8–12 Exhortation and Blessing for All
    3:13–17 Suffering While Doing Good
    3:18–22 Christ as Model of Suffering and Victory
    4:1–6 Separation from the Gentile Life
4:7–5:11 The End Is Near
    4:7–11 Love within the Community
    4:12–19 Suffering as Judgment
    5:1–5 Elders and Their Flocks
    5:6–11 Concluding Call to Suffering
5:12–14 Epistolary Postscript

Theology

For all the debates about authorship and literary structure, there is agreement among readers of 1 Peter that this text presents an intriguing and challenging theology. As with most early Christian letters, the theology is embedded in the rhetoric and exhortation of the letter. The theology of 1 Peter is intensely contextual. It is built around the problem of abuse from neighbors and the suffering it causes. The most obvious purpose of the letter is to provide encouragement. This is done by creating a theological narrative that not only gives meaning to suffering but also treats suffering as a blessing. The story of Jesus, for instance, becomes a story that exemplifies and sanctifies suffering. A variety of traditional Christian theological images are fed into the problem of suffering. These diverse images unpack the mystery of suffering even as the inscrutable character of suffering transforms the images themselves. The result is a letter that challenges its readers to embrace righteous suffering as a blessing and as a sign that the spirit of God rests upon them.

This focus upon encouragement does not mean that classical Christian ethics is neglected. First Peter continuously calls upon the diverse ethical traditions of early Christianity. Furthermore, 1 Peter does not soften or suppress the rigors of these ethical demands simply because the community might suffer because of them. Instead, various traditions are combined into a theological narrative that is in some ways typical of early Christianity and in other ways unique to 1 Peter. The traditional ethical values of early Christianity, which are being tested by persecution, are reaffirmed. In fact, the key to suffering serving as a blessing is that good behavior surrounds the abuse. Only a particular sequence can transform the terror of suffering into a blessing. If a person engages in good behavior, and this good behavior inspires animosity and abuse from neighbors, and the person responds to this abuse with more good behavior—only thus is suffering connected to blessing. Most of the theology of 1 Peter is gathered around this sequence.

The core theological move in 1 Peter lies in the articulation of a cosmic narrative into which Christians are called. God is portrayed as the author and primary actor in this narrative. The opening blessing gives the basic outline of God's activity (1:3–5). God has caused these Christians to be born again into a new life. This life is shaped by hope for an inheritance that God is keeping for them. Not only is God keeping the inheritance safe; God is also keeping them safe. In this passage and throughout the letter, 1 Peter describes a new past, a new present, and a new future.

First, God authors a break from the past. Although God is the primary actor in this break, God acts through Jesus Christ or, as 1:3 states it, "through the resurrection of Jesus Christ from the dead." There is a suggestion of a further role for Jesus in 1:18–19, where Jesus is the sacrificial lamb whose blood has ransomed the Christians from their futile lives. Much of 1 Peter focuses on the break and distance from the past. While there are a variety of cosmic groundings for this break, the primary concern in 1 Peter is with the ethical character of this break. Though much of the exhortation to the ethical life will focus on the positive, 1 Peter also demands the negative. Former lives are described as driven by desires and ignorance (1:14) and dominated by drunkenness and idolatry (4:2–4). The battle between the old life and the new is described as warfare (2:11). Christians are called to resist. This resistance is complicated by the abuse they receive from their neighbors (4:2–4). The temptation is to drift back into old social patterns, to give in to the passions, and thereby to avoid persecution. Thus 1 Peter narrates the theological groundings of this break from the past and exhorts ongoing refusal to return to that past.

Second, God orders a holy life in the present. The weight of the exhortations in 1 Peter falls not upon resistance to the past but upon life in the present. First

Theology

Peter constantly pleads with these Christians to live the lives they have been called to live. The dominant image is that of holiness: "You shall be holy, for I am holy" (1:16). The traditional OT image of holiness reinforces the special identity of these Christians. They are "a chosen race, a royal priesthood, a holy nation" (2:9). In fact, they "were once not a people, but now are a people of God" (2:10). They are separate, distinct, and holy. Even the terms "alien" and "sojourner" connect to the sense of separation in the word "holy."

However, the present life is characterized not so much by separation from other people as by connection. The letter demands that its readers "honor everyone" (2:17). In some ways, this command announces the central concern of 1 Peter. The social patterns that once organized the lives of these Christians are no longer viable. In their place is a Christian ethic demanding that these Christians honor everyone, whether that person is a member of the Christian community or a neighbor who is abusing them. Within this ethic of personal encounter, distinctions are made about which virtues are appropriate for which person. While everyone deserves honor, not everyone deserves love. In 1 Peter, love is directed to the community of Christians. The necessity and propriety of loving other Christians does not appear to be a matter of controversy. First Peter does not try to define or even describe what this love looks like. In fact, its rhetoric about behavior within the community is couched more as reminder than as critique.

The controversy lies in how Christians can behave in a holy way toward people who are abusing them. Is there an appropriate Christian way to honor people who are causing suffering? First Peter's response to this puzzle is to call upon the story of Jesus. In fact, the primary role of Jesus in 1 Peter is to model a pattern of behavior in the face of suffering (and a pattern of divine response to that suffering). As 2:21 declares, Jesus "suffered, . . . leaving for you a pattern, so that you might follow in his footsteps." This pattern involves not sinning and not giving in to the desire for revenge when faced with abuse. Jesus, it is noted, "when he was abused, did not abuse in return; . . . when he suffered, did not threaten" (2:23). This refusal to return evil for evil is common in early Christianity. (The force of the Sermon on the Mount on early Christian ethics is difficult to overestimate, although Jesus' command to love enemies [Matt 5:44] is modified in 1 Peter, where everyone deserves honor but only the Christian community deserves love.) Greco-Roman ethics is filled with similar challenges. The key to wisdom lies in always living the virtues. Returning vice for vice is not a virtue. Thus 1 Peter is not proposing an ethical pattern unknown or unattractive to the Gentile neighbors of these Christians. This shared recognition of the virtue of not returning abuse for abuse is what leads to the Gentiles ultimately recognizing that the irritating behavior of their Christian neighbors is in fact good (2:12, 15; 3:1–2, 16).

All of this means that good behavior is the key to the Christian life. First Peter shows little concern for questions of orthodoxy. The purpose of a theological account of God or Jesus or the cosmos lies less in its capacity to produce theological correctness and more in its capacity to produce good behavior. Knowing the truth about what God is doing in Christ inspires and enables Christlike behavior. While it is the case that "the word of the Lord endures forever" (1:25), the purpose of this word is not its mere endurance. Obedience to this word, to the truth, leads to love (1:22). First Peter inevitably returns all theological accounts to the crucible of human behavior. In some ways, the willingness to live as Jesus lived is the true content of faith. The sequences of 4:12–19 are typical. After a series of assertions about the true character of suffering and judgment, the passage concludes with the admonition "So then, may those who are suffering in accordance with the will of God entrust their lives to the faithful creator by doing good." The challenge is to do good in a world that abuses those who do. The purpose of theology is to convince these Christians that good behavior secures their place in the saving narrative of Jesus Christ.

Finally, in the future God judges all people. God judges not according to proper or improper confessions of faith but "without partiality according to the deeds of each person" (1:17). The narrative of Jesus forms the paradigm. When Jesus was abused, he did not return abuse for abuse, rather he "handed over himself to the one who judges justly" (2:23). Jesus is not only raised from the dead (1:21) but "is at the right hand of God, having gone into heaven, with the angels and authorities and powers being made subject to him" (3:22). This Jesus sequence is the potential sequence of all people. First Peter uses the traditional OT language of hope (1:3), inheritance (1:4), and salvation (1:5, 9, 10) to fill out this narrative. Unlike much of Greco-Roman ethics, where the reward for practicing virtue in the face of vice lies in the virtue itself, 1 Peter insists that good behavior will lead to salvation and glory, just as it did for Jesus. The promises of 5:10 are typical: "But the God of all grace, who has called you into his eternal glory in Christ, will himself, after you have suffered a short time, restore, support, strengthen, establish you." Good behavior depends to a great degree on believing that this narrative of reward is true.

God's coming judgment is also a threat. This threat falls, of course, upon non-Christians, who disobey the word (3:1, 20; 4:17). "They will give an account to the one who is ready to judge the living and the dead" (4:5). First Peter appears to be more than a bit skeptical about how these disobedient Gentiles will fare at this judgment (4:17–18). This threat also falls upon the Christian readers. The call to holiness leads to the warning "If you call father the one who judges without partiality according to the deeds of each person, in fear live the time of your exile" (1:17). Belief in Jesus does not in itself lead to glory. The believer must also live the holy life that Jesus lived. In this regard, suffering plays a dual role. In agreement with most people, whether Jewish, Greek, or Roman, 1 Peter affirms the refining power of suffering. Suffering refines and ultimately proves the quality of a person, just as fire refines gold (1:7). But 1 Peter affirms something a bit more unique about suffering when it claims that the abuse being endured by these Christians is the beginning of God's end-time judgment (4:17). Suffering is the ultimate test as to whether a person is willing to live the Christian life. The temptation is to return to social patterns that avoid suffering.

While 1 Peter speaks of the power of God that sustains the Christian life (1:5), the primary way God seems to empower this Christian life is through words. The narrative of Jesus is crucial, but so are the words of the OT. While Isaiah, the Psalms (esp. Ps 34), and Proverbs are the texts most frequently cited, 1 Peter cites at least eleven different OT texts, usually preferring the Septuagint to the Masoretic text. The frequent Scripture citations do not seem to function as prophetic proof for the holiness of the story of Jesus and the community, as they often do in early Christian texts. First Peter quotes and alludes mostly to enrich and illustrate. Citations are given no special authority. There is no discernible difference between the force of an image from Scripture and an image from Christian tradition. The imagery of Scripture and the peculiar images of the Jesus story become interchangeable. This is understandable since, as 1:10–12 asserts, the prophets were testifying about the story of Jesus, and they were doing it for the benefit of future Christians.

Crucial to all the theological rhetoric in 1 Peter is the context of suffering. Suffering is a testing and refining fire. The purpose of theology of 1 Peter is to offer guidance and assurance in the face of this test. The power to resist the trials of suffering depends in part upon belief that the theological narratives articulated in 1 Peter are indeed true. Yet belief by itself is not enough. These Christians, empowered by this theology, must live holy lives, in which they honor everyone.

Text and Translation

The Greek text of 1 Peter is reasonably well represented in the early manuscripts. However, among the papyrus manuscripts, only $\mathfrak{P}^{72}$ contains the full text. There are sections in $\mathfrak{P}^{74}$ and $\mathfrak{P}^{81}$. All of the major uncials except for Codex D (Bezae) offer a version of the Greek text of 1 Peter. The text is completely absent in D, and only some sections are present in Codex C (Ephraemi Rescriptus). A full Greek text is present in the early uncials ℵ (Sinaiticus), B (Vaticanus), and A (Alexandrinus). It is also fully represented in Koine and Majority text traditions. Its absence from D, its unevenness in the Latin tradition, and its omission from the Muratorian Canon suggests an underrepresentation in the so-called Western tradition of manuscripts.

Among the existing texts, the disagreements are mostly minor and understandable. The variations usually represent slight differences in grammar or terminology. This commentary cites two kinds of variants. Sometimes it is not possible to decide with any confidence which of the variants is most likely to be the earliest. In such instances, the relevant variants will be cited and a suggestion will be made as to the preferable text. Sometimes variants are simply interesting because they illustrate theological arguments within early Christianity. Many of these will also be cited.

Readers of this commentary will notice that the English translation is at times somewhat awkward. As all readers of Greek are aware, Greek syntax and English syntax are structured quite differently. It is often not possible to express in normal English the grammatical tensions that are crucial to the force of the Greek. The translation offered here intentionally tries to capture the rhythms and forces in the Greek syntax. While this results in English that is on occasion a bit infelicitous, one hopes that this translation will engage the reader of this commentary with the felicities of the Greek.

COMMENTARY

1 Peter 1:1–2 Epistolary Prescript

The classic Greek letter opening of "sender to recipient, greetings" had been expanded, prior to NT times, by Jewish writers. They divided the classic greeting into two lines, in which the first named the sender and recipient and the second evoked a blessing on the recipient (e.g., Dan 4:1; *2 Bar.* 78.2). Forms of this salutation occur, of course, in Paul's Letters and here in 1 Peter.

The question for readers of 1 Peter is how to hear the series of theological terms that pile up in this salutation. If salutations are largely stylized and symbolic openings, wherein terms are collected not in order to make or anticipate an argument but simply to evoke the feel of a proper greeting, then we should not get bogged down in the theological subtleties that these terms suggest. However, most readers of 1 Peter detect an anticipation of later arguments in the terms collected here. The author's theology is already emerging. Thus interpreters of 1 Peter typically read the salutation with an eye on the larger theology of the letter.

> 1:1 Peter, an apostle of Jesus Christ, to the elect sojourners[a] of the dispersion[b] in Pontus, Galatia, Cappadocia, Asia, and Bithynia, 2 (who have been elected)[c] in accordance with the foreknowledge of God by the sanctification of the Spirit for obedience and sprinkling of the blood of Jesus Christ, may grace and peace be multiplied for you.

> a. The precise meaning of the word *parepidēmos*, which is rendered here as "sojourner," is much debated. Especially the distinctions among *parepidēmos*, *paroikos* (2:11), and *xenos* have puzzled readers. It is possible that careful political distinctions are being made, wherein a *parepidēmos* is someone living in exile from their home, whether the exile is willing or not; a *paroikos* is a person with the specific legal status of resident alien; and a *xenos* is any kind of stranger. But the metaphorical reach of the terms in 1 Peter suggests that together they evoke the recipients' outsider status, legal and otherwise. Some texts insert *kai* between "elect" and "sojourners," probably in order to simplify the syntax. But it is probably better to leave "elect" in the somewhat awkward position of an adjective.

b. Some readers have suggested a partitive genitive for "of the dispersion" so that the phrase would read "the elect sojourners among the exiles." Such a reading emphasizes the legal implications of the term "sojourner." It is better to read a qualitative genitive, whereby names and titles are being added to the portrait of the recipients: "elect sojourners dispersed in Pontus."

c. It is possible to connect the foreknowledge of God with "apostle," so that Peter is an apostle "in accordance with the foreknowledge of God," or with the blessing, so that grace and peace are multiplied "in accordance with the foreknowledge of God." Both are a bit awkward. It is far easier to connect the foreknowledge of God with the elect character of the recipients.

[1] Peter is named in the expected way as "an apostle of Jesus Christ." However, there is no real exploration of his status as an apostle in the letter. In fact, when the peculiar voice of Peter emerges in 5:1, Peter's unique status as an apostle is not evoked. Instead, his equality with the recipients is explored.

The weight of the salutation falls not upon the character and authority of Peter but upon the theological status of the recipients. The series of opening images, "elect sojourners of the dispersion," in brief compass evokes the dominant imagery of the letter. The sense of being chosen pervades the letter. Although this election is ultimately good news, for it leads to the "unfading crown of glory" (5:4), it also connects readers with the suffering of Christ. Being called to follow in Christ's footsteps creates the constant tension in the letter, between suffering and glory, the cross and resurrection. This opening phrase evokes that tension in the coupling of election with being a sojourner, with being dispersed. To be chosen will mean that one no longer belongs to the world in which one lived. To follow Jesus is to walk no longer among the Gentiles. The scandal of the cross, which animates so much of the letter, emerges here, albeit in a gentle way.

The image of the diaspora and the geographical names that follow further evoke the outsider status that election creates. Although there are debates about the precise areas being named here and the reason for the order of the names, the general reference is clear enough. Almost the entire area of modern Turkey north of the Taurus Mountains is included in these five names. Although we know of Pauline missions and of existing churches in the first century in the general areas of Asia and Galatia, we know nothing with any assurance about Christian presence on the borders of the Black Sea (Pontus and Bithynia) until the Trajan-Pliny correspondence (ca. 111 C.E.; see the introduction), nor of the more isolated areas of Cappadocia, apart from the brief reference in Acts 2:9. There is no particular reason to call these areas the diaspora, although they might be included in the reach of the term. More likely, we have a Christianizing of Jewish and Roman terms. Christians are now metaphorically sojourners, living in the metaphorical diaspora. The very real outsider status, evoked by these metaphors, is both social and spiritual. There is no evidence, not even in this letter, that these areas were undergoing persecution that other areas were not (see 5:9). Rather, we should understand that these areas, along with Rome, from where the letter claims to be sent (5:13), must compose the primary Christian world of the author.

[2] Although God, Jesus Christ, and the Spirit are all named here, there is no attempt to work out any Trinitarian doctrine or even to specify the relationship among the three "persons." Rather, we have a further gathering of the theological themes that drive the letter. It is no surprise that election is in accordance with the foreknowledge of God and that it is empowered by sanctification. These are standard early Christian ideas, and they are fundamental to 1 Peter. Election must lead to holiness. What is affirmed here, mostly by implication, will become a threat in 1:16–17.

The image of sanctification leads naturally to an insistence on obedience. As we shall see, obedience sits at the heart of 1 Peter's theology. The readers will be called "children of obedience" (1:14), and much of the letter seems to be couched to exhort obedience. The classic early Christian tension between election and judgment is evoked here. On the one hand, Christians are called, chosen, and sanctified; but on the other hand, these assurances do not eliminate the necessity of obedience or spare anyone from judgment. The elect must obey, because the elect will be judged. Much of the theology of 1 Peter is carved out of this classic tension.

What is surprising is that all of this also leads to "sprinkling of the blood of Jesus Christ." As readers have long noted, the blood of Jesus ought to coincide somehow with God's act of sanctification and thus precede the obedience that follows. Atonement should lead to sanctification and obedience, not vice versa. This puzzle has caused many readers to suggest that the blood here is not the blood of atonement but the blood of covenant. In Exod 24:3–8, for example, the people promise obedience, and then the blood of sacrifice is sprinkled on both the altar and the people. This sprinkling seals the covenant. This fits perfectly with the syntax of 1 Peter. However, the only other reference to Christ's blood in 1 Peter clearly refers to atonement (1:18–19). Furthermore, given the constant call to suffering in the letter, it is difficult not to hear echoes of that suffering in the reference to blood. "Sprinkling of the blood of Jesus Christ" may occur in the abuse that Christians endure when they follow in his footsteps (2:21). The salutation ends with the standard Jewish and Christian epistolary blessing.

Already in this brief salutation, we have entered the complex and troubling theological world of 1 Peter. The fundamental and disconcerting tensions between belonging and not belonging, between the cross and the resurrection, between obedience and salvation, are briefly sketched in these two verses. The letter of 1 Peter will take us deep into the wonders and terrors of these conflicts that are at the heart of the Christian life.

1 Peter 1:3–12 Opening Blessing

In the common style of Christian, Jewish, and to some extent Greek letters, 1 Peter opens with a blessing to God for God's blessings to "us." These verses then move to an account of the role of suffering in the Christian life, to an account of the Christian's relationship with Christ, and finally to an account of the relationship between the prophets of the past and the gospel of today. Because of this shift in topic, these verses are often divided into four sections. However, such a division obscures the ongoing force of the blessing. The echoes of the opening blessing are still in force in 1:12. Thus the fact that angels desire to peek into the details of the gospel (1:12) is still a sign of how much God has blessed these people.

A gentle progression of thought around the concept of faith may structure the order of these topics. The opening blessing includes the notion that "we" are being guarded "through faith." The following verses (1:6–7) highlight the centrality of faith by declaring that faith can be seen as the reason for Christian suffering. Suffering demonstrates the genuineness of faith. That genuineness in turn leads to the final glories of God's blessing. The familiar not-yet character of faith is being developed in these verses. In faith, there is suffering now and glory later; in the life of faith, the present contains a lack and a terror that God's future will overcome. This tension at the heart of faith structures the readers' relationship with Christ: they do not see Christ now and yet have faith in him (1:8–9). This not-yet character of faith may even structure the section on the prophets who testify beforehand and who learn that "not for themselves but for you they were serving these things" (1:12).

On the other hand, epistolary blessings such as this often gather diverse theological images without subsuming them to strict logical control. This blessing has a liturgical feel in that the force of the rhetoric seems designed more to evoke the wonders of God's blessings than to make a theological argument.

The basic rhetorical character of 1 Peter is reflected in the eclectic composition of this blessing. First Peter does not offer careful theological arguments. It does not even follow any of the common progressions of rhetorical arguments. Instead, it evokes a theological and ethical world by way of diverse metaphors and wandering rhetoric. Such a disorder is sometimes permitted in classic rhetoric as effective for persuading an audience. If there is a fundamental difference between argument (or proof) and persuasion, then 1 Peter must be classed as almost entirely persuasion.

> **1:3** Blessed be the God and father of our Lord Jesus Christ, who in accordance with his great mercy has caused us to be born again into[a] a living hope through the resurrection of Jesus Christ from the dead, **4** into[a] an

imperishable and undefiled and unfading inheritance, kept in the heavens for you **5** who are being guarded by the power of God through faith for[a] a salvation ready to be revealed at the last time. **6** For this reason[b] you rejoice,[c] even if[d] now for a short time[e] it is necessary that you are grieved by various trials, **7** in order that the genuineness[f] of your faith, [a genuineness] more precious than gold, which though it is destroyed is tested by fire, might be found to result in praise and glory and honor at the revelation of Jesus Christ, **8** whom, though you have not seen, you love, in whom, now not seeing but believing, you rejoice with an inexpressible and glorified joy, **9** for[g] you are receiving the goal[h] of your faith, the salvation of your lives,[i] **10** concerning which salvation, the prophets who prophesied about this grace intended for[j] you sought and searched, **11** searching for what[k] and what sort of time the Spirit of Christ within them was indicating[l] when it testified beforehand about the suffering intended for[j] Christ and the glories after them, **12** to whom it was revealed that not for themselves but for you they were serving these things, which things have now been announced to you through those who proclaimed the good news to you by the Holy Spirit sent from heaven, things into which angels desire to peek.

a. Three similar prepositional phrases follow the participle about rebirth ("caused us to be born again"). While all three begin with *eis*, they seem to have different meanings. The first two seem to have the sense of place and thus are translated "into," while the third has more the sense of purpose and thus is translated "for." The preposition *eis* can refer to both place and purpose.

b. The relative pronoun in the phrase *en hō* can be either masculine or neuter. If masculine, the antecedent would probably be "time" in the phrase "at the last time" (v. 5). It could also refer back to God or Christ in v. 3. All of these options are a bit awkward. Thus it is best to read the pronoun as neuter. The antecedent would be the overall content of what preceded.

c. The verb *agalliasthe* (you rejoice) could be imperative or indicative. However, it reads more naturally as an indicative, and the obvious indicative of "you rejoice" in 1:8 suggests an indicative here.

d. The phrase *ei deon* presents considerable difficulties. It is grammatically possible to read the phrase as introducing either a factual or hypothetical condition. If factual, the translation would run something like "For this reason you rejoice, although now . . ." A bit more likely is the hypothetical translation given here. However, as we shall argue below, the hypothetical structure of the syntax is rhetorical and does not prove either the reality or unreality of the suffering.

e. "For a short time" could also be rendered "a little bit," but the latter fits awkwardly with the theology of suffering in the letter.

f. The Greek *dokimion* conveys the sense of something having been tested and approved. Its meaning here seems to be something like "the approved status" of your faith or as translated above, "the genuineness" of your faith.

g. The present participle *komizomenoi* can be either temporal "as" or a causal "for" or "because." A causal reading clarifies the theological logic of the verse.

h. The Greek word *telos* can have both the sense of being on the way toward a goal and the sense of having reached that goal, thus of being finished. Its translation here as "goal" tries to keep both nuances in play.

i. The word *psychai* is often translated as "souls." This is not so much incorrect as misleading for it suggests an anthropology that may not be present. First Peter will make a distinction between the body and the spirit, but not between the body and the *psychē*. Thus *psychai* should be translated as "selves" or "lives."

j. The phrases "the grace intended for you" and "the sufferings intended for Christ" both employ the preposition *eis*, translated here as "intended for." The point of the phrases is not possession: "your grace" or "Christ's sufferings." The edge here is prophecy. The prophets are searching for grace and suffering that belong not to their time but to the future.

k. *Tina* can be read as an adjective, "what," modifying "time," or as a pronoun, "who." Both readings are quite plausible here.

l. The grammar of this verse is confusing because it is not clear what is the direct object of the verb *edēlou* (was indicating). The direct object could be "what and what sort of time," as translated here, or "the suffering intended for Christ and the glories after them." Either works grammatically, although the former is a bit simpler.

[3] The Greek practice of opening letters with a prayer for the recipients was often modified in Christian letters by the OT language of blessing (cf. 2 Cor 1:3; Eph 1:3). First Peter opens with the standard syntax of blessing. The only striking moment in this initial phrase lies in the notion that God is the God of Jesus Christ and not just the Father. Although this language might prove awkward for later Trinitarian formulations, the supremacy of God evoked here is in force throughout the letter. Even if the story of Jesus is the key to how God is behaving, it is still God who is the primary actor and the author of human blessings. This supremacy is reiterated in the notion that it is God who has "caused us to be born again" through the resurrection of Jesus. God is acting through Jesus.

Almost every word in this opening sentence becomes crucial to the theology of 1 Peter. Images of mercy, new birth, a living hope, and resurrection will return throughout the letter. God's mercy will be explicitly detailed in the exploration of what it means to be a chosen people (2:9–10). But mercy also underlies much of the Christology of the letter (e.g., 1:18–21). At the heart of the gospel story lies the inexplicable mercy of God.

The image of rebirth returns explicitly in 1:23 and 2:2, wherein readers are encouraged to seek the new food of the word as suckling babes seek milk. Furthermore, the notion of rebirth funds the entire worldview of the letter. Christians are a new people, chosen, reborn. They are cut off from the old life, in both their beliefs and their behavior, and are now living new lives, with new forces and faces governing them and their fate.

Opening Blessing

Finally, hope and resurrection evoke the ultimate conviction of the letter. This letter is a letter of hope in the midst of suffering, an affirmation of the resurrection under the terror of death. First Peter favors the image of "glory" to call forth the coming blessings awaiting faithful readers. While they must suffer, wait, and endure the terrors of life and the abuse of outsiders, they do so under the glow of God's glory, a glory that shall be given to them, just as it already has been given to Christ.

[4–5] Hope, perhaps especially Christian hope, escapes precise definition. Since the fulfillment of Christian hope depends upon God, the complete nature of that fulfillment remains hidden in the mystery of God. Thus it is no surprise that these verses do not detail the precise content of the hope announced in 1:3. Instead, we encounter the typical Christian theological move in the face of this mystery. Rather than speaking what cannot be spoken, 1 Peter points to the surety of this hope, to the eternity of the unimaginable reward.

In the Greek, a series of *alpha* privatives (conveyed in English as *im*perishable and *un*defiled and *un*fading) announce in rather poetic fashion the eternal character of the inheritance. The notion of inheritance is fundamental in much of biblical thought. From Israel's inheritance of the land, to notions of eschatological inheritance in the prophets, to Christian notions of inheritance in Christ, the Bible offers a rich vision of a promised inheritance. The working nuance of inheritance, as opposed to language of reward, lies in the sense of ownership that the word suggests. This "inheritance" belongs to the readers. Furthermore, this inheritance is "imperishable and undefiled and unfading." The imagery here is creating a feeling of surety, almost of guarantee.

This sense of surety is reinforced with an image of God watching over this inheritance. It is "kept in the heavens for you." God is keeping "your" inheritance safe. In evoking, albeit indirectly, this act of keeping by God, 1 Peter reinforces the larger syntax of the passage. It is God who "has caused us to be born again into a living hope" and thus "into an . . . inheritance." The logic of "into" is not clear. This much at least can be asserted: by God's act in Christ, "we" are living in a new situation. This new situation, reality, and condition assure hope and inheritance and God's keeping. Overstating things a bit, the whole of 1 Peter can be read as an exploration of this "into." The letter explores the forces and faces, the promises and obligations, the terrors and wonders that emerge from God's rebirthing "us."

Not only is the inheritance kept safe, but so also are these believers. They "are being guarded by the power of God through faith." God is keeping both the inheritance and the heirs safe. However, the guarding of the heirs by the power of God includes a human element. While the safekeeping of the inheritance requires only the attention of God, the safekeeping of believers requires proper behavior from the believers. The little aside "through faith" opens up the constant exhortation in the letter. The readers must be faithful; they must follow in

Jesus' steps; they must live the full ethics of the Christian life. God keeps them safe, not by protecting them from the violence of outsiders, but by protecting them from themselves. It takes faith to live the Christian life.

Thus a hint of uncertainty about ultimate salvation enters the discussion. The readers are being guarded "for a salvation ready to be revealed at the last time." In the Greek the "for" in this phrase actually parallels the "into" in the phrases above (see note a). If the first phrases suggest a dislocation of place (people are here and the inheritance is in heaven), this phrase suggests a dislocation in time. Salvation is not yet revealed. Rather, it is "ready to be revealed." Living in temporal and spatial dislocation structures faith. Faith demands a believing in the reality of what is not quite in hand. There is a distance in both space and time between the heir and the inheritance. Faith lives in this distance. The nuance of trust in the Greek root *pistis* is in play here. People must trust God, who is reliable but who remains nonetheless a mystery. Their belief in God is not simply an assertion of God's existence. They also trust that God is a certain kind of God who behaves in a certain way. However, 1 Peter will also insist that these Christians must live holy lives (1:15–16). Salvation depends upon both God and human behavior. God judges all people according to their deeds (1:17). Thus they should live their lives in fear (1:17). However, they should not live just in fear because they are "being guarded by the power of God." This language is reminiscent of Phil 2:12–13, where people are called to "work out your own salvation with fear and trembling, for it is God who is at work in you."

[6–7] In the usual rhythm of theology, a statement of God's action leads to a statement about human action. God's act of giving new birth into this place of hope and inheritance leads to rejoicing. The phrase "for this reason" is appropriately vague. It is, of course, difficult to be precise about the connection between God's blessings and the readers' rejoicing.

This rejoicing over what God has done and is doing leads to 1 Peter's initial foray into the complexities of Christian suffering. First Peter does not, at this point at least (see 4:13), declare that the readers should rejoice because of or even in suffering. Suffering comes into the condition of rejoicing as an aside, an exception. Whether we translate the phrase *ei deon* as "even if" or "although" (see note d above), a gap between suffering and rejoicing is still in place. The decision between "even if" and "although" is, however, relevant to how we imagine the social situation of the community. Is the community actually suffering at this point, as the translation "although" would suggest? Or is suffering only a possibility, as "even if" might suggest? Yet the hypothetical condition suggested by "even if" may be, as noted above, rhetorical and not factual. It is, or may be, a theological "even if" rather than an uncertainty about the social situation. Thus the syntax here is not of the kind that enables us to draw social portraits with any certainty. First Peter's tendency to theologize about suffering means that a confident reconstruction of exactly what was happening is beyond us.

Opening Blessing

The theological question that is hinted at, and which will find further treatment later, lies in the nature of "it is necessary." Christians, who are rejoicing in God's blessings in Christ, suffer. And questions are Why? Who or what dictates that necessity? An initial response is offered in 1:7 and perhaps in 1:8 as well.

As readers have long noted, 1 Peter employs a loaded word in the phrase "you are grieved." The Greek root is *lypē*, the traditional word for "grief" or "pain." It is both physical and mental pain and is akin to *dolor* in Latin. Thus 1 Peter chooses perhaps the most negative word possible to evoke Christian suffering. Later 1 Peter will employ the more theologically ambiguous word *pathēmata* (1:11; 4:13; 5:1, 9). Here he seems to highlight the offensiveness of the suffering. Part of what makes a philosophy or religion worthy is its capacity to rescue humans from *lypē*. In a provocative way 1 Peter points out (or admits) that being the elect of God does not include an escape from *lypē*.

The readers, we are told, are grieved "by various trials." The Greek word *peirasmos* can mean "trial," "test," or even "temptation." All those nuances seem to be in play in 1 Peter. We cannot say what is happening to the community in these trials. Instead, the author points to the theological role of the trials. These "trials" that are testing the readers, whatever they are, can both make the readers better and destroy them. On the one hand, these trials examine who the readers are. As 4:17 notes, these trials are a form of judgment. Only in these trials does the true character of Christians emerge. This could be for good or ill. Thus there is a sense here of being tempted. Trials that come with being the elect can tempt one to cease being the elect. On the other hand, these trials have the capacity to improve, to refine. The trials become almost a good thing. As 1:7 will note, for gold to become gold, it needs the fire.

We are given in 1:7 the first explanation for why trials (or suffering) are necessary. They are necessary "in order that the genuineness of your faith . . . might be found to result in praise and glory and honor at the revelation of Jesus Christ." As readers have long noted, it is not faith that leads to praise and glory and honor; it is the genuineness of faith. The Greek *dokimion* (genuineness) conveys the sense of something that has been tested and approved. Trials test faith. This is a dangerous thing because Christians can fail such a test. However, trials that are endured can produce a proved quality. A faith that has been tested and approved will lead to praise and honor and glory at the revelation of Jesus Christ. The triad of "praise and glory and honor" together evoke the wonders of the heavenly inheritance. In this context, these terms cannot be precisely defined because they are evoking events and realities beyond the reach of theology. There is no way to know, for instance, for whom the praise is intended and what the content of the praise is, or what the nature of the glory and honor might be. In a sense, only God knows the full character of those blessings. This triad works rhetorically as the destiny and reward for enduring trials. In what follows, 1 Peter will explore how faith proves itself in the midst of trials. Jesus will be the model. The letter will call upon its readers to display in their suffering the same virtues that Jesus displayed in his suffering.

The theological complexity of 1 Peter is already beginning to emerge. While the letter insists that God has caused the readers to be born again into a new life of hope, inheritance, and salvation, the letter also insists that the journey is not finished. The readers are not yet approved for judgment. The journey of suffering, of Christian ethics, of submission, of love, of walking in the steps of Jesus—all this is still before them. Even if the glories of Jesus' resurrection somehow already belong to them, being kept safe in heaven for them, this does not mean that the cross is behind them. They still have the journey of Jesus ahead of them. Even if they are already redeemed by the blood of Christ (1:18–19), they will suffer as Christ suffered.

In some ways, the exception clause in 1:6 proves to be misleading. Suffering is not an unfortunate aside on the journey of rejoicing. In the theology of 1 Peter, the terrible and lamentable suffering of Christ becomes, in the hand of God, a blessing. Yet this blessing is at present incomplete, unfulfilled, and even absent. As noted above, there is both a spatial and temporal distance created by this blessing. Praise, glory, and honor are not present until the "revelation of Jesus Christ."

[8–9] The role of Christ that is hinted at above receives further treatment here. Even if God is the primary actor in the theology of 1 Peter, God is acting through Christ. Thus, the theology of 1 Peter emerges primarily through Christology. The story and person of Jesus will become the key to the identity of both God and the elect.

These verses, however, explore less the story of Jesus and more the present relationship with Jesus. Although these verses do not explicitly address the issue of suffering, they do explore the problem of distance. Jesus is not here, or at least not in some sense. This absence of Jesus creates the space in which faith and hope exist. First Peter's language is simple and classical, "whom, though you have not seen, you love; in whom, now not seeing but believing, you rejoice with an inexpressible and glorified joy." Jesus' absence is expressed as a visual absence: they have not seen Jesus and do not see Jesus now. This visual absence will not be overcome until "the revelation of Jesus Christ." Thus, the eschatological event may include not only praise, glory, and honor, but also a full visual sighting of Jesus (and perhaps of the heavens). But for now this lack, this absence, gives space for the Christian virtues.

First, even though they have not seen Jesus, these verses insist that they love him. Love will, of course, become the central force in how these Christians should treat one another (see 1:22; 2:17; 4:8). But at this point it is not one another they love but Jesus, whom they have not seen. This capacity to love God and Jesus, who remain a mystery to people, is a constant in theology. First Peter is certainly not unique in insisting that believers must love a God they do

Opening Blessing 35

not fully know. In the theology of 1 Peter, as in most early Christian theology, love is not perfectly dependent on knowledge. People can love someone who remains mysterious to them, whether that be God or neighbor.

Second, this verse declares that even though they do not see Jesus now, they believe in him. This is a nearly ubiquitous claim in early Christianity. Faith is always shaped by a disjunction between what people believe to be true and the truths of the present. For example, in the language of Hebrews, faith is "the assurance of things hoped for, the conviction of things not seen" (Heb 11:1). What is striking about 1 Peter is the christological shape of this disjunction. It is Jesus' visual absence that provides the space for faith. The sense of trust that is contained in the Greek word *pistis* and its cognates seems to be highlighted in the tension created by this absence. Even though they do not see and cannot see Jesus, they trust that the glory and honor and praise given Jesus after his resurrection await them. These readers are portrayed as giving their lives to the story of a person they have never seen. Faith cannot exist without hope, and both exist in this lack.

Third, although they have not and do not see Jesus, they "rejoice with an inexpressible and glorified joy." This call to rejoice in response to the absence of Jesus and to the suffering of the Christian life, a call that 1 Peter will repeat in various ways throughout the letter, has always raised questions among readers. How can people rejoice in contexts that seem to promote laments? How can grief, suffering, and a sense of Jesus' absence lead to rejoicing?

Perhaps 1 Peter gives a hint in the unusual closing clause "You rejoice with an inexpressible and glorified joy." Both of these adjectives enlighten the problem. This joy is "inexpressible." It is not a joy that submits to language. Furthermore, this joy is "glorified." An eschatological dimension emerges here. This joy already partakes of glory. The glory that these Christians will enjoy at the revelation of Jesus Christ is already shining in this rejoicing. The source of their rejoicing lies not within them, neither in theological logic nor in feelings. True joy, according to 1 Peter, comes from heaven.

This sense of already experiencing the heavenly blessings is further articulated in the participial clause of 1:9. The participle *komizomenoi*, which is translated "for you are receiving," is in the present tense. Thus, whether the participle is temporal ("you rejoice . . . as you receive") or causal ("you rejoice . . . for you are receiving"), the fact remains that the readers are already receiving the "goal of their faith." Somehow, in the present, they are already enjoying the salvation that awaits them at the revelation of Jesus Christ. The contrast is striking. On the one hand, they have not and do not see Jesus now. There is a distance from the final inheritance experienced in their relationship with Christ. On the other hand, even in this distance they rejoice because they are already receiving their salvation. A crucial tension, or even contradiction, is being established. Their inheritance is hidden in the future, but this future inheritance is in some sense already being enjoyed. Almost all Christian theology articulates an already/ not yet tension of this kind. One can argue that this tension, this contradiction, is fundamental to Christian theology. It is a tension that theology does not try to resolve or overcome but to articulate. First Peter articulates it beautifully.

The imagery of "goal of your faith" is particularly effective. As noted above, *telos* can evoke both the sense of being on the way and the sense of being finished. This range of meaning works nicely here. The readers are both on a Christian journey with a long road before them, and they are at the end of that journey already partaking of heavenly blessings.

In the syntax of 1 Peter, it is faith that has the unique capacity to track this tension. People are described as believing without seeing. In this believing they already enjoy a future that they cannot see. This ongoing tension means that faith in 1 Peter plays an essential role. It is "through faith" that God is guarding the elect (1:5). And faith has this goal, this end, this destiny (*telos*), which is salvation.

[10–12] While prophecy and its fulfillment are crucial to the theology of 1 Peter, their function in the opening blessing is not clear. Some readers have suggested that the issue of time structures the opening blessing: verses 3–5 address the future, 6–9 address the present, and 10–12 address the past. While such a reading is a bit subtle, a close attention to the periodization of salvation history fits with the general apocalyptic tenor of 1 Peter. However, it is also the case that many of the key elements of the theology of 1 Peter are introduced in this blessing. As we shall see, prophets and their prophecies are indeed key to the theology of 1 Peter. Thus the general gathering force of the blessing may account for the introduction of the topic.

In any case, these verses offer both a series of exegetical puzzles and a series of insights into the theology of 1 Peter. The initial puzzle concerns the identity of the prophets. Are these OT prophets or early Christian prophets? The main argument in defense of the suggestion that these are Christian prophets is the lack of an object for the verbs "sought and searched." If we imagine the prophets as Christian prophets, then they can be searching Scripture. This reading, however, creates a series of other problems. In particular, the sense of future articulated in 1:11–12, which fits perfectly with OT prophets, makes little sense with Christian ones. More important, reading this passage as a reference to Christian prophets undoes the theological logic of 1 Peter. Much of 1 Peter's theology is exegetical. In the theology of 1 Peter, Scripture tells the story of Jesus and the elect. Thus much of the theological imagery of 1 Peter is derived from a reading of Scripture. These prophets must be OT prophets.

The prophets and their prophecies are seen exclusively through the story of Jesus and his followers. These verses offer a radically christocentric reading of OT prophecies. The character of these prophets is determined by their relationship to the Christian story: "the prophets who prophesied about this grace intended for you." Prophets are not prophets because of their relationship to ancient Israel; they are prophets because they foretold Christian grace. According to 1 Peter, their task was not to call ancient Israel back to the covenant but to search out the salvation of Christian lives. The two verbs translated as "sought" and "searched" have almost identical meaning. If there is a difference, it would be that the first has more the sense of "looking for" and the second more the sense of "examining." In this passage, their usage together probably serves to reinforce the searching of the prophets—something like "they searched and searched."

As noted above, the grammar of 1:11 is difficult, even though the point is rather much the same whichever way it is translated. The OT prophets are searching out and examining the salvation of Christians. As they are doing this, searching for what (or who) and what sort of time, the "Spirit of Christ" reveals to them the peculiar nature of this future salvation. It is not clear precisely what is intended by the phrase "Spirit of Christ," since the phrase could refer to the preexistent Christ or to the Spirit that somehow belongs to or is sent by Christ. What seems to matter is a connection of some kind to Christ. What clarified Christian salvation to OT prophets was not just any spirit, not even the spirit of God, but the Spirit that belongs to Christ. Thus, it is the Christ story, not any other story, that was revealed to them. This does not necessarily mean that all prophecies in the OT are about Christ. This just means that some of them are.

It is crucial to the theology of 1 Peter what the Spirit of Christ disclosed. The scandal and the crux of 1 Peter's theology is the centrality of suffering. Thus it is no surprise that this is what the Spirit of Christ reveals. The Spirit reveals "the suffering intended for Christ and the glories after them." In 1 Peter there is no real puzzle about what this prophetic revelation looks like because the letter is filled with examples. As we shall see, Isaiah provides the primary material, but the Psalter and other texts contribute. The revelation to the prophets will not simply be the fact that Christ suffers and then is glorified. The revelation will include a description, or partial description, of how Christ behaves in the midst of suffering. First Peter thus presents an early form of an argument crucial to ancient Christian apologists. Christ's crucifixion is not a sign of failure; Christian suffering does not disprove the goodness of the Christian life. All of this, the crucifixion and the subsequent sufferings of Christians, was foreseen by the prophets. In fact, Christians, or at least the apologists, were quite capable of pointing out the precise texts. Whether 1 Peter believes that the presence in prophecy of "the suffering intended for Christ and the glories after them" proves the ultimate truth of Christianity is never made clear. What is clear is that 1 Peter finds the details of the Christian life written down already in the OT prophets. Thus, for Christians to know who they are, they must read these texts.

The final verse consists of three delightful pieces. First, the verse notes that it was revealed to the prophets that "not for themselves but for you they were serving these things." The prophets did not write oracles that they did not understand.

They did not write about their own time and in so doing, unknown to themselves, actually wrote about the future. They knew they were writing about "you." First Peter does not say that they knew and understood every detail of the Christian story, but he does say that the basic destiny of their texts was clear to them.

Second, "these things" that the prophets foretold have now been told to "you" through Christian preachers. The word, the truth of Jesus, the story of this Jesus whom they have never seen, was told to the recipients of the letter by Christian preachers. This same story was also written in Scriptures since the "Spirit of Christ" revealed this story to the prophets. This again sets up the theological structure of 1 Peter. The readers can find themselves, the version of themselves told them by Christian preachers, in the ancient Scriptures. It is probably the case that the specifics of Christian preaching inform the Christian how to read Scripture. There is an aspect of recognition. However, this is not the explicit argument. The argument is that the prophets told ahead of time what the Christian preachers preach.

Third, there is a final note about the angels. We probably do not need to pursue questions of whether these angels are actually messengers of some kind. The point seems to be that even those who are privy to the secret counsels of God are eager to peek into the secrets of the gospel. It is an inviting image that returns the reader to the opening mood of blessing. God is to be blessed, because the secrets of this rebirth, this salvation in Christ, are a delight even to the angels.

According to the norms of ancient letter writing, a letter should begin with a thanksgiving or blessing. This expectation does not mean, however, that the blessing should be executed as a mere formality, a rhetorical obligation to be passed through quickly. The blessing in 1 Peter conveys the feel of a genuine thankfulness and celebration. It is also an effective introduction to the theological issues of the letter.

The prevailing context of both the rhetoric and theology of 1 Peter is suffering. The challenge of responding to the ongoing experience of abuse in the context of the promises implied in becoming God's elect creates the theological energy of this opening. These verses (1:3–12) accomplish in brief form what the letter as a whole also accomplishes. This opening blessing articulates the tension essential to 1 Peter's vision of the Christian life. It is, on the one hand, a life shaped by mercy, resurrection, rebirth, a heavenly inheritance, hope, glory, and the power of God. It thus is a life of joy, celebration, and confidence. These verses convey all of that. The Christian life is, on the other hand, shaped by suffering, abuse, temptation, testing, and patience. It is a life lived more in faith and hope than in the possessing. These verses also convey all of that.

In the somewhat chaotic style of 1 Peter, these verses gather a considerable variety of theological images. This letter has a somewhat remarkable capacity to include a large number of images and ideas in one syntax. Furthermore, nearly every image in this opening blessing will surface again in the letter. These verses are an initial gathering of the core images of the letter. They are also the first of a series of explorations of how the experience of suffering can be connected to the "grace of God" (5:12).

1 Peter 1:13–2:10 The Holy Life

1 Peter 1:13–21 Call to Holiness

One of the most intriguing words in Christian thought (perhaps in all religious thought) is the "therefore" that connects theology to ethics. First Peter moves continuously from theological confessions to exhortation, asserting in various ways that the readers must behave a certain way because certain things are true about God. Despite the centrality of this move from confession to exhortation, the logic of the connection is never perfectly clear. Even when the relationship between the indicative and the imperative appears to be quite direct, as in "You will be holy, because I am holy" (1:16), the theological indicative does not lead in a formally logical way to the ethical imperative. There are many possible conclusions that one might draw from the theological claim that God is holy. After all, why must the readers be holy just because God is?

Much of 1 Peter is written traversing this gap from confession to exhortation and from exhortation to confession. In some ways one cannot understand the theological confession until one sees what the ethical response might be. In the straightforward claim of 1 Peter, the ethical exhortations in 1:13–21 (and perhaps further) come directly from the confessions in 1:3–12. However, one could hardly derive the content of 1:13–21 from even the closest reading of 1:3–12. Thus, not only do the ethics derive their content from the theology; the theology also derives its content from the ethics. We cannot understand 1:3–12 until we read 1:13–21.

However, the rhetoric of 1:13–21 is not simply an exhortation echoing the themes of 1:3–12. It is more complicated than that, for 1:13–21 is not simply exhortation. It is also a complex interweaving of ethical calls and theological warrants. In fact, the shifting rhetoric of these verses displays the theology. The character and behavior of God are intertwined with the character and behavior of the readers. This cosmic truth creates an intertwined rhetoric.

As we noted in the introduction, this rhetorical style makes any attempt to outline 1 Peter difficult. In 1 Peter it is always hard to know how far the rhetorical force of a theological claim extends. For instance, the call to holiness in 1:15–16 may extend beyond these verses up to 2:10 or even further. By all accounts, there is a rhetorical and theological shift that sets these verses apart. The rhetorical shift comes by way of the "therefore" in 1:13 and the direct imperatives that frequent these verses. The theological shift centers around the image of holiness. The God who is saving people by way of Jesus Christ is still the classic God of holiness. And the people who are thus being saved are also holy people.

This call to holiness comes in two sections. The first, which runs from 1:13–16, centers upon the theological claim that God is holy. The second, which runs from 1:17–21, focuses upon the threat of impartial judgment and the preciousness of redemption in Christ. The rhetorical anchor of both sections is probably the imperative "You yourselves become holy in all your behavior" (1:15).

> 1:13 Therefore, having girded up[a] the loins of your mind and being sober,[a] set your hope completely[b] upon the grace being brought to you at the revelation of Jesus Christ. 14 As obedient children,[c] do not be conformed to the passions that you formerly had in your ignorance, 15 but instead, as the one who called you is holy,[d] you yourselves become holy in all your behavior. 16 For it is written, "You will be holy, because I am holy."[e] 17 And if you call father the one who judges without partiality according to the deeds of each person, in fear live the time of your exile,[f] 18 knowing that not with perishable things, silver or gold, were you ransomed from your futile ancestral way of life, 19 but, as from a blameless and spotless lamb,[g] with the precious blood of Christ, 20 who was known before the foundation of the world but who was manifested at the end of times[h] because of you, 21 who through him trust[i] in God, who raised him from the dead and gave him glory so that your trust[i] and hope are in God.

a. The aorist tense of the participle *anazōsamenoi* (having girded up) and present tense of *nēphontes* (being sober) means that "having girded up" precedes "being sober."

b. The adverb *teleiōs* could grammatically and logically modify either the participle "sober" or the imperative "hope." However, since adverbs typically precede the verb they modify and the sentence seems to highlight the act of hope more than that of being sober, it is preferable to connect the adverb to the imperative.

c. Whether the genitive in the phrase "children of obedience" is a form of the Semitic "children of" construction or just a genitive of quality ("obedient children"), the phrase identifies the essential quality or character of these children.

d. The adjective *hagion* can be understood as a substantive adjective, and the phrase would be translated "in conformity with the holy one who called you." In fact, the use of *kata* with a substantive indicating the reason for an action is common in 1 Peter (cf. 1:2, 3; 4:6, 19; 5:2). However, *hagion* can also be understood as standing in the predicate position to the substantive "the one who called you," and the phrase would be translated as above. The latter preserves the verbal sense of the exhortation in 1:15b and thus is preferable.

e. This entire verse is filled with textual problems. Some texts (B, Ψ) include *hoti* (that) before the quote, and some ($\mathfrak{P}^{72}$, ℵ, A, C) do not. Some texts (K, P, 𝔐) read "you

Call to Holiness

become" instead of "you will be." Some texts (ℵ, A, B) omit *eimi* (I am) at the end of the quote. None of these variants really change the meaning.

f. If the word *paroikia* is being used in a technical way, it means having the status of being a resident alien. But a technical use of the term is hard to maintain. It is unlikely that all the recipients of 1 Peter are of this peculiar legal status. In fact, they seem to have once been living quite at home with everyone else (4:3–4). Thus, the term must be used metaphorically. The recipients are not legally aliens, but they are so theologically.

g. The phrase "as from a blameless and spotless lamb" intervenes awkwardly in the Greek between "precious blood" and "of Christ." Both "lamb" and "Christ" are in the genitive case. By placing "Christ" at the end of the phrase, it becomes clear that the participial phrases in 1:20, which are also in the genitive, modify Christ and not the lamb.

h. The phrase "end of times" with its singular "end" (*eschatou*) and plural "times" (*chronōn*) led to textual variants that make both nouns singular and plural in various combinations. The best textual evidence (A, B, C) supports the singular "end" and the plural "times." In any case, little difference in meaning is at stake.

i. The adjective *pistos* carries the dual connotation of "being faithful to" or "trusting in." Unlike the verb (*pisteuō*) or the noun (*pistis*), the adjective rarely carries the nuance of belief. The context of the verse suggests that it is God rather than "you" who is the reliable one. Thus, "trust in" is the better translation.

[13] The explicit consequence of the theological narrative in 1:3–12 is the imperative to "hope." Because of what God has done through the resurrection of Christ, "you" should and even must hope. The expressed object or ground of this hope is "the grace being brought to you at the revelation of Jesus Christ." Early Christians rarely try to articulate the specifics of hope. They do not pretend to foresee the precise configurations of heaven. Instead, sentences about the final day, about the ultimate end, tend to offer a loose syntax of the most fundamental theological terms. Such is the case here. Readers should probably recall the imagery of 1:3–5. This grace that will be "yours" connects to the eternal and perfectly preserved inheritance of 1:4. Even at the very end, the entry into salvation will not be managed by holiness, no matter how essential that holiness might be. Rather, it will still be God's grace that opens whatever doors there might be in heaven.

Two participial phrases introduce the imperative to hope, pointing to the ethical dimensions of the new birth of 1:3. The difference in tenses between the aorist "having girded up the loins of your mind" and the present "being sober" come from the basic meaning of the images and not from some sense of order attendant to the act of hoping. The girding of the loins is a common ancient image that is derived from the need to tie up one's robe before attempting any vigorous physical act. Here it means something like "having gotten ready for action" (cf. Luke 12:35; Exod 12:11 LXX). It is most easily imagined as a single act, and thus the aorist. The image of being sober fits most naturally in the present tense, since it is best imagined as an ongoing state.

The ethical challenge hinted at in this verse opens upon one of the fundamental challenges of 1 Peter. To have hope is not simply to feel a certain way or to think certain things or even to trust in God. To have "a living hope" (1:3), people must behave in a certain way. Hope lives in deeds that display who these Christians believe God is. In 1 Peter, the readers will be able to love and suffer and be holy because of their conviction that there is indeed "an imperishable and undefiled and unfading inheritance, kept in the heavens for you" (1:4). Moreover, there is a double implication: hope that does not live in such deeds is not really hope, and also, deeds and not words display who these people truly are. This is a classic early Christian claim, perhaps seen best in the Sermon on the Mount (Matt 7:15–20).

[14–16] These verses point to several of the core ethical claims of 1 Peter. The logic of naming, the call to turn away from the old life, and the challenge of holiness are all essential aspects of the ethical vision that animates this letter. These core images are woven into an argument about the nature of God and the consequent nature of God's children.

First Peter uses the comparative particle *hōs* (as) twenty-seven times. Typically in 1 Peter, the particle functions less to introduce the strict comparison "as if" and more the real condition "since." However, it is actually the slight distance between "as if" and "since" that creates the space for the exhortation. In this slight ambiguity, 1 Peter is exploring the gap between theological fact and ethical behavior. They are obedient children; therefore, they must behave as obedient children. Being reborn into this new life of hope does not automatically and inevitably lead to the virtuous life. Effort is required.

The image of "obedient children" recalls the language of rebirth in 1:3 and anticipates the discussion of God as father in 1:17. In 1:2, obedience is portrayed as the proper destiny of the readers. Thus the phrase "obedient children" is revealing of the core outlook of 1 Peter. They are God's children. A child can be disobedient or obedient. The nature of their obedience will be derived from the character of God. Anticipating the logic of what follows, since God is holy and "you" are obedient children, "you will be holy."

The phrase "do not be conformed to the passions that you formerly had in your ignorance" takes the modern reader into the complex social and theological tensions of 1 Peter. The letter will devote much energy to exploring the Christian rejection of the Gentile life. Here two classical ideas are briefly sketched. First, the description of the virtuous life as involving the rejection of the passions runs through nearly all ancient thought. Greeks, Romans, Jews, and Christians employed the term *epithymiai* (passions) to denote the chaos, selfishness, and sensuality of a life without reason or virtue. The term is such a central term to ancient thought that by itself it actually tells us very little about the character of the readers' former lives. The description in 4:3 on the surface seems to give a bit more information (see also 2:1,11). But even there it is not

Call to Holiness

completely clear what about their former lives warrants the term *epithymiai*. Thus, the term here may function more ideologically than descriptively. By attributing *epithymiai* to the former lives, 1 Peter invokes a pervasive negative image in the ancient world and thereby denigrates the non-Christian life. First Peter does not describe the peculiarities of this former life and does not need to. It was a life driven by *epithymiai*; that is all one needs to know.

Second, 1 Peter claims that in their former life these Christians held these passions "in your ignorance." The relationship between knowledge and virtues was much debated in the ancient world. However, the initial point in 1 Peter seems clear enough. Before they knew about the salvation into which "angels desire to peek," they were unable to avoid the terror of passions. Two things are implied here. First of all, they are no longer ignorant. Although 1 Peter does not specify in this verse precisely what they know, the larger context makes it clear enough. Second, the implication is that now, with their new knowledge, they are able not to be conformed to these former passions that they held in their ignorance. Again, the uncertainty of how one traverses the distance from knowledge to virtue creates the rhetorical space of 1 Peter.

The relationship between this text and Rom 12:2 has long fascinated readers of 1 Peter. Both the general context and the precise syntax of Rom 12:2 and 1 Pet 1:14 are nearly identical. The striking similarity suggests a common tradition of some kind. Readers have often suggested a shared baptismal catechesis, but the precise provenance of this shared tradition remains unclear. However, the close relationship between these texts does suggest that 1 Peter stands in the mainstream of early Christian theology. One may suspect that, even when there is no explicit evidence in 1 Peter of connections to larger Christian arguments, those connections are there.

Verses 15–17 are structured around the dual images of calling and holiness. In the standard rhetoric of ethical exhortation, these verses form the contrast to the life of ignorance and passion. The dynamics of calling will create a peculiar irony for the readers. First Peter 1:15 employs the central biblical image of God calling God's people. This image is crucial for 1 Peter and will appear again in 2:9 and 5:10. There is nothing surprising in 1 Peter's use of this image since the image is so prevalent in Jewish and Christian literature. Nevertheless, the imagery of being called fits perfectly with the overall rhetoric of 1 Peter because it bridges the gap between who the readers are theologically and who they are in their deeds. God is calling across this gap. The letter of 1 Peter can be read as part of this calling. The letter calls readers, who are God's obedient children, to live as though they are.

This image of calling is combined with the equally classical image of holiness. The one who calls is holy. Few terms in theology are more difficult to define with any precision than that of "holiness." Holiness typically includes the sense of otherness, of separation. God's holiness is part of what separates God from humans and makes God other and unknowable. Furthermore, this separateness of God effects a separateness in God's people. Israel is set apart from the nations. This aspect of holiness certainly seems to be in force in 1 Peter. Holiness in 1 Peter involves not being conformed to former passions (1:14). This holiness will thus inaugurate the sense of estrangement and the experience of suffering that frequents the syntax of 1 Peter. However, the holiness of God is not a quality distinct from God's righteousness and justice. Thus the call in 1 Peter to love each other (1:22) should not be understood as somehow separate from the call to holiness. This combination of holiness and morality is not an innovation of 1 Peter. The Holiness Code, for instance, in Lev 17–26 is full of calls to justice and righteousness. The command to love your neighbor as yourself, which Jesus promotes as the one of the two great commandments (Matt 22:34–40; Mark 12:28–31; Luke 10:25–28), comes from the Holiness Code (Lev 19:18).

Thus 1 Peter opens its ethical challenge with a classical theological move. Israel was called by the holy God to be a holy and just people. And now 1 Peter claims that Christians are being called by this same holy God to be a holy and just people. Although Christology will transform the equation somewhat, the core dynamic remains the same as in the call to Israel. God is holy. God calls Israel or, in this case, Christians to be a holy people. The called ones must respond by pursuing holiness. Thus, both the OT and 1 Peter are filled with commandments and calls to obedience.

Given this pervasive tradition, the response in verse 15b to the assertion of God's holiness seems inevitable. If anything, the imperative in 1 Peter is striking for its simplicity: "You yourselves become holy in all your behavior." This is a rather overwhelming challenge, reminiscent perhaps of the equally overwhelming demand in the Sermon on the Mount to be "perfect . . . as your heavenly Father is perfect" (Matt 5:48). The sweeping language of this challenge suggests that this imperative functions almost as a first principle for all the ethics that follows. Each command and challenge in 1 Peter can be understood as an aspect of this demand for holiness "in all your behavior."

It is not helpful to try to tone down the theological problems of this imperative. Readers have often complained that this imperative, and others like it in 1 Peter, undercuts the sufficiency of God's act of making people holy (cf. 1:2). However, it is this tension, this gap, between what God does and people do that creates the theology of 1 Peter. For humans to be holy in all their behavior requires the act of God and the actions of people, and the roles of each cannot be precisely delimited. The quoting of Lev 19:2 (see also Lev 11:44, 45; 20:7, 26) not only articulates the theological logic of the call to holiness; it also conveys the essential connection between Scripture and the new life as obedient children. As 1:10–12 asserts, the prophets were searching for the story of Jesus, and what they prophesied applied not to them or their time but to "you" and to this time. Thus the assertion "You will be holy, because I am holy" is speaking about "you" who are obedient children.

In 1 Peter Scripture functions as it does in most of the NT. First of all, Scripture is employed as a source of true sentences. In this sense it provides an unimpeachable warrant for the call to holiness: "You will be holy." Second, Scripture is read prophetically. In the language of 1:12, it was revealed to the prophets that "not for themselves but for you they were serving these things." The prophecies of Scripture that cohere with the Christian story demonstrate the divine character of Christian reality. Furthermore, the completeness of God's plan for humanity is displayed in this coherence between the text and Christian experience. The unfulfilled and even broken character of the visions in Scripture find wholeness in the stories of Jesus and his followers. Thus, God, Scripture, and the Christian community are all vindicated in these scriptural citations.

[17] This verse is a typical transitional sentence in that it completes what precedes it and introduces what follows. Both the image of being called and that of becoming holy are employed in a rather ironic way in this verse. The calling that has been presented as promise and challenge becomes threat in this verse. Furthermore, the image of being God's child, of calling God "Father," is not one of being cared for and protected but one of living in the presence of the holy judge.

The "if" in the phrase "and if you call father . . ." again creates the space between reality and possibility. The assumption is that the readers do indeed call God "Father," but the slight sense of unreality in the syntax creates a nice opening for the imperative that follows. Calling God "Father" is not peculiar to early Christianity even if the predominance of so doing is unusual (e.g., Ps 89:26; Mal 1:6). What is unusual is the combination of father and judge. The parent image will be used in a strikingly different way in 2:1–2, where the image of being newborn babes is connected with the goodness of mother's milk and the kindness of God. However, the syntax of 1:17 creates a reversal in the implied status of the readers. The sentence begins with the comforting notion of calling God "Father" and then undercuts the security implied in that name by combining it with the image of God as judge. A father in the ancient Mediterranean world had the duty both to protect and to discipline.[8] Thus the reversal accomplished here does not go beyond the range of the term "father."

The contention that God judges impartially is traditional in Judaism and early Christianity. Impartiality is articulated here as God judging "according to the deeds of each person." Hence, calling God "Father" does not entitle one to escape the righteousness and impartiality of God's judgment. All people, whether called or not, whether part of the new people, the royal priesthood, or not, will be judged by exactly the same standards. The notion that each will be judged by deeds, and deeds alone, is also traditional to both Judaism and early Christianity.

---

8. Suzanne Dixon, *The Roman Family* (Ancient Society and History; Baltimore: Johns Hopkins University Press, 1992).

All of this means that the exhortation to live the holy life is not an aside or an addition to the gospel. The assurance in 1:3–5 that both Christians and their inheritance are being kept safe, or the command in 1:13 for them to place their hope in grace, does not mean that somehow they will not be judged. Grace is a proper part of judgment, and grace does not cancel impartiality. The conviction that God on the day of judgment will be full of absolute justice and absolute mercy is also the classic Christian and Jewish notion. First Peter shares the usual early Christian refusal to mark the precise boundaries between God's justice and mercy. Only God can do that.

The command to live "in fear" is also the standard response to affirmation of the holiness and impartiality of the final judge. The phrase "in fear" has occasioned debate because the Greek *phobos* means both fear and reverence. In a given context *phobos* can thus have either a negative or positive connotation. Both connotations seem to be in force in 1 Peter. God is to be both feared and revered. "The Lord is kind" (2:3), and the Lord judges impartially according to your deeds. In 1 Peter both kindness and impartiality are essential to the portrait of God.

As noted above, "the time of exile" is not referring to any real legal status. This exile, this status of being an alien, comes from being reborn as obedient children of God. Calling God "Father" attests to an exile that is both social and spiritual. On the one hand, calling God "Father" means that one lives in the house of God and no longer in the house of the Gentiles. Membership in the new community means alienation from the old. Furthermore, there is a sense of incompleteness in this new household. Full membership in the household of God only comes on the last day. Yet as these verses insist, even that future membership is dependent on living a holy life. Thus 1 Peter can insist that, in this time of exile, these members of God's house must live their lives in fear because they know that this father is holy and impartial in judgment. Fear is offered here as a proper grounding for ethics. They must live holy lives because God is holy. This does not mean that these Christians should imitate God out of gratitude for already-complete salvation; it means that they must live holy lives because they will be judged by a God who is absolutely and impartially holy.

[18–19] Here as elsewhere in the NT (1 Cor 15:58; Eph 6:8, 9; Col 3:24; 4:1; Jas 3:1), the participle "knowing" (*eidotes*) seems to introduce material that is already known to the readers and about which there is no controversy. Thus the rhetoric of 1:18 is that everyone (the author and all the readers) knows and believes the following to be true. The feel of the rhetoric is that of reminder. However, if this is the case, some of what is agreed upon is surprising.

The imagery of being ransomed is common in the NT even if the verb *lytroō* occurs only here and in Luke 24:21 and Titus 2:14. As often noted, the idea of being ransomed in the ancient world normally referred to either the ransoming of prisoners or the manumission of slaves. This largely political event is somewhat spiritualized in the NT. Christians were once prisoners or slaves to the powers of their old lives. These powers could take many forms, as they do in 1 Peter. Furthermore, the ransoming of Christians is typically connected with the cross and/or the blood of Christ (cf. Rom 3:24–25; Heb 9:12). Thus the core theological move in these verses is the standard early Christian one. The blood of Jesus has ransomed Christians from the powers of their old lives. The contrast between ransoming by "silver or gold" (1:18) and "the precious blood of Christ" (1:19) creates space for the standard Christian proposal that the move from the old life to the new Christian life was accomplished by a ransom offered by the death of Jesus Christ. First Peter will add two particular arguments to this common view.

The first is suggested in the phrase "your futile ancestral way of life." The adjective *mataios* means "futile" or "vain" and (with its cognates) is used in LXX to denigrate the Gentile way of life (e.g., Lev 17:7; Jer 8:19; 10:15) and in the NT to describe the uselessness of the former lives of Christians (e.g., Acts 14:15; Rom 1:21; Eph 4:17). Thus its usage here conforms with standard Jewish and Christian rhetoric. More striking is the adjective *patroparadotos* (ancestral) because this is a classically positive term in Greco-Roman literature (e.g., Dio Cassius, *Roman History* 52.36). For something to be handed down by the fathers assured its truth and value in conservative Roman society. Thus, when 1 Peter combines "futile" with "ancestral," the ongoing social tensions in the letter are connected with the ransoming by Jesus. It is this ransoming power of Jesus' blood that inaugurates the tensions between these Christians and their neighbors.

The second move surfaces in 1:19. The ransoming of Jesus was accomplished by something of inestimable value: "the precious blood of Christ." An unusual warrant for the call to holiness is implied here. These Christians should be holy because they were ransomed by something of such value. According to the normal values of exchange, of ransoming, gold and silver carry the most weight. Christians' ransoming occurs from something of even more value than gold and silver.

It has often been pointed out that the "perishable" (*phthartos*) nature of gold and silver and the "precious" (*timios*) character of Christ's blood do not form obvious opposites. But the point is not to analyze the inadequacy of a ransom by gold and silver but to highlight the value of ransom by Christ's blood. Thus the acknowledged value of gold and silver is not the basis for an opposition but for a comparison to something much better. The word *timios* with its sense of "costly" and "valuable" fits naturally with gold and silver. Hence, gold and silver, which might warrant the adjective "precious," instead acquire the adjective "perishable." And blood, which seems to be the most perishable of all things, instead is called "precious."

The exact nature of the connection between blood and ransoming is not obvious. In 1:2, the author combined obedience with "sprinkling of the blood of Jesus Christ" in such a way as to suggest more the idea of covenant and perhaps of Christian suffering than that of atonement or ransom. In the larger context of 1:19, blood is connected once again to obedience. The readers were named "obedient children" in 1:14, and the whole passage is a call to live the holy life. Thus most readers of 1 Peter connect the imagery of blood and ransom, not to the political sphere, but to the cultic, wherein obedience and blood are constantly connected. The reference to "a blameless and spotless lamb" reinforces that connection. However, echoes of Passover and the redemption from Egypt are also unavoidable. Passover imagery may fit better with 1:2 than 1:19, but a rigid line between Passover and temple sacrifices cannot be maintained, since the stories and sacrifices of the Passover find ongoing life in the sacrifices in the Jerusalem temple. Thus the blood of Christ in 1 Peter can be the redeeming blood of a sacrifice (1:19) or the sprinkled blood that seals a covenant (1:2) or even the apotropaic blood of the Passover lamb. In any case, in whatever way the blood of Christ is conceived, this blood leads to obedience.

[20–21] The balanced participial couplets in 1:20 and the relative clause in 1:21 suggest to many readers the formal syntax of liturgy. It thus is possible that 1 Peter is actually quoting directly from the liturgy of the early Christian readers. The author could, of course, just be writing in a nicely balanced way. Nevertheless, the force of the participle "knowing" in 1:18 is still in place. Whether these verses are from Christian liturgy or not, they are offered as something already known by the readers. Furthermore, the attributes of Jesus that are detailed here connect to other christological statements in the letter, suggesting that even if the author is quoting, he is quoting from material that coheres with his own theology.

The initial claim is that Jesus "was known before the foundation of the world." The passive voice of the participle "was known" coupled with the timing "before the foundation of the world" means that God is the one who knew Jesus. This foreknowledge of Christ by God echoes the foreknowledge of "your" sanctification in 1:2. The phrase "before the foundation of the world" becomes a common phrase in Christian thought (John 17:24; Eph 1:4; cf. Matt 13:35; 25:34; Luke 11:50; Rev 13:8; *Barn.* 5.5). God's redemptive act through Jesus is not the result of God having authored a failed creation. Furthermore, God's foreknowledge grounds the foresaying of the prophets (1:11). First Peter shares one of the constant early Christian convictions: this new thing that God has done and is doing in Christ is, in God's eyes at least, not a new thing at all.

What is new is that Christ has now been "manifested" (*phanerōthentos*). The same verb occurs in 5:4, where it refers to the manifestation on the last day. In spite of the language "at the end of times" (1:20c), this manifestation has already occurred and thus seems to be the first historical appearance of Jesus. In Jewish and Christian apocalyptic literature, the precise temporal referent of phrases such as "at the end of times" cannot be determined by the structure of

Call to Holiness

the phrase itself but only by context (cf. Jude 18; 2 Pet 3:3; Heb 1:2; *4 Ezra* [2 Esd] 3.14; 12.9). Thus, the phrase "at the end of times" does not date the manifestation chronologically but rather theologically. First Peter shares the widespread early Christian conviction that God's final plan for salvation is now unfolding in the events of Christ's story and in the experiences and callings of the community of believers.

All of this has been and is being done "because of you." This centering of the entire story of salvation upon "you" is one of the central convictions of the letter. Perhaps this high status given to "you" is best displayed in the series of names in 2:9-10: "You are a chosen race, a royal priesthood, a holy nation, a people for keeping safe. . . ." The whole letter focuses upon the astonishing and unique character of the salvation that God is offering "you."

This section ends (1:21) with a further description of "you," or at least of "you" in your relationship with God. The threat of God's holiness and the invoking of fear of the God who judges impartially (1:15-17) gives way to "trust" and "hope" in a God who raises people from the dead and gives them glory. The explicit ground for this shift in attitude is Christology. It is "through him [Christ]" that "you" now trust in God. Furthermore, it is in what God has done for Christ, raising him from the dead and giving him glory, that "you" are able to trust and hope in God. This trust and hope do not cancel out fear. The God who raised Christ and who offers grace is still the God of holiness.

In the classic pattern of early Christian theology, the affirmation of God's blessings in 1:3-12 leads to a call for holy behavior in 1:13-21. In the eclectic rhetoric of 1 Peter, this call for holiness employs a variety of images and strategies. At the core of this exhortation sit two theological affirmations. The first is the holiness of God. God's holiness is the ground of human holiness. This holy God functions both as parental instigator of holiness and as threatening judge. The second is redemption from the "futile ancestral way of life" by "the precious blood of Christ." The immense value of that blood reinforces the sense of trust and hope that these Christians have in their holy God.

Also in the classic pattern of early Christianity, the ground for ethics in 1 Peter is both fear and trust. This passage explicitly calls for both. On the one hand, these Christians are called to live "in fear" the time of their exile (1:17). On the other hand, they are called to place their trust and hope in God (1:21). This combination of fear and trust pervades the entire letter. First Peter will use a considerable variety of theological images to enforce this call to fear and trust. In fact, this passage by itself contains a rather impressive range of images. Not only does this range of imagery provide the modern reader with a glimpse of the richness of early Christian theology; this range also, according to the norms of ancient rhetoric, adds to the persuasiveness of the letter.

1 Peter 1:22–25 Love and the Word

In one sense these verses are simply a continuation of the call to holiness in 1:15–16. The straightforward rhetoric of 1:22 is that the call in 1:15 has been obeyed. And now that it has, a new command enters. "You" have been obedient and thus have become holy. Therefore, "you" can move on to love. However, to read 1 Peter as moving progressively from one argument to another is to misunderstand the nature of ancient ethical rhetoric. First Peter does not build its case one piece at a time. It exhorts by gathering all sorts of ethical, theological, scriptural, and even liturgical imagery.

There are, in any case, two somewhat new ideas in these verses. First is the straightforward command to love one another. Second is a rich and even ironic exploration of the image of the word. At the center of the exploration of "word," 1 Peter cites Isa 40:7. Thus, these verses are like most of 1 Peter in that they are neither pure doctrine nor pure ethics, but a combination.

> 1:22 Having made your lives holy by[a] your obedience to the truth,[b] which leads to an unfeigned mutual affection, love one another intensely from a pure[c] heart, 23 because[d] you have born again not from a corruptible seed but from an incorruptible one, through the living and enduring[e] word of God.
>
> 24 For all flesh is like grass
> and all the glory of it like a flower of grass.
> The grass withers
> and the flower falls off,
> 25 but the word[f] of the Lord endures forever.
>
> This is the word that has been proclaimed to you.

a. The *en* could be instrumental, "by means of obedience," or locative, "in the practice of obedience." The general tone of exhortation suggests an instrumental translation. Yet even a locative translation suggests some sense of agency.

b. The genitive *tēs alētheias* could be a genitive of quality, "true obedience." However, an objective genitive, "obedience to the truth," better sets up the ensuing examination of the "word." "Truth" is used here almost as a synonym for "the word." There is good textual support for the addition of "through the spirit" (*dia pneumatos*) after the phase "obedience to the truth," although most of the best witnesses omit it.

c. The adjective *kathara* is not included in several important manuscripts. Its omission may be the result of confusing the repeating *ka-* of *katharas kardias*. However, it is possible that *kathara* was interpolated here as it was in Rom 6:17. Nevertheless, the weight of the manuscript tradition suggests that *kathara* is original.

d. The participle *anagegennēmenoi* is the second one attached to the imperative "love" (the first being *hēgnikotes*). Although it is possible to render this participle temporally, as was the first, it is more grammatically sound and fits the sense better to render the circumstantial participle *anagegennēmenoi* as causative.

e. The adjectives "living and enduring" could modify either "word" or "God." The Vulgate and most other traditional translations have placed them with God, since it is God who is classically the source of all things that endure (cf. Dan 6:27 LXX). However, the contrast between the corruptible and incorruptible seed (1:23a) suggests that it is the endurance of the "word" that is being affirmed. Furthermore, the quotation from Isaiah asserts the endurance of the word of the Lord, not the Lord (1:25a).

f. A difficulty for translation into English is created by two different words for "word" in these verses. "Word" in 1:23 is *logos*. Its use in 1:23 is not surprising, for not only is *logos* the more common term in Christian theology; its nuance of "seed" also fits with the "seed" (*spora*) of 1:23a. However, "word" in 1:24–25 is *rhēma*. The use of *rhēma* in these verses presumably occurs because this is the term used in the LXX version of Isa 40:8. The problem with translating all three instances as "word" is that such a translation implies that the "word" of 1:23b is unequivocally the same word as the "word" of 1:25b. In the Greek, there is some room for doubt.

[22–23] This section opens with the perfect participle *hēgnikotes*, suggesting thereby that the call to holiness has been and still is being accomplished. However, the fact that the participial phrase leads to an imperative shows that "having made your lives holy" does not mean that holiness is an accomplished and stable fact. The syntax of these verses conforms to the general syntax of 1 Peter, wherein theological facts and ethical exhortations to realize those theological facts are woven together into a complex relationship that defies a stable ordering. The passage from doctrine to ethics is traversed in many ways. Verses 22–23 in some ways form a classic example of how labyrinthine this passage can be.

As noted above, the opening phrase is a declaration that "you" have made your lives holy. Translating *psychas* as "lives" rather than "selves" or "souls" gives a better sense of the ethical drive of the phrase. It is striking that "you" and not God have made your lives holy. This focus on the power of the human deed is amplified by the subsequent assertion that "you" have done this "by your obedience to the truth." Holiness is apparently the result of human obedience. The naming of the readers as "children of obedience" in 1:14 prior to the call to holiness in 1:15 may not be accidental.

However, it is significant that "your obedience" is "to the truth." The precise content or pedigree of "the truth" is not declared at this point. First Peter does not use the word again, although the adjective "true" is attached to God's grace in 5:12. But the context suggests that truth be connected to "seed" (1:23) and then to both forms of the "word" (1:23, 25). The presence of the "truth" in this process toward holiness breaks the purity of human accomplishment. Humans cannot make themselves holy by obedience, unless there is the truth, the word of the Lord, which they can obey.

The passage then turns back to human behavior when it notes that all of this leads to "an unfeigned mutual affection." *Philadelphia*, which is translated here as "mutual affection," is a central term in Greek, Roman, Jewish, and Christian thought.[9] The term denotes the special obligations and feelings that sustain a family. *Philadelphia* was not confined to blood relations or to males. It signals the constant Christian conviction that if the story of Jesus is true, then the followers of Jesus should be living together as a family. The holiness that emerges from being called by God and by obeying the truth must lead to people loving each other.

Given the constant shift from theological fact to imperative, it is no surprise that 1 Peter insists that the result of holiness and love is the command to "love one another intensely from a pure heart." In the theology of 1 Peter, those who are called never stand outside the imperatives to live holy lives and to love one another. It is not that holiness and love are the same thing; it is rather that both belong to the Christian life. The consequence of being called apart by this holy God is that "you" must love one another "intensely." The language of loving from a "pure" (*kathara*) heart echoes perhaps the purity of holiness.

Although verse 22 gives the general feeling that humans are the primary actors in the journey to love and holiness, the next three verses complicate that. Verse 23 begins with the perfect passive participle *anagegennēmenoi*, which recalls both the perfect participle that began the verse and the same word (*anagennēsas*) in 1:3, where it is God who "caused us to be born again." Thus verse 23 shifts from the activity of humans to the activity of God, or to the activity of God toward humans.

The metaphor of rebirth extends into the image of the seed (*spora*), and it will extend into 2:2 and perhaps even until 2:10. *Spora* can refer to the seed of plants or to human seed. Both images seem to be evoked here. Though the quote from Isa 40:6–8 suggests an agricultural context, the image of rebirth as God's children suggests divine seed. This is, furthermore, the point of the contrast between corruptible and incorruptible seed. The incorruptible seed is God's seed. The God who "caused us to be born again" (1:3) is here portrayed as a male father, producing progeny through seed. This male image will be balanced by the motherly image of God's milk, but here the passage uses the image of male seed as the organizing metaphor of 1:23–25.

The seed (*spora*) in 1:23a is then connected to the "word" (*logos*) in 1:23b. The term *logos* can also have connotations of procreation as well as its more common connotations of speech and reason. It is probably the capacity of the word *logos* to evoke the image both of procreation and of words that makes

---

9. The classic Greco-Roman account comes from Plutarch, *Peri Philadelphias*. On general usage, see Bruce J. Malina, *The New Testament World: Insights from Cultural Anthropology* (rev. ed.; Louisville, Ky.: Westminster/John Knox Press, 1993), esp. 28–62.

Love and the Word 53

all of this imagery work. Its sense of "seed" connects *logos* to *spora*, while its sense of "word" connects it to the word *rhēma* (and perhaps to Scripture itself) in 1:25. On the one hand, these verses offer a clever metaphorical connection among a series of images; on the other hand, something about the nature of God's presence and the power of rebirth is hereby affirmed. By combining the image of words with that of procreation, these verses enrich the sense of how God is working. In one sense, God is working outside of words, in unnameable powers that work as the seed of a father works in his child. In another sense, God is working in words, words such as the words of 1 Peter or Isaiah. And this word is both living and enduring.

It is not explicitly explained why the enduring quality of the divine seed should lead to love. As noted before, the connection between the specific content of a theological claim and the specifics of the ethics that ensue is often mysterious in 1 Peter. Perhaps the endurance of the word that seeds the Christian life gives support to trusting and hoping in God (1:21). Believing that God's word will not fade enables one, perhaps, to risk the vulnerability of love. Or perhaps a better guess would be that the seed that gives the new life makes "you" the child of a Father who demands holiness and love. "You" are now a member of the family, reborn from an incorruptible seed, and this leads to "mutual affection" (*philadelphia*).

Readers have often noted the baptismal allusions in these verses. Although there is no direct reference to the washing of baptism, the language of holiness, obedience, and rebirth all point to ancient baptismal liturgies. These verses have even been seen as primary evidence that the core of 1 Peter was a baptismal homily.[10] Although few readers hold such a precise connection between 1 Peter and baptism, most readers hear baptismal echoes in these verses.

[24–25] The quote from Isa 40:6–8 is not introduced as Scripture, unless the reference to "the living and enduring word of God" in 1:23b counts. The citation seems to be closer to the LXX, since 1 Peter, as does the LXX, omits 40:7, which is in the MT, although the phrase "all its glory" follows the MT. Both the MT and the LXX have "God" where 1 Peter has "Lord," in the phrase "the word of the Lord" (1:25a). It is possible that "Lord" is used in order to affirm that it is the word of Jesus that endures forever. However, "Lord" can refer to both God and Jesus. Scriptural citations are notoriously loose in the NT, and this may be just such a loose rendition.

Scriptural citations in 1 Peter do not simply reinforce with divine warrant an argument already made; they also push the argument in new directions. Into the social problems of the community, 1 Peter places the classic biblical contrast between the impermanence of the things of the world and the eternity

---

10. On the baptismal possibilities in 1 Peter, see Frank L. Cross, *1 Peter: A Paschal Liturgy* (London: Mowbray, 1954).

of God. Thus the image functions in much the same way as it does in Isaiah. These Christians are caught between the old way of life and the new. Much of 1 Peter is written on the borderline between the old and the new. The letter claims that there is a new family and even that the way of life inherited from their ancestors was futile (1:18). The quotation from Isaiah gives a new view of the borderline. Here flesh is declared to be as fragile and impermanent as grass and the flowers of grass. What lasts is not a person's soul or life, but the word (*rhēma*) of the Lord. This is the word from which they were born anew. Thus the eternal comes to these Christians not in the form of a gift that somehow becomes their possession. The inheritance is not in their personal possession, but is "kept in the heavens for you" (1:4). The eternal belongs to the seed that gives them this new life. Hence their trust and hope are not in their obedience to the truth; their trust and hope are in God or God's word.

This incorruptible seed is then declared to be "the word [*rhēma*] that has been proclaimed to you" (1:25b). The images of seed and word are now connected to the image of proclamation of "the good news" that evoked the desire of the angels (1:12). The things that endure are now at least three: the seed of the father that gives new birth, the words of prophetic Scripture, and the new words of Christians. In the last category, the text of 1 Peter is probably to be included. Thus the act of reading 1 Peter unleashes the incorruptible seed into the lives of the readers. In fact, their flesh will wither and die, but the words of this letter will give life and love that endures forever.

In the usual rhetorical style of 1 Peter, this passage (1:22–25) combines several images into a celebration and affirmation of the life of holiness. This passage enriches the image of the holiness by including two traditional ideas. First of all, holiness comes from obedience and issues in love. Apart from the necessity of turning from the passions of their former lives, the dominant image of holiness in 1 Peter concerns how people treat one another. The call to "love one another intensely from a pure heart" is common in early Christianity. At the center of the holy life sits a Christian community that loves one another. Second, this passage points to the enduring quality of the word of God. Using the familiar language of Isaiah, this passage affirms the eternity of the word that orders the lives of these Christians. While the life of suffering will fade, the life of holiness and glory that is built upon God's word (or seed) endures forever. First Peter insists that suffering is not only real but also essential to the Christian life. Nonetheless, suffering is temporary. Meanwhile, "the word of the Lord endures forever."

Finally, the baptismal imagery of rebirth leads naturally into the next section, where the readers are described as babies hungry for their mother's milk. The image of the father's seed giving birth will give way to the complementary image of a mother nursing her children.

1 Peter 2:1–3 Milk of the Lord

In some ways, these verses belong to the preceding since they continue the image of new birth and its ethical consequences. They also continue the play on the image of the "word" by combining "word" with "milk." Their relationship to 2:4–10 is less explicit, although the call to desire the Lord's milk sets up nicely, if only implicitly, the call to the living stone. These verses, then, form a nice link in a complex chain of images in the call to "obedient children" that begins in 2:13. The grammar follows the combination of participles and imperatives that structures the whole section from 1:13 to 2:10.

These verses also offer a progression and even an innovation in the imagery about God that drives these exhortations. Though the preceding verses focus upon the holiness of God the Father and even advise fear in the face of that holiness, these verses focus upon the kindness of the Lord and point to the more motherly imagery of God's nourishing milk. Thus the rhetoric of these verses follows the usual pattern of 1 Peter. There is no explicit development of an argument but a gathering of images and exhortations that gradually create a picture of the Christian life.

2:1 Having put away all evil and all deceit and hypocrisies[a] and envies and all slandering, 2 as just-born babes desire the verbal undeceitful milk,[b] in order that you might grow by it into salvation, 3 since[c] you have tasted that the Lord is kind.[d]

a. In a few manuscripts (B) both "hypocrisies" and "envies" occur in the singular. However, the majority supports the plural form. *Hypokrisis* retains some of original meaning of "actor" and could be rendered "pretenses" or even "deceits." Thus it is close in meaning to *dolos*, which is translated above as "deceit."

b. The phrase *to logikon adolon gala* poses the difficulty of how to render two adjectives that normally do not modify "milk." The force of the rhetoric is fairly clear. *Logikon* is playing off the various terms for word in the preceding verses, and *adolon* evokes *dolon* in the previous verse. The difficulty is how to turn these adjectives into English. The primary question is whether to convert the first adjective into a noun ("the undeceitful milk of the word") or to keep both adjectives as adjectives ("the verbal, undeceitful milk"). The former underlines the connection between *logikon* and the "words" of 1:23–25, while the latter maintains the emphasis on "milk." Even though "verbal" does not quite convey the etymological connections between word and word, keeping *logikon* as an adjective better retains the syntax of the Greek and thus is preferable.

c. Some key early manuscripts (C, Ψ, 𝔐) have *eiper*, which is the strengthened form of *ei*, in place of the slightly better attested *ei*. Both are conditional particles and are normally translated as "if." However, both can occasionally have the causal meaning of "since." Exactly where to place this *ei* or *eiper* on the scale of reality from "if" to "since" is not clear. Probably the aorist "you have tasted" conveys a certain sense of an accomplished fact, thus giving warrant to the translation of "since." However, "since" in the translation here should have at least echoes of "if."

d. There is the almost expected variant of *chrēstos* (kind) as *christos* (Christ) in several manuscripts ($\mathfrak{P}^{72}$, K, L).

[1] All the vices listed here are common in early Christian ethics, although there is nothing peculiarly Christian about any single one of these. If there is anything peculiarly Christian about this list, it is the overall selection of vices. The exact force of the terms in early Christian vice (and virtue) lists is never perfectly clear. Some lists seem to work by piling up negative images; others seem to pick the vices with more precision. This list seems more carefully drawn than many. "Evil" (*kakia*) is an extremely common term and may serve as the covering image. Unspecified "evil" could be almost anything. Thus the vices that follow give "evil" its content. It is also in the vices that follow "evil" that the special concerns of 1 Peter emerge. Deceit, hypocrisy, envy, and slander are all vices that damage the community (cf. 4:3). They are, if not the opposite, at least contrary to the "unfeigned [*anhypokriton*] mutual affection" that is called for in 1:22. Ethics in the NT is almost exclusively communal in character. The vices to be avoided and the virtues to be pursued are those that impact the life of the community. These vices are contrary to and even undermine love; this is what makes them vices.

The language of "putting away" (*apothemenoi*) vices is frequent in the NT (Rom 13:12; Eph 4:22, 25; Col 3:8; Heb 12:1; Jas 1:21). The necessity of turning away from the former life of passion is crucial to the theology and sociology of 1 Peter. These Christians have rejected their former lives, and this rejection leads to abuse from their neighbors (2:11–12; 4:1–6, 12–19). This language of putting away also suggests a context of baptism. Such imagery was a frequent part of early Christian baptismal homilies (e.g., Hippolytus, *Trad. ap.* 21). However, none of the aforementioned NT texts explicitly mentions baptism; nor does 1 Peter. Thus a certain modesty suggests that the imagery in 1 Peter be seen as a frequent part of early Christian ethical exhortations and that wonderings about liturgical settings be somewhat constrained. The imagery of "putting away" coheres with the overall social and theological situation of the recipients. They need to put away the old life, the old self, because they have been reborn (1:3; 2:2). In this sense, the language of "putting away" leads naturally to the language of rebirth in 2:2.

[2] This striking verse leads the reader not only into a new image of God but also into the question of male and female imagery for God. First Peter, as noted above, uses the comparative "as" more than any other book in the NT (27x). In general, 1 Peter does not use "as" in order to introduce an unreality but a reality. The sense here would be "as the newborn babes that you are, desire milk," rather than "desire God's nourishing word, with the same intensity and need as newborn babes desire milk." However, the whole question of language about God is implicated here. Is some of it factual and some of it just evocative?

Perhaps the question suggested by this verse would be this: Is God really our father and only metaphorically our mother?

Brephē (babes) does not mean the recently born but the just-born. In fact, *brephos* often refers to the not-yet-born, to a fetus. Furthermore, the *arti* in *artigennēta* conveys the sense of "just now." First Peter is calling the recipients "just-born babes." This does not mean that all of them were converted only a moment ago. This is, rather, a permanent condition. They are all helpless babies, in need of their divine mother's "verbal, undeceitful milk." As noted above, the two adjectives "verbal" and "undeceitful" connect this imagery to the preceding imagery. Each adjective brings its own echoes. Furthermore, the "word" (*logos*) and the "word" (*rhēma*) are part of the character of the milk on which these just-born babes live. This does not mean that this milk is really speech and nothing more. It means that the divine milk that makes these just-born grow partakes of the verbal. The undeceitful character of this milk imposes not only a contrast to the deceit that the recipients are to put away but also an association with the "truth" that lies at the source of obedience (1:22).

Milk (*gala*) in the ancient world, to state the obvious, does not come from bottles; it comes from women. Thus God is portrayed in this text as a mother suckling her babies with her "verbal, undeceitful milk." God is not directly named "mother" in this verse, though God is named "father" in 1:17. It is also striking that God as father is judge and is to be feared, while God as mother suckles her babies and is "kind" (2:3).

All of this imagery comes couched as an imperative. The recipients are challenged to "desire" this milk as the just-born babes they are. This drift from theological principles to ethical exhortations, from indicative to imperative (and vice versa), is perhaps the fundamental rhetorical move of 1 Peter. The letter, over and over again, combines assertions of God's presence and power with exhortations to live out of this presence and power. In this verse, it is affirmed that the result of these babes suckling this unusual milk is that they grow by the power of this milk into salvation. This is classic 1 Peter theology. It takes a combination of God's power and human effort to accomplish salvation.

[3] This verse is a loose quotation of the Septuagint version of Ps 33:9 (34:9 MT; 34:8 NRSV). This psalm will be quoted at length in 3:10–12. First Peter is full of imagery from this psalm. Most readers have guessed that the sense of consolation that animates the psalm inspires its employment in 1 Peter. And the overall mood of the psalm fits beautifully with this passage in 1 Peter. The maternal imagery of 2:2 extends naturally into the insistence on the Lord's kindness. The verse continues the suckling imagery of 2:2 with the verb "taste." In fact, *chrēstos* can even mean "good" in the sense of something that tastes good, although both the context in the psalm and 1 Peter is that of "kind." The aura of motherhood is reinforced in spite of the male term "Lord." It is hard not to think of God in these verses as a kind, nursing mother.

The sense of unreality contained in the particle "if" reinforces the imperative mood of these verses. Nothing here seems automatic. God may be a nursing mother, but salvation cannot be accomplished by God alone. There must also be people who are just-born babes and are hungry for God's milk.

After an opening exhortation about putting away vices, this passage (2:1–3) offers one of the most explicitly female images of God in the Bible. God is portrayed as a kind mother, nursing her newborn children. Readers are portrayed as babies hungry for the kind milk of their mother. Though female imagery and especially maternal imagery for the divine is common in the Greco-Roman world, it is unusual in Christianity. God is typically father, and Jesus is typically son. Yet female language will eventually gather around Mary, who in later Christian theology will become in some ways mother not just to Jesus but also to everyone. In this passage, however, it is the "Lord" who is depicted as mother.

In Heb 5:12, the imagery of Christians as babies living on milk is used to describe their immature status. Here the almost identical image is used quite differently. First of all, the status of being a suckling babe does not suggest theological immaturity; here it suggests the intense need and dependence of these Christians for the "verbal, undeceitful milk." They need the word of God with the same desperation that a baby needs its mother's milk. Second, this imagery is used to reinforce the kindness of the Lord. While the image of God as father leads to warnings of judgment (1:17), the image of God as mother leads to affirmations of the kindness of God's milk.

1 Peter 2:4–10 The Living Stone

This is one of the most carefully organized passages in 1 Peter. The opening two verses articulate the themes that are unfolded in what follows. Thus they function almost as a thesis, although the imagery is more evocative than argumentative. Just as the opening two verses begin with the image of the living stone and move to a theological description of the priesthood of the recipients, 2:6–10 opens with a development of the centrality of this stone and concludes with a careful naming of the recipients that includes the idea of priesthood.

One of the striking features of this passage is the number of scriptural allusions in it. Practically every verse echoes a text or two from the OT. The image of the stone gathers "stone" texts from Psalm 117 (LXX; 118 NRSV) and Isaiah. But there are loose citations from Hosea and Exodus and perhaps other places as well. This accumulation of scriptural echoes has led readers to wonder about the origin of the text: whether, for instance, such a gathering of scriptural images is better explained as emerging from communal liturgies than from the hand of a single author. However, the text itself offers no definitive evidence of its origin.

The Living Stone

In any case, it shows how complex the role of Scripture is in 1 Peter. Scripture certainly provides warrant and support for the overall argument of the letter, but it does much more. It provides imagery and even syntax for the argument of the letter. And it provides argument itself. Scriptural citations and allusions in 1 Peter often do not simply provide warrant but also push the argument in new directions. In this passage its role is so complex as to defy analysis. In fact, the border between the text of 1 Peter and the texts it cites almost disappears.

This passage is usually understood by readers as forming a conclusion to the exhortations beginning in 1:13. A line of thought beginning with the idea of rebirth, continuing through the idea of growth, finds its conclusion in the call to be "built up" into a holy people in this passage. Yet it is probably better not to confine the voice of this passage to such a rigorous logical order. As is the case throughout 1 Peter, this passage mostly adds voices and gathers more imagery. It does not really argue a point. Jesus is here named with the famous scriptural image of the rejected and chosen stone. And the recipients are named with a series of scriptural names. These images help the readers to understand both who Jesus is and who they are. This is the primary role of the passage: to provide another set of images to perceive who God is and who they are. These images do, of course, cohere with other images in 1 Peter. They not only draw from the images that precede them, as noted above; they also connect to the exhortations that follow. For instance, the exhortations to the household in 2:18–3:7 combine effectively with the building images of this passage.

2:4 When[a] you come to him, a living stone, rejected by people but to God chosen, honored, 5 you yourselves, as living stones, are being built up,[b] a spiritual house,[c] to be[d] a holy priesthood, in order to bear spiritual sacrifices acceptable to God through Jesus Christ. 6 Wherefore it is included in scripture,[e]

> Look, I place in Zion a stone,
>   a cornerstone,[f] chosen, honored,
> and the one who trusts in it will never be put to shame.

7 For you, therefore, who trust, there is honor, but for those who do not trust, there is a stone that the builders rejected; this has become the head of the corner, 8 and a stone of stumbling, and a rock of offense.[g] They stumble by disobeying the word[h] and for this purpose they were placed.

9 But you are a chosen race, a royal priesthood,[i] a holy nation, a people for keeping safe, in order that you might announce the virtues[j] of the one who called you out of the darkness into his amazing light. 10 You who were once not a people, but now are a people of God, who had not received mercy, but now have received mercy.

a. The circumstantial participle *proserchomenoi* is often translated as an imperative: "Keep coming to him." However, there is no good reason to impose an imperative sense on a participle that functions quite well as a normal circumstantial participle.

b. It is much debated whether *oikodomeisthe* is an imperative or an indicative. Grammatically it could be either. In support of it being an imperative is the persistent pattern in this section of 1 Peter, in which circumstantial participles are gathered around imperative verbs. In support of its being an indicative is both the overall indicative mood of this passage and the general sense in this passage that God is the one acting.

c. The phrase *oikos pneumatikos* is the nominative and thus should be translated not as the result of being built up but in apposition to the subject: "You, who are a spiritual house, are being built up to be . . ."

d. Connecting the infinitive phrase *eis hierateuma hagion* with the verb *oikodomeisthe* leads to a rendering of the prepositional phrase as purpose. Though this is a quite normal use of *eis*, it produces the awkwardness of having a purpose clause following a passive verb. Thus some readers separate the main verb from the rest of the sentence: "You . . . are being built up; you are a spiritual house, intended to be a holy priesthood. . . ." But this exchanges one awkwardness for a greater one. Thus most translators opt for the somewhat awkward purpose clause following a passive verb (see similar usages in the LXX of *oikodomeō*: 1 Chr 22:5; 28:10; Tob 14:5).

e. Some texts (P, 𝔐) have *graphē* in the nominative: "scripture contains." But the weight of the manuscript tradition ($\mathfrak{P}^{72}$, ℵ, A, B) favors the dative.

f. Since *akros* can mean either "extreme" or "highest," *akrogōniaion* could mean either "keystone" or "cornerstone." However, the context in both Isa 28:16, where the stone serves as a foundation, and 1 Peter, where one can trip over the stone (2:8), suggests "cornerstone."

g. The word *skandalon* can mean "a stumbling block," "a snare," "a trap," and even "an offense." It is hard to envision how a rock could be a snare. And it is perhaps better not to repeat the image of stumbling. Finally, "offense" works nicely in the flow of the passage.

h. It is not clear whether the participle *apeithountes* is a substantive participle that connects to the article *hoi*, which opens the phrase ("the disobedient stumble over the word") or a circumstantial participle, as it is rendered above. The latter fits better with the usual style of 1 Peter.

i. The word *basileion* can grammatically be either a noun or an adjective. If it is noun, then the phrase would be two substantives: "a royal residence, a priestly community." But this breaks up the series of nouns with modifying adjectives. Thus most readers see *basileion* as an adjective modifying *hierateuma*.

j. The word *aretai* can mean "virtues," "virtuous deeds," or "powers." There is rarely a clear demarcation among all these. To possess a power, to have an ability, is to possess a virtue; and these powers and virtues must issue in virtuous deeds.

[4] The passage opens with the prepositional phrase *pros hon* (to him), which links the entire passage to "Lord" in 2:3. This gives the entire passage the sense of being a christological exploration. The recipients come to this Lord out of the desire for milk and words and other forces of salvation.

The Living Stone

The appositive phrase "a living stone" opens upon the christological core of the passage. This image anticipates the Septuagint language of Ps 118:22 (117:22 LXX), cited in 2:7, and that of Isa 28:16, cited in 2:6. These stone texts were popular in early Christian literature and were used a variety of ways in various christologies (see, e.g., Matt 21:42; Mark 12:10; Luke 20:17; Acts 4:11; Rom 9:33). By modifying "stone" with "living," the author declares the interpretation of these passages before citing them. This stone is no longer a real stone, although connotations of a holy site remain.

This living, christological stone then becomes a force of division and identity. The stone is, first of all, "rejected by people." The rejection of Israel that is evoked in the stone imagery of Ps 118 and Isa 28 becomes in 1 Peter the rejection of Jesus and then of his followers. The stone imagery blends so easily with the story of Jesus and that of the early church that it is understandable how popular this language would become.

The rejected, living stone then becomes, in the language of Isa 28, "chosen" and "honored" before God. These terms create a coherence among Israel, Jesus, and Jesus' followers, since all of them are rejected, chosen, and honored. This coherence serves not so much to validate the experience of the recipients, although it does do that, as to expose something persistently true about how salvation occurs.

[5] The intensive *kai autoi* (you yourselves) signals a shift in the imagery of stone from Jesus to the recipients. The stone imagery of Isa 28 and Ps 118, which will be quoted, albeit loosely, in 2:6–7, is here connected with people in ways reminiscent of texts from Qumran. The theological complexity of this verse is mirrored in its grammatical complexity.

The verse begins with the basic metaphorical move of the verse: "you yourselves as living stones." Although people are called "stones" in both the OT and Qumran, the adjective "living" seems to come from the single "living" stone in 2:4, thus reinforcing the theological and metaphorical link between Jesus and the recipients of the letter. The force of the "as" in "as living stones" probably has the usual usage in 1 Peter: "as the living stones that you are . . ." Thus, the metaphorical force of the phrase does not come from the "as" but from the disjunction between living humans and real stones.

The uncertainty, mentioned in note b, of whether *oikodomeisthe* is imperative or indicative fits with the constant drift in 1 Peter from declaration of theological truths to exhortations for the holy life. It can be argued that the rhetorical force of this verse is much the same whether the verb is indicative or imperative. The command "Let yourselves be built up" focuses almost more on the action of the God who builds up than upon those who let God do so. And the assurance "You are being built up" implies a call to let this happen.

The real difficulty of this passage results less from the grammatical uncertainties than from the combination of images in this verse. Each of the images in the verse brings an uncertainty over its intended meaning, and the combination of these uncertainties builds into an awkward grammatical syntax that creates further problems. The opening images of living stones and being built up lead to a third building image. The recipients are called "a spiritual house." *Oikos* can refer to all kinds of houses and buildings. Most often it refers to a human "household." Such a rendering evokes the sense of God as father (and perhaps mother) and the consistent sense of being a new family, a new people, that frequents 1 Peter. However, it is almost impossible to read this passage and not think about the temple. Priests, sacrifices, and stones evoke the temple more than the household. Thus a neutral translation such as "house," which opens in both directions, works best. The adjective "spiritual" does not signal some kind of unreality, as in "you are kind of like a house." "Spiritual" has its normal function of inscribing divine presence. Thus God's somewhat effaced presence in the passive "you are being built up" emerges in the more straightforward way in the adjective "spiritual."

The purpose clause gives the reason God is building the recipients into a spiritual house. They are designed to be a "holy priesthood," which offers sacrifices acceptable to God. It is probably significant that priesthood is singular. Each person is not a priest; rather, they together form a priesthood. Although the word *heirateuma* occurs only here and in 2:9 in the NT, the concept of a called people being a priesthood is a frequent part of OT covenant language. In both 2:5 and 2:9, then, 1 Peter seems to quote Exod 19:3–8. Israel may have priests within its midst who perform special tasks, but the whole nation is called to function as a priesthood for the rest of humanity. It is this priestly role toward outsiders that 1 Peter is inscribing here.

Since so many of the images in 1 Peter can be connected to the general concept of priesthood, it is possible to see this priestly role as one of the organizing images of the letter. As Exod 19:3–8 demonstrates, the concept of priesthood, with its connotations of holiness and service, can function as the key metaphor in explorations of the covenant. Thus being "obedient children" (1:14) who are called to be "holy" (1:16) leads naturally to their designation as a "holy priesthood" (2:5). However, the only explicit detailing of what it means to be a priesthood happens in the second purpose clause: "in order to bear spiritual sacrifices acceptable to God through Christ."

The possible connotations of "spiritual sacrifices" are numerous. A parallel with Rom 12:1 is tempting but not very helpful. The most common suggestions are two. The first is the rather explicit reference to witnessing in 2:9b. The recipients' role as witness is crucial to the theology of 1 Peter. They are called again to this role as witnesses in 2:12, where they witness with their good behavior. In fact, the entire section from 2:11 to 4:11 can read as an exploration of how the recipients are to witness. The second suggestion is simply a narrowing of the first. The primary way the recipients are to witness is by suffering (see, e.g.,

The Living Stone

3:1–2, 16). The idea of suffering fits naturally with the language of sacrifice, since sacrifice always involves loss and sometimes death. Furthermore, in both Christian and Jewish thought, martyrdom is connected to temple sacrifice and is understood as having the power to make things and people holy. The language of being "acceptable to God" is what makes sacrifice not just a loss but a gain as well. Only a loss, a suffering, an offering, a sacrifice, acceptable to God can make anyone holy. In 1 Peter, it is the story of Jesus that defines what is an acceptable sacrifice and what is not.

The final phrase "through Jesus Christ" introduces or reinforces the sense of violence that haunts this passage. The imagery will shift back from stones to the stone, and to the story of rejection that belongs to that living stone. There is also a hint of sacrificial mediation in the notion that it is through Christ that sacrifices are "acceptable to God."

[6] The unusual phrase "it is included in scripture" does not seem to signal anything unusual in the force of the scriptural citation. *Graphē*, which means "writing," is a standard way in the NT of referring to OT Scripture. The logic of "wherefore" cannot be completely detailed. As is almost always the case in NT scriptural citations, the precise relationship between the larger arguments of a text and the cited Scripture remains a bit mysterious. It is also not clear how far this introductory phrase extends. Pieces of Scripture are included not just in this verse but in each of the next four verses (2:7, 8, 9, 10).

The basic imagery of verse 6 derives from Isa 28:16, which is also cited by Paul in Rom 9:32–33. The syntax of 1 Peter does not coincide with either the MT or the LXX. There is no way to know in what form the verse was known by the author. In any case, as the verse stands, it reinforces what precedes and also pushes the imagery in a new direction. It reinforces the image of the chosen stone, and it introduces the power of this stone to divide. The power of this stone to divide comes from the standard christological notions of early Christianity, but also probably from the context in Isa 28, where the laying of the stone is a moment in the arrival of God's justice. Thus the stone in Zion has two narratives. First, it is, in the imagery of Ps 118, a rejected, chosen, and then honored stone. Since Jesus and the recipients are both stones, both Jesus and the recipients are also rejected and then chosen. Second, it is also, in the imagery of Isa 28, a dividing stone. Jesus has this same power to divide, and it may be the case that the recipients do so as well.

The precise phrase "and the one who trusts in it will never be put to shame" does not come directly from Isa 28, but the basic ideas do. Following the imagery of a cornerstone, people do not so much believe in the stone as trust it to be a reliable cornerstone. Thus *pisteuō* is better rendered here as "trust" than as "believe." Furthermore, the question of trust fits better with the question of shame. Is there shame in being rejected by the world? Is there shame in attaching oneself to Jesus, who was also rejected? By all accounts, in the ancient world the question of shame and its opposite, honor, were crucial to almost everyone, not just to Jews and Christians. Apparently much of the hierarchy in ancient Mediterranean culture was structured around shame and honor.[11] In fact, 1 Peter does not bother to make a case for the positive value of honor or the negative of shame; it simply assumes those values. Into the pervasive dynamic of honor and shame, 1 Peter injects the classic religious claim: it is God and not humans who ultimately decides who is ashamed and who is not. The change in voice reinforces the sense that it is God who is acting, since it is God who placed in Zion this stone: "Look, I place in Zion a stone. . . ." God is creating a new dynamic of shame and honor around the person Jesus, the living stone. The recipients are not directly being challenged to trust in God; rather, they are being reassured, by way of this theological narrative, that their trust in God does not end with shame. Their rejection (and perhaps their initial feeling of shame) is a necessary moment in the journey to honor (*entimon*).

[7–8] These verses lay out explicitly the dividing power of this stone. It is not perfectly clear who is speaking in these verses. The voice of God, which is speaking directly in verse 6, seems at a minimum to authorize the declarations of verses 7–10. In fact, God may still be speaking. In any case, it is difficult not to hear echoes of God's voice in all the declarations of verses 7–10. The porousness of the border between the ancient text and the letter of 1 Peter is crucial to the power of each.

The opening assertion affirms the journey to honor the recipients: "For you, therefore, who trust, there is honor. . . ." The affirmation is not that these people are trusting people, but that they trust in the living stone. The issue is that of Christology. Jesus is the cornerstone of the building. Thus Jesus establishes the pattern and orientation of the building (the readers). In the language of 2:21, Jesus leaves "for you a pattern, so that you might follow in his footsteps." The assurance is that this strange pattern, characterized by rejection and suffering, is ultimately a path to honor.

For those who do not trust the stone, those who are not willing to be part of a building orientated by such a strange stone, there is a different narrative. As noted above, this narrative comes primarily from Ps 118 or, perhaps more accurately, Ps 118 as seen through the lens of the story of Jesus. The sequence of the quote places those who trust and those who do not in different predicaments. First Peter assumes that early Christian readers already know that this verse from Ps 118 is messianic, that it tells the story of Jesus and thus the story of themselves. Unlike Isa 28:16, in early Christianity Ps 118:22 becomes a popular messianic verse (Mark 12:10–11; Matt 21:42; Luke 20:17; *Barn.* 6.4). Since Ps

---

11. David D. Gilmore, *Honor and Shame and the Unity of the Mediterranean* (American Anthropological Association Special Publication 22; Washington, D.C.: American Anthropological Association, 1987).

The Living Stone

118 was traditionally understood as a psalm of David, the creativity of Christian exegesis consists only in deciding what parts of the psalm are most fitting. The rejection of the stone by the builders becomes not only a central moment in the story of salvation but also a permanent and necessary moment in how God saves anyone and everyone. As in nearly all Christian thought, the cross is not a tragedy to be avoided but the terrifying path to resurrection. This rejection instigates the irony of the rejected stone rejecting those who rejected it.

The precise meaning of all these building images is a bit allusive. The stone becomes "the head of the corner" (*kephalē gōnias*). In the *Testament of Solomon* the same phrase refers to the keystone at the pinnacle of the temple (22.7–9). But here in 1 Pet 2:7, *kephalē gōnias* parallels *akrogōniaion* of verse 6, and thus both must be understood as "cornerstone." The fact that the stone they rejected has become the head of the corner probably remains a secret to the builders. The real status of the rejected stone and thus the ultimate destiny of those who do not trust in it will be revealed at the very end.

The images of "a stone of stumbling" and "a rock of offense" come from Isa 8:14. The text of Isa 8:14 is notoriously diverse. The MT, the LXX, and the Greek versions of Aquila, Symmachus, and Theodotion are all different. The fact that Paul seems to quote the same version of Isa 8:14 in Rom 9:33 suggests that both shared a common Greek source that we do not have. The imagery in 1 Peter illustrates that for those who do not trust the stone to be a cornerstone, it is a stone in the wrong place, in their path perhaps, that people stumble over. For those people it is the wrong stone in the wrong place, but for those who trust it, this stone of stumbling, when seen through lens of theology, is the cornerstone of God's building.

The end of verse 8 offers an explanation for the predicament of those who reject the stone. "They stumble" over the stone "by disobeying the word." The "word" could refer to the stone and thus be Jesus Christ, or more likely, in consistency with "word" in 1:23–25, refer to words. The precise content and extent of these words is not perfectly clear. As in the case of 1:23–25, "word" could include Scripture, the gospel about Jesus Christ, and even the words of 1 Peter. It also is not perfectly clear what it means to disobey the word. First Peter uses the same phrase for husbands in 3:1, when exhorting wives to win over without a word husbands who disobey the word. Judgment is pronounced in 4:17 on those who disobey the "gospel of God." Something more than a synonym for not trusting or believing must be intended. Perhaps those who do not trust in the stone also reject the call to holiness and love.

The notion that "for this purpose they were placed" invokes the always-controversial notion that God ordains disobedience and its subsequent punishment. It is possible that "for this purpose" refers only to the act of stumbling: they disobey the word out of their own freedom and then are placed by God in the position of stumbling over the stone that they rejected. But it is more likely that "for this purpose" refers to the entire sequence, including the disobedience. As has often been noted, the ancient world had a different notion of human freedom. The absolute power given to human freedom in some modern theology is absent from ancient thought. God is implicated in all humans' deeds, even those contrary to God's word.

The role of God in all this is emphasized by the choice of the passive *etethēsan* (they were placed). This is the same verb used in verse 6b: "I place in Zion a stone." God is the one who places in Zion the stone, the people who trust it, and those who reject it. The entire gathering of forces and persons around the gospel of Jesus Christ is "placed" by God.

[9–10] The rather emphatic *hymeis de* (but you) creates a sharp contrast with what precedes. After defining those who reject the stone, the letter addresses those who trust. The imagery of verse 9, which names "you," comes from a combination of Exod 19:6 and Isa 43:20–21. The notion of a "chosen race" (*genos eklekton*) connects to the chosen stone in 2:4. The recipients of the letter are, like Jesus Christ, chosen. Both terms (chosen, race) come from Isa 43:20. There is little attempt in the letter to pursue the connotations of *genos*, which refers to a people of common origin. However, the concept of election is crucial to most biblical thought and seems to be the central force of the phrase "chosen race." To be elect not only connects the recipients to Jesus and to ancient Israel; it also forms a poignant contrast to those who were placed for disobedience and stumbling.

The two phrases "a royal priesthood" and "a holy nation" derive from Exod 19:6. Both images recall the exhortation to holiness in 1:15. It is significant that both images are collective. The recipients are not priests; instead, together they form a priesthood. The phrase "a people for keeping safe" has roots in both Exod 19:5 and Isa 43:21. Obviously, the recipients are acquiring for themselves classic names that once belonged to Israel. It is less clear whether the names have extensive content beyond this identification with Israel and the ongoing echoes of holiness. Perhaps the priestly function of the recipients lies in the purpose clause. They announce the virtues of God. And the notion of being kept safe echoes God's keeping them and their inheritance safe in 1:4–5.

This new status is "in order that you might announce the virtues of the one who called you." The choice of the word "virtues" as that which is announced is interesting because virtue is more a classical Greek image than a biblical one. However, as noted above, the word *aretai* can mean "virtues," "virtuous deeds," or "powers." These virtues belong, in an intensely biblical phrase, to "the one who called you." And while the idea of being called from darkness to light is fairly common in the Greco-Roman world, it is also a classic biblical image. This purpose clause articulates again a crucial aspect of the theology of 1 Peter. In 1 Peter this new status with God carries with it responsibilities for others. In fact, God seems to bless these people not just in order to bless them but in order also to bless others through them.

The clipped and balanced contrasts of verse 10 offer a nice conclusion to this section. It is perhaps overstating the case, as some readers have done, that this verse serves as a climax to the entire first part of the letter. First Peter is not so carefully structured, and this verse seems mostly to provide another image of who "you" are. The image is potent: they "who were once not a people, but now are a people of God."

The imagery of verse 10 is drawn loosely from Hosea (see esp. 1:6, 9; 2:1, 25), where these terms are the names given to the children of Hosea and Gomer. Paul also uses these images (also in a loose way) in Rom 9:25–26. First Peter does not pursue the subtle change in status for Israel that is implied by these terms in Hosea; instead, 1 Peter seems to use these terms to reinforce the new status of believers. In fact, the general force of verse 10 is to underline the sense of safety that is included in being a people of God. First Peter only uses the image of mercy in this verse and in 1:3. In both places "mercy" reinforces the surety of salvation by locating its origin not in human behavior but in the character of God.

In this passage (2:4–10), 1 Peter's evolving description of the holy life takes on several classical biblical images, all of which focus on the core image of the "living stone." The stone imagery works in a variety of ways. First of all, it offers a connection to the central narrative of Jesus' suffering and subsequent glory. Jesus is the rejected cornerstone. The rejection of this precious stone anticipates 1 Peter's ongoing treatment of the suffering and abuse of Jesus himself and of his followers. The stone imagery also puts in place the classic narratives of the temple, of priesthood, and even of spiritual houses. The recipients of the letter should see themselves not only in the Jesus story but also in the story of Israel. The language of Isa 28 and Ps 118 belongs to Jesus and his followers. Thus the disconcerting experience of suffering and abuse that these Christians are enduring is recast in this passage as another moment in an ancient pattern. God's chosen have always been rejected.

1 Peter 2:11–4:6 Life as Aliens and Sojourners

1 Peter 2:11–12 Call to Beautiful Deeds among the Gentiles

Nearly all readers of 1 Peter notice a rhetorical shift in these verses. First of all, a general shift in topic seems to occur. While 1:3–2:10 points mostly to God's offering of salvation through Christ, 2:11 begins an extensive exploration of how believers are to behave toward outsiders and one another. Some readers see this new section as extending only to 4:11. A different section, which functions as conclusion and restatement of the themes of 2:11–4:11, is perceived as beginning in 4:12. The repetition of the direct address "beloved" in 2:11 and 4:12 is also seen as formally marking these two sections. In addition, the audience seems to be more carefully defined, especially in 2:18–3:7 where specific groups are named.

On the other hand, 1 Peter does not seem to be organized around rigorously defined sections. The rhetoric is repetitious and informal, as it often is in early Christian letters. At a minimum, 1 Peter evidences the standard transition from an opening blessing or theological introduction to ethical exhortation. Thus the organizing force of these verses may be more ideological than rhetorical. In fact, these two verses may even serve a thesis, albeit a soft one, for the ethics that follow. They lay out, in succinct fashion, the basic ethical argument of 1 Peter.

> 2:11 Beloved, I exhort you, as aliens and sojourners,[a] to abstain[b] from fleshly desires, which fight against life, 12 by keeping[c] your behavior among the Gentiles beautiful,[d] so that when they slander you as evildoers, as a result of seeing your beautiful works, they might glorify God on the day of visitation.

a. As noted above (see note on 1:1) *paroikos* and *parepidēmos* can have both technical and metaphorical meanings. The sense here is not that each and every recipient of the letter is a legal noncitizen of some kind. The sense is that the alienation endured by such people is now endured by the recipients on account of their faith.

b. The earliest manuscripts are about equally divided between the infinitive *apeches-thai* (ℵ, B, Ψ, 𝔐) and the imperative *apechesthe* ($\mathfrak{P}^{72}$, A, C, L). Both are fine grammatically. Most readers prefer the infinitive since having an infinitive follow the imperative "I exhort you" is the more common construction.

c. Grammatically *echontes* serves as a circumstantial participle, modifying the infinitive "to abstain." It is often rendered as a separate imperative since it seems to many readers that abstaining from fleshly desires and keeping your behavior beautiful are complementary acts. However, there are no real problems in translating the participle as a participle. It just means that "keeping your behavior . . . beautiful" becomes an instance or means of abstaining from fleshly desires.

d. The word *kalos* has both moral and aesthetic meaning, although the aesthetic meaning, "beautiful," is more common than the moral meaning, "good." Furthermore, being the object of sight by the Gentiles suggests the aesthetic "beautiful."

[2:11] The challenging exhortations that compose the heart of 1 Peter are introduced with the epithet "beloved." This popular Christian self-designation, repeated in 4:11, puts in place a sense of God's blessings, protection, and love as the context for the difficulties of the Christian ethical life. The exhortation opens with two interesting dynamics. The first is the ambiguous "as aliens and sojourners." As noted above, 1 Peter uses "as" (*hōs*) in the sense of both "as if" and "since." The usage here must be more "as if" than "since." The recipients of the letter are not legally "aliens and sojourners," but they share the predicament of such persons. The life of suffering that these Christian sojourners are called to live includes spiritual alienation. However, there may also be a real social exclusion forced upon them by the "Gentiles." If the latter is the case, then this exhortation can have the sense of calling them to live well among the Gentiles, even though the Gentiles exclude them. Even if that is the case, it is the sense of spiritual alienation that really drives this exhortation. The recipients are called to stand apart from society, to take on an outsider status, and to think of themselves as aliens, as noncitizens. They may not legally be outsiders, but they are to imagine themselves as such. This spiritual move is essential to the entire exhortation to suffering.

The second dynamic comes from the direct call "to abstain from fleshly desires." The language of "fleshly desires" is so traditional and so pervasive that it becomes almost meaningless in itself. In the theology of 1 Peter, it becomes shorthand for the forces that pull believers away from their calling as people of God. It is not a reference to modern sins of the flesh, with overtones of sexuality, although it might include that. Instead, fleshly desires are the powers of the world and the old self that stand against the challenges of being aliens and sojourners. It is in this basic ethical sense that abstaining from fleshly desires can be the ground of behaving well among the Gentiles.

It is also in this fundamental sense that these desires "fight against life." This phrase is an effective summary of the ancient view of passions: they destroy life. It is perhaps significant that the recipients are not admonished to go to war against these passions. Rather, it is the passions that employ violence. In the theology of 1 Peter, the people of God endure violence; they do not practice it themselves.

[12] The recipients abstain from passion by keeping their behavior among the Gentiles beautiful. The causal force of this phrase suggests that the key move in the new believer's separation from the passions of the world is behaving well toward the Gentiles. This is not easy. As 1 Pet 4:2–4 notes, these new believers used to be Gentiles. Now they must live among them, not as one of them, but as outsiders. Furthermore, they are not called simply to separate themselves but to model Christlike behavior toward these Gentiles. The choice of the word *kalos*, "beautiful," evidences the author's understanding of classic Gentile values, for *kalos* evokes the public prestige of an honorable and ethical life. These new Christians, these no-longer Gentiles, display toward the hostile Gentiles, among whom they live, the highest Gentile value. They keep their behavior beautiful. This shared value allows for the purpose clause that follows. The purpose clause probably does not exhaust the reasons why Christians are called to behave well, for the call to a holy life is essential to salvation whether the Gentiles see it or not. Nevertheless, the force of witness is crucial to the argument of 1 Peter. It

is possible that these hostile Gentiles will, by "seeing your beautiful works," become Christian. However, the main force here seems to be that they will only admit the beauty of these deeds and glorify God on the last day. God's judgment on "the day of visitation" includes both mercy and punishment.

These verses (2:11–12) offer the first clear articulation of a central image in 1 Peter. Christians are to practice virtues in the face of abuse. The syntax of 2:12 will be repeated almost verbatim in 3:16. The idea of responding to abuse with good deeds will dominate much of the letter. In 2:19–23 Jesus himself models this behavior by refusing to return abuse for abuse, "thus leaving for you a pattern, so that you might follow in his footsteps" (2:21). While these followers of the pattern of Christ find themselves to be "aliens and sojourners" in the midst of their Gentile neighbors, the behavior they practice connects to the values shared with these Gentiles. The Gentiles themselves will recognize this alienating Christian behavior as "beautiful."

1 Peter 2:13–17 Submission to the Authority of the Gentiles

In some ways this passage serves as the first example of how Christians are to live out the exhortations in 2:11–12 to abstain from fleshly desires and to keep their behavior beautiful among the Gentiles. In another sense, however, the opening imperative "be subject to every human creature" serves as the governing phrase for the call to the slaves and wives to submit to lords and husbands. In fact, the participles in 2:18; 3:1; and 3:7 probably derive their imperatival force from the grammatical imperative of 2:13. This passage can thus be seen as the opening of a diverse and complex call for submission.

The passage itself seems to be organized around the peculiar issue of the relationship with persons in positions of authority in Roman political life. There also seems to be a rather imprecise inclusio in 2:13 and 2:17, with the dual imperatives to submit first to everyone and then to the emperor. Thus the rhetoric of the passage declares that the Christian's relationship to the emperor is one of kind with the Christian's relationship to any and all persons. However, the passage will draw a subtle distinction between how Christians submit to emperors and how they submit to others. This initial distinction initiates a series of distinctions in how Christians submit to different persons. Slaves, for instance, will submit to their lords in particular ways (2:18–20), as will wives to husbands (3:1–6). Christians should submit to different people in different ways.

Central to the meaning of the passage is the force of *hōs*, which occurs five times in these four verses. As noted above, *hōs* can mean "as if," denoting a sense of unreality and pretense, or it can mean "since," denoting a real if tentative condition. The question is whether every instance of *hōs* in this passage, or in all of 1 Peter, contains identical percentages of reality and unreality, or whether some instances of *hōs* suggest more reality or unreality than do other instances. Are governors actually sent by God to effect justice, or are Christians only to pretend that they are?

> 2:13 Be subject to every human creature[a] because of the Lord, whether to the emperor as if[b] to the one who is superior 14 or to governors as if[b] sent by him[c] for justice upon those who do evil and for praise of those who do good; 15 because in this way it is the will of God that by doing good you silence the ignorance of foolish people, 16 doing this[d] as[b] free people, and not using your freedom as a covering for evil, but as[b] slaves of God. 17 Honor everyone, love the community,[e] fear God, honor the emperor.

a. The noun *ktisis* can mean a "founding," "an act of creation," and "something created." The created thing could be a person or a thing. The term has typically been translated in English as "institution," but it is unlikely that this is what is intended. The ancient world rarely spoke of "institutions" in the modern sense of the word. Furthermore, the examples that follow are all of persons. Thus, the best rendering is "creature."

b. The adverb *hōs* can express a variety of degrees of reality. In this passage it is translated both "as if" and "as," depending on the context.

c. The antecedent of him is clearly the emperor, not God.

d. The grammatical structure of verse 16 is not clear. Since the verse lacks a main verb, the verb must be supplied from either what follows or what precedes. It is possible that v. 16 anticipates the imperative to honor everyone in v. 17. But it is also possible that all these unattached phrases are subject to the opening imperative in 2:13 to "be subject to every human creature" or even to the exhortation in 2:12 to keep "your behavior among the Gentiles beautiful." The persistent looseness of the grammar in this section suggests that no one phrase grammatically governs the rest. The ongoing mood here is exhortation, and there is no single term that controls the rest. Thus an ambiguous connection such as "doing this," wherein "this" remains unspecified, offers the best translation.

e. The Greek *adelphotēta* literally means "brotherhood." To modern ears "brotherhood" hints of a gender exclusiveness not necessarily implied by *adelphotēta*. The translation "community," offered above, conveys both the open character of the group and the sense of one unit suggested by the singular *adelphotēta*. However, "community" does not adequately convey the family echoes contained in *adelphotēta*.

[13] The verb *hypotassō* occurs six times in 1 Peter (2:13, 18; 3:1, 5, 22; 5:5). The basic etymological meaning of the word is "to arrange under." Its primary usage in Greek literature is to evoke proper participation in the social order, in the sense of calling one to submit to someone superior in the social order.[12] This order could range from the household to the courtroom or even

---

12. For a survey of the call to submission, especially in the context of household codes, in Greco-Roman and Christian literature, see Balch, *Let Wives Be Submissive*.

to the army. The translation "be subject to," while awkward for modern theology, conveys nicely the sense of social hierarchy in the term. The problem with the opening phrase of the verse lies not with the command to submit but with the object. The call to "be subject to every human creature" is so absolute and universal as to be almost unthinkable. There is no sense here of any recognizable social hierarchy. Every single human being becomes the social superior to every Christian. Such a command does not enforce a social order; it *undermines* all order because all Christians, no matter what their social position, are called to submit to every human creature, no matter what their social position. This dynamic is not friendly to any stable social order.

The only order enforced in such a command is a christological one. Christians are to do this "because of the Lord." It is not clear whether "Lord" refers to God or to Jesus, but the general theological context is clear enough in 1 Peter. Jesus himself, as described in 2:21–25, is the model. Christians are to live the pattern of submission that is best displayed in Jesus. Yet the submission of Jesus is not eternal; it is prelude to an exaltation in which the cosmic powers submit to him (3:22). Furthermore, this submission is a moment in the general program of witnessing to outsiders. The submission of Christians will silence the "foolish people" (2:15) and lead to the Gentiles glorifying God (2:12).

First Peter moves from the comprehensive principle of submitting to everyone, to the particular problem of submitting to ignorant public officials, crooked personal lords, and unbelieving husbands. It is as though the discomforting general principle is explored by way of three equally discomforting examples. These three examples might be the most problematic ones in the community. Should Christians submit to such negative figures?

The first figure named is perhaps the most problematic because it raises the basic question of the nature of society and the face of justice. The Greek term *basileus*, which means "king," probably refers to the Roman emperor. It is thus equivalent to the Latin *imperator*. The emperor, as 2:14 shows, becomes the primary symbol for Roman civil authority. The call to submit includes submission to the authorities that order the Gentile world that these Christians have rejected.

Christians are to submit "as if [*hōs*] to the one who is superior." The sense of pretense in "as if" is crucial here. The emperor is not in fact superior to the Christian. This same emperor is probably included in the group of "foolish people" in 2:15. Furthermore, the reason for submission does not lie in the real superiority of the emperor; the reason lies in the pattern that Christ has provided and in the goal of witnessing. Christians are to submit because of the Lord, but they will do it "as if" the emperor were superior to them, when in fact this emperor is not. Thus the presence of an inferior emperor of an unjust kingdom does not undo the call for submission. And there is no confirmation of the inherent justice or propriety of Roman society, or of any society, for that matter.

[14] This sense of pretense extends to the "governors" who are "sent by him." The traditional Roman notion of the authority of the emperor being extended through his officials is hereby affirmed, although in an ironic way. The Roman ideal is that civil officials enforce justice. The Roman concept of justice focuses a bit more on the fairness of the process than on the results,[13] but the overall sense is not that different from the biblical one. First Peter employs the classic Greco-Roman terminology of "justice" for "those who do evil" and "praise" for "those who do good." However, as all Greeks and Romans know, civic officials rarely enforce true justice. By using classic terms, 1 Peter invokes the irony of this ideal. Romans, perhaps more than anyone else, were well aware of the hypocrisy of the Roman claim to justice, but that hypocrisy did not negate the ideal.[14] For 1 Peter, even the ideal is probably suspect since Christians no longer hold to the same social values that they once did when they were good Gentiles. There is therefore an inescapable irony in the imagery here. Ideally, praise and not punishment should fall on those who do good. However, Christians can and will suffer while doing good. The irony is not absolute, since the same people who abused the Christians who do good will, in the end at least, recognize the Christian good as good.

[15] The enigmatic "because of the Lord" in 2:13 is given content in this verse. In the exhortation to household slaves that follows this passage, 1 Peter gives the fullest articulation of the christological grounds for Christian suffering (2:21–25). Here, however, "because of the Lord" is not grounded, explicitly at least, in the suffering of Christ, but in the missionary and witnessing duties of Christians toward outsiders.

This exhortation to good behavior is not couched in the imperative but in the common biblical idiom of a declaration of God's will. The imagery of God's will sets up the dynamic in 2:16, where Christian freedom emerges from being "slaves of God." In the rhetoric of the verse, it is not clear how far God's will extends. Does God's will include not just the doing good by Christians but also the silencing of foolish people? Does the purpose of Christian behavior lie in the purity of deeds, wherein Christians do good no matter what the consequences or the reaction of others? Or is the purpose of Christian behavior carefully configured so as to produce certain reactions by non-Christians?

The phrase "doing good" nicely summarizes 1 Peter's basic approach to the conflict between Christians and non-Christians that dominates so much of the letter. Furthermore, this position will become the most common one throughout the Christian history of persecution. Christians are to do good no matter what.

---

13. See, e.g., Socrates' speech in Xenophon (*Oec.* 9.14) and the affirmations of the good ruler in Pliny the Younger (*Pan.* 70.7) and Dio Chrysostom (*Or.* 39.2).

14. For a survey of Roman sense of justice and injustice, see J. A. Crook, *Law and Life of Rome: 90 B.C.–A.D. 212; Aspects of Greek and Roman Life* (Ithaca, N.Y.: Cornell University Press, 1967).

Bad emperors, bad governors, mistreatment by neighbors, even martyrdom, do not change the fundamental Christian obligation to God. The call to the holy life (1:15) is absolute. Christians must be holy because God is holy. It does not matter how they are being treated or by whom they are being mistreated.

The language of silencing foolish people by doing good echoes the earlier call in 2:12. The terminology is identical. In 2:12 people accuse you of "doing bad" but will glorify God on the day of visitation when they see your "good works." In 2:15 Christians silence foolish people by doing good. The eschatological context of 2:12 suggests an eschatological reading of 2:15. The silencing of foolish people does not happen now. At this point, foolish people remain foolish people. They live according to their ignorance. They will be silenced, apparently, "on the day of visitation" (2:12). The eschatological context of this silencing adds to the terror of the present. Christian good behavior does not mitigate, transform, or undo their mistreatment. Until the day of the Lord, foolish people will remain ignorant of the goodness of Christian behavior.

However, this ignorance may not be absolute or unassailable. The recipients of the letter were themselves once living in ignorance (1:14). First Peter never explicitly asserts that witnessing to outsiders will convert them into Christians. Nevertheless, since all the early Christian readers of the letters were once living and thinking exactly as were these "foolish people," it can be assumed that all this witnessing can bear fruit before the day of the Lord.

[16] As mentioned above in note d, the grammar of this verse is not clear. However, the looseness of the grammatical connection of this verse to the passage does not really affect the meaning. This verse makes its own exhortation, creating a standard that could fit in many contexts.

Christians are to do all of this "as free people." On the one hand, the declaration of freedom in the context of submitting to civil authorities suggests a certain political status. In some ways, only a free person can really submit, for there is a fundamental difference between how a slave submits and how a free person does so. Thus the freedom that gives space for this call to submission evokes classic political freedom. On the other hand, as the verse also asserts, this freedom comes out of theological slavery. To act as free persons turns out to be the same thing as acting as slaves of God. Thus the grounding and motivation for this political submission does not lie in any explicit political philosophy. Submission is a necessary part of the holy life. Perhaps the sense of pretense in *hōs* is again in force. Christians are to submit "as if" they enjoy the political status of free citizens, whether they have that status or not.

The grammar of this verse, with "free people" and "slaves of God" in apposition, creates an equivalency or identity between being free and being God's slave. The idea of being a slave of God is classically biblical. Being a slave of God denotes not only a command of obedience to God's will (2:15), but also the impossibility of being anyone else's slave. As slaves of God, Christians stand before any and all emperors as free persons. Hence it is always God's will and not the emperor's that drives Christian behavior. Probably for this reason, 1 Peter never asks Christians to obey the emperor; it does not even ask for obedience from slaves to their human lords. Christians are to "honor" the emperor. It is not clear in practice where the line between honor and obedience would lie. Nevertheless, 1 Peter insists on a line of some kind.

The warning not to use this theological freedom as "a covering for evil" reinforces the theological ground for this call to submission. If the new life as God's slaves means that Christians stand as free persons before civil authorities, this does not mean that Christians are perfectly free. Christian freedom is not absolute because this freedom is derivative of an earlier slavery. Perhaps a free citizen is permitted to dissimulate before the authorities, pretending at good deeds that hide bad ones; but a slave of God is not.

[17] This passage ends with a series of four imperatives. The verse itself is structured by the inclusio of "Honor everyone" and "Honor the emperor." In between are two imperatives that focus more on internal relations than external. This verse also seems to function as a conclusion and even as a clarification of the call to submit that began this passage. Submitting and honoring seem to define one another. The call to submit to every human creature does not mean that Christians are to treat everyone the same. First Peter insists that Christians treat different people differently. Christians are to submit to everyone; Christians are to honor everyone. However, honor and submission must be gauged for the person.

The opening imperative to "honor everyone" is in the aorist, while the remaining imperatives in the verse are in the present. Typically the present tense in the imperative indicates ongoing action, while the aorist would suggest onetime action. However, since the aorist is often used in statements of general principle, such a distinction does not always hold. Probably the aorist is used to indicate that the command to "honor everyone" is a permanent command for the community. It is not the case, however, that the command to "honor everyone" is the general principle of which the next three imperatives serve as examples. The command to "fear God" can hardly be an instance of honoring everyone.

The parallel between "be subject to every human creature" and "honor everyone" indicates a connection between submission and honoring. "Honor" is a common word in Greek and thus can have many meanings. In a way the broad range of its usage prohibits a precise definition. However, the general range of the word does provide a possible clarification of what it means to submit. While submission often has the sense of obedience, honor focuses more on offering the respect due to someone given their position in society. To honor the emperor does not mean to obey the emperor, although it would not prohibit such. In the honor-and-shame dynamics of the ancient Mediterranean world, the giving of respect is crucial to maintaining the order of ancient society. Somehow Christians are to find a way to "honor everyone" while being "slaves of God."

The command to "love the community" by all accounts exceeds anything implied in the commands to honor or to submit. Members of the Christian community deserve special treatment, which transcends honoring. First Peter does not define love, and the NT itself never defines love. Even in 1 Cor 13, Paul is more exploring and celebrating the power of love than he is defining it. Love apparently resists precise definition. Nevertheless, love is crucial to the life of the Christian in 1 Peter. Believers are called "beloved" (2:11; 4:12), and 1 Peter uses the command to love as a summary of the internal behavior in the community both here and in 4:8. Christians are to love other Christians while they honor everyone.

As noted above, the translation "community" fails to convey the sense of family in the Greek *adelphotēta*. Love is not an indiscriminate act; it should be offered only where appropriate. Thus the sense of a family collective creates the proper object for love. Love belongs to the internal life of the believing community. It does not belong to everyone or to the emperor. In 4:8, the command to "keep your love for one another intense" indicates that Christians are to love every individual Christian. However, in 2:17 Christians are to love the "community." This distinction is probably not unlike the modern distinction between loving the institutional church and loving each person in the pews. As has been often noted, the sense of bias in this usage of love seems quite different from the command to love your enemies in the Sermon on the Mount (Matt 5:44).

While the verb *phobeō* can often have the sense of "fear," it can also mean something closer to "awe" or even "respect." Thus the phrase "fear God" does not necessarily evoke the name of God solely as a threat. On the other hand, the English word "awe" strips *phobeō* perhaps too much of the feeling of dread and even terror contained in the term. Fear of God is crucial to the theology of 1 Peter (see 1:17; 3:2, 6, 14, 16). Although Christians are to live in hope of the resurrection (1:3–5) and God is full of mercy (1:3), the sense of threat conveyed in 1:16–17, for instance, gives a certain energy to a Christian's attempt to live the holy life. The God who has acted to save these new believers is a holy God who demands holiness from these same believers. The thought of final judgment should evoke both hope and fear.

The final imperative to "honor the emperor" now comes across as a bit tame. After the commands to love and to fear, honor is not asking too much. By creating these distinctions in how Christians are to treat different people, some of the terror in the commands to submit to everyone, to honor everyone, and finally to honor the emperor is reduced. The kind of vulnerability included in the command to love is not included in the command to honor or even to submit. God and other Christians have a greater claim on Christians than do any outsiders, including the emperor. Nevertheless, the emperor and, in fact, all people do have a claim on these Christians. First Peter does not, unfortunately, detail precisely what is involved in an act of honoring or submitting.

Submission of Servants to Masters

This passage (2:13–17) inaugurates what is to modern readers, at least, the most controversial section of 1 Peter. The opening imperative to submit to everyone issues in three troubling examples. This passage commands submission to people with political authority. The ensuing passages command slaves to submit to their lords, including "crooked" ones, and wives to submit to their husbands, including ones that are "disobedient to the word." It is significant that, while modern readers chafe at these commands, there were few complaints in antiquity.

Loyalty to social order was almost universally affirmed in early Christianity. The source of this loyalty is much debated among historians. The most popular theory had been that early Christian fondness for social order comes from the pervasive Greco-Roman ethical norms of submission within the household and within society. The presence of numerous passages in the NT that discuss order within the household (see, e.g., Eph 5:21–6:9; Col 3:18–4:1; 1 Tim 2:8–15; 5:1–6:2; Titus 2:1–10; 3:1–2) suggests that hierarchical household norms were shared by Christians and non-Christians. It is argued that early Christians not only affirmed these norms within their own households but also injected these patterns into the churches, which were typically regarded as a peculiar form of an extended household. Perhaps the primary reason Gentiles will see the submissive behavior of these Christians as good behavior is because this behavior affirms social hierarchy. Apparently these Christians were not a threat to social order within the house or within public space.

Though this passage seems to build its argument upon this shared loyalty to hierarchy, 1 Peter will build even more extensive arguments on Christology. In the final analysis these Christians do not submit to others as a tactic for evangelism or for avoiding conflict, although submission might accomplish these things. They submit because this is what they are called to do (2:21; 3:9). They submit because they follow in the footsteps of Christ, who left for them a pattern of not returning abuse for abuse (2:21–23). According to 1 Peter, submission is an essential aspect of the Christian life.

1 Peter 2:18–25 Submission of Servants to Masters

This passage begins with an exhortation to household servants that they must submit to their human masters. It then offers a brief justification for this call to submission based on a definition of "grace." To endure while suffering unjustly is "grace with God." This rather stunning and disconcerting definition of grace gives way to an extended articulation of the christological basis of Christian suffering. The suffering of Christ, in all its details, provides the pattern for all Christian suffering. In this way the theological arguments offered in support of the exhortation to the household slaves implicitly provide warrant for all Christian suffering.

This exhortation to household slaves and then to wives (3:1–6) and husbands (3:7) has raised the issue of the genre and purpose of such household exhortations. The long-standing suggestion that NT exhortations to members of households belong to a widespread Greco-Roman household code tradition, in which submission and order are enforced on various members, has some credibility but oversimplifies the actual arguments in the NT. First Peter certainly affirms the common household hierarchies of the Greco-Roman world, but it cites that tradition in a peculiar way. The alienation that these Christians have from their neighbors does not seem to include alienation from the propriety of social hierarchies. Everyone seems to agree with the ideal. People should occupy their social roles with appropriate submission. However, early Christianity, including 1 Peter, offers a unique reason for this submission. First Peter does not explicitly defend the virtue of these hierarchies. In fact, 1 Peter consistently notes the flaws in the character of those in power. Thus there is no argument for submitting because the social order deserves it. Instead, Christians are to submit because they are following in the steps of Christ. Christ submitted to the powers. Thus Christians must submit as well. This does not mean that the political dominance of Rome or the social dominance of masters and husbands is ordained in the heavens. What is ordained in the heavens is not returning abuse for abuse.

It is striking that no specifics are provided to household slaves on how they are to submit. This entire section (2:11–3:7) lacks ethical details. These Christians are not told how to submit to or how to honor everyone (2:13, 17). Household slaves are not told what submission to their masters looks like in an actual deed (2:18–20), nor are wives' submission to their husbands detailed (3:1–6). First Peter offers general principles along with theological warrants for them. In fact, the theology may precede the ethics. Given the weight on theology and the lack of specific ethical examples, it seems more likely that theological traditions are creating an ethic rather than theology is being created to support an existing ethic. It does not seem that the portrait of Jesus as one who suffers is being debated; the passage reads as if the portrait of Jesus is traditional and credible, and what is at stake is whether and how Christians are to suffer.

Thus, this passage, like the entire section, requires a creative reader. In order for the ethical force of these passages to be realized, the readers must be able to connect these general principles and the pattern of Jesus Christ to particular deeds in their lives. They must find a way to endure while they suffer for doing good. They must find a way to "follow in the footsteps" of a Jesus who did not abuse in return when he was abused, who suffered but did not sin.

2:18 Household servants, do this[a] by being subject in all fear to your masters,[b] not only to those who are good and gentle, but also to those who are crooked.[c] **19** For this is grace[d] if someone out of consciousness[e] of

Submission of Servants to Masters

God bears grief while suffering unjustly. 20 For what fame is it if, sinning and being beaten,[f] you endure? But if, while doing good and suffering, you endure, this is grace with God. 21 For you were called for this purpose, because Christ also suffered[g] for you, thus leaving for you a pattern so that you might follow in his footsteps,

22 who did not a commit a sin,
    nor was deceit found in his mouth,
23 who, when he was abused, did not abuse in return,
    who, when he suffered, did not threaten,
    but handed over himself[h] to the one who judges justly,[i]
24 who himself bore our sins in his body upon the wood,[j]
    in order that by being removed from our sins we might
        live to[k] righteousness,
    by whose wounds you were healed.
25 For you were wandering[l] like sheep,
    but you have now been turned to the shepherd and overseer
        of your lives.

a. Circumstantial participles without main verbs are frequent in NT exhortations (1:14; 2:1, 18; 3:1, 7, 9; 4:8, 10; Rom 12:9–21; 13:11; Eph 4:2–3; Col 3:12–17; Heb 13:5). The tendency to translate them all as the equivalent of imperatives is probably overdone, since the evidence for freestanding participles functioning as imperatives is slight. The question in this passage is whether general imperatival mood of this section imparts an imperatival sense to the participle ("be subject to your masters") or a specific imperative from the larger context governs this participle ("Do this by being subject to your masters"). If the latter, then the question remains as to which imperative should be imported. It could be the initial exhortation in 2:11, the general imperative to submit to everyone in 2:13, or perhaps what is most likely, the command to honor everyone in 2:17. The translation "do this by being subject" conveys both the grammatical ambiguity of the Greek and the dependence of this circumstantial participle on the larger arguments of the section.

b. While the term *despotēs* can refer pejoratively to a "despotic" ruler, it can also have the more benign meaning of "master of the house" (e.g., 1 Tim 6:1; Titus 2:9).

c. The word *skolios*, which means crooked, bent, twisted, does not normally have a moral meaning, although the word is used in the LXX to describe the generation of Israel (Deut 32:5; see also Acts 2:40; Phil 2:15).

d. Some key manuscripts (C, Ψ) read "this is grace with God if on account of a good conscience someone bears grief." The text used above is somewhat better attested, although both readings are possible.

e. The manuscript tradition includes not only "consciousness [*syneidēsis*] of God" and the "good conscience" (*syneidēsis*) mentioned above, but also "good consciousness [*syneidēsis*] of God." In the NT *syneidēsis* without an object means something close to the English term "conscience." However, with an objective genitive it means "consciousness," "awareness," or "mindfulness."

f. Some texts ($\mathfrak{P}^{72}$, P, Ψ) have the more general *kolazomenoi* (punish), but the more unusual *kolaphizomenoi* ("beaten with fists") has better textual support (א, A, B, C, 𝔐).

g. Several key manuscripts ($\mathfrak{P}^{81}$, א, Ψ) have *apethanen* (died) instead of *epathen* (suffered). The idea of suffering fits better with the theology of this passage. And it is likely that "died" came from the common Christian confession that "Christ died for our sins" (e.g., Rom 5:8; 1 Cor 15:3).

h. The verb *paredidou* has no object, although both Cyprian and Augustine cite the text while adding "himself." "Himself" is perhaps the best suggestion, especially in light of 4:19, where people entrust their *psychas* ("lives" or "souls") to the Creator, but it is also possible that Jesus hands "them" or even the whole situation over to the one who judges.

i. A few late manuscripts read "unjustly," in which case Jesus would be handing himself over to Pontius Pilate, his unjust human judge.

j. The Greek *xylon* means "wood" or occasionally "tree." Under the probable influence of Deut 21:23, the NT sometimes refers to the cross as *xylon* instead of *stauros* (Acts 5:30; 10:39; 13:29; Gal 3:13).

k. The dative *tē dikaiosynē* could be rendered "in," "with respect to," or even "on the basis of." A slightly ambiguous "to" is perhaps the best, since this evokes the classic biblical sense of "righteousness" as a standard.

l. Instead of the nominative masculine plural *planōmenoi*, several manuscripts ($\mathfrak{P}^{72}$, C, Ψ) have the neuter *planōmena*, producing the reading "You were like wandering sheep."

[2:18] The use of *oiketai* (household servants) rather than the more general *douloi* (slaves) signals a shift from the public arena to the private. The choice of this term may obviate, at least on a rhetorical level, the problem of being a "slave of God" and the slave of a human lord. The private context of the household is continued in 3:1–7 in the exhortation to wives. The rhetorical force of these exhortations seems to reach beyond the unique concerns of both slaves and wives, although those concerns are both real and specific. The specific predicament faced by slaves and wives occasions exhortations to Christlike suffering, which becomes a model for all Christians, no matter what their status and predicament. In fact, the only specific command to slaves comes in this verse in this general exhortation to submit. After this verse, the rest of the passage is couched in terms applicable to all Christians.

Whether the imperatival force of the participle *hypotassomenoi* is self-contained or derives from the imperative in 2:17, a command to household slaves that they submit to their masters is hardly surprising. This is the general standard of antiquity.[15] It is significant that no clarification is provided in 1 Peter as to what this submission might actually look like. First Peter does not really provide much help to slaves as to how they should behave in the complexities

---

15. On the history and social norms of Roman slavery, see Keith Bradley, *Slavery and Society at Rome* (Key Themes in Ancient History; Cambridge: Cambridge University Press, 1994).

Submission of Servants to Masters

of the household. Instead, the general standard of submission is evoked in the briefest way possible, and then this standard is explored theologically.

The dominance of theology is evoked immediately in the phrase "in all fear." It is possible that this fear is in regard to their human masters. However, the call to "fear God" in 2:17 and the earlier command in 1:17 to live "in fear" the time of your exile exert some force over the use of the word "fear" in this verse. To this point in 1 Peter, fear has been directed to God, while honor, submission, and love have been directed to humans. Furthermore, directing fear to God and not humans fits with the imagery in 2:19 of bearing grief "out of consciousness of God." Thus, even if fear may be appropriate for "crooked" masters, the sense here seems to be that slaves submit to human masters "in all fear" of God and not in fear of masters.

The frequent concern in the NT over the relationship between Christian slaves and their human masters receives a unique treatment in 1 Peter. The explicit question is less whether a slave should submit and more whether slaves should submit only to "good and gentle" masters and not to "crooked" ones. This distinction is key to the whole perspective of 1 Peter on the relationships of Christians to the non-Christian Roman world. The core message of this passage is that slaves, and actually all Christians, are to behave as Jesus behaved. The model of Jesus that is articulated in 2:22–24 is embodied by slaves who submit no matter what the character and behavior of their masters.

[19–20] The sentence "This is grace" is one of the most difficult sentences in 1 Peter. The immediate context in verses 19–20 suggests that "grace" here means something like "credit." Most readers of 1 Peter parallel *charis* in 2:19 with *kleos* in 2:20, thereby giving *charis* the meaning of "favor" or "credit." The final phrase of verse 20, *para theō*, would mean "credit with God," and the force of these verses would be that unjust suffering gives credit with the God who will judge all people. Such a translation is certainly possible since *charis* often has this meaning in Greek literature and is used this way at least one other time in the NT (Luke 6:32). However, in the other usages of *charis* in 1 Peter (1:2, 10, 13; 3:7; 4:10; 5:5, 10, 12), it seems to have its more theologically loaded sense of "grace." In the NT it is 1 Peter and Paul that use the word *charis* as a, or even the, fundamental theological image. Central theological terms are often difficult to define or translate because they carry so much weight and range. In 1 Peter *charis* can mean "kindness," "favor," "the gospel," and even something like "the new reality in which Christians live." Therefore, when this sentence declares "this is grace," it is nearly impossible to silence the complex theological range of the term. Thus, even if these verses bring out the sense of "credit" in the word *charis*, this does not mean simply that unjust suffering gives credit with God, but that the grace that belongs with unjust suffering includes credit with God.

These two verses offer a succinct articulation of 1 Peter's troubling definition of grace. The phrase "this is grace" begins verse 19 and concludes verse 20, thereby forming a nice inclusio. Within this inclusio is a positive, negative, and then another positive definition of grace. All three come in the form of simple conditional clauses, implying thereby a general truth. Furthermore, all three pieces together are needed in order to give an adequate portrait of the striking account of grace in 1 Peter.

The initial positive definition has three parts. The phrase "if someone endures grief" hints at the provocative account of grace in these verses. Many voices in the ancient world understood the peculiar blessings found in grief and suffering.[16] And the notion of "suffering unjustly," given by 1 Peter, was often seen as preferable to suffering for a vice. Thus, in some ways, finding the good in unjust suffering is not particularly provocative. The third piece, however, hints at the provocative nature of 1 Peter's argument. Grace is when someone suffers unjustly "out of consciousness of God." Unjust suffering is not grace, but unjust suffering out of a consciousness of God is. The phrase "out of consciousness of God" is, on its own, not very specific. The specifics could be supplied by the christological assertions in 2:21–25. However, the rather open syntax of this verse makes the key point that for unjust suffering to be grace, God must be involved.

The negative assertion in verse 20 eliminates the possibility that there is something magical in suffering itself. Suffering was often understood in antiquity as a great teacher, and even Paul, in a quite different context, evokes such a notion (see Rom 5:3, where Paul actually discusses *thlipsis* rather than *pathēma*). But this does not seem to be what is in force here. The argument is theological, or more precisely, christological. This negative assertion does not really advance the argument, but instead makes explicit the obvious objection. Enduring while you sin and are beaten gives no fame (*kleos*). Thus it is not suffering in itself that teaches; rather, the suffering must be unjust. Furthermore, this unjust suffering does not necessarily teach; this suffering is perceived as "grace."

The final clause modifies only slightly the images of the first two clauses by adding the notion of "doing good." This addition highlights the peculiar theological character of this argument. It is not suffering that is key, but the injustice of it. Unjust suffering is in itself not sufficient. For all of this to be "grace," doing good must be part of the formula. The process begins with a doing good that in itself evokes mistreatment. The good of the Christian life provokes abuse. This sequence is not derived from observations about the nature of the world, although one might do so, but from the pattern of Christ. The apparent

---

16. On righteous suffering and sacrificial death in the ancient world, see Arthur J. Droge and James D. Tabor, *A Noble Death: Suicide and Martyrdom among Christians and Jews in Antiquity* (San Francisco: HarperSanFrancisco, 1991). For a selection of texts, see Jan Willem van Henten and Friedrich Avemarie, *Martyrdom and Noble Death: Selected Texts from Graeco-Roman, Jewish and Christian Antiquity* (The Context of Early Christianity; London: Routledge, 2002).

Submission of Servants to Masters 83

tension between this verse and the claims of good treatment for good behavior in 2:14 and 3:13 is only apparent, for both 2:14 and 3:13 assume in their larger arguments this same abuse.

[21] In many ways, this verse takes the reader to the heart of 1 Peter's theology: it asserts not only that unjust suffering is an inevitable aspect of the Christian life, but also that such suffering constitutes the essential character of Christian life. It is to this suffering that believers are "called." The statement "You were called for this purpose" is repeated verbatim in 3:9 in a somewhat similar context. Doing good and suffering for it, out of consciousness of God, in the pattern of Jesus Christ—this is the core of the Christian life. To be a follower of Jesus is to be called to suffer. The apologetic feel of arguments such as 1:5–6, which try to explain suffering as temporary, gives way to the conviction that suffering is necessary. This sense that suffering is the central moment of the Christian calling goes beyond the usual accounts of suffering in the New Testament. First Peter seems to elevate suffering from being one of the necessary moments of the Christian to being the single most important moment. Christians are called to suffer. First Peter says other things about the Christian life, but all those things emerge from the shadow of suffering.

The explicit reason for this striking claim about suffering comes from the suffering of Christ. The familiar early Christian idea of atonement is suggested in "Christ also suffered for you." It is possible that atonement is not evoked here, since the phrase might simply mean that Christ suffered for you so that you might have an example. However, the notion of atonement is unmistakable in 2:24. Thus it is preferable to hear "for you" (*hyper hymōn*) as implying some kind of atonement (cf. 1:18–19). In any case, suffering is not connected primarily to atonement in 1 Peter. Instead, suffering places one on the path to salvation. Christ's suffering shows the way. The suffering of Christ does not end Christian suffering; the suffering of Christ calls forth more suffering.

The language of example or pattern (*hypogrammos*) in this verse is but one instance in 1 Peter in which the suffering of Jesus and the suffering of believers are connected (3:17–18; 4:1, 13). *Hypogrammos* might literally mean "writing-copy" or "trace"; yet when connected to the image of following in his steps, it means "example" or "pattern." Furthermore, while the language of following after Jesus is frequent in the NT, 1 Peter creates a unique image by combining these two ideas. Believers follow Jesus' steps or tracks (*ichnos*), not simply into the unknown, out of a faith that has no expectations, but in accordance with the particular pattern of Jesus' suffering. This pattern will be sketched in 2:22–24.

[22–24] The origin of these verses is much debated. The shift from second person to first person, the use of the relative pronoun *hos* and the introductory *hoti* in 2:21, plus the shift in audience, have all suggested to some readers that a traditional christological piece is being taken up by 1 Peter. However, most readers see these verses as coming from the hand of the author of 1 Peter.

In fact, the peculiar combination of Isa 53 and Jesus' suffering as an ethical example articulates so effectively the theological position of 1 Peter that there is no reason to imagine a composed source. The sources are Isaiah, the story of Jesus, and the author's theology of suffering.

The righteous sufferer is a popular figure in Jewish, Greek, and Roman literature (see, e.g., Plato, *Apologia*; 4 Maccabees). Thus there would have been little controversial in pointing to the nobility of people who suffer unjustly and maintain their virtue in the midst of this injustice. First Peter's discussion of suffering will insist over and over again on the centrality of virtue. Good behavior must be practiced no matter how unjust the suffering might be. All of this would be expected in the Greco-Roman world. However, in 1 Peter virtuous suffering does not validate itself, either by teaching or as a manifestation of nobility. Virtuous suffering connects a person to the story of Jesus, and the Jesus story is the story of salvation. Thus what makes the righteous suffering of Christians salvific is that it partakes of the suffering of Christ.

Nevertheless, this sense of being taken up by God's grace (2:19–20), of being on a trajectory of salvation, does not undo the centrality of virtues. This precise configuration of these virtues does not, however, derive from any Greco-Roman model, but from a combination of the Jesus story and Isa 53. In fact, 1 Pet 2:22 repeats precisely the Septuagint wording of Isa 53:9b, except for having "sin" (*hamartia*) instead of "lawlessness" (*anomia*). Jesus does not sin and does not deceive. The denial of deceit (*dolos*) on Jesus' part anticipates the admonition to believers to be ready to offer with gentleness and reverence an account of their faith (3:15–16). Believers should not lie or deceive or abuse even if they are being threatened. It is hard not to hear echoes of later Christian debates about what should and should not be said under threat of persecution.

There is also an implication about the normalcy of persecution and suffering. As 1 Peter asserts, "Do not be surprised at the burning among you" (4:12), because this ordeal fits the classic pattern. This same pattern of suffering is described in Isaiah, was manifested in the life of Jesus, and is now being manifested in the life of believers.

There is no explicit citation of Isa 53 in 2:23, although there may be slight echoes of the silence of the lamb in Isa 53:7. Instead, 2:23 seems to be anchored in a general memory of Jesus' passion. No specific detail of Jesus' passion seems to be in play here. Instead, a sense of Jesus' unjust suffering is couched in the language of example and virtue. The language of abuse by outsiders takes different forms in 1 Peter (cf. 2:12; 3:16; 4:4, 14). The diversity of terminology enables the syntax to be applicable to more situations. The footsteps that believers are called to follow are not precisely laid out. This verse focuses on what people say. The term *loidoreō* invokes more the sense of verbal than physical abuse. This verbal sense fits with the imagery of Jesus' not threatening when he suffers. Finally, the claim that Jesus "handed over himself to the one who judges justly" evokes the theological grounding of the ethic. Jesus did not abuse or threaten when suffering unjustly because he trusted God to judge righteously. It is the same with believers; they can follow in Jesus' steps not because it makes them virtuous but because God will reward them.

Just as 2:21 contains the dual images of Jesus' suffering as model and Jesus' suffering as redemption, these verses shift from model to redemption. Most of 2:24 echoes Isa 53, although only verse 24c comes close to being a direct quote. As typical of 1 Peter, these verses suggest a thorough knowledge of Isaiah. The author pulls images and sentences from a wide variety of verses in Isaiah. The phrase "who himself bore our sins in his body upon the wood" echoes Isa 53:4, 11–12. The peculiar narrative of Jesus' crucifixion and the theology that emerges from that narrative produce a reconfiguration of the sacrificial imagery of Isaiah. Christ is not the sacrificial animal, and the wood is not the altar. Instead, 1 Pet 2:24 evokes the redemptive power of Christ's death on the cross. The precise theology of that redemption is not detailed. Jesus carries not a sacrifice but "our sins," not to the altar but "in his body upon the wood." Somehow Jesus' body contains the sacrifice but is not the sacrifice.

The language of verse 24b seems more Pauline than anything else in its contrasts between sin and righteousness, and between dying and living, although the precise wording is not mirrored in Paul. The force of verse 24a is detailed in 24b. By "being removed from our sins," we "live to righteousness." While the exact theological geography of this is not detailed, the basic imagery fits the constant theme of 1 Peter. The suffering of Christ enables the righteous life. The dual themes of suffering and virtue may be configured many ways in 1 Peter, but it is these two themes that constantly return.

The wording of verse 24 follows the language of Isa 53:5. The phrase "by whose wounds you were healed" changes only the person of the verb from first person to second person. Nevertheless, the specific sense of the phrase is not clear, since "wounds" could refer to Jesus' scourging or to his general suffering during his crucifixion. This imprecision seems almost productive in 1 Peter. The precise shape and content of suffering is left open, as is the precise shape and content of the righteous and virtuous response to that suffering. This means that all kinds of righteous suffering in the lives of the readers can connect them to the story of Christ. Suffering heals, at least when it is Christlike suffering.

[25] The shift in imagery in this verse is likely occasioned by the syntax of Isa 53:5–6, which makes the same shift. This shift from atonement imagery to shepherding language is not in itself surprising, since the logic of sacrifice theology would be to include both. Processes of atonement should lead to a return to God's care. Not only is this sequence to be expected; a movement from atonement to shepherding also is crucial to the theology of 1 Peter.

The reference to wandering like sheep presumably refers to the pre-Christian life since 1 Peter is fond of references to the "futile" life of the Gentiles, in which the readers once lived (1:14, 18; 4:3). Although God is classically referred to as shepherd, it is more likely that Jesus is the referent here (cf. 5:4). There is no reason to understand the term "overseer" (*episkopos*) as designating a formal church office. It conveys the general sense of one who protects and thus pairs nicely with "shepherd."

This passage (2:18–25) is typical of 1 Peter in that it combines a variety of different images and patterns of speech. The movement from doctrine to ethics, from indicative to imperative, the gathering of diverse theological and ethical figures, and even the shift from specific to general audience—all this is frequent in the letter. This mixed rhetoric means that the letter lacks extended, sequential theological argument. Instead, the letter's theology is built more by gathering than by sustained argument. It takes the readers to complete the argument, since the readers must decide, for instance, how Jesus' footsteps might be followed in their own lives.

In some ways, it is puzzling how this passage opens with a direct address to household slaves and moves to a general ethic applicable to any reader. Slaves in ancient literature are not usually treated as being like normal people. Their disconnection from normal social obligations, their lack of family ties, their prohibition from public space, and their suppressed legal position meant that ordinary human virtues and vices were not expected from them. However, 1 Peter gives no hint that slaves are not seen as full ethical agents. There is, for instance, no attempt to rehabilitate slaves in the letter; they are assumed—quietly yet perhaps radically—to have ethical freedom and understanding. It is possible that the assumption of humanity in household slaves by 1 Peter indicates that the letter comes from a different social class than most of the social commentary we possess from the ancient world, nearly all of which is upper class. But it may also be an instance of the social leveling that frequented early Christianity. In any case, this passage depends upon slaves being on the same moral plane as the rest of the readers of the letter. The same could be said for the logic of the address to women in 3:1–6. Every reader of 1 Peter needs to be able to see oneself in the behavior of both slaves and women. The specific command to slaves to submit to crooked masters becomes an occasion for an exploration of Christian suffering. In fact, it is not simply that readers can see themselves in the general rhetoric of 2:19–25; whatever their social standing, they can also see themselves in the command in 2:18 to household slaves to submit.

In this passage, suffering has the dual force that it has throughout 1 Peter. On the one hand, it is redemptive and salvific. Christ's suffering redeems, and the suffering of believers connects them to salvation. On the other hand, suffering examines the genuineness of faith (1:7; 4:12) and occasions, in these verses in particular, the extraordinary virtue of righteous suffering. First Peter's account of suffering is never simple or one-sided; it will actually become even more complex as the letter progresses. Believers are asked to trust that suffering places them in God's care. They may have had images from Isaiah and perhaps from the Greco-Roman world of the righteous sufferer. From Isaiah they certainly received notions of suffering as redemptive and salvific. What is striking is the centrality given to suffering: "For you were called for this purpose" (2:21). First Peter is almost heterodox at this point. Early Christianity commonly asserted the redemptive and salvific import of suffering, and even perhaps that it is necessary. But the singularity of suffering as the universal path of all Christians was mostly avoided.

1 Peter 3:1–7 Submission by Wives and Honoring by Husbands

This controversial admonition to women (or wives) to submit to their men is part of 1 Peter's extensive examination of Christian behavior toward non-Christians, which runs from 2:11 to 4:6. Most of this material, while focused upon the relationship toward outsiders, spills over into an analysis of virtuous behavior in general. Even this passage, which in its explicit form confines its rhetoric to the specific interaction between women and men (or wives and husbands) in the household, creates an ethic that is applicable and valuable to any reader of the letter. Women, in their virtuous submission to their men, model Christlike behavior.

Ancient Greco-Roman and Jewish literature frequently admonished the submission of women to men and especially of wives to their husbands.[17] The critique of adornment and the value of silence is commonplace in these admonitions.[18] However, the tendency in this literature to see this submission as necessary to the good of society is lacking in these verses of 1 Peter. This is to be expected, for 1 Peter displays a consistent indifference to the fate and health of the Roman social order. On the one hand, these verses do not really change what kind of behavior of women toward men is regarded as virtuous. On the other hand, the purpose and force of virtuous submission is transformed.

> 3:1 Women,[a] in the same way, do this by being subject[b] to your own men, in order that even if some are disobedient to the word, they shall be won over without a word by the behavior of their women, 2 because they observe your holy behavior, done in fear.[c] 3 Let not be yours the external adornment[d] in the braiding of hair and the wearing of gold or the putting on of clothing, 4 but let be yours the secret person of the heart, with the incorruption of a meek and quiet spirit, which[e] is very precious to

---

17. On the Roman family, see Keith R. Bradley, *Discovering the Roman Family: Studies in Roman Social History* (Oxford: Oxford University Press, 1991).

18. See texts in Jane F. Gardner, *The Roman Household: A Sourcebook* (London: Routledge, 1991).

God. **5** For in the same way formerly also the holy women who hoped in God adorned themselves by being subject[f] to their own men, **6** as Sarah obeyed[g] Abraham when she called him lord, whose children you became by doing good[h] and not fearing anything frightening.[i]

7 Men,[j] in the same way, do this with understanding by living with[k] the women[l] as with the weaker vessel, the womanly, assigning honor as even to fellow heirs[m] of the grace of life, so that your prayers[n] are not cut off.

a. The article *hai* is missing in several key manuscripts ($\mathfrak{P}^{81}$, ℵ, A, B). The inclusion of the article ($\mathfrak{P}^{72}$, C, P, Ψ) emphasizes the vocative force of the phrase and has somewhat better textual support. The word (*gynaikes*) means "women." However, when the term occurs in marriage contexts, it carries the sense of "wives." Here the phrase "your own men" (*tois idiois andrasin*) suggests that it is wives who are being addressed and not women in general. The translation given here maintains the basic referent of "women" and "men," letting the context provide the sense of wives and husbands. However, the imagery of 3:7 suggests that more than husbands and wives may be included here. Women are obligated and subject to men other than their husbands.

b. See above, note a for 2:18.

c. The phrase *en phobō* (in fear) modifies the adjective "holy" (*tēn en phobō hagnēn anastrophēn*). Rather than translating the phrase as another adjective ("reverent and holy behavior"), and in consideration of the other occurrences of the phrase in 1 Peter (1:17; 2:18; cf. 3:14, 16), it is preferable to render it as a separate prepositional phrase.

d. The word *kosmos* does not mean "world" here as it does in most of the NT but "adornment." The core meaning of *kosmos* is "order," which can lead naturally to "arrangement," "decoration," "the order and arrangement of the universe," and finally "world."

e. The antecedent of the neuter relative pronoun *ho* (which) could be the neuter *pneuma* (spirit), but it more likely refers to the entire preceding clause.

f. The circumstantial participle *hypotassomenai* could be instrumental ("by being subject") or attendant circumstance ("while being subject"). The choice is difficult since both make sense in this passage. The centrality of submission, which is signaled by the same participle *hypotassomenai* in v. 1, suggests an instrumental reading.

g. Some manuscripts have an imperfect *hypēkouen* instead of the aorist *hypēkousen*. The imperfect, with its sense of continuous obedience, is probably the more difficult reading. But the aorist is better attested and thus preferable.

h. The present participles *agathopoiousai* and *phoboumenai* could be continuous ("You became her children and now are doing good and not fearing"), instrumental ("You became her children by doing good and not fearing"), or even conditional ("You will become her children if you do good and do not fear"). Since the general force of this passage lies in the imperative to virtuous submission, an instrumental reading is the most likely.

i. The word *ptoēsis* has the sense not only of "something fearful" but of "passionate excitement." It might function as a cognate accusative, intensifying fear ("Do not be afraid at all"). If it is an objective accusative, its precise referent is unclear, but the context suggests something fearful about the husbands ("Do not be afraid of the fearful anger of your husband").

j. In context, "men" probably refers, first of all, to "husbands," but may include any man in any household.

k. The participle *synoikountes*, following the same syntax as the participles in 2:18 and 3:1, stands alone and derives its imperative force from the larger context. The variant *synomilountes* (converse with) has the support of Sinaiticus (ℵ), but all other major manuscripts have *synoikountes*.

l. The participle *synoikountes* has no explicit object, but the context leaves little doubt that men are addressed as living "with the women" rather than "together."

m. Several key manuscripts (A, C, Ψ, 𝔐) have the nominative *synklēronomoi* instead of the dative *synklēronomois* ($\mathfrak{P}^{72}$, $\mathfrak{P}^{81}$, B). A nominative participle would make the men the "fellow heirs of the grace of life." Thus men would assign honor to women not because women are fellow heirs but because the men are. However, the dative fits the syntax of the verse and gives a clearer warrant for both the assigning of honor and the protection of prayers.

n. Several manuscripts ($\mathfrak{P}^{81}$, B), instead of the accusative *tas proseuchas*, have the dative *tais proseuchais* ("so that you are not cut off with respect to your prayers"). The accusative has better support and makes perfect sense.

[3:1–2] These verses open as a continuation of the argument about submission. The phrase "in the same way" locates this exhortation in the series that begins in 2:11. In fact, the logic of these two verses echoes the logic of 2:12, where Gentiles verbally attack "you" but then see "your beautiful works" and "glorify God" (cf. 3:16). The audience for this exhortation is not completely stable. It is not just that all readers can see themselves in the predicament and calling of "women," but also that the precise profile of "women" is not clear. While all the exhortations from 2:11–4:6 focus upon the relationship between believers and outsiders, they do not confine themselves to that. These verses display the same fluidity in audience. They focus upon the behavior of wives toward unbelieving husbands, but they are not limited to that. It is only "some" of the husbands who are "disobedient to the word." Thus the women being addressed here cannot be confined to the women married to unbelieving husbands.

An imperative to wives that they be subject to husbands reflects the almost universal standard in antiquity. Given the regularity of this standard, a simple command to submit lacks much content. The content must come from either context or further comment. The context of 2:11–4:6 suggests many possibilities, from the salvific force of righteous suffering to the imitation of Jesus to the furtherance of the word. This last possibility is explicitly named here, although other purposes surface later in the passage. The purpose of submission is not for the good of society, or the peace of the church, or the divine ordering of life inside or outside the believing community. There is no sense here that women are divinely ordered to be submissive to men. The purpose of submission is evangelical. Submission converts disobedient husbands. These disobedient men are "won . . . by the behavior of their women."

It is not just any submission that does this. Two images crucial to the character of this submission are offered. The phrase "without a word" suggests that silence is central to this submission. The virtue of silence is well known in the ancient world and was applied to the behavior of women toward their men (Sophocles, *Ajax* 293; Aristotle, *Pol.* 1.5.8). The virtue of silence is most often suggested when power is out of balance. Jesus is silent at his trial. Women are silent before the authority of their men. The violence against neither Jesus nor women is hereby being affirmed; it is the silence of both that is validated here. Yet there is something terrifying in a recommendation of silence. But this silence is not complete. Both Jesus and these women speak with deeds. The play on words wherein husbands who are disobedient to the "word" are won over without a "word" underlines the irony of this silent proclamation.

The second image is that of "holy behavior, done in fear." The precise configuration of holy behavior is not described. As 1:15–16 attests, 1 Peter can use the word "holy" as the general designation of the Christian life. The meaning of holiness must be derived from other values articulated in the letter. Thus the whole range of virtues attested to in this letter is suggested in this phrase. The earlier claim that the holiness of believers is grounded in the holiness of God (1:16) is reflected in the phrase "done in fear." Given the prohibition against fear of the husbands in 3:6 and the connection between holiness and fear of God in 1:15–17, the fear enjoined on the women is fear of God. Then fear of God shapes the behavior of women toward their men. Given the language of seeing both here and in 2:12, the fear of God may be manifested in deeds. Holy behavior makes those who witness it think about God.

In this way witnessing has a certain ironic character in 1 Peter. While readers are enjoined to have a "defense" ready for anyone who asks (3:15), even this defense must be offered with "meekness and fear" (3:16). The consistent pattern that comes from Jesus and is expected of his followers is that witnessing is done with deeds rather than words. As the admonition to women continues, the sense of the silence and hiddenness of this witness will only be emphasized. Moreover, the act of witnessing seems to occur primarily in the context of unjust suffering. It is virtuous behavior in response to unjust suffering that has the unique capacity to attract the attention and curiosity of Gentiles. In all of these arguments is an assumption that Christians and non-Christians share sufficient values for non-Christians to recognize the good in the behavior of Christians.

[3–4] The awkwardness of the Greek produces a slight uncertainty over the meaning of these verses. Although they are often translated as arguing for a distinction in the kind of adornment appropriate for women ("Let not your adornment be external, . . . but let your adornment be the secret person"), the Greek actually makes a distinction between adornment and the secret person as though the secret person were not an adornment. However, as 3:5 makes clear, submission can be an act of adornment. Nevertheless, it is perhaps important to maintain a distinction between adornment and the secret person since adornment has a sense of something external and nonessential.

Ancient literature has extensive discussions about proper and improper adornment of women (e.g., Epictetus, *Ench.* 40; Pliny the Younger, *Pan.* 83.7). As might be expected from the fact that this literature comes from males, most of them elite and conservative, the standard argument is against ostentation and for simplicity and modesty. The popularity of this condemnation of ostentation by women makes it uncertain whether this warning counts as evidence of rich women in the audience of 1 Peter. Instead, the author's condemnation of adornment by way of hair, jewelry, and clothing may be an appeal to a value already shared by the women in his audience. It is striking that 1 Tim 2:9-11 also cites this tradition in a way similar to 1 Peter. In 1 Timothy this same condemnation of adornment is coupled with a call to submission and silence similar to that of 1 Peter. It is not possible to construct a full picture of early Christian thinking on the proper social role of women, but it does seem that the gathering of images and concepts that we encounter in these verses is not likely to be unique to our author. It appears instead that the author of 1 Peter may be using rather widespread early Christian notions about propriety in women. The fact that 1 Peter never bothers to inform women about how to dress in a proper manner lends further credence to the notion that dress and adornment is not the issue. The issue is submission.

The positive appeal is for having a "secret person" with a particular kind of spirit. The precise geography of this secret person is difficult to map since the images in this verse can be understood in various ways. The adjective *kryptos*, which modifies "person" (*anthrōpos*), has the sense of both "secret" and "hidden." Thus there is a hint here that this self is intentionally hidden from others. The silencing of even the virtues of the women is necessary to the character of the witness. The heart is named as the realm of this secret person, probably indicating not only the standard contrast between outer and inner selves but also the place of one's intentions and true will. Thus the real self of these women must remain secret.

This secret self is connected to the "incorruption of a meek and quiet spirit." The nature of this connection is not clear, since the dative *aphthartō* is probably just a dative of accompaniment. This kind of loose association of theological terms is typical of 1 Peter, which avoids precisely ordered theological maps. First Peter prefers to gather diverse images into these rather loose associations. The spirit is not the Holy Spirit but the spirit of the individual women. This spirit is characterized as "meek and quiet," two virtues essential to 1 Peter. These are perfect virtues for the spirit of those who must submit and who must silence and hide their true selves. These virtues are also conventional in ancient accounts of the proper wife. Jews, Greeks, Romans, and early Christians all praised the gentle, quiet, submissive wife. Thus these virtues are not peculiarly Christian even when they play a crucial role in a Christian theology.

Although the spirit named here is not the Holy Spirit, there is a hint of divine presence in the language of "incorruption." Neither virtuous acts nor silent spirits can produce incorruption. Only God has such power. The difficult demands of 1 Peter makes sense only if there is a God who can reward the people who follow this Jesus and live this ethic. As 3:5 will suggest, it is only the women who hope in God who might behave this way. Thus the assertion that this behavior is "very precious to God" is essential to the logic of the admonition. The ultimate value of this behavior is not established by its potential power to win disobedient husbands, although that power is clearly an important good. The final value of this behavior is that it connects these women to the Jesus story and thus promises them salvation.

[5–6] Given the example of Sarah in verse 6, it is generally assumed that "the holy women" in verse 5 are the Jewish matriarchs. First Peter seems to cite them as proof that "holy women" submit to their husbands. Furthermore, since this submission is the manner of their adornment, these holy women are, by implication, examples of modesty in dress and appearance. The proper conclusion is that all holy women adorn themselves, not with braiding of hair or nice clothing, but with submission.

It is crucial that these holy women place their hope in God. The assumption of this argument is that the predicament of women has never changed. Women cannot trust the value of their lives to the social order or the processes of history. First Peter presumes some kind of injustice and unfairness in this necessity of women's submission to their men. Thus women can only submit if they place their hope in God. God, then, is put in a position of repaying women for this injustice. The theology of 1 Peter is that God repays all such righteous suffering, including that of women in the world of men.

The reference to Sarah as the prime example of such submission is curious. The only explicit instance where Sarah calls Abraham "Lord" is in Gen 18, where the three visitors promise to Abraham the birth of a son. In the Septuagint account of this event, Sarah "laughed to herself, saying, 'This has not yet happened to me even until now, and my lord [*kyrios*] is old'" (18:12 LXX). This is hardly an exemplary moment of submission, yet 1 Peter recalls this moment with the claim "Sarah obeyed [*hypēkousen*] Abraham when she called him lord." The relationship between a text and the text it cites is never completely stable, since it is never clear how much voice the cited text should have. In this instance it is not clear whether the laughter of Sarah should be reverberating in the syntax of 1 Peter. In Genesis, Sarah tries to keep her laughter a secret, thereby hiding her true self much as the women of 1 Peter hide themselves (18:15). In any case, the obedience of Sarah has a bit of the qualified feel of the submission of the women in 1 Peter. Perhaps, in an echo of the centrality of words and no words in 3:1, the focus is upon the words of Sarah. In the midst of her laughter, she called Abraham "lord."

The purpose of these references to holy women and Sarah surfaces in verse 6b. The sense of the aorist *egenēthēte* suggests that the wives in 1 Peter have already become the children of Sarah. Although it is obvious from the context that being called a child of Sarah is a high compliment, it is not explicit in 1 Peter what Sarah's status might be. Sarah is probably to be understood at least as a holy woman who hoped in God and who obeyed her husband (3:5). Whether she partakes of the salvation promised in Christ is not stated, but the logic of the argument certainly suggests that such would be the case. The relationship between Christ and the patriarchs and matriarchs is a vexing question in early Christianity, although there is general (but not universal) agreement that the holy persons, male and female, of Israel are saved. Since the author of 1 Peter appears to have no need to explain the status of Sarah to his readers, it may reasonably be assumed that Sarah would be seen by all as in some sense a mother of the faith.

In any case, these wives become Sarah's children "by doing good and not fearing anything frightening." The notion of doing good is not only a central image in 1 Peter (2:14, 15, 20; 3:10, 11, 16, 17; 4:19; cf. 2:12); it is also an image that would be appreciated by nearly anyone in antiquity. There is nothing peculiarly Christian in the term, and thus its precise content must be supplied by the context in 1 Peter. As the passages cited above show, the term seems to be used most often as a way to summarize the character of Christian behavior when it is approved by non-Christians. Both 2:12, which uses *kalos*, and 3:16, which uses *agathos*, declare that non-Christians will recognize the good behavior of Christians as good. However, the concept of "good behavior" in 1 Peter carries connotations of vulnerability. Christians behave in a "good" way even if persecution and violence is the result. Thus "good" is an effective term for summarizing the behavior of these women since they are being called to engage in behavior, in a context of violence, that their non-Christian husbands will recognize as good, even noble.

This context of violence makes it likely that the obscure phrase *mē phoboumenai mēdemian ptoēsin*, translated above as "not fearing anything frightening," is referring to the potential violence of the husbands (cf. 3:14). The precise character of the frightening behavior of these husbands is not detailed and probably did not need to be so. These wives needed no instruction about the potential violence of their husbands. The term *ptoēsis*, with its connotations of passion and excitement, may be referencing the sudden anger of husbands. In any case, the challenge to these wives is to not fear the dangerous behavior of their husbands. The implication is that they should fear not humans but God (1:17) and that by trusting God in the face of such violence, they are imitating Jesus (2:23; cf. 4:19).

The centrality of ethics in 1 Peter surfaces again in the insistence that one becomes a child of Sarah, not by election, faith, or progeny, but by good behavior. First Peter refuses to separate ethics from salvation. Good behavior is not an appendage to or even a result of being saved; it is a necessary moment in how God is saving them.

[7] The grammar of this verse mirrors that of the call to slaves and women, making this exhortation dependent on the initial call to good behavior and honor in 2:11–17. The men are addressed as having power and being, in the context of the household, without fear. The initial call to these men is to recognize the reality of power in the household. Men are called, not simply to live with their women but to live with them "with understanding." The content of this understanding is supplied by the rest of the verse. First of all, women are named as the "weaker vessel, the womanly." The emphasis here is on weakness, since by implication men are vessels too. There was much discussion in antiquity about the weakness of women, specifically as to whether physical weakness signaled other kinds of weaknesses. Given 3:1–6 and the conclusion of this verse, it appears that 1 Peter is highlighting and even insisting upon the physical weakness while denying any other weaknesses, moral or spiritual, in women. Given the context of fear and violence in 3:1–6, the initial challenge to men in this verse appears to be a reminder that the physical weakness of women makes men the objects of fear. Men create fear in their women simply because of their physical strength. This imbalance must be recognized by the men.

Although women are named, first of all, as "the weaker vessel," they are also named as "fellow heirs of the grace of life." The phrase probably does not warrant careful unpacking of its theological structure since the main point is to affirm the complete equality of men and women in their right to salvation. Grace (1:2, 10, 13; 4:10; 5:5, 10, 12) and life (1:3, 23; 2:5, 24) are fundamental terms in 1 Peter's description of salvation. And their purpose here is not to detail the precise forces of salvation but simply to evoke that salvation. The reminder in force is that women are "fellow heirs [*synklēronomoi*]." First Peter is fond of expressing unity by means of the preposition or prefix *syn* (cf. *synoikeō*, 3:7; *sympathēs*, 3:8; *sympresbyteros*, 5:1; *syneklektos*, 5:13), typically uniting different persons or groups by their shared status in the Christian narrative. This shared status as Christians means that men must "assign honor" to their women. Since honor is such a prevalent term in the ancient world, it is not possible to detail exactly what men are to do. A shared sense of how a household assigns honor to its various members must be assumed here. It is significant that men are addressed as the ones who have the power to assign or not to assign honor to their women. There is no threat to ancient household hierarchies. Patriarchal dominance is affirmed even as Christian unity is affirmed.

This plea to men comes with a threat that is lacking in the plea to slaves and women, who actually receive promises. Men, on the other hand, in their position of power and in their connections to violence, receive a warning. Do this "so that your prayers are not cut off." The idea that the efficacy of prayers and worship in general depends upon ethics is prevalent in both Judaism and early Christianity

Exhortation and Blessing for All 95

(e.g., Amos 5:21–24; Matt 5:23–24; 1 Cor 11:20–29). The standard nature of this appeal makes it unlikely that "your" in "your prayers" refers to both men and women. This is an appeal to those whose behavior is unjust. In 1 Peter, it is assumed throughout that one's behavior affects and almost determines one's status before God. Salvation requires ethics. Men must give honor to their women as to "fellow heirs," or their own status as heirs is put in question.

As it does in much of 1 Peter, violence haunts these verses (3:1–7). And as in the rest of 1 Peter, the character of this violence is never made explicit. It operates as a force over the argument but is only described in general terms. These verses are penned in the context of violence by men against the women in their house. Yet these verses never address that violence directly.

Instead, this violence is understood and ordered by the paradigmatic violence in the story of Jesus. All violence against Christians, or at least all unjust violence, belongs to the same order as the foundational violence against Jesus. Thereby the enduring of this violence leads to salvation. This is the primary response of 1 Peter to the terrors of persecution in the public world or to the terrors of violence in the house. Jesus suffered unjustly; therefore in the journey to salvation, so must his followers.

Furthermore, practicing "good" behavior while enduring this unjust violence witnesses to the gospel. Husbands can be won over to the word without a word. There is no argument in 1 Peter as to why or how such witnessing speaks to non-Christians. It is simply assumed that all humans will see the power and goodness of such a witness. Non-Christians are not completely evil; they are all potential Christians. But they are prone to violence. Gentile neighbors and non-Christian husbands (perhaps Christian as well) are prone to violence against Christians under their power. They can be converted from this violence by the suffering of those they abuse. But for now, they are potentially violent.

In these verses, it seems that Christian husbands are forbidden such violence. In fact, these verses seem to assume that no Christian husband will practice violence even if the hierarchies of the household permit such. This argument is picked up at a later stage. The very potential for violence that is built into the structure of the ancient household is a danger that requires special attention from the men, even if these men would never practice such violence themselves. The patriarchal hierarchies in the ancient household are left in place, but the violence permitted by such is not only prohibited but also lamented.

1 Peter 3:8–12 Exhortation and Blessing for All

Gathering images from preceding verses, this general exhortation to "all of you" works as a summary of the admonitions to slaves, women, and men. There is almost no image in here that is not anticipated in 2:11–3:7. However, the change in audience creates a change in tone. Though the admonitions to slaves, women, and men contained principles that could be generalized for all readers, the address to "all of you" is itself couched in the form of a series of general truths.

Although the opening participle in 3:8 mirrors the grammatical structure of 2:18; 3:1; and 3:7, these verses build a graceful syntax of their own. A chiastic series of adjectives in 3:8 leads to a contrasting set of participles in 3:9. This in turn leads in 3:10–12 to an effective rewriting of the awkward Septuagint version of Ps 34:13–17 (Ps 33 LXX). The most striking rhetorical feature is a series of five third-person imperatives, each ending in *-atō*. Together these five imperatives intensify the challenge to "do good." These verses also gather some of the core images and themes of the letter, while using some new terms and images. This combination of fluent syntax and striking theological images produces one of the more forceful moments of paraenesis in the letter.

Readers have long noted the similarity in imagery between 1 Pet 3:8–9 and Rom 12:14–17, with some readers suggesting literary dependence of 1 Peter on Romans.[19] It is more likely that both texts share a common Christian tradition, which includes the gentle virtues enumerated in 3:8 and the theme of nonretaliation in 3:9. First Peter locates this ethic in the life of Jesus, and this is its likely historical source. These themes emerge from the life and teachings of Jesus and are developed in many ways in early Christian literature.

The citation of Ps 34 in 3:10–12 has occasioned speculation about extensive influence of this psalm on the theology of 1 Peter.[20] Psalm 34 anticipates the themes of suffering, living as resident aliens, fear of the Lord, blessing, hope, and the general question of how to find a good life in the midst of violent neighbors. The settings are not precisely the same, the understanding of what is the good life is probably different, and each contains lots of images not contained in the other, but there is no reason to doubt influence. As with Isaiah, the imagery, themes, and theology of the psalm are combined in 1 Peter in a variety of ways with the imagery, themes, and theology of the Jesus story. The theology of 1 Peter emerges in large part from an interaction among the Jesus story, the OT, and the experiences of the community.

Finally, there is uncertainty about context of these verses. The prevalent context of 2:11–3:7 is that of Christians living with hostile Gentiles. However, some of the imagery in these verses (e.g., "loving toward the brothers and sisters") suggests a context of conflict within the community. There is a question, then, whether the abuse mentioned in 3:9 is coming from insiders or outsiders. Given the general force of 2:11–3:7, the specifics of 2:2–23, and the outsider context of the verses that follow (3:13–17), it is easier to detect the

---

19. See the comparative chart in Elliott, *1 Peter*, 602.
20. See the discussion in Achtemeier 225–27, esp. 225 n. 70.

Exhortation and Blessing for All 97

threat of outsiders rather than insiders in the danger of abuse of 3:9. Thus there is a shifting context in these verses. This shifting underlines a key argument of 1 Peter: Christian virtues must be practiced in any and all contexts, with both friends and enemies.

3:8 Finally, all of you, do this[a] by being like-minded, sympathetic, loving toward the brothers and sisters,[b] compassionate, humble-minded, 9 not returning evil for evil or abuse for abuse, but on the contrary blessing, because to this[c] you were called, in order that you might inherit a blessing.

10 For the one who wishes to love life
      and see good days,
   let that one keep the tongue from evil
      and the lips from speaking deceit,
11 let that one bend away from evil and do good,
      let that one seek peace and pursue it;
12 for the eyes of the Lord are upon the righteous
      and his ears are toward their prayers,
   but the face of the Lord is upon those who do evil.[d]

a. See above, note a for 2:18.

b. Given the reference to women in 3:1–6 and the communal sense of this passage and all of 1 Peter, *philadelphoi* must be translated as referring to love of both brothers and sisters. "Loving of the community" does not adequately convey the personal sense of the word.

c. The demonstrative *touto* (this) could refer to either what precedes or what follows. If it refers to what follows, the sense would be that one blesses others because one is to receive a blessing of one's own. Thus the followers of Jesus bless others out of a response to their own blessing. If it refers to what precedes, the sense would be that one blesses in order to receive a blessing of one's own. Given the language of 2:21; 3:7; and 3:10–12, "this" probably refers to what precedes. Thus the followers of Jesus are called to bless in the way that Jesus blessed in order to receive a blessing of their own.

d. A number of minuscules and the Vulgate follow Ps 33:17 LXX (34:16 NRSV) and add "to eliminate them from the earth."

[3:8] This series of five qualities that are enjoined upon "all" create a classic early Christian virtue list. Many readers have noted the chiastic structure in the repetition of *phrones* in *homophrones* and *tapeinophrones*, and in the similar meaning in the first and fifth terms and in the second and fourth. The first term, *homophrones*, "like-minded," although unique here in the Bible, occurs in Greek literature in much the same sense as here. Of course, the idea of thinking together is frequent in the NT. First Peter 4:1 conveys something similar in the call to "arm yourselves with the same understanding" (*tēn autēn ennoian*).

The Pauline phrase "think the same thing" (*auto phronein*) conveys a similar idea (Rom 12:16; 15:5; Phil 2:2; 4:2). The fifth term, *tapeinophrones*, "humble-minded," in this form is rare in the Bible, although the idea of humility is common enough in both the NT and Jewish literature. It has often been noted that humility is not a typical virtue in the honor-shame society of the Greco-Roman world. While hubris is regarded as a vice, humility is too resonant of shame and thus is seen as contrary to the pride in oneself that is key to social order and meaning. However, Christians and Jews adopt humility as a central virtue, and not just humility before God, but also before other humans. God's concern in the OT and Jesus' in the NT for people of low status impress this peculiar virtue on much of early Christianity, not just upon 1 Peter. In any case, these terms, when taken together, promote an attitude in thinking that encourages harmony and unity in the community.

The second term, *sympatheis* (sympathetic), literally means "suffer with," but in common usage it denotes compassion and tender feelings. Thus it can be linked with the fourth term, *eusplanchnoi*, which literally means "good bowels or innards," but in common usage also denotes compassion and tender feelings. These are feelings that also promote harmony and cohesiveness in the community. The middle term, *philadelphoi*, also conveys a commitment to community but does so more by way of deeds. In Greek, brotherly love involves obligation rather than feelings. This obligation includes personal loyalty but focuses upon the material support of food and shelter and upon the provision of protection and aid in public life. Thus these five terms work best in combination with one another. They call believers to feelings of compassion, to thinking that binds the community, and to deeds that support the material and social needs of community members.

Given this focus upon community, it is appropriate that these virtues are addressed to "all." First Peter will have more to say about life in the community, especially in chapters 4 and 5. There the imagery will be different, although the general sense will remain the same. The imagery of this verse and the next, like most of 2:11–3:7, is governed by imagery in the Jesus story in 2:22–23.

[9] Early Christian critique of the OT *lex talionis* is persistent and mostly uniform. There are, of course, counters to this principle within the OT itself, and Judaism will mostly reject the *lex talionis*.[21] Christian tradition locates the origin of this critique with Jesus himself, who gives an uncompromising negation of the principle of equal exchange of damage in the Sermon on the Mount (Matt 5:38–42; Luke 6:29–30; *Gos. Thom.* 95). First Peter evokes this Jesus tradition in 2:23, applying its norms to both slaves and women. Here the Jesus principle of nonretaliation is enjoined upon "all."

---

21. James F. Davis, *Lex Talionis in Early Judaism and the Exhortation of Jesus in Matthew 5.38–42* (JSNTSup 281; London/NewYork: T&T Clark, 2005).

Exhortation and Blessing for All

The opening phrase "not returning evil [*kakon*] for evil" makes this principle as universal as possible. As is the case in the Sermon on the Mount, there are no limiting contexts here. First Peter is stating a principle that all believers should carry into all moments. The following phrase "abuse [*loidorian*] for abuse" may reflect the peculiar situation of 1 Peter. The term *loidoria* can have the general meaning of "abuse" but can also designate "verbal abuse" or "insult." This seems to be its primary meaning in 2:23, and such a verbal sense anticipates the admonition about speech in the following verses. This focus upon the verbal aspects of evil has suggested to many readers that the context of the conflict in 1 Peter is primarily verbal. Christians are being insulted and shamed by their Gentile neighbors. It is likely that the various trials (1:6) that Christians are enduring includes more than being insulted by neighbors, though it certainly includes such insults and the loss of social status that such abuse implies.

Whatever the context, early Christian rejection of the law of retaliation meant that maintaining one's honor and avoiding shame could not be accomplished by the normal means of returning verbal abuse for verbal abuse. In fact, not only must Christians remove themselves from the cycle of retaliation; they also must respond to abuse with blessings. Although *eulogountes* can have its etymological meaning of "speaking well of," it is likely that 1 Peter is being even more provocative than suggesting that these Christians respond to insults with praise. Since later in this verse *eulogia* has the sense of God's blessing, it probably does so here. In the Sermon on the Mount, rejection of retaliation includes more than simple rejection. The follower of Jesus is called to respond to persecutors by praying for them (Matt 5:44). A similar challenge is given in 1 Peter. Believers are to respond to abuse by invoking God's blessings on those who are abusing them.

The offensiveness of this challenge is recognized in the two warrants that ground this call to bless those who abuse. The phrase "to this you were called" repeats the almost identical wording of 2:21. In 2:21 slaves are called to endure unjust suffering. They are told that to do so earns them "grace with God" (2:20). This behavior is then grounded in Jesus' example. The same logic seems to be in place here. To be a follower of Jesus means to follow his example of unjust suffering, of not abusing in return, and of trusting God and not humans to render accounts (2:23). Although some readers argue that 1 Peter does not mean that such behavior earns grace or blessings, the syntax of 1 Peter suggests that it does. Here the assertion is not only that it is to this specific kind of suffering that followers of Jesus are called, but also that they should do this "in order that [*hina*] you might inherit a blessing." The *hina* clause should be read not as an object clause but as a purpose clause. The language of inheriting a blessing recalls the imagery of 1:3–5 and thus should be understood eschatologically.

[10–12] As noted above, there is considerable thematic coherence between Ps 34 and 1 Peter. The psalm, for instance, is set in exile and deals with questions of suffering and hope. The language and the theology of the psalm correspond closely with the language and theology of 1 Peter. There are several changes from the syntax of the psalm, most notably the change from second to third person. Though it is possible that the author of 1 Peter has a slightly different Greek text of the psalm from the Septuagint, it is also likely that 1 Peter transforms the psalm text in order to make a better rhetorical fit. In any case, the assertion made here is central to the theology of 1 Peter, and the presence of imagery and syntax from the Psalter adds weight and credibility to these claims.

The citation of the psalm begins with a thematic echo of the blessing in 3:8–9. The path to this blessing is described in 3:8–9 by way of christological themes; here it is by way of classic OT calls to righteousness. The language of loving life and seeing good days suggests historical blessings in present life, while the language of blessing in 1 Peter typically refers to the future life. The present reality of these blessings is not, however, a misleading consequence or an unintentional remainder of OT imagery that contradicts the future cast of Christian blessings in 1 Peter. While often focusing upon Christian blessings in the future, 1 Peter insists that the present life is blessed as well. Present suffering does not strip life of all its goodness. The sequence of the Christian life in 1 Peter is not pure terror now and pure blessing in the future. Thus, even if the blessing that believers "inherit" in 3:9 is "kept in heaven for you" (1:4), the call to the "good life" in 3:10 evokes the possibility of enjoying aspects of this blessing now.

The theological logic of this citation agrees with the overall theological logic of 1 Peter. Those who want to love life now should live in certain ways. When they live in these prescribed ways, God will bless them. Thus even if the specific imagery is not typical of 1 Peter, the theological structure of the argument is. In 1 Peter, partaking of God's blessings requires not just faith but also certain virtues and specific behavior. Five ethical admonitions are given: to keep tongues from evil, to keep lips from deceit, to avoid evil, to do good, and to seek peace. Such admonitions about speech are common in the OT, but they are also central to the christological virtues of 1 Peter. In the same way, the prohibition against evil and the admonitions to do good and pursue peace also reflect the christological logic of 1 Peter. The psalm and 1 Peter offer a similar challenge. The proper response to abuse from others is to live the righteous life. This is done not only because righteousness is good, but also because God responds to righteousness with blessings.

The account of God's response to such behavior in 3:12 is couched more in the language of the Psalter than that of 1 Peter. The eyes, ears, and face of God that are named here are classic ways of describing God in God's relationship to humans. The idea that God's eyes and ears look upon and listen to the righteous, while God's face is against the unrighteous, is peculiar to this text. In the OT, God's face is not more dangerous than God's eyes or ears, nor is one or the other persistently attached to either the righteous or the unrighteous. Thus the argument is not about what aspect of God is directed upon what kind of people, but that God, in God's capacity to bless and punish, looks upon everyone. The notion of the universal judgment is essential to 1 Peter. Christians and non-Christians shall be judged, each "without partiality according to the deeds of each person" (1:17). This conviction perhaps calms the need for personal vengeance since God will deal with the unrighteous. But its main function in 1 Peter is to challenge believers to Christlike behavior.

It is often difficult in the NT, and certainly in 1 Peter, to determine the precise border between a citation from the OT and language peculiar to the NT text. The imagery, syntax, and theology of 1 Peter emerges from and depends upon OT imagery, syntax, and theology. Thus confusion between language of the OT and that peculiar to 1 Peter is essential to the character of the theology of this text. If there is a conscious point to be made in citing the Psalter at this point, it would be that the surprising (cf. 4:12) necessity of suffering and the call to respond to such suffering with good deeds is not only patterned in Christ but also in the OT. This pattern of life may be new to the readers, but it is not new to God and God's people. Thus to wander along this blended way from the story of Jesus, to the story of contemporary believers, to the story of Israel, is to articulate a theological truth.

The story of Christ is the hermeneutical key. The Christ pattern of manifesting virtue in the midst of unjust suffering provides the lens to both the OT and the lives of the believers. Christology holds all of this together.

To suffer unjustly may be essential to the Christian life, but suffering and injustice are not the final word. First Peter insists that both the suffering of believers and the rule of injustice shall end. Believers will receive blessings, and God will effect justice. The powers that rule history are not the final powers. In the end, the very end, righteousness and justice will be victorious. Thus it is not simply that a willingness to suffer unjustly is essential to the Christian life, but rather that believers are called to do this with the conviction that such suffering is the path to heavenly blessings. Faith includes the conviction that God will judge everyone with impartial justice.

1 Peter 3:13–17 Suffering While Doing Good

Although there is little new thematically in this passage, there is a shift in the rhetorical style. The opening question and the series of general imperatives that follow reflect more of the conversational character of Greco-Roman paraenesis. Both the informality and the conversational format of ethical exhortation were typically understood as assisting in the persuasiveness of the rhetoric. A conversational style invites hearers both to identify with the argument and to respond to it. Much of the second half of 1 Peter reflects this informal style.

This shift in style has led many readers to identify this passage as the beginning of the final section of the letter. However, this part of 1 Peter seems to defy all attempts to identify its precise rhetorical structure. For instance, this passage belongs thematically both to what precedes and what follows. A looseness of form is typical of ancient paraenesis. First Peter is, in some ways, a classic example of this functionally disorganized rhetoric.

The challenge of unjust suffering is still the dominant theme. In some ways, this passage gathers a collection of insights from what precedes, adding the notion of readiness to make a defense. In fact, the general assertions in these verses feel inadequate on their own; for their cogency they need other arguments in the letter. This collection is also rhetorically effective and quite diverse. It includes ongoing exhortation to submit to unjust suffering, theological warrants for doing so, advice for how to manage such, and some new comments about evangelizing those who might "do bad to you."

3:13 Who then will do bad[a] to you if you become[b] zealots[c] for the good? 14 But even if you should suffer on account of righteousness, you are blessed. Do not fear them at all[d] and do not be troubled,[e] 15 but sanctify Christ[f] as Lord[g] in your hearts, being ready always to present a defense to anyone who asks you for an account of the hope that is in you, 16 but do it with meekness and fear, keeping[h] a good conscience, so that when you are slandered[i] those who disparage[j] your good behavior in Christ may be put to shame. 17 For it is better when doing good, if it should be God's will, to suffer, than when doing bad.

    a. While the participle *kakōsōn* has the general sense of doing "harm," a translation doing "bad" better displays the contrast with "the good."

    b. The subjunctive *genēsthe* has better textual support (A, C, P, 𝔐) than numerous variants that include the indicative *genesthe*, the optative *genoisthe*, and the copulative *este*.

    c. While many later manuscripts (K, 𝔐) read *mimētai* (imitators), the early manuscripts prefer *zēlōtai* (zealots).

    d. The phrase *ton de phobon autōn mē phobēthēte* literally means "Do not fear their fear." Although this phrase recalls the similar "not fearing anything frightening" in 3:7, the use of the cognate accusative suggests intensification. The modifying *autōn* would then become an objective genitive.

    e. Some of the best early witnesses ($\mathfrak{P}^{72}$, B, L) omit "and do not be troubled." The weight of the manuscript evidence supports the inclusion of the phrase, and its omission may occur from haplography, resulting from the similar endings of *phobēthēte* and *tarachthēte*.

    f. Most later texts (P, 𝔐) read *theon* instead of *Christon*, probably in attempted conformity with normal Christian usage.

    g. The sequence *kyrion de ton Christon* can be read as predicative, "Sanctify Christ as Lord," or as appositional, "Sanctify the Lord, that is, Christ." While the syntax of

Isaiah and the presence of *de* suggests an appositional reading, the presence of the article in *ton Christon* indicates a predicative structure. Furthermore, the translation "sanctify Christ as Lord" clarifies the meaning of sanctification.

h. The participle *echontes* could be read as an imperative introducing a new argument about the question of slander ("Keep a good conscience, so that when you are slandered . . ."). However, it is simpler to read it as part of the ongoing collection of images occasioned by the call to sanctify Christ as Lord.

i. The somewhat awkward passive *katalaleisthe* (You are slandered) is preferable to the equally well-supported variant *katalalousin hymōn hōs kakopoiōn* (They slander you as evildoers), which is probably derived from 2:12.

j. The verb *epēreazō* (disparage) includes the sense of both threatening and despising.

[3:13] The question that opens this passage seems somehow misstated. Not only does all of 1 Peter assume that doing good will not forestall abuse by others; the very next verse also declares that possibility. The core imagery is probably derived from Isaiah (50:9; 53:7). Neither in Isaiah nor in 1 Peter does this question suggest that people will not treat the righteous badly. Thus the force of the question cannot be found in the simple response of "no one." Perhaps the point is that it is unrighteous humans, and not God, who "do bad to you." The power of humans to inflict harm is nothing compared to what God can do. Most readers, however, suggest that this question points to the protective power of God more than to the limits on the capacity of any human to do bad to another. The question is an indirect reminder of the power and promise of God to protect those who do good. In this way, the question is a continuation of the assertion in the preceding verses and throughout 1 Peter that God will bless those who become "zealots for the good."

The phrase "zealots for the good" has occasioned speculation that 1 Peter is intentionally using a term associated with violence. The normal response to violent abuse is pursuit of violent revenge, in the manner perhaps of the Jewish Zealot party. The readers of 1 Peter are exhorted to become nonviolent, submissive-to-abuse zealots, driven not for revenge but for "the good." While the echo of violence is possible and hard to muffle completely, the primary edge in this phrase is the sense of radical commitment to the good that is expected from believers.

[14–15] There are about forty beatitudes, or makarisms, in the NT, two of which are in 1 Peter (3:14; 4:14). The form is also common in Greco-Roman literature.[22] The primary context for these beatitudes, whether in the NT or not, is theological. A beatitude typically asserts a logical contradiction: Someone who appears not to be blessed in a particular way is declared just so. The force

---

22. On the Beatitudes, see Hans Dieter Betz, *The Sermon on the Mount: A Commentary on the Sermon on the Mount including the Sermon on the Plain (Matthew 5:3–7:27 and Luke 6:20–49)* (Hermeneia; Minneapolis: Fortress, 1995), 91–105.

of the blessing comes not from finding an inherent good hidden in the bad, as if suffering were in itself not really suffering, but from the action of God. It is God who maintains the truth of the beatitude.

First Peter sometimes speaks of suffering as conditional (1:6; 2:19–20; 3:17), sometimes as a reality (2:12; 3:9; 4:12–19). Reference to suffering as conditional does not mean that believers are not suffering now or have not in the past; it simply means that doing good does not automatically induce abuse by others. The form of the condition *ei kai* with the optative gives no definitive direction on how likely suffering would be. The question of the degree of probability of suffering is not the point. The beatitude asserts a theological truth, perhaps the single most important theological truth of 1 Peter.

The language of suffering "on account of righteousness" recalls Jesus' beatitude in the Sermon on the Mount (Matt 5:10). However, the sense of *dikaiosynē* (righteousness) in 1 Peter, unlike the Sermon on the Mount, cannot be derived from classic Jewish notions of the law. Righteousness in 1 Peter (cf. 2:24; 3:12) is equivalent to "doing good" (3:11, 17; 4:19) and thus refers to the general virtuous character of the behavior of Jesus' followers. This beatitude, though it depends for its theological logic on the larger narratives of 1 Peter, functions as an effective summary of much of the letter. The beatitude gives the reason why "you should not fear at all" those who mistreat you. It is not because they will not "do bad to you" but because God will bless you.

To address the question of whom to fear, 1 Peter returns to Isaiah. Isaiah 8:12–13 is an exhortation to the prophet Isaiah not to share in the people's fear of conspiracy but to fear the Lord. First Peter follows the basic syntax of the LXX version of Isaiah but makes several changes appropriate to a different context. By changing the *phobon autou* of Isaiah to *phobon autōn*, the identity of the "people" is changed from a fearful Israel to non-Christians who threaten the Christians. But the point is similar. Fear should only be directed toward God. The second part of the quotation from Isaiah deviates dramatically from the LXX syntax: only the terms "sanctify" and "Lord" are maintained. First Peter effects these changes in order, first of all, to assert that it is Christ who is being sanctified, and second, to clarify the character of this act of sanctification.

While the notion of holiness or sanctification (*hagios* and its cognates) is central to the theology of 1 Peter, the term is often difficult to define. The term has a wide range of meanings in the OT, but in 1 Peter "holiness" occurs primarily in two contexts, that of ethics and that of fear. As 1:14–17 asserts, the holiness of God inspires both holy behavior in believers and fear of God's holiness. The same connection seems to be in place in these verses. The act of sanctifying Christ as Lord "in your hearts" means both living the holy life in obedience to Christ and fearing God (and Christ) and no one else.

The call for readiness to make a defense in 3:15b reestablishes the social context of these exhortations. There is good cause to fear nonbelievers because

Suffering While Doing Good 105

they may "do bad to you." These verses insist that such fear is prohibited, since fear belongs only toward God. Typically, 1 Peter orders the relationship of believers to nonbelievers through the images of doing good and the example of Christ. In suggesting readiness to make a defense, this verse pushes in a new direction. The wordless witnessing of women toward men by way of good deeds (3:1–2; cf. 2:12) gives way to a readiness to use words. Both *apologia* (defense) and *logos* (account) often have connotations of public, legal defense. However, the language of "always" and "to anyone" suggests readiness for all kinds of situations and inquiries. Furthermore, since the content of the account is "the hope that is in you," the defense seems to be more a theological account, a statement of gospel, than a legal defense against a public accusation. Thus the purpose of the defense would not be to protect the believer but to persuade the nonbeliever of the truth of the gospel. The word "hope" certainly includes anticipation of future reward, but it also has the more general sense of trust in the gospel (cf. 1:3, 13, 21; 3:5).

[16] This verse echoes both the argument and syntax of 2:12, although the context of 3:16 changes its force somewhat. While 2:12 seems to hold out the possibility of conversion of the Gentiles or at least the possibility that the Gentiles might desist in their abuse of Christians, here the assumption is that the Gentiles will persist in their abuse. Both passages exhort, in quite similar language, good behavior in the face of abuse.

Though the content of good behavior is not made explicit here, the images of "meekness" and "fear" provide a basic orientation for the good behavior. Most readers see in the term "meekness" a warning about "the account" that should be given to those who ask about Christ (2:15). Somewhat in the tone of the admonition to wives for silence (3:1), this passage insists that any account of Christ offered to anyone must be done with restraint and humility. The reference to "fear," on the other hand, probably invokes the fear of God (2:17) and not fear of the Gentiles. Accordingly, apologies for Christianity must be offered with a dual respect for the Gentiles and for God.

It is not clear what the language "keeping a good conscience" might mean, but "conscience" probably means what it does in 2:19 and 3:21. In 2:19 the phrase *syneidēsis theou* was translated "consciousness of God." In 1 Peter *syneidēsis* seems to have the common meaning of "mindfulness" or "awareness." In both 2:19 and 3:21 this mindfulness has something to do with God. It is likely, therefore, that "keeping a good conscience" means something akin to "fear of God." Such a rendering fits the general context of this passage and the theology of 1 Peter, wherein holiness and righteousness come not from any human sense of right and wrong but from the will of God.

As noted above, the last clause in this verse echoes 2:12. The explicit purpose of meekness, fear, and a good conscience is the eventual shame of those who "disparage" and "slander" the good behavior of the Christians. Once again, the precise content of this slander is not described in the text. The general feel of the passage is not that of formal legal proceedings or courtroom settings. Instead, this slander recalls the vague sense of 2:12, where neighbors and fellow Romans are ridiculing Christians. The abuse seems to involve loss of social status and friendship but not formal persecution. In 2:12 the result of good behavior in the face of persecution is that the Gentiles give glory to God on the last day. Here the result is shame, and the time frame is not made explicit. In a society much more attuned than modern Western culture to dynamics of honor and shame, shame could be accrued in a variety of ways. It is possible that this shame is acquired by having the Roman community recognize that the slanders against Christians are false. They are engaged in good behavior, not bad. It is also possible, and perhaps a bit more likely, that this shame is inflicted upon the Roman abusers by God on the "day of visitation" (2:12).

In any case, once again the author of 1 Peter assumes some shared values between nonbelievers and believers. The logic of this passage, and much of 1 Peter, depends upon non-Christians recognizing the good in peculiar Christian behaviors. Thus it is significant that the phrase "in Christ" is included in the syntax of "good behavior." In spite of the assumption of shared values, the origin of Christian good behavior is not in the character of common humanity, but in Christ. This is especially the case when this good behavior is behavior carved out in the face of abuse, since Christ is the one who models such.

[17] Just as 3:16 recalls the syntax of 2:12, so does this verse echo 2:20. In 2:20 the receiving of grace or fame was the explicit motivation for doing good while suffering. This passage is less specific about the immediate theological destiny of such behavior. The inevitability of suffering seems initially to be assumed in this verse, since the distinction is being drawn between suffering when doing good and suffering when doing bad. However, the unusual optative phrase "if it should be God's will" suggests that suffering is not inevitable. Thus the ordering force seems to be the doing of good rather than of suffering. In 1 Peter, suffering is not pursued for its own sake. Suffering is inflicted upon believers by unrighteous outsiders. Of course, in the theological irony of 1 Peter, this suffering becomes a good since it connects the one who suffers unjustly to the saving narrative of Jesus. Thus the proviso "if it should be God's will" is important because it reinforces the secondary character of suffering. Hence, this verse assumes that suffering does not in itself mean that one is doing good. One can suffer while doing bad. The gentle distinction that it is "better" to suffer when doing good than when doing bad proves to be an understatement. As the argument in 4:15 will show, there is nothing good in suffering for doing bad.

Once again, there is no explicit indication of the character of this suffering. As noted above, the general sense of this passage is that these believers are enduring social slander. The proverbial character of this verse makes it difficult to know not only what the character of the suffering might be, but also what theological narratives make it better to suffer when doing good. Most readers detect in 3:17 an inclusio with 3:14a. The verse is clipped and its references unspecified because its main function is to evoke and to summarize the preceding arguments.

These verses (3:13–17) belong to the ongoing argument about the necessity for doing good. They build on the imagery of 3:9 and 3:11. If 3:11 calls on the readers to "do good," then these verses explicitly address the questions of what happens to people who obey these imperatives and become "zealots for the good." After the declaration "If you should suffer on account of righteousness, you are blessed," these verses address the difficulty posed by the experience of fear.

This fear is analyzed in the potent ancient language of shame. The suffering endured by believers seems to be mostly of the kind that would lead to social shame and not to death. The social force of slander and ridicule lies in the power to induce shame. Christians have lost social status and, even worse, are subject to ongoing ridicule and attack. Shame is the natural consequence. First Peter reverses the economy of shame. In the normal human accounting, shame should fall on the ones being slandered. But in the theological accounting of 1 Peter, shame falls on the ones who are slandering. While these verses do not give an account of who gets "glory," which in this context is the opposite of shame, elsewhere (see 2:12; 4:11–14, 16; 5:1, 4, 10) 1 Peter makes it clear that glory belongs to God and that this glory, given first to Jesus, will eventually be given to Jesus' followers. Thus the ongoing plea of 1 Peter is to not be ashamed of experiences that feel shameful because God will reverse and is reversing the present economy of shame and glory.

The familiar challenge to continue in good behavior in the face of abuse and slander receives several general theological warrants in this passage. Perhaps the simplest warrant is the claim that one is "blessed" when one behaves thus. But the precise ordering of this blessing is not pursued here. The challenge to "sanctify Christ as Lord in your hearts" suggests a connection to the saving narrative of Christ. And the promise that those who are presently slandering the readers will themselves be shamed, either now or in the eschatological judgment, evokes the surety of eventual justice. All of this gives a sense of a rather fluid and diverse theology. This becomes even more apparent in the following verses (3:18–22) which on the one hand provide further theological reasons for good behavior in Christ, and on the other hand introduce a completely new set of theological images.

1 Peter 3:18–22 Christ as Model of Suffering and Victory

Most readers of 1 Peter regard these verses as the most perplexing in the letter. On one level, the passage consists of a straightforward series of theological images that undergird the ethic of doing good in the face of suffering. However, on another level, the difficulties are numerous. The images themselves can be understood in a variety of ways; the connection among the images is not explicit; the literary structure of the passage seems, at first reading at least, to be confused; and even the relation of these images to the ethic of 1 Peter and to the other theological images in the letter is difficult to trace. Some readers consequently conclude that the passage is a rather ineffective intrusion into an otherwise fairly clear argument, observing that the language of 3:17 connects readily with that of 4:1.

As is typically the case, answers to the larger questions of how the passage functions in the argument of 1 Peter depend upon a series of particular exegetical decisions. The identity of both the "unrighteous" and the "spirits in prison," the nature of the distinction between flesh and spirit, the possible allusion to *1 Enoch*, the force of the reference to Noah and baptism, and finally the identity of the powers in 3:22—these are all debated. How each of these exegetical issues is resolved determines one's understanding of the passage's overall direction.

In spite of the difficulties of this passage, most readers see it as an integral moment in the letter. For all their obscurity, the theological images are intriguing. They add potent new voices to the theological mix of the letter. For instance, the christological narrative in 1 Peter becomes, hereby, richer and more complex. Finally, some glimpses, opaque though they be, are provided into the implicit traditions behind the letter's explicit syntax.

3:18 For Christ also suffered for sins[a] once and for all, the righteous for the unrighteous, so that he might bring you to God, having been put to death in[b] the flesh, but having been made alive in[b] the spirit. 19 In which[c] also[d] going he made a proclamation to the spirits in prison, 20 who once did not obey,[e] when the patience of God waited in the days of Noah, while the ark was being prepared, into which a few,[f] that is, eight lives,[g] were saved through water. 21 In a corresponding way to all of that,[h] baptism now saves you also, not as a putting off of the filth of the flesh but as a pledge[i] to God of a good conscience,[j] through the resurrection of Jesus Christ, 22 who is at the right hand of God, having gone into heaven, with the angels and authorities and powers being made subject to him.

    a. The textual variants of the phrase "suffered for sins" are numerous. The main changes are the occurrence of "died" in the place of "suffered," the addition of prepositional phrase "for you," and the addition of the adjective "our" to sins. Although there is a bit more textual support for "died" than "suffered," the more unusual "suffered" fits the theology of 1 Peter. A change to "died" along with various additions of "you" and "us" can best be seen as coming from the influence of the common Christian language of Jesus "dying for our sins" and from the language of death later in the verse.

    b. There are numerous possibilities for how to translate the dative forms of flesh and spirit. A locative reading, while adequate grammatically, creates a bifurcation of

Christ as Model of Suffering and Victory

the person into a fleshly part and a spiritual part. This reading seems unlikely because the NT persistently resists the later Christian notion that in death the body (or flesh) dies while the spirit lives on. Furthermore, the claim is that Jesus is "made alive," not that his spirit somehow survives the death of his flesh. Thus two other readings are suggested. The dative could be one of respect or reference, in which flesh and spirit do not refer to parts of the self but, in agreement with the rest of the NT, to modes of being. The dative could also be read instrumentally. This works adequately in the second phrase, which would mean that Christ is made alive by the spirit of God. This is a bit puzzling since it is typically God, not the spirit of God, that gives life to the crucified Jesus. However, a reading of the first phrase as Christ's being put to death by the fleshly powers is obscure at best. It seems unlikely that any reader would actually hear the word *sarx* as a reference to Pilate and the high priests. An instrumental reading also complicates the transition to 3:19. Thus most commentators read these as datives of respect.

c. The prepositional phrase *en hō* can be read as a temporal conjunction, translated "when"; as a circumstantial conjunction, translated "in which condition"; or more literally as a preposition, with the relative pronoun referring back to spirit, thus translated "in which." The phrase occurs four other times in 1 Peter. In both 2:12 and 3:16 *en hō* clearly has a temporal meaning, while in 1:6 and 4:4 the sense is ambiguous. Few readers render the phrase in 3:19 temporally, since the *kai* that follows becomes confusing and it remains unclear "when" any of this would have happened. In later Christian tradition, Christ's descent into hell occurs between the crucifixion and the resurrection. However, the temporal sequence in this verse would place the event after the resurrection. The reading "in which," with "spirit" as the antecedent, is grammatically the simplest, but "in which condition" makes somewhat more sense exegetically. Therefore, an ambiguous "in which" is probably the best translation.

d. Although there is no textual evidence of any problem with *kai*, a clever confusion has been proposed wherein an original *enōchkai* (Enoch also) or *enōkaienōch* (in which also Enoch) was mistranscribed as *enōkai* (in which also). Detecting a lost "Enoch" in this phrase is not completely unlikely, since in *1 Enoch* it is Enoch (and not Jesus) who goes into heaven and preaches condemnation to the rebellious angels (see, e.g., 12.4–6; 13.1–10; 18.12–14). Inserting Enoch as the subject might explain the origin of the imagery of this verse, but it creates an enormous problem with the overall sense of the passage. What is Enoch doing in the middle of this christological account? And as noted above, there is no textual evidence for a problem with *kai*. It is best to retain "in which also."

e. The participle *apeithēsasin* could be circumstantial and rendered causally: "because they were disobedient." It could also be rendered attributively: "who were disobedient." The difference in meaning is admittedly slight since both renderings connect disobedience to the spirits in prison. The traditional division of the verse before the participle may support a circumstantial reading, but most readers prefer the somewhat simpler reading: "who were disobedient."

f. Most ancient witnesses have the masculine *oligoi*, which would be a generic reference to people. But some witnesses, including the Majority text (𝔐), have the feminine *oligai*, which emphasizes a connection to the following *psychai* ("souls" or "lives").

g. While the word *psychē* can on occasion refer to the "soul" as a specific aspect of a person, here the word has the common meaning of "life" or "self."

h. The textual and grammatical problems in the beginning of this verse are nearly unsolvable. Most ancient texts begin the verse with the neuter relative pronoun *ho*. However, some texts have the pronoun in the dative, while some texts omit the pronoun altogether. In addition, the word *antitypon* could be an independent noun or an adjective modifying baptism. As an adjective it could be either in the predicate position or the attributive. The simplest solution is to read a dative pronoun ("corresponding to this, baptism..."). The dative is likely a clarification of the much more difficult *ho*. However, reading an opening *ho* makes the opening phrase almost impossible to translate into idiomatic English. There are many suggestions. The neuter relative is commonly used to refer back, not to a particular word (such as "water"), but to an event or sentence as whole. Such a use is likely here. The word *antitypon* could then be understood as a predicate noun in apposition with *baptisma*. Admittedly, such a reading is more than a little awkward, but any reading is awkward. This one seems to create the fewest problems.

The word *antitypon* only occurs again in the NT in Heb 9:24. In general usage an *antitypon* is the inferior copy of a *typos*. Since it is not at all clear in this instance what the prototype of the antitype might be, it is best to see the word as simply evoking a sense of correspondence.

i. The Greek noun *eperōtēma* normally means "question" or "request," although in some papyri it can have the technical meaning in a contract of "pledge." Both translations make grammatical sense in this verse. However, the idea of baptism as a prayer or request to God is difficult to comprehend in the theology of early Christianity, while the notion of baptism as a pledge to God fits perfectly with standard early Christian language.

j. The word *syneidēsis* occurs two other times in 1 Peter (2:19; 3:16). Although it is possible that both 2:19 and 3:21 use the word with its later Christian nuance of conscience in the sense of a moral guide, all three usages in 1 Peter can and should be read with the Greek word's ordinary sense as "consciousness."

[18] The conjunction "for" (*hoti*) asserts that what follows validates what precedes, although it is not possible to track precise correspondences between the theological assertions in 3:18–22 and the admonitions in 3:13–17. The opening phrase "Christ suffered for sins once and for all" in some ways sounds like a piece of common Christian tradition and in other ways like a formulation peculiar to 1 Peter. The image of Christ's suffering strikes the persistent chord in 1 Peter of Jesus as a model of suffering (2:21–25), but the addition of the phrases "for sins" and "once and for all" evokes dynamics of atonement (2:24). Christ is not just a model. This shift to an assertion about what Christ does for believers inaugurates a series of statements about the activity of God and Christ on behalf of people. Thus the admonitions in 3:13–17 find warrant in a conviction that God and Christ are able and willing to reward those who suffer unjustly.

The phrase "the righteous for the unrighteous" can also be read as a reference to atonement or at least to vicarious suffering. While the term "the righteous" is a common designation for Christ in the NT, it is not confined to that referent. Humans in general can be called righteous. The other two occurrences of the adjective in 1 Peter (3:12; 4:18) refer to followers of Christ and not to Christ himself. Thus, while it is hard to resist hearing some version of atonement, the original background may be that of martyrdom, in which the primary setting is human politics and not the temple. Even if some kind of temple economy is included in the language of "for [*peri*] sins" and "for [*hyper*] the unrighteous," the political context of unjust suffering is still in place.

This uncertainty over the precise force of these assertions means that there are several ways in which Christ "might bring you to God." Christ can lead "you" to God by "leaving for you a pattern, so that you might follow in his footsteps" (2:21). Such a reading connects nicely with the imagery of 4:1 that Christians arm themselves with the same way of thinking as did Christ. But Christ can also lead by opening an atoning door (cf. 2:24). The willingness of 1 Peter to combine both exemplary and atoning images in 2:21–25 suggests that both might be in place here. The theology of 1 Peter works more as a gathering of images than an ordering of images.

The real difficulties in these verses begin with the contrasting aorist passive participles "put to death" and "made alive." Though these terms echo the persistent contrast in the NT between Jesus' death and resurrection, the syntax here is unique. The passive construction implies the contrast between the killing activity of human opponents and the saving activity of God. It is this contrast that structures the theological argument of much of 1 Peter. When human opponents cause unjust suffering for the righteous, God responds with the giving of life and glory. The use of the terms "put to death" (*thanatoō*) and "make alive" (*zōopoieō*) emphasize the contrast between death and life that is essential but sometimes only implicit in the crucifixion and resurrection language of Christian tradition.

It is the contrast between flesh and spirit that poses the real puzzle in this verse. An instrumental reading of the dative simplifies the puzzle, since flesh could then refer to human opponents and spirit could refer to the spirit of God. But the more likely reading (see note b) as a dative of respect leads to the difficult question of what 1 Peter intends in this contrast between a mode of being in the flesh and a mode of being in the spirit. The distinction is probably not between viewpoints, as if from a human point of view Christ was put to death, while from a spiritual point of view God made Christ alive. It is more likely that the phrases are pointing to some kind of realm or forces. Christ—living in the realm of the flesh, under the powers of the flesh, himself a proper member of the world of the flesh—was put to death; yet living in the world of spirit where God rules, Christ was made alive. The cosmic conflict between fleshly powers and spiritual ones should not be divided temporally (in terms of era) or spatially (as parts of the self or the world). Flesh and spirit work in the same place, at the same time. Christ, as subject to fleshly powers, is put to death. Christ, as cared for by God, is made alive. Admittedly, no straightforward reading of these phrases has proved to be completely persuasive; still, references to realms or kingdoms seems to work better than any alternative.

[19] This verse may be the most obscure verse in the NT. Basically every phrase, even every word, is unclear. The traditional, although not the most ancient, interpretation is that Christ's spirit, after his crucifixion and before his resurrection, descends into hell where he (or it) preaches the gospel to the deceased of Noah's generation in order to save them. This exegesis has been contested at every single point.

The uncertainty begins with the translation of *en hō* (see note c). However, the exegetical key to the verse lies in the identity and location of "the spirits in prison." The bundled questions of when and how and who and what was said, all revolve around the identity of these spirits. Furthermore, their identity exerts impact on the meaning of 3:20 and probably 3:22 as well. Since 3:20 locates these spirits in the time of the "days of Noah" and describes them as disobedient, two options are possible. These spirits could be the disobedient humans who were destroyed in the flood and whose prison is the place of the dead. The reference to the "dead" having the gospel preached to them in 4:6 seems to reinforce this reading. However, the problems with this reading are considerable. The word "spirits" (*pneumata*) only rarely refers to humans (see, e.g., Heb 12:23). More often the term refers to supernatural beings of some kind. Furthermore, the word "prison" (*phylakē*) is not typically used for the place of the dead. Thus, most modern readers prefer a second option, which not only fits the terminology of 2:19 but also coheres with 3:20 and 3:22.

In Jewish tradition the rebellious angels of Gen 6:1–6 both cause the Noachian flood and are subsequently imprisoned (e.g., *Jub.* 7.21; 10.1–9; *1 En.* 6–16; 13.6; 15.4–7; 18.12–19.2; *2 En.* 7.1–3). Thus "the spirits in prison" could refer to the rebellious angels of Genesis, as developed in this tradition. This reading is reinforced by stories in *1 Enoch*, wherein Enoch journeys to this prison and announces to these angels their final destruction. This reading also explains the reference to Noah in 3:20 and anticipates the subjection of "the angels and authorities and powers" to Jesus Christ in 3:22.

An interpretation of this verse is now possible. As a result of "being made alive in the spirit," Jesus Christ journeyed to the site of the imprisonment of those disobedient angels of Gen 6, who caused the Noachian flood, and there Jesus "made a proclamation" (*ekēryxen*). There is no definitive evidence in either the Jewish tradition or 1 Peter where this prison might be, but it does not have to be below. The content of the proclamation is not made explicit in this verse. However, the imagery of 3:22 and the example of Enoch suggests that Christ does not offer forgiveness but instead announces to the spirits their final defeat and subjugation. Perhaps the victories of Christ described in 3:18 and 3:22 provide the content.

Christ as Model of Suffering and Victory

[20] The flood reference in this verse connects to the preceding both by the narrative structure of Gen 6 and by the theological logic of these verses. Jesus' victory over death and the cosmic powers, announced in verses 18 and 22, is prefigured in the story of the flood and experienced now in baptism (v. 21). In some ways this verse is a simple evocation of the narrative of the disobedient angels and the flood story of Noah as narrated in Gen 6, although the details of the argument suggest some knowledge of the complex Jewish tradition about these stories.

It is puzzling that the flood story is cited here as a sign of God's patience and not God's impatience, especially since the narrative of Gen 6 suggests that God floods the earth because God has run out of patience with humanity. Nevertheless, this verse places certain limits on God's patience. God waits while the ark is being prepared but does not wait forever. There is no hint in this verse of the later Christian notion of the ark being a symbol for the church. Nor is there any explicit account of the nature of the angels' disobedience during the time of the ark's preparation. The precise configuration of the tradition behind these verses cannot be reconstructed. What matters in 1 Peter is that, even while God was acting to save a "few" from the judgment of the flood, the angels were acting disobediently. The flood narrative in this way parallels the contemporary narrative of the readers of 1 Peter. The cosmic powers (see v. 22) are still dangerous and disobedient, even as God is acting to save a few.

For all the importance of the flood narrative in early Christianity, the figure of Noah has little role. Such is the case here. Noah has no active part in this narrative. He is not a model of obedience. It is not even made explicit that he is the one who builds the ark. The passive "while the ark was being prepared" may actually reflect the tradition in *1 Enoch* 67.2 that the ark was built by angels. The mention of the number "eight" probably has nothing to do with later Christian interpretations of the number as a holy number; rather, it is a simple counting of Noah, his wife, their three sons, and the three wives of those sons. Finally, it is unlikely that the phrase "through [*dia*] water" should be understood instrumentally, even though such a reading might make the analogy with baptism more complete. The water of the flood is not a saving water but the cosmic waters of chaos "through" which Noah and his family were saved.

[21] For all the difficulties in establishing and translating the beginning of this verse, the basic assertion is clear. There is a theological analogy between God's saving Noah and his family from the flood and God's now saving through baptism the followers of Jesus. However, the explicit syntax suggests that it is baptism itself and not God that does the saving. Furthermore, the saving is done "through the resurrection of Jesus Christ" and not "through water."

Once again it is difficult to reconstruct a full account of the theological narrative implied in this verse. The general tradition of early Christian baptism[23] is that water functions as it does in Jewish purification rituals, but the analogy with the flood suggests that water in this baptism may represent the waters of chaos, waters aligned with the disobedient angels of verses 19 and 20 and with "the angels and authorities and powers" of verse 22. A connection by way of water to these powers reinforces the connection to the theological images of verse 18 and to the phrase "through the resurrection of Jesus Christ." Baptism saves people from the watery grasp of death and the evil powers, even as Jesus was raised from the dead and just as eight lives were saved from the waters of the flood. Furthermore, as verse 22 will assert, all the evil powers, in chaotic waters and anywhere else, are ultimately subject to Jesus Christ.

This theological narrative includes an aside about the proper domain of baptism. First of all, 1 Peter claims that baptism is not "a putting off of the filth of the flesh." The precise contours of this imagery are, once again, difficult to reconstruct. While attempts to recognize in these images classic Jewish ritual washing or subtle references to circumcision are unconvincing, the general context of ritual purity makes sense. However, in 1 Peter this ritual imagery is transformed. First Peter is claiming that baptism is not a putting off of filth whereby the one baptized becomes ritually clean. It is even possible, as some readers suggest, that the phrase should be rendered "a putting off of filth from the flesh" since there is no indication in 1 Peter that flesh is either morally or ritually evil. Instead, baptism is "a pledge to God of a good conscience." Thus in 1 Peter the realm of baptism is not ritual purity but moral commitment. Baptism is or includes a promise to God to have a "good conscience." As noted above, *syneidēsis* in 1 Peter has the regular meaning of "consciousness." The promise is not to have a clean conscience, in the sense of having no awareness of any unrepented personal sins. The promise is to maintain ongoing proper awareness, mindfulness, and consciousness of God.

[22] This verse partakes of the common early Christian tradition of Christ's ascension and exaltation, coupled with the subjugation of the cosmic powers to Christ. The phrase "who is at the right hand of God" occurs in exactly the same form in Rom 8:34 and with slight variations in numerous passages elsewhere in the NT (see, e.g., Mark 14:62; Acts 2:34; Heb 1:13). This language comes from Ps 110:1. The imagery of Christ "going into heaven" occurs in various forms throughout the NT (see, e.g., Acts 1:10–11). The imagery of subjugation of cosmic powers to Jesus occurs with slight variations throughout the Pauline corpus (see, e.g., 1 Cor 15:24; Eph 1:21; Col 2:10). Thus 1 Peter is clearly employing common Christian tradition in this brief christological narrative. Yet the specifics of this tradition are key to the theological force of this passage.

---

23. For a survey of these early Christian baptismal traditions, see Everett Ferguson, *Baptism in the Early Church: History, Theology, and Liturgy in the First Five Centuries* (Grand Rapids: Eerdmans, 2009).

Though the terms *angeloi*, *exousiai*, and perhaps even *dynameis* could refer to human figures, in the context of these verses and in the NT's prevailing usage, they denote cosmic powers. Furthermore, in common Christian usage and certainly in this passage, they refer to cosmic powers that oppose God and threaten the Christian community. They are evil, spiritual, cosmic forces. It is not, however, possible to identify precisely the face and duty of each of these powers. The three terms together do not identify a generally acknowledged division of the cosmic powers into three categories. Rather, the three names create a sense of comprehensiveness.

The basic theological issue is that of power. This verse affirms the cosmic power of Jesus. The image of being at the right hand of God is, of course, an image of power and authority. The result of Jesus' exaltation is that he is at the right hand of God and that all the evil powers of the cosmos are subject to him. This imagery forms a fitting conclusion to the entire passage. The unifying theme of the passage is that of God's power over the evil cosmic forces that threaten the community. The resurrection of Jesus, the story of the flood, the experience of baptism, and the exaltation of Jesus collectively proclaim to both the evil powers and to threatened believers that God is victorious.

If this passage (3:18–22) is read in the context of *1 Enoch* and the battle between cosmic powers, then the initial impression of disorder and interruption in this passage is replaced by an impression of an ordered and coherent theological narrative. The diverse theological images of this passage and their lack of explicit narrative are misleading. These verses have a clear theological narrative and a rather focused argument.

Jesus Christ has broken the power of sin and led people to God. This victory over sin and deliverance of people came from the reversal of crucifixion and resurrection. The evil cosmic powers could not hold Jesus in death because he was made alive by God. God's action broke the hold that the cosmic powers had over him. Jesus then journeyed to the prison that already held some defeated fallen angels, where he announced his victory. These were the very angels who caused the flood and who were disobedient to God even as God was saving a few from the terrors of chaotic waters. In the same way, God saves people today from the cosmic powers through baptism. This baptism is empowered by the resurrection of Jesus Christ, wherein these cosmic powers are defeated. And Jesus is now at the position of highest authority in the cosmos: all the powers, fallen angels and otherwise, are subject to him.

In the context of 1 Peter, this victory of Jesus in the resurrection, which is received today in the power of baptism, announces to all the evil powers, including Roman political powers, their ultimate defeat and subjugation to Jesus Christ. Thus the imbalance of power in the lives of persecuted Christians is misleading, for already all the powers of the cosmos are subject to Jesus

Christ. Read in this context, this passage fits beautifully into the complex theological argument of 1 Peter.

Excursus: The Tradition of Enoch and the Fallen Angels

First Peter, 2 Peter, and Jude appear to assume that their readers have some knowledge of a tradition concerning the imprisonment of the fallen angels of Gen 6. In the midst of a series of reminders of how "the Lord" judges the unrighteous, Jude 6 declares "And the angels, who did not keep their own position of authority, but left their proper dwelling, he has kept under darkness in eternal chains for the judgment of the great day." In probable dependence on Jude 6, 2 Pet 2:4 begins a series of similar warnings with "For if God did not spare angels when they sinned, but casting them into hell handed them over to chains of darkness, to be kept for judgment . . ." The brief note in Gen 6:4 about "the Nephilim" does not include any account of the subsequent imprisonment of "the sons of God." Later Jewish tradition does.

While pieces of this story surface in numerous Jewish texts, it is in *1 Enoch* that the fullest form of the story is encountered. Given the composite character of *1 Enoch* and the generally inconsistent pattern of apocalyptic texts, it is no surprise that there is not perfect uniformity in the many references in *1 Enoch* to the fallen angels of Gen 6. However, the basic story is given in the so-called "Book of the Watchers" and remains consistent throughout *1 Enoch*. The angels desire the beautiful daughters of humans (*1 En.* 6). Two hundred angels bind themselves with an oath and take human wives for themselves (*1 En.* 6–7). They teach dangerous arts that produce violence and evil on earth (*1 En.* 8–9). God decides to destroy the earth (*1 En.* 10). (The link between the activity of the Nephilim and the flood is not explicit in Genesis, but it is constant in these later accounts.) The angels are bound and thrown into a dark place, where they await final punishment (*1 En.* 10).

Throughout *1 Enoch* a variety of details are added to this core narrative. In *1 Enoch* 54, Enoch sees a valley burning with fire, where "iron fetters of immense weight" are being forged for "the armies of Azael" (on these chains or bonds, see also *1 En.* 13.1–2; 14.5; 56.1–2; 88.1). This binding in chains is echoed in Jude 6 and 2 Pet 2:4. The pervasiveness of this image is highlighted by Josephus, who connected the Jewish traditions of the fallen angels to the ancient Greek myth of Titans, who were giants that rebelled against Chronos and were bound in chains in Tartarus (*Ant.* 1.73). The announcement of doom to the fallen angels, which is accomplished by Jesus in 1 Pet 3:19, is carried out in *1 Enoch* by Enoch himself (12.4–6; 13.1–3; 15.1–16.3). This tradition of an announcement of doom is complicated in *1 Enoch* by a request made to Enoch by the fallen angels that he pray on their behalf. The watchers send Enoch to announce punishment on the angels (12.4). When he does this, the angels beg him to write for them "a memorial prayer" that will be a "prayer of forgiveness" (13.4). Enoch writes down this prayer, but then sees in a vision that these prayers will not be heard, that judgment has been pronounced, and that the angels will be imprisoned "inside the earth" forever (14.3–6). The place of the angels' imprisonment seems quite fluid, even if the core image is that of "inside the earth." In *1 Enoch* 10.12, God binds the angels "underneath the rocks of the ground until the day of their judgment." In *1 Enoch* 21, their imprisonment is in "an empty place," where Enoch sees "neither a heaven above nor an earth beneath, but a chaotic and terrible place." In *1 Enoch* 67, it is a burning valley in the west (67.4), where ironically rivers of water are the means of punishment (67.7). However, outside of *1 Enoch*, the primary location seems to be the second heaven (2 *En.* 7.1–3; *T. Levi* 3.3). Throughout *1 Enoch* and other Jewish texts, this core story is developed and enriched in a variety of ways. The pervasiveness and diversity of these accounts, on the one hand, reinforces the likelihood that 1 Peter, 2 Peter, and Jude can assume their readers' knowledge of the core story of the fallen angels; but on the other hand, this diversity makes reconstruction of the precise details of the story assumed in each impossible to reconstruct.

In any case, the story of God's victory over the rebellious angels, along with their subsequent imprisonment and forthcoming punishment, as narrated in the visions and journeys of Enoch, was portrayed in these early Christian texts as instructive for the Christian story. While 1 Peter, 2 Peter, and Jude incorporate this story into their own theological frameworks, the initial force of the story is similar in all. In the current life of Christians, it appears as though their enemies and the enemies of God (who are one and the same) are prospering and will continue to do so. Enoch's account of the punishment of the rebellious angels illustrates what will happen to all God's enemies. All three letters devote attention to the discord between the promises of glory in the Christian story and the ongoing experience of suffering and abuse. In all three letters, the story of the fallen angels provides warrant for the hope that animates the Christian life. Your enemies may be flourishing now, but remember the fate of the fallen angels and have faith that God will, in God's own time, punish all who rebel.

1 Peter 4:1–6 Separation from the Gentile Life

The ongoing challenge to do good receives a peculiar twist in this passage. The call to good is combined in these verses, as it typically is in 1 Peter, with both the example of Christ and the necessity of suffering. However, the assertion in 3:22 of Christ's victory over the cosmic powers leads to an emphasis on judgment, especially the judgment of the Gentiles. In the common rhetorical pattern of 1 Peter, wherein the major theological themes are not treated one at a time but repetitively in different combinations, the idea of judgment receives fuller treatment in 4:12–19. Whereas 3:13–16 concentrated on the positive behavior of Christians in response to the abusive behavior of others, envisioning ongoing connection between Christians and non-Christians, these verses concentrate on Christian rejection of Gentile behavior, envisioning distance and separation. Christians are to cease "accomplishing the will of the Gentiles" not just because they are called to do good in Christ but also because the Gentiles will be judged. To return to the Gentile way of life is to fall under God's judgment.

Along the way, this passage gives the single best hint for the nature of the conflict between these Christians and their Roman neighbors. The imagery here suggests that the suffering endured by these Christians is not the result of legal persecution but of social and personal conflict. The disagreement seems to be between former friends, not between the Roman religious order and a perceived disloyalty and atheism of Christians.

These verses contain two well-known and much-debated exegetical puzzles. Both the grammar and general sense of the concluding clause of 4:1, "because the one who has suffered in the flesh has ceased from sin," are uncertain and have occasioned much debate. However, the reference in 4:6 to the gospel being preached even "to the dead" is even more controversial. Its meaning depends in part on the relationship between this verse and 3:19.

4:1 Therefore, since[a] Christ suffered in the flesh,[b] you also arm yourselves with the same understanding,[c] because[d] the one who has suffered in the flesh has ceased from sin, 2 so as to live[e] the remaining time in the flesh no longer according to human desires but according to the will of God. 3 For the time that has passed is sufficient for accomplishing the will[f] of the Gentiles, going about in licentiousness,[g] desires, drunkenness, inebriating feasts, drinking parties, and lawless idolatries. 4 In this they are surprised,[h] that you no longer run with them in the same pouring out of wastefulness, and thus they slander.[i] 5 They will give an account to the one who is ready to judge[j] the living and the dead. 6 For this reason the gospel was proclaimed[k] also to the dead, in order that although they were judged in the flesh according to human standards,[l] they might live in the spirit according to God's standards.[l]

a. The genitive absolute *pathontos* (suffered) is best rendered causally.

b. Some key texts (A, 𝔐) add "for us," while a few minor texts add "for you." These additions are likely to have come from scribal conformity with traditional Christian language of suffering.

c. The Greek word *ennoia* often has the more dynamic sense of "understanding" rather than the more static meaning of "thought." The verb can even mean "to conceive a plan." Furthermore, "understanding" in this dynamic sense fits the overall viewpoint of 1 Peter. The focus in 1 Peter is not upon simply knowing something that is true but upon reaching an understanding of the gospel that leads to the Christian life.

d. The conjunction *hoti* can be read as an explanatory "that" or a causal "because." The reasons for rendering the *hoti* as causal are given below.

e. The implied subject of the infinitive could be the one who suffers. However, it is easier to read the "you" of v. 1b.

f. A few manuscripts (P, 𝔐) read *thelēma* in concord with the *thelēmati theou* of 4:2. Both *thelēma* and *boulēma*, which most texts have here, mean "will," although *boulēma* carries the sense of "counsel" or "intention."

Separation from the Gentile Life 119

g. The word *aselgeia* denotes uncontrolled behavior, especially sexual licentiousness.

h. The verb *xenizō* in the active voice means "to welcome a stranger." In the passive it typically means "to be surprised, amazed, or even offended" at something or someone strange. The word suggests not only that Gentiles are "surprised" at the new behavior of Christians, but also that Christians have become strangers to them.

i. The verb *blasphēmeō* means "to speak ill" of something or someone. It can mean to speak ill of a person, "to slander," but its more common meaning is to speak ill of something sacred or of a god, "to blaspheme." It is possible that 1 Peter is asserting that the Gentiles, in criticizing Christians, are actually criticizing God. However, the context suggests that the implied object of the verb is the Christians, who no longer "go about" with the Gentiles. Here some texts (א, C) have the conjunction "and" along with a present indicative verb instead of the present participle, probably in an attempt to clarify the syntax.

j. The rather complex but perfectly correct syntax of this verse (lit., "to the one readily having to judge") is simplified in numerous texts ("to the one who judges readily" or "to the one ready to judge").

k. On the impersonal translation of *euēngelisthē*, see discussion below.

l. The parallel phrases *kata anthrōpous* and *kata theon* in the context of judgment probably have the sense of "according to human/God's standards" rather than "on a human/divine level."

[4:1] The exact logic of the opening "therefore" is not obvious. Since 1 Peter typically connects arguments in an imprecise way, this "therefore" probably refers to the ongoing connection in 1 Peter among suffering, ethics, and judgment. More significant is the question of precisely what is being evoked by the phrase "Christ suffered in the flesh." "In the flesh" probably does not mean in the flesh as opposed to the spirit. Flesh refers here simply to Christ's life as a human being. The question is what aspect of Christ's suffering is being evoked. Since the theological sequence offered in these verses is once again that of good conduct, followed by suffering, followed by more good conduct, the general narrative of 2:18–24, which relates this sequence explicitly, seems to be in place here. However, all the images of Christ's suffering in 1 Pet 2 and 3 fit well enough. It is also striking that the precise sequence of 2:24—he "who himself bore our sins in his body upon the wood, in order that by being removed from our sins we might live to righteousness"—is repeated here. The suffering of Christ leads to freedom from sin. The Christian's own suffering is added to this sequence, and freedom from sin becomes freedom both from the sins and company of the Gentiles and from the earlier Gentile life of the Christian.

However, the emphasis here is not upon the redemptive power of Christ's suffering but upon the example that Christ provides. Believers are called to "arm" themselves with "the same understanding" that Christ had. The use of military imagery in contexts of ethics is common in Greco-Roman philosophy and in the NT (e.g., 1 Pet 2:11; 2 Cor 10:3–5; Eph 6:11–17). The battle imagery also connects effectively to the social conflict between these Christians and their Roman neighbors. The phrase "the same understanding" apparently means the same understanding that Jesus had. If the *hoti* is read as explanatory, then Christ's understanding would have been that "the one who has suffered in the flesh has ceased from sin." However, this hardly seems an adequate account of Christ's own "understanding" as narrated in 1 Peter. Reading the *hoti* causally eliminates this awkwardness but also leaves the content of this "understanding" unspecified. This imprecision is functional, to some degree at least, since the relationship among suffering, sin, virtues, and salvation in 1 Peter cannot be easily summarized. As noted above, the christological narrative of 2:18–24 provides the best hint of what this understanding might involve. It is the view of God and reality that could warrant such astonishing behavior.

A causal reading of *hoti* means that the concluding phrase is not the core theological truth that funded Jesus' own behavior but a conclusion drawn from the example of Christ and ongoing experience of his followers. Readers have long debated the identification of "the one who has suffered in the flesh."[24] Since it is not true that every Christian who suffers has ceased from sin, and since the constant ethical appeal in 1 Peter to suffering Christians shows that 1 Peter assumes that sin is still an option for suffering Christians, a few readers argue that the one who suffers and ceases from sin must be Christ. But this would be a curious affirmation at this point in the argument, since the passage is an exhortation to Christians to cease from Gentile sinning. Thus some readers have suggested that this phrase is not a christological truth but a bit of Jewish gnomic wisdom that affirms the pedagogical power of suffering. In the rhetoric of such proverbs, this affirmation is not a simple fact, since not all who suffer cease from sinning. Rather, the power of suffering to subdue vice and unrighteousness is here couched as a proverbial truth. Though the specific Jewish martyrdom tradition might be included in this assertion, both Jewish and Greek wisdom traditions affirm the power of suffering to teach the ethical life. However, both of these readings unnecessarily limit the force of this affirmation. A reader of 1 Peter is hard pressed not to hear both Christ and suffering Christians in this phrase. Suffering disciplines the flesh. This is demonstrated in the life of Christ and in the lives of his followers.

[2] This verse expresses the purpose of having the same understanding as Christ had, which is to live as Christ lived. The syntax here is ordered around the circumstances of the followers of Christ who have turned away from their old lives. The language recalls that of 1:14; 2:1; and 2:11, which imagines

---

24. Compare, e.g., Elliott, *1 Peter*, 713–18; and Goppelt 278–82.

a rejection of the old ways and a taking up of a new moral battle. Thus "the remaining time in the flesh" probably does not refer to the remaining time before the Parousia but to the time remaining before their individual deaths (cf. "the time of your exile" in 1:17).

First Peter envisions the moral life, or at least one key moment in the moral life, as a choice between opposing ways of living, that are here named as living "according to human desires" or "according to the will of God." The difference between these two ways of living is not obvious. The following verses will provide a hint, but just a hint, about the content of a life in accord with human desires. It is striking that the imagery of the moral battle is that of classic Stoicism. The noun *epithymiai* is the standard term in Stoicism for the forces within humans that frustrate the virtuous life. Desires, passions, cravings are the negative powers in the moral warfare of the Stoic. In fact, the vices listed in 4:3 are those that the Stoic and most other Romans would recognize as vices. Even as Christians are called to reject the Gentile life, they claim many of the values of that Gentile life. Most Gentiles want to subdue their "desires."

[3–4] Given the normal intensity of the rhetoric of 1 Peter, 4:3 uses a rather understated and perhaps ironic syntax: "the time that has passed is sufficient." This verse assumes, at least rhetorically, that the recipients of the letter used to accomplish "the will of the Gentiles." The "will of the Gentiles" in this verse appears to refer to the same thing as the "human desires" of 4:2. If so, this language rhetorically suggests that Gentiles approve of living according to human passions. But this surely is not the case. In fact, the Gentiles' blaspheming of Christians in 4:4 assumes a disapproval of people who live "according to human desires." Thus the rhetoric of 4:4 is ironic. First Peter says to the Gentiles that their criticism of Christians amounts to an approval of life dominated by the passions. The argument assumes that Gentiles would not want to be giving their approval to such a life.

The brief vice list is unusual in its focus. Vice lists (and virtue lists) typically include diverse and wide-ranging topics (See, e.g., Wis 14:25–27; Sir 7:1–21; Gal 5:19–21; Col 3:5–8; 2 Tim 3:2–4). Their purpose is, more often than not, to evoke every possible aspect of the ethical life. But this list does not do that, and this focus may provide key data about the character of the conflict between Christians and their Roman neighbors. The sequence of "drunkenness, inebriating feasts, drinking parties" recalls the infamous dining and drinking parties that dominated much of Roman life. Romans and Greeks formed all kinds of associations and clubs for all kind of purposes, ranging from business interests to religious devotion to burial.[25] Almost all of these had religious overtones. In

---

25. See Hans-Josef Klauck, *The Religious Context of Early Christianity: A Guide to Graeco-Roman Religions* (trans. Brian McNeill; Minneapolis: Fortress, 2003), 42–54.

fact, *kōmoi*, which is translated here as "inebriating feasts," originally referred to village (*kōmē*) celebrations in honor of Dionysus. Thus, while the accusation of "lawless idolatries" is often used by Christians and Jews as an unspecific charge of vice against Gentiles, in the context of this verse it probably refers to the religious groundings of these public feasts. This suggests that the terms "licentiousness" (*aselgeia*) and "desires" (*epithymiai*), which also can refer to many kinds of vices in many different contexts, in this context refers to the excess reveling of these drinking parties.

While the central social entity in the Greco-Roman world was always the family, these various collegia had grown enormously in social importance in the period of the empire. As the imperial political system grew, the prestige and power of local political systems and political office decreased. These collegia provided needed social glue. They were celebrations and articulations of mutual social, economic, and religious interests. Apparently Christians had ceased to attend them. The syntax of 1 Peter does not give a reason for the decision by Christians not to participate in these groups and their parties. Their reasons were probably complex. These celebrations are portrayed here as being immoral. They are a "pouring out of wastefulness," a giving in to human desires, and a denial of Christian holiness. They were also acts of idolatry since these meals often included homage to gods and goddesses.

It is unlikely that Gentiles would have used the language of 1 Pet 4:3–4 to describe the sudden social withdrawal of the Christians. Though the language of drinking parties and inebriating feasts might have seemed accurate enough, the imagery of wastefulness and lawless idolatry would not have. It is more likely that the slander by Gentiles would have conveyed the same attitude as did the second- and third-century accusations against Christians: harboring hatred of humanity. To withdraw from these crucial groups and events was seen as a rejection of Roman civilization itself, as hatred. These first-century Christians would have agreed, at least in part, with this "slander." They are indeed rejecting Roman society even if they do not hate their neighbors. Unfortunately, we cannot reconstruct precisely what was said or done in this slandering. Nevertheless, the slander was serious enough to inspire 1 Peter's meditations on suffering.

[5] The accusation of "slander" against the Gentiles leads to this announcement of punishment. The Gentiles will give "an account" (*logos*) to the one who will judge all people. In 1 Peter the revelation of God's power "at the last time" (1:5) functions primarily as assurance of salvation and reward for suffering and faithful Christians. Here the imagery is one of threat and punishment. The forensic terminology of giving an account is standard in Jewish and Christian references to final judgment, as is the assertion that this judgment will fall on "the living and the dead." Thus 1 Peter uses accepted Christian notions

Separation from the Gentile Life

of judgment to assert the coming punishment of the Gentiles, who are now slandering the Christians. Christians will have their retribution.

It is not explicit whether Christ or God is the one who will judge. Though Christ is often described as judge in the NT (e.g., Matt 25:31–46; Acts 17:31) and such a role may be implied in 3:22, it is God who is most often the judge, both in the NT and in 1 Peter (1:17; 2:23; 4:17–18). In any case, this verse complicates, in the usual Christian way, God's role in final judgment. In 1:17 and 4:19 that role is to protect and reward Christians. In this verse, God's role is to punish those who abuse Christians. Thus, when Jesus in 2:23 "handed over himself to the one who judges justly," he may have been entrusting to God both his own safety and the punishment of those who abused him.

[6] The exegetical difficulties of this verse have caused more than one reader to conclude that this verse simply defies interpretation. The most striking difficulties are (1) What or who is being proclaimed? (2) Who are the dead? (3) What is the relationship of this verse to 3:19? (4) What is the connection between this verse and what precedes? (5) What is the context and meaning of the judgments in the *hina* clause? None of these questions has a simple solution. And upon none of them is there much agreement.

(1) Since an impersonal use of *euangelizomai* is rare in the NT and since the verb normally takes Jesus as the object, many readers suggest that Jesus is the implied subject. However, the two other occurrences of the verb in 1 Peter suggests that "gospel" is the implied subject. In 1:12 the things (*ha*) about Christ are proclaimed (*euangelisamenōn*) by unspecified people "to you." And in 1:25 it is "the word [*rhēma*] of the Lord" that is proclaimed (*euangelisthen*) "to you." In fact, 1:25 employs a passive participle form of *euangelizomai* with an impersonal subject. First Peter seems to prefer an impersonal use of the verb. Thus it is best to read an imprecise "gospel" as the implied subject.

(2) The question of the identity of "the dead" depends in large part upon the answers to (3) and (4). If this verse is read as referring to the same event as 3:19, and if "for this reason" means that this verse explains how God can judge the dead, then both 3:19 and 4:6 can be read as a classic harrowing of hell. The dead spirits of humans, trapped in hell, hear the good news from Christ, who journeys in the spirit to their prison. Thus both the dead and the living have access to the gospel, and God can thereby judge all people, dead and alive, fairly.

But there are considerable difficulties with such a reading. As noted above, this rendition of 3:19 is difficult to sustain. Furthermore, the point of 4:1–6 does not seem to be that of justifying God's judgment of the Gentiles. Both the reality and probity of this judgment is assumed. The passage functions instead as exhortation and comfort to Christians undergoing abuse from their Gentile neighbors. Thus few modern readers follow this account.

Instead, most readers make a distinction between the events of 3:19 and 4:6 and do not identify "the dead" with "the spirits in prison." Furthermore, "for this reason" is better understood as referring not simply to the necessity for the Gentiles to give an account and thus be judged, but also to the originating call in 4:1–3 for Christians to arm themselves with the same understanding as Christ and to reject the Gentile life. Such a reading coheres not only with the overall context of the passage but also with the concluding imagery. The ultimate purpose of this proclaiming of the gospel to the dead and the coming judgment is that they "might live in the spirit." This concluding positive note, which affirms life as the destiny of the dead, does not fit naturally with the implied threat of 4:5.

This leaves unresolved the question of the identity of the dead. If they are not human spirits imprisoned somewhere in death, who are they? Some readers, including many in the early church, suggest that the dead are the spiritually dead and not the physically dead. But this would require that the dead in 4:5 have no relation to the dead in 4:6. Furthermore, the notion that these dead, by way of God's judgment, end up living in the spirit suggests that these are people who not only hear but also follow the gospel. Thus "the dead" are probably the dead Christians. The issue here may be the same as or similar to that of 1 Thess 4:13–18, which addresses the problem of Christians who have died before the final judgment. Christians, who have heard the gospel and perhaps been abused by Gentiles, have died. This verse affirms that God judges and saves not only the living but also the dead. The force of the gospel is not undone by death.

(5) This message of hope and comfort provides a clue for how to read the curious contrasts of the *hina* clause. The imagery of this clause is without precise parallel in the NT and, consequently, has occasioned much debate. At the center of the debate is the series of contrasts between "judged" and "might live," between "according to human standards" and "according to God's standards," and between "in the flesh" and "in the spirit." The meaning of each phrase depends on the meaning of its opposite. And there are many possibilities. However, much of the sense of this clause depends upon the identity of the dead. If the dead are dead Christians, then a rather straightforward reading emerges. This becomes a brief narrative of the fate of dead Christians.

Since God obviously does not judge "according to human standards," and since it seems unlikely that the point would be that Christians judge each other according to human standards, the reference must be to the Gentiles who are judging Christians when they "slander" them. This means that this judgment is not final judgment or even judgment unto death. Furthermore, in this context, "in the flesh" does not mean "in their sinful selves" but simply "in their mortal lives." Thus the first sequence of the clause asserts that dead Christians in their mortal lives were judged negatively and slandered by the Gentiles according to the standards of the Gentiles. But the second sequence affirms that this is not the end. Ultimately these same Christians will "live in the spirit according to God's standards." The imagery is that of the resurrection. God will bestow life on these dead followers of the gospel.

Readers have long noted the parallel between this clause and 3:18, which describes Jesus as "having been put to death in the flesh, but having been made alive in the spirit." The same historical, cosmic, and theological sequence that constitutes Jesus' death and resurrection constitutes that of all Christians. This parallel reinforces this interpretation of "the dead" and their judgment as referring to dead Christians who will ultimately, in the final judgment, partake of life and glory.

As is typically the case in 1 Peter, this passage (4:1–6) has more than one purpose. It begins with an exhortation to cease from "accomplishing the will of the Gentiles" and living "according to human desires." This plea is anchored christologically. The initial christological anchor is to "arm yourselves with the same understanding" that Christ had. This understanding is narrated in 2:21–24. Jesus models two things. He responds to vice toward himself with virtue toward others; he refuses to meet abuse with abuse. Christians are to do the same toward the Gentiles who are slandering them. Jesus also models trust in God. Jesus "handed over himself to the one who judges justly." Jesus trusts God, as final judge, to effect justice. This claim logically, although not immediately, leads to the second christological anchor. The passage concludes with the affirmation that as Christ was "made alive in the spirit" (3:18), so will Christians "live in the spirit according to God's standards." Thus Christians should trust God as final judge just as Jesus did. There is "an imperishable and undefiled and unfading inheritance, kept in the heavens for you who are being guarded by the power of God through faith for a salvation ready to be revealed at the last time" (1:4–5).

In the midst of this challenge and promise is an exploration of the life of the Gentiles, a life that Christians used to live. The description of the Gentile life focuses not upon day-to-day business or family dynamics or even the Gentile attempt to accomplish virtue, but rather upon the various collegia and their parties. These celebrations are described as occasions of drunkenness, but also as a giving in to human desires, and finally as idolatry. Though this description itself would justify the plea to cease from that life, the passage adds an eschatological warning. People who live this way and slander those who do not will have to give an account to God, who judges all. Thus God's judgment, both as threat and promise, theologically controls this passage. God will punish and reward. The readers are called to live accordingly.

1 Peter 4:7–5:11 The End Is Near

1 Peter 4:7–11 Love within the Community

Almost all readers see this wonderful compendium of early Christian ethics as providing a transitional moment in the letter. The question is whether this passage functions more as conclusion to what precedes or as introduction to what follows. The echoes of 2:11–12, its general feel of a summary, and its concluding doxology lead some readers to understand this passage as the conclusion of a rhetorical piece that begins in 2:11 and ends here. However, most readers detect a change in subject matter from a focus on communal suffering amid abuse by outsiders to a focus on the community's internal life. Furthermore, the announcement that "the end of all has drawn near" inaugurates a focus on eschatology that continues until the end of the letter. Consequently, these readers see this passage as the beginning of the concluding section of the letter, which focuses on internal communal life in the context of final judgment. Of the two readings, the latter is more appropriate.

The ethical imagery of these verses has numerous, in fact almost countless, parallels to other Christian texts. However, there is no suggestion of direct literary dependence on any single text. First Peter is not citing other texts but is speaking from the rich fund of early Christian ethical tradition. The virtues of self-control, love, hospitality, and service are central not only to 1 Peter but also to most of early Christianity.

> 4:7 The end of all[a] has drawn near. Therefore, be self-controlled[b] and be sober for prayers. 8 Above all keeping[c] your love for one another intense,[d] because love covers[e] a multitude of sins. 9 Be hospitable[c] to one another without grumbling. 10 Let each person, as each has received a gift, serve[c] it to one another, as excellent[f] stewards[g] of God's varied[h] grace. 11 If someone speaks, speak as if speaking[i] the oracles[j] of God; if someone serves, serve[c] as if serving out of the power that God supplies,[k] so that in everything God might be glorified through Jesus Christ, to whom[l] is the glory and the power forever and ever. Amen.

a. While it is possible to read "all" (*pantōn*) as referring to all people, so that the phrase becomes a warning that everyone will in time die and thus should do the following, it is much easier to read the "all" as an eschatological "all things" or "all ages."

b. Although the two imperatives *sōphronēsate* and *nēpsate* could function as a hendiadys governed by the prepositional phrase "for prayer," giving the reading of "be self-controlled and sober for prayers," the weight of the verb *sōphroneō* suggests separating the verbs. The verb *sōphroneō* is difficult to translate. It has the sense of maintaining balance, exercising sound judgment, keeping moderation, and being self-controlled. The noun *sōphrosynē* was often named as the virtue that balances the other virtues.

Love within the Community 127

c. In the unusual but consistent syntactical style of 1 Peter (cf. 2:18; 3:1, 7, 8), this passage has an opening imperative that gives imperatival force to the various clauses that follow. The participles in vv. 8 (*echontes*) and 10 (*diakonountes*), along with the adjective (*philoxenoi*) in v. 9, derive their imperatival force from v. 7. The elided syntax of v. 11 requires the implied imperatives to "speak" and to "serve" in order to make any sense.

d. The adjective *ektenē* can modify the noun "love," producing the translation "maintain fervent love for one another." However, the article *tēn* before *agapēn* suggests that the adjective is predicative. The word *ektenē* can mean "constant," but its basic and more common meaning is "intense."

e. Some key texts ($\mathfrak{P}^{72}$, א, P) read the future *kalypsei* instead of the present *kalyptei*, thereby emphasizing the sense of final judgment. The occurrence of the present tense in *1 Clem.* 49.5 and *2 Clem.* 16.4, which may be quoting 1 Peter, along with a possible scribal assimilation with Jas 5:20, give support to the present tense.

f. The adjective *kalos* is often equivalent to *agathos* (good) but has more the sense of public good, of the communal ideal. It can mean "beautiful," "proper," or "noble." Here it has the sense of being "honorable" or "excellent" in the performing of public duty.

g. An *oikonomos* was typically a slave who managed the household, but the term is also used for a variety of public officials, especially those responsible for public goods, such as food or money. The term here probably combines the sense of "household servant" with that of a "steward" assigned to care for goods of the house.

h. The adjective *poikilē* literally means "many-colored" or "spotted." Here it has the more metaphorical meaning of "various" or "diverse."

i. In the typical elliptical style of ancient Greek, the verse actually says, "If someone speaks, as the oracles of God; if someone serves, as out of the power that God supplies."

j. While *logia* can mean simply "sayings," in religious contexts, whether Christian or not, it has the sense of sacred "oracles." Grammatically, *logia* could be nominative, giving the sense of the oracles of God speaking through the speaker. It is more likely that it is accusative, yielding the sense that the speaker speaks the oracles of God.

k. The verb *chorēgeō*, which originally meant "supply or pay for a chorus on stage," in later usage came to mean "to supply or pay for anything." Its echoes of patronage make it an appropriate term for God supplying the needs of God's household.

l. The antecedent to *hō* could be Jesus Christ, since the NT has other doxologies to Jesus (2 Pet 3:18). However, given the context of glorifying God, the likely referent is God.

[4:7] The threat and promise of judgment in 4:1–6 is continued here but more in the sense of a reminder of urgency and duty. The phrase "the end of all has drawn near" is unique to 1 Peter in early Christianity. However, the concept is common and almost universal. Most of early Christianity shares a belief in an impending cosmic day of the Lord. Unlike some Christian texts, 1 Peter gives few hints about the precise sequence of this coming judgment. The only "sign" might be the suggestion in 4:17 that the suffering of Christians is the beginning of God's final judgment. The "all" that is coming to an end is probably, in light of 1:20 and perhaps 4:11, all the ages (cf. 1 Cor 10:11). It is historical time, not the cosmos, that is ending. The perfect *ēngiken* (has drawn near) conveys a sense of urgency and necessity without giving a precise date or sequence. Most early Christian eschatological imagery displays this same tension and balance. Furthermore, the reminder of an impending end functions here, as it does in the rest of 1 Peter and in most of early Christianity, as a provocation for ethical living.

The opening imperative "be self-controlled" uses a term with a long and significant history in Greek ethics. As noted above, the verb *sōphroneō* is difficult to translate because it has so many connotations. This semantic range makes the word ideal as an opening description of the Christian ethical life. Nearly everyone in the Roman Empire, Christian and non-Christian, would aspire to living in accord with this virtue. The context of drinking parties (4:3) and sobriety for prayer suggests that the nuance of *sōphroneō* in this verse would be that of balance and self-control. Christians are being reminded to control themselves. In the same way, the call to "be sober for prayers" recalls the insobriety and idolatry of their former lives (4:3). In contrast to a time when they were living according to the will of the Gentiles, Christians should control themselves and pray in perfect sobriety. This is a rejection of the Dionysian model of religion.[26] Christian worship is not ordered by the insanity of drunkenness, and the God who judges all is not praised thereby. Christian worship is ordered by moderation and is offered with complete control of the mind and body.

[8] The fact that an exhortation to love one another is standard in early Christian ethics does not mean that this imperative to love is merely formal. The language here recalls that of 1:22: "Love one another intensely [*ektenōs*] from a pure heart." There is no attempt to define or even describe precisely what love is or what it means to keep your love intense, suggesting thereby that 1 Peter is evoking the accepted language of the community. The syntax assumes larger conversations about love in the community. In accord with the distinction in 2:17, wherein Christians are called to honor outsiders, including the emperor, and to love the community (*adelphotēta*), love in this verse is for "one another." Love assumes a vulnerability that is not appropriate for one's enemies. This version of love is in some disagreement with that of the Sermon on the Mount (Matt 5:44).

The meaning of the theological proverb "Love covers a multitude of sins" is not obvious. It is not clear whose sins are covered and what it means to "cover" sins. If it is the sins of the one doing the loving, then to cover sins means to have them forgiven. Thus Christians are called to love because God is then more inclined to forgive them their sins. We love others in order to obtain forgiveness from God. If it is the sins of the one being loved, then to cover sins means to forgive sins in others. Thus the proverb reminds Christians that love is not

---

26. Thomas H. Carpenter and Christopher A. Faraone, eds., *Masks of Dionysus* (Myth and Poetics; Ithaca, N.Y.: Cornell University Press, 1993).

directed toward those who deserve it but toward sinners. We love others in spite of their sins. In some ways, it is difficult to avoid either of these readings. The syntax of the verse produces both. Furthermore, such tension over the purpose of love is normal in early Christianity and is perhaps inherent in love itself. In any case, this verse insists that love for another is essential to the Christian life, probably for both the character of the community and the individuals in it.

[9] Hospitality was seen as an essential virtue throughout the ancient Mediterranean world. It was an almost sacred duty for both Greeks and Jews, the violation of which pollutes the whole community. Hospitality is normally construed as the act of offering shelter, food, and protection to strangers. However, the hospitality enjoined here is not to strangers but "to one another" (*eis allēlous*). This limitation of hospitality to members of the community parallels the same limitation on love, although it is more unusual in that it violates one of the essential aspects of ancient hospitality. Early Christianity became famous for its hospitality to strangers, as long as those strangers professed Christianity. It is possible that this is an admonition about traveling Christians. However, it seems more likely that the verse is concerned that the community behave as a single household. To be hospitable to one another would mean to offer the comfort and protection of each house to every member of the Christian community. The note to do so without grumbling reflects the ongoing trouble and burden of welcoming visitors in one's home. Perhaps the prevalent early Christian concern that no member of the community be left in need is being recalled here.

[10] The obvious echoes of 1 Cor 12:4–11 and Rom 12:6–8 do not indicate direct literary dependence but a sharing of common ethical terminology. Paul, for instance, connects the imagery of multiple gifts (*charismata*) to the image of the body and its many members. First Peter, on the contrary, retains its focus on the household, so that the various gifts become forms of service in the household. First Peter appears to assume a diversity of gifts and then to exhort individuals on how to serve one another out of this diversity. Thus the grammatical shift to the singular "each" does not signal a shift to an individual ethic but is, on the contrary, an attempt to subsume this diversity of gifts under the same duty.

Although the origin of these gifts is not made explicit, the language and syntax of this verse squares nicely with the theology of Paul. In Rom 12:6 Paul speaks of a "proportion to faith" and of a singular grace (*charis*) that results in different (*diaphora*) and plural gifts (*charismata*). This sequence coheres with 1 Peter's imagery of a varied (*poikilē*) and singular grace (*charis*). This grace results in a gift (*charisma*) to each person in the household. It is not clear whether persons receive more than one gift. The exhortation in this verse, which assumes this theological sequence, calls on each person to serve (*diakoneō*) that gift "to one another" and to do so as excellent stewards (*kaloi oikonomoi*) of

God's grace. Early Christianity's fondness for the verb *diakoneō* and its noun equivalents, *diakonos* and *diakonia*, along with its wide usage in non-Christian Greek, makes precise translation difficult. The root *diakon-* in itself does not automatically connote selfless service or even domestic service. The word simply means "to serve" and can be used in a variety of contexts. Thus its ethical force is derived from the character of the relationship in which it occurs and the content of the deed.

The context of this call to service is the familiar 1 Peter image of the household of God (2:5; 4:17; cf. 2:18–25). Normally a given household has one steward, who manages the goods of the house. In 1 Peter each member of the household is named as a steward because each has received a gift (*charisma*). This gift, however, does not belong to the one who has received it. It is destined for the good of the house, for "one another." Furthermore, these gifts come from God, from God's grace. God's varied, perhaps even multicolored, grace creates multiple gifts and many stewards. Furthermore, God maintains a claim on these gifts that determines not only the destiny of these gifts but also, as the next verse makes clear, the character of the service that offers them.

[11] The Pauline diversity of gifts (*charismata*) is not detailed here. While 1 Cor 12:7–11 lists nine gifts and Rom 12:6–8 lists seven, 1 Peter only names speech and service, neither of which may be a specific gift. Nevertheless, the language of 4:10 suggests the presence in the household of different and diverse unnamed gifts. First Peter assumes awareness of such gifts in the community and focuses not upon naming them, but upon their origin and the attitude with which they are to be served. The phrase "if someone speaks" probably does not refer to a specific *charisma* but includes any gift that involves speaking. The same is probably the case with the phrase "if someone serves." The reference may be to any gift, since all gifts, in the language of 4:10, involve service. The emphasis is upon the attitude of the server or the character of the service.

The first admonition is that, if one speaks, one should speak as if speaking the oracles of God. Since the phrase "oracles of God" (*logia theou*) could refer to almost any form of divine revelation, there is little limitation on the setting or content of this speaking. The point seems to be that when people speak in the household of God, they speak not their own words but sacred words that belong to and come from God. The same point is reinforced in regard to service. When serving in the household of God, people are to do so not out of their own power, but "out of the power that God supplies." Both the gifts of the community and the capacity to administer those gifts come not from the inherent virtues of the individuals but from God. People are not to be praised for their gifts because these gifts do not come from them or belong to them. They come from God and belong to others.

Thus the brief doxology reinforces this account of the gifts of the household of God. The proper response to the blessings of these gifts is not to praise one another but to praise the God who supplies and empowers these gifts. The doxology is similar in form and content to many other early Christian doxologies. The combination of "glory" (*doxa*) and "power" (*kratos*) occurs also in Rev 1:6, but the combination in 1 Peter probably comes from the general themes of the preceding verses. The idea of glorifying God through good works is common in the NT and early Christianity (e.g., 1 Cor 6:20; 10:31) and is a central theme of 1 Peter (2:12; 4:16).

In the midst of a series of comments about mistreatment and abuse from outsiders, the author inserts these exhortations (4:7–11) designed to support life within the household of God. The shift in focus can be read as an understandable plea to a beleaguered community: even if others are treating them badly, they can treat one another well. These exhortations also make a crucial theological point. In the imagery of 1:4–5, God has not only destined Christians for an inheritance in the heavens; God is also protecting Christians now. God protects in part by supplying the virtues and gifts for a loving Christian household. Thus glory belongs not only to Christians who persevere (1:7; 5:1, 4, 10) but also to God, who protects and rewards (2:12; 4:11, 16).

While the language and imagery of these verses are typical and common in early Christianity, these exhortations are fundamental to the theology of 1 Peter. Christians are called to the holy life, and they are challenged to emulate the behavior of Jesus. They do this not only by practicing the virtues of love, hospitality, and service, but also by recognizing that God is the source of all such communal gifts. In 4:1–3 these Christians were challenged to cease from sin and to live according to "the will of God." These verses sketch such a life. They read almost as a reminder. Thus it is likely that larger and familiar ethical conversations are evoked in these brief allusions.

1 Peter 4:12–19 Suffering as Judgment

Readers of 1 Peter have long detected a rhetorical, and perhaps even historical, shift in 4:12. Some readers have even argued that 4:12–5:11 is a disorganized collection of mismatched material written at a later time and then added, more or less awkwardly, to the rest of the letter. It is pointed out that 4:11 contains a concluding doxology and that the address "beloved" signals the beginning of a new section, as it does in 2:11. It is further argued that the view of suffering has shifted. While most of 1 Peter only assumes the potential for suffering, this section not only declares its reality but also looks back on it.

However, such a theory is both unlikely and unnecessary. And these days few readers of 1 Peter detect a radical rhetorical or historical break. It may be pointed out, to the contrary, that doxologies in the NT occur in many contexts, not just at the end of the letter. Furthermore, the doxology in 4:11 emerges from the immediate context of the enumeration of communal gifts. It does not signal the end of a letter. The address "beloved" does not indicate the beginning of a new letter, but just as in 2:11, it inaugurates a personal appeal. Finally, there is no real evidence of any shift in either the historical context of suffering or the letter's attitude to it. While 1:6; 3:14, 17 do refer to suffering by way of conditional clauses, this is rhetorical and not historical. The rest of 1 Peter treats suffering, both rhetorically and historically, as though it is presently occurring in the community. Nowhere, including this passage, does 1 Peter detail the precise character of this suffering.

The issue then becomes what kind of shift occurs here. The tendency among recent readers is to see 4:12–5:11 as the conclusion or even the climax of the letter, but it is hard to know precisely what this means. This section certainly does not summarize or even rehearse (in the classic form of a *peroratio*) the preceding. If a climax is the most forceful rhetorical moment in an argument or even the ultimate destination of an argument, then these verses are not a climax. In some ways these verses simply mark another discussion of the central theme of the letter, the reality of suffering for being a Christian. If there is a shift, it lies mostly in the theological categories that are used to address the question. Most of the letter thinks christologically about suffering. Jesus is the epitome and paradigm of all Christian suffering. While this passage includes this, it also returns to the initial images of 1:6–7. Suffering is a testing. And this testing is connected to final judgment. Furthermore, this placing of suffering into the context of final judgment returns to the announcement of the end in 4:7. In some ways, this passage flows beautifully from the passage that precedes and can be read as part of a larger meditation on final judgment that begins in 4:7.

> 4:12 Beloved, do not be surprised[a] at the burning[b] among you that is coming upon you for a test[c] as though something strange[a] were happening to you; 13 but, as you share in the sufferings of Christ, rejoice so that you may also rejoice with exultation[d] at the revelation of his glory. 14 If[e] you are insulted[f] in[g] the name of Christ, you are blessed because the Spirit of glory and of God[h] is resting upon you.[i] 15 But let none of you suffer as a murderer or thief or evildoer or as a mischief-maker.[j] 16 But if as a Christian, let that one not be ashamed, but let that one glorify God in this name.[k] 17 For it is time for judgment to begin with the house of God; and if first with us, what will be the end of those who disobey the gospel of God?
>
> 18 And if the righteous person is scarcely[l] saved,
>   where will the impious and sinful person appear?
>
> 19 So then,[m] may those who are suffering in accordance with the will of God entrust[n] their lives[o] to the faithful Creator by doing good.[p]

Suffering as Judgment

a. "Do not be surprised" (*mē xenizesthe*) and "strange" (*xenou*) come from the same Greek root (*xen-*). This play on words cannot be adequately reproduced in English although the connection between surprise and something strange is common enough.

b. Since the word *pyrōsis* can refer to all kinds of burning in all kinds of contexts, here it is given the neutral translation "burning." However, in 1 Peter it is connected in both this verse and 1:7 to a burning that tests and refines.

c. In 1:7 the fire of suffering is connected with *dokimazō*, which means to test or to prove by means of testing. Here the fire of suffering is connected with *peirasmos*, which can refer to temptation as well as testing.

d. The present participle *agalliōmenoi* (lit., exulting) modifies and thus intensifies the verb "rejoice." The same root is used in 1:6 in the same context.

e. The grammatical structure here is that of a simple condition, which indicates nothing positive or negative about the reality of the condition. However, 1 Peter has a tendency to use simple conditions as real conditions (cf., 2:19, 20; 4:11, 16). Thus, "if" (*ei*) can be read almost as "when."

f. The verb *oneidizō* means "reproach" or "insult." Joined with *katalaleō* ("slander," 2:12; 3:16), *loidoreō* ("abuse," 2:23), *loidoria* ("abuse," 3:9), *epēreazō* ("slander," 3:16), and *blasphēmeō* ("slander," 4:4), the word conveys a sense of public, verbal abuse.

g. Though it is possible that the lack of the definite article before Christ permits a causative reading of *en* ("because of Christ"), the wide range of meanings of the Greek dative suggests that "in the name of Christ" probably has the same basic meaning as *hōs Christianos* (as a Christian) in 4:16.

h. The awkwardness of the grammar (lit., "the of glory and the of-God Spirit is resting upon you") creates uncertainty as to what modifies what. The simplest explanation is to see one Spirit with the two modifiers "of glory" and "of God."

i. Several later texts (P, Ψ, 𝔐) add "for them, it is to be slandered, but for you, it is to be glorified."

j. The numerous textual variants seem to be attempts to comprehend the otherwise unknown Greek word *allotriepiskopos*. These variants attempt different spellings and different divisions of the word into its roots. The word *allotriepiskopos* is apparently composed of *allotrios* and *episkopos*, which etymologically should mean something like "overseer of another person's affairs." While we do not have exact parallels in ancient literature to this word, the partial parallels we do have suggest either the rather benign meaning of a busybody, a meddler in the affairs of others, a "mischief-maker," or a more egregious meaning of one who defrauds others. Of the two, the more benign "mischief-maker" has the better parallels in meaning.

k. The phrase "in [*en*] this name" is usually read as referring to a state or condition, thus meaning something like "by virtue of bearing this name." This is a common meaning of *en*, and the later and pervasive textual variant "in this respect [*merei*]" suggests that some scribes read the phrase this way. However, *en* often has an instrumental use both in the NT and in 1 Peter. In this reading, Christians, accused of being Christian, would ironically glorify God by means of the name itself. The accusation would become an honor. Nevertheless, it is more likely that *en* has its common referent of state or condition and that the phrase has the same meaning as the phrase "as a Christian" at the beginning of the verse.

l. The scarceness affirmed here obviously does not refer to some inadequacy in the blessings of salvation but to the difficulty in attaining that salvation. The adverb *molis*, which means "scarcely" or "hardly," is a later form of the more common *mogis*. The noun *mogos* means "toil" and "trouble." Thus, *molis* probably has the connotation of "with toil and pain."

m. The *kai* in the opening phrase *hōste kai* could be connected either with the participle "those who are suffering" or with the imperative "may [they] entrust," adding the adverbial emphasis "also." Such a reading produces an awkward connection to the rest of the passage. Thus it is best to read *kai* with *hōste* with the meaning "so then" or "therefore."

n. The verb *paratithēmi* means to deposit something of value with someone for safekeeping. The noun *parathēkē* is used in the Pastorals (1 Tim 6:20; 2 Tim 1:14) to refer to the apostolic tradition that has been entrusted to Timothy, for him to guard.

o. In 1 Peter the noun *psychē* refers to a person's life or their entire selves, not just "souls."

p. The prepositional phrase *en agathopoiia* can be the temporal "while doing good" or the instrumental "by doing good." The overall context slightly favors the latter.

[4:12] The personal address "beloved," both here and in 2:11, is seen by many readers as indicating the beginning of a new section of the letter. But it is hard to know how far this slight change in voice should carry. It is not clear that 2:11–4:11 and 4:12–5:11 are distinct sections. The address fits in both places with the personal and even delicate character of the appeal. "Beloved" echoes nicely in the context of suffering.

Given the christological foundations of suffering that the letter has already detailed, an appeal not to be surprised at the "burning among you" seems unnecessary. Suffering has already been established as an essential aspect of belonging to Christ. The language of being surprised at suffering and of suffering as something strange suggests the extent of theological difficulty that suffering was creating. Obviously, few people became Christian just in order to suffer. Furthermore, while Jews were well acquainted with the notion of suffering for their beliefs, this is less common in Gentile circles. Gentiles certainly knew about suffering on behalf of a cause. However, in most Greco-Roman religious narratives, suffering is a sign that something is broken in one's relationship to the gods.

The imagery of suffering as a burning whose purpose is to test is familiar to most Jews and will become familiar to most early Christians. It is apparently becoming familiar to the Gentile Christian readers of 1 Peter. Thus 1:7 uses the analogy of gold, which is tested and proved by fire. This suffering is couched in 1:6 as possible but not necessary. As the letter proceeds, however, suffering is treated as being essential to the Christian life. The christological core of this necessity is expressed nicely in 2:21: "Christ also suffered for you, thus leaving for you a pattern, so that you might follow in his footsteps." In 4:12 suffering as a Christian is not only essential; it is also a test, perhaps even a temptation. At

Suffering as Judgment

this point in 1 Peter, the burning of suffering connects the person to Christ and demonstrates the genuineness (1:7) of a person's faith. However, in this passage the burning of Christian suffering will be connected to the fire of final judgment.

[13] This call to rejoice in suffering is the centerpiece of the passage. It combines the language of present rejoicing in suffering while anticipating eschatological glory (1:6–7) with the language of suffering as Jesus suffered (2:20–21; 3:17–18). It combines these in such a way as to emphasize not only the necessity of Christian suffering but also the necessity of rejoicing in that suffering. Instead of being surprised over suffering, they should rejoice. In fact, rejoicing "at the revelation of his glory" seems to depend not simply on whether one suffered as a Christian but whether one rejoiced in that suffering.

The language of sharing (*koinōneō*) in the suffering of Christ evokes less the sense of participation in the being of Christ and more the sense of repeating Christ's suffering. The logic of 2:21 is in place here. Christ left "for you a pattern, so that you might follow in his footsteps." The suffering of Christ does not eliminate suffering; it creates even more suffering. To repeat this suffering is cause for rejoicing, both now and in the future.

This future rejoicing will occur "at the revelation of his glory." It is not precisely clear what this means. By itself the phrase could refer to Jesus' present status of sitting at the right hand of God "with the angels and authorities and powers being made subject to him" (3:22). However, in light of the imagery of judgment in 4:18–19, this revelation of glory is most likely eschatological. Furthermore, this reading coheres with the use of the term *apokalyptō* in 1:5, where this revelation happens explicitly "at the last time."

Thus this passage rearticulates the logic of 2:19–20, wherein unjust suffering accrues credit (*kleos, charis*) with God. To this logic is added this notion of rejoicing. In 2:20 this imagery of suffering while doing good is contrasted with suffering while sinning. Jesus' refusal to return abuse for abuse is then presented as the model for how to endure suffering. A similar contrast will be played out in the following verses.

[14] The verse opens with a beatitude that is reminiscent not only of the earlier beatitude in 3:14 but also of Jesus' beatitude, found in the Sermon on the Mount (Matt 5:11) and the Sermon on the Plain (Luke 6:22). Each piece of the blessing is crucial. People are pronounced blessed not simply when they are publicly abused but also when they are insulted "in the name of Christ." The positive content of what it means to be "in the name of Christ" is not made explicit. Apart from the general imagery of doing good in 4:19 (cf. 2:20; 3:13), the content will be established by way of the negatives in 4:15. It is likely that the withdrawal from drunken revelry that is detailed 4:3–4 is still in place. Thus the abuse from non-Christians seems to arise not from any negative public behavior, not even from a refusal to worship the gods (of which nothing is said in 1 Peter). Christians are abused mostly for what they are not. Somehow they are perceived as not quite Roman anymore. This lack of provocation is essential. Neither vice nor provocative attempts to convert others (3:1, 15–16) can occasion abuse that leads to divine blessing. Only a peculiarly Jesus-like suffering, the suffering of a silent wife (3:1), warrants a beatitude.

Beatitudes in Judaism, the New Testament, and early Christianity tend to bless people who do not appear to be blessed.[27] Thus they often provide an explanation for why such an apparently unblessed person is actually blessed. The beatitude in 3:14 does not include a specific explanation for why suffering "on account of righteousness" results in a blessing, although the larger context suggests several reasons. The beatitude in 4:14, however, does offer a specific explanation. The explanation appears to be a modification of the Septuagint version of Isaiah 11:2, which promises that the spirit of the Lord will rest upon the root of Jesse. The citation is a bit too loose and clipped for 1 Peter to be asserting that Isaiah's prophecy is being fulfilled in the suffering of the Christian community. The argument seems simpler. The spirit of God is present when a person suffers as a Christian, and that spirit connects the one who is suffering to God's glory.

[15] This verse depends grammatically and logically upon the preceding. It creates an exclusion to the gracious blessing on those who suffer. Not all suffering warrants a blessing. Given the contrast in 2:20, where "doing good" is contrasted with "sinning," and in 3:17, where "doing good" is contrasted with "doing bad," this abbreviated vice list may simply function to evoke the opposite of "doing good." It is unlikely, for instance, that there is a pressing problem with murder or theft, although the constant warnings in early Christianity about abuse of money suggest that a problem with theft is at least possible. In any case, the use of the catchall term "evildoer" (*kakopoios*) reinforces the feeling of this list as a general warning about bad deeds of any kind.

However, the unusual term *allotriepiskopos* ("mischief-maker" or "busybody") raises the possibility that a specific problem is being addressed. A mischief-maker, someone who meddles in the affairs of others, would exacerbate the already-tense relations with outsiders. The social context implied in 2:12; 3:16; and 4:4 is still in place. Christians are being slandered by their neighbors. Any "bad" behavior that creates negative perceptions in the surrounding non-Christian community must be avoided, whether that behavior is of the flagrant kind, such as murder or theft, or just an irritating messing in the affairs of others. It is probably important that there is nothing peculiarly Christian about this list. Both Christians and non-Christians would agree that these are bad behaviors.

[16] The positive contrast to the negative in 4:15 does not offer a corresponding list of positive behavior but simply invokes the name "Christian." The elided verb in the phrase "but if as a Christian" is probably "suffer" of

---

27. See survey in Betz, *Sermon on the Mount*, 91–105.

4:15 and not "abused" of 4:14. The suffering in 1 Peter appears mostly to take the form of verbal abuse. In any case, the word "Christian" is striking because it is so rare in the NT. According to Acts 11:26, the first use of the term "Christian" was in Antioch. Though it is possible that the Acts account could be read as Christians calling themselves "Christians," it is more likely that it is a term used by outsiders. The Latin, rather than Greek, inflection of *Christianos* suggests that term came from the Romans. It would have been unlikely that Jews would have bestowed the messianic name on this renegade sect. In any case, the pattern of naming a group after its leader or founder is common in the ancient Mediterranean. Finally, the name "Christian," at least early on, appears to have mostly negative connotations. Herod's lament in Acts 26:28, "Are you so quickly persuading me to become a Christian," illustrates the pejorative force of the word.

Thus it is possible that the readers of 1 Peter are being called "Christian" as an act of ridicule. The word would be an instance of the abuse and ridicule to which 1 Peter constantly refers (2:12, 13; 3:9, 14, 16; 4:4). Whether the name is being used publicly this way or not, this verse seems to assume its pejorative force while working to rehabilitate the name. First, the verse nods to the real possibility that public ridicule, perhaps even the name "Christian" itself, is a cause for shame (*aischynē*). In short time the accusation of being a "Christian" will carry the threat of death. Such a legal threat does not seem to be in place at this point. The name or the ridicule that goes with the name occasions shame rather than death. Shame is not simply a personal feeling, although it certainly includes that; it also involves loss of social status. Shame, in the ancient Mediterranean world, has more to do with disgrace, public dishonor, than with bad feelings.[28] Given the description of suffering as a "test" in 4:12 and the occasional Christian use of "shame" as denial of faith (e.g., Mark 8:38), it seems likely that the public ridicule and loss of social status that Christians are experiencing is tempting some to abandon their Christian convictions.

In some ways, the opposite of shame (*aischynē*) is glory (*doxa*). To have glory is to have status and the praise that goes with it. To have shame is to lose status and to have the ridicule that goes with such. It is striking that readers are called not to be ashamed but to "glorify [*doxazetō*] God in this name." Thus the call to "glorify God" has two edges. First, readers should not give in to shame over the name "Christian" but take glory in it. The name "Christian" is one of high status, not low. Second, these Christians who are tempted to deny their faith should instead give glory to God. While the phrase "glorify God" can refer to all kinds of specific deeds, it must include here claiming the name "Christian" and the behavior that goes with it.

---

28. See survey in Jerome H. Neyrey, *Honor and Shame in the Gospel of Matthew* (Louisville, Ky.: Westminster John Knox Press, 1998), 14–34.

[17–18] While most of this passage reworks, in a creative way, ideas and images that are common in 1 Peter, these verses offer two new ideas. Both of them are rather stunning. First, now is the time of final judgment. Judaism and early Christianity both extensively explore the relationship between the present, especially present suffering and trial, and final judgment. In both traditions the connections between present judgment and final judgment are so complex as to defy categorization. Nevertheless, 1 Peter has an unusual and perhaps even unique way of describing the connection. Present suffering—the abuse and ridicule of the community by outsiders, which tempts, tests, and refines the community—is the first act of final judgment. It is not simply that this test will issue in a favorable report on the final day; this test is the final-day test.

Second, final judgment begins with "the house of God" (*ho oikos tou theou*). This idea is certainly not unique to 1 Peter. The prophets often speak of God's judgment falling first on the people of Israel (e.g., Isa 10:11–12; Jer 32:29). In fact, readers have often pointed to Ezek 9:6 as the source of 1 Peter's imagery. Ezekiel 9 is a call by the Lord to the "executioners of the city" (9:1) to "pass through the city . . . and kill" (9:5) everyone without the saving mark. In the Hebrew text it is clear that they are to begin this slaughter with the sanctuary or at least at the sanctuary (9:6). But the Septuagint is less clear, giving an ambiguous *apo tōn hagiōn* (either "from the holy places" or "from the holy ones"). In both Greek and Hebrew, "the house" is the primary setting for this punishment. This raises the question of whether "house of God" in this verse refers to the temple or to the people of God. Both the uncertainty of the influence of the Ezekiel passage on 1 Peter and the clear use of the house imagery in 1 Pet 2:5 as referring to people makes it quite unlikely that a specific reference to the temple is in place here. The force of naming people as "the house of God" depends on echoes of the temple.

Unlike Ezekiel and Revelation, where the righteous or the elect are marked and thereby protected from God's wrath, 1 Peter argues that God's initial judgment falls only on the followers of Jesus. While the prophets frequently announced God's focused and singular judgment of Israel, the notion of end-time judgment beginning in the persecution of the righteous by the unrighteous is unusual. This somewhat unexpected and offensive claim is immediately balanced by the announcement of coming judgment on "those who disobey the gospel of God." The verb *apeitheō* is used in 2:8 and 3:1 to refer not just to unbelievers but also to those who behave contrary to the word of God. The "gospel of God" that they disobey does not refer solely to notions of grace and forgiveness but to the whole narrative of Jesus Christ, including the call to holy behavior. Thus these people are not just outsiders or nonbelievers, but the unrighteous, whose unrighteousness probably includes persecution of Christians. In any case, the ultimate justice of God's judgment, which was brought in question to some degree in the insistence that the current persecution of

Christians is engendered by God, is reaffirmed in the suggestion that the suffering of those who disobey will be even worse.

The severity of the coming judgment on those who disobey "the gospel of God" is announced by way of two comparative questions, both of which depend on the unfairness, even seeming injustice, of God's initial judgment falling only upon these Christians. The first states the comparative logic in its simplest form. "If it begins with us, what will be the end of those who disobey . . . ?" This question only has force if the reader is properly troubled by the initial act of God in judging Christians by way of persecution. The second (v. 18), while using the same logic, is an almost precise quote of Prov 11:31 LXX. In some ways Proverbs makes the exact argument of 1 Pet 4:17b but with a slight difference in the terminology of the contrast. The language of "the righteous person" as opposed to "the impious and sinful person" reinforces the emphasis on behavior rather than election. As 1 Peter insists throughout, God "judges without partiality according to the deeds of each person" (1:17). This is both the terror and comfort of God's justice. The advantage of the Christian does not lie in escaping judgment but in the combination of redemption, inheritance, and a pattern of righteousness and holiness, all of which are founded in Christ.

[19] This verse returns to the mood of exhortation with which the passage began. The opening call not to be surprised and the subsequent theological explanation now issue in a more challenging imperative. Those addressed are defined as "those who are suffering in accordance with the will of God." This naming invokes both the affirmation of this passage that the persecution of Christians by their neighbors is actually the beginning of God's judgment and the warning of this passage not to suffer for doing unrighteous deeds. To these quite specifically defined persons, this verse offers two challenges.

First, they are called to entrust their lives to God. This call suggests that persecution has the power to bring into question the reliability of God. It is appropriate that God is named "the faithful Creator" since this term affirms both the power and character of God. In spite of the experience of suffering, this God can be trusted. Thus those who are suffering should entrust their very selves, their whole lives (*tas psychas autōn*), to this faithful creator God. Second, they should do so while or by doing good. As 4:1–6 noted, it is "doing good," as Christians understood it, that sparked the persecution. The ancient Mediterranean was enormously tolerant of diverse religious beliefs, but its social norms were less flexible. Christians, trying to live the Christian life by turning from their past passions and dissipations, alienated and offended their neighbors. The obvious way to avoid trouble is to conform with the behavioral expectations of their non-Christian neighbors. This call to keep doing good requires an enormous trust in God. They must believe that God is both able and faithful. And more than believing, they must keep "doing good" no matter what the social consequences.

The ongoing argument in 1 Peter about suffering and the Christian life takes on a slightly different shape in this passage (4:12–19). The opening call not to be surprised at persecution suggests that these Christians were surprised. Yet any reader of 1 Peter would, by this point in the letter, expect and almost welcome such abuse. The letter has carefully drawn a portrait of Jesus as one who suffers and yet continues to behave righteously. It has also pointed to Jesus' experience of suffering and his behavior in that suffering as a model. There are echoes of this Christology in the claim that "the Spirit of glory and of God" resides on them when they "are insulted in the name of Christ" (4:14). However, this passage focuses more on the claim in 1:6–7 that suffering is a test and even a refinement. This fairly common understanding of suffering as refinement and proof grows in this passage into the striking argument that this suffering is a test, a temptation, that is part of God's final judgment.

Throughout 1 Peter, suffering is not simply an occasional and lamentable addition to the lives of some unlucky Christians; it is, rather, a necessary and inevitable part of the Christian life. To this point, the abuse has been described as originating in the resentment and animosity of non-Christian neighbors. This passage goes further, by building on the common biblical notion that God sends humans to punish God's people. These verses transform that common notion and argue that God is not sending this social abuse in order to punish but in order to test. God is discovering, in the fire of persecution, who they truly are. The temptation is to give in to the abuse and to abandon Christian behavior. Thus the proof that they are gold (1:7) is that they continue "doing good." Simply being a Christian in name does not protect one from God's holiness and judgment. However, being a faithful Christian who lives the holy life connects one to the faithful, creator God and to "an imperishable and undefiled and unfading inheritance, kept in the heavens for you" (1:4).

1 Peter 5:1–5 Elders and Their Flocks

This passage effects a transition common in 1 Peter, moving as it does from comments about relationships with outsiders in 4:12–19 to these comments about relationships among insiders. The focus on elders and young persons recalls the similar shift in 2:18, with its focus on household servants and wives. Even if the beginning transition is obvious enough, it is not clear where this passage ends. Many readers connect the call to humility in verse 5b with the next passage. There are good reasons for this. The call to subjection and humility connects to the call to humility before God in verse 6. The audience shifts in verse 5b as well, moving from an address to the elders and young people to an address to all in the community. However, most readers connect verse 5b with this passage because it forms a fitting rhetorical conclusion and because the call to be humble before God in 5:6 makes an effective beginning to the general exhortation of 5:6–11. Admittedly, there is little at stake in the question of the proper division in the overall meaning of 1 Pet 5 since the whole section is nicely interlaced.

A more difficult question concerns the meaning and context of the word "elders" (*presbyteroi*). In Christian literature, the term can refer either to elderly people in general (in this context almost certainly men) or to a group among the elderly who hold a specific office or play a specific role in the community.[29] Given the discussion of how to tend the flock in verses 2–4, the word here most likely refers to a group of elderly people who have a specific role in the community. However, by itself this tells us little about who they were since 1 Peter tells us almost nothing about the duties of these people, and early Christianity is too diverse in organizational patterns for the term itself to disclose much. All we know for certain is that their role warrants comparison with shepherds and occasions this exhortation.

The form and imagery of this passage has parallels with Paul's speech to the Ephesian elders in Acts 20:17–35 and with exhortations in the Pastorals to bishops (1 Tim 3:1–7; Titus 1:7–9), deacons (1 Tim 3:8–13), and elders (1 Tim 5:17–19; Titus 1:5–6). In all of these exhortations, little is said about the specific duties of these people, probably because ancient readers all knew what they were. Instead, the focus is on the ethic and attitude with which the duties are carried out.

> **5:1** Therefore, the elders[a] among you I exhort, I who am a fellow elder and witness[b] of the sufferings of Christ, who am also one who shares[c] in the glory that is about to be revealed: **2** Shepherd the flock of God that is in your midst,[d] exercising oversight[e] not under compulsion but willingly in accord with God,[f] and not for shameful gain but eagerly, **3** not as those who dominate[g] their charges[h] but being examples for the flock; **4** and when the chief shepherd is manifested, you will obtain[i] the unfading[j] crown of glory.[k] **5** In the same way, younger people,[l] be subject to the elders. And all of you, clothe yourselves[m] with humility toward one another, because
>
> God opposes the arrogant, but gives grace to the humble.

a. Although the word *presbyteroi* means simply "old men" or "older men," in political contexts it often means "ambassador." In Christian contexts it can have and probably does have here the semitechnical meaning of elderly men who have leadership roles in the community. It is possible, but historically unlikely, that the masculine ending is not gender-specific but refers to elderly people.

---

29. A thorough discussion of elders in early Christianity can be found in R. Alastair Campbell, *The Elders: Seniority in Early Christianity* (Edinburgh: T&T Clark, 1994); and A. E. Harvey, "Elders," *JTS* 25 (1974): 318–32.

b. A *martys* is a person who has seen something and who testifies to it. In the NT it sometimes means "eyewitness" and sometimes "one who bears witness." In later times, it comes to mean "one who confesses Christianity and dies for that confession." Given the context of persecution, some anticipation of that later meaning may be in place here. In any case, the phrase could be translated as "witness of the sufferings" or "one who testifies about the sufferings."

c. The noun *koinōnos* means "sharer," "participant," or "partner."

d. The exact meaning of the dative prepositional phrase *en hymin* is not clear. The dative could express interest or belonging ("the flock that is under your care") or more likely association or distribution ("the flock that is in your midst or around you").

e. The circumstantial participle *episkopountes* is missing in several key manuscripts (ℵ, B). Its omission is perhaps the result of not wanting to confuse the role of elder and bishop (*episkopos*). The weight of the manuscript evidence ($\mathfrak{P}^{72}$, A, P, Ψ, 𝔐) supports its inclusion. The participle could be translated either as agency ("shepherd . . . by exercising oversight") or accompaniment ("shepherd . . . [while] exercising oversight"). Since the content of what follows has more to do with manner of shepherding than with the duties, the participle more likely expresses accompaniment.

f. The prepositional phrase *kata theon* could underline the force of "willingly" in the sense of being willing as God wants, or it could add a qualifying note that oversight must be done "according to the standards of God." Both cohere nicely with the theology of 1 Peter, but the context of 5:1–5, with its emphasis on attitude, makes the former more likely.

g. Although this verse continues the contrast of "not/but," the presence of the circumstantial participle *katakyrieuontes* connects the verse back to the original imperative "shepherd" (v. 2). Thus elders are called to shepherd, but not in a domineering manner. While the verb *kyrieuō* can mean simply to "rule," the prefixed preposition *kata* makes the ruling negative and even violent.

h. The noun *klēros* means "lot" or "that which is assigned by lot." In early Christianity it was often used to refer to ecclesiastical office. If that is the meaning here, the elders are being admonished not to be domineering in their assignment of office. Since *klēros* can refer to people (see Deut 9:29 LXX) and the syntax of 1 Peter parallels *klēros* with flock, the plural *klēroi* probably refers to groups of people that are assigned to the care of various elders.

i. The future middle form *komieisthe* has the sense of acquiring for oneself.

j. The adjective *amarantinon* (unfading) is probably derived from the flower of that name proverbial for not fading.

k. The genitive "of glory" is best read as epexegetical, in which the crown is a sign of glory and honor. In the ancient Mediterranean a crown (*stephanos*) came in many forms and was used in many contexts. Thus there is no way from the word itself to know what kind of crown is envisioned.

l. Though the basic meaning of the term *neōteroi* (younger people) is clear enough, it has proved difficult to determine the exact composition of "younger people." It could mean "young people" as opposed to old people (elders). However, the term "elders" suggests not just age but also role. It is unlikely that "young people," in parallel to the "elders," refers to a fixed group with designated roles. Thus it is easiest to see "young

Elders and Their Flocks

people" as a rather imprecise way to designate a loose configuration of those young in faith and young in age.

m. The imperative *enkombōsasthe* has an etymological connection to the noun *enkombōma*, an apron worn by slaves, and so conveys the sense of tying on an apron in preparation for service.

[5:1] The force of the conjunction "therefore" probably lies in the pervasiveness of the call to do good. The obligation to live in the footsteps of Christ is in place not only when enduring persecution but also when living in the Christian community. More difficult is the question of who these "elders" are and why they are addressed at this point in the letter. The term *presbyteros* was used by Greeks in many settings to refer not simply to the elderly but also to the elderly who had acquired a certain leadership status and who were due appropriate honor.[30] In synagogues, ancient Jews used the term to designate a formal group of leaders (e.g., 1 Macc 11:23; 12:35). This synagogue pattern is repeated, and perhaps even borrowed, by early Christian communities. In the NT, when the term is used of Christians in churches, it seems to refer to a specific office or role (see, e.g., Acts 20:17; 1 Tim 5:17–19; Titus 1:5; 2 John 1; 3 John 1). However, it is never made clear in the NT what that role is. It is probably misleading to import later Christian organizational hierarchies into the NT times. Thus the only real data we have about the role of these elders in 1 Peter emerges from the instructions in 1 Pet 2–4.

The imagery of 1 Peter suggests a loose organizational structure at best. A specific office seems unlikely. The call to shepherd the flock suggests the ancient Mediterranean pattern of giving honor and responsibility to the elderly in the community. It is, nevertheless, unclear why they are addressed at this point in the letter. Early Christian letters, including those in the NT, often end with a series of admonitions to different people in the community. This fits that pattern. Furthermore, the discussion in 4:12–19 of tension with outsiders issues naturally in the call for harmony and good order in the community itself.

"Fellow elder" (*sympresbyteros*) is an unexpected term to be used for the apostle Peter. Nowhere else in the NT is Peter called "elder," much less "fellow elder." In 1 Pet 1:1 he is named apostle, not elder. The term *sympresbyteros* seems to place Peter on the same status as the elders in these communities. Yet in the rhetoric of the letter, the apostle is also the author of the letter. Herein lies the probable reason for this term. The protocols of exhortation in ancient letters include such rhetorical identification between unequals. Furthermore, in its early years Christianity works against the strict social hierarchies of the ancient

---

30. Adolf Deissmann, *Bible Studies* (trans. A. Grieve; Edinburgh: T&T Clark, 1901), 154–57, 233–34.

world. This term also suggests a tradition in which Peter's official authority in Rome was that of an elder rather than a bishop.

As observed above (note b), the term *martys* has several connotations within its core meaning of "witness." Peter's witnessing is connected to "the suffering of Christ," but it is not clear exactly how. It can be argued that Peter is, first of all, someone who witnesses the actual suffering of Jesus himself. It is true that he is never described as present at the crucifixion, but he was an intimate participant in the passion week. It can also be argued that he becomes a witness to others about the sufferings of Christ. In this sense, he is "witness of the sufferings of Christ" in the two standard ways. At this point it seems that the suffering to which he is witness is the personal suffering that Jesus himself endured. However, 4:13 complicates this account with the notion that all the Christian recipients of this letter can "share in the sufferings of Christ." The suffering of an individual being abused by a neighbor is the suffering of Christ. Thus Peter may be witness in a third sense: he himself suffers. It is hard to suppress the echoes of any of these readings. All of them reinforce the credibility of the one witnessing.

The third term ascribed to Peter changes the mood, while emphasizing again the commonality between Peter and the readers of the letter. He is described as one who shares in or participates in "the glory that is about to be revealed." While there are faint echoes in this imagery of Peter's presence at the transfiguration and his witness of Jesus' glorification (see 2 Pet 1:16–18), 1 Peter is undoubtedly thinking of future glory (see 1:7; 4:13; 5:4, 10). In both 1:6–7 and 4:13 the sequence is first suffering and then glory. In 1:11 Jesus himself partakes of the same sequence. Thus present suffering, as long as it is the "sufferings of Christ," is the first moment of a theological sequence. As 4:14 insists, if "you are insulted in the name of Christ," this means that "the spirit of glory" is resting upon you. The centrality of this sequence raises the possibility that being "witness of the sufferings of Christ" includes the personal experience of suffering. Finally, it is probably participation in suffering and glory that, in the first instance, gives Peter the authority to exhort the elders, and, second, gives the elders authority to exhort the community.

[2] The command to shepherd the flock invokes one of the most common and persistent biblical images. God is the primary shepherd (see, e.g., Pss 23:1–4; 28:9; Isa 40:11). The Jesus tradition portrays Jesus as shepherd (e.g., John 10:1–18), and the disciples are described as tending the flock (e.g., Matt 10:6). This familiar imagery is used here to promote a certain kind of leadership that is defined in the following verses and elicited in the traditional gentle profile of the biblical shepherd. Early Christianity will persistently use the image of shepherds and sheep to promote a sense of gentleness and tenderness within its hierarchies.

This gentle style of leadership that the image of the shepherd evokes is immediately detailed. Usage of the verb *episkopeō* (exercising oversight) suggests

Elders and Their Flocks

the familiar early Christian mixing of the terms "elder" and "bishop" and of their duties. However, *episkopeō* and its cognates is perhaps the most common Greek term for official oversight. Thus the profile of the later Christian bishop should probably not be imported here. Exercising oversight is what elders in any community do. The force of the argument lies, instead, in the qualifiers. A series of "not/but" contrasts offer an effective portrait of the usual early Christian insistence on gentle and loving leadership.

The first contrast focuses on the question of whether to undertake the role of leadership at all. The warning that leadership should be done "not under compulsion but willingly" suggests such that leadership duties in these communities were not light. Such leadership may even have involved a certain public visibility that made leaders subject to more abuse than otherwise. The second contrast recalls the familiar problem of money. Christianity was not more haunted than other groups by money scandals, but they did occur. The shamefulness in the warning about "shameful gain" probably does not lie in something illicit or unethical in how the money is acquired. The acquisition of money by any means through the perks of office is in itself shameful. The general sense of these two contrasts is that leadership should be undertaken out of a pure eagerness for service. This is a common admonition in ancient Christianity and throughout the Greco-Roman world. Leadership undertaken for ulterior motives is dangerous and immoral.

[3] The third contrast is built grammatically upon the command to shepherd and creates a traditional contrast. The negative warning not to "dominate their charges" is nearly identical to Jesus' command (Matt 20:25; Mark 10:42; Luke 22:25) not to be like Gentile rulers who dominate (*katakyrieuō*) the people. Of course, Greco-Roman literature and culture is filled with warnings against tyrants and exhortations to rulers not to dominate. Greeks, Romans, Jews, and Christians all agree that rulers should not dominate. Furthermore, the reference to being examples (*typoi*) finds numerous parallels in Greco-Roman literature. The Greco-Roman ethical tradition insists that teachers teach primarily by example. Students learn more by imitating the life of the teacher than by studying their words.[31]

First Peter creates a Christian version of this familiar ancient ideal. While the call to humility in 5:5 provides some explicit content to the shape of Christian leadership, for the most part the content is implied. The various ethical norms that occur throughout the letter are certainly included in the behavior of the elders, but the primary source for content comes in the model of Christ. Even the precise nature of Christ's leadership is mostly implicit. The explicit use of

---

31. On the Greek and Jewish background of these terms and their usage in early Christianity, see Elliott, *1 Peter*, 811–44; and Hans von Campenhausen, *Ecclesiastical Authority and Spiritual Power in the Church of the First Three Centuries* (Stanford, Calif.: Stanford University Press, 1969).

Jesus as a model for how to respond to persecution in 2:21–25 provides patterns that are useful here. It is certainly significant that Jesus is named in that passage as "the shepherd and overseer [*episkopos*] of your lives," which anticipates his naming as "chief shepherd" in 5:4. Nevertheless, readers would probably need to rely on stories of Jesus and christological narratives current in these communities that are not detailed here.

[4] At this point 1 Peter returns to eschatological imagery. The time of the return of the chief shepherd is clearly the last days. Although 1 Peter did not coin the term "chief shepherd," its other usages offer little help in its usage here. Most likely nothing mysterious or technical is intended here. Jesus is the chief shepherd in the sense that he is the shepherd of everyone, including all elders and all under their care (2:25). Any elder engaged in shepherding is doing so in the context of a chief shepherd who will return to care for and judge everyone. The rhetoric here is entirely positive. There is no explicit threat in the reminder of the coming of the chief shepherd. The syntax assumes that the elders shepherd willingly, eagerly, becoming examples for the flock. Thus, when the chief shepherd is manifested, it will be for purposes of dispensing rewards. The emphasis on a future crown of glory (or honor) that does not fade creates a contrast to any honors accrued now that derived from the status of leadership. Those honors will fade.

[5] This three-part conclusion begins with the specific command to young people to "be subject to the elders." The word "submit" (*hypotassō*) is used for all Christians in 2:13, for slaves in 2:18, and for wives in 3:1. Early Christianity, like most social groups in the Greco-Roman world, enjoined submission to the proper social order. The term *hypotassō* is primarily used to enforce the submission of the weaker to the stronger, or of the person of low social status to the person of higher. Early Christian notions of equality before God did not, for the most part, undo social hierarchies. However, it is not clear in this verse who is being asked to submit to whom and what the character of that submission might be. The most likely explanation is that "elders" and "young people" refer loosely to both age and status in the community. The admonition to elders not to rule in a domineering way does not permit the young people to ignore their authority. This admonition reads as an all-inclusive call for the maintenance of normal social order. Elders should rule, but they should do so in a gentle way. Young people should, in turn, submit to this noncoercive authority.

This call for submission on behalf of the young flows quite naturally into a general call to "all" in the community to "clothe yourselves with humility toward one another." The verb *enkombōsasthe* (clothe yourselves) and the noun *tapeinophrosynē* (humility) suggest the behavior and status of a slave. This echo is lacking in the English word "humility," but its presence is crucial to the meaning of the verse. All Christians are called to behave as slaves toward one another. The offensiveness of this call invites a theological warrant in the form of a quote from Prov 3:34. The placing of the quote reiterates the constant theological logic of 1 Peter. If Christians live the Christian life now, with its gentle and submissive ethic, it will reduce their social status in the present, but God will reward them at the end.

In some ways this passage (5:1–5) offers little new to the theology of 1 Peter. The theological values and the images of the Christian life are anticipated elsewhere in the letter. The gentle ethic, modeled on Jesus the shepherd, that is articulated throughout the letter is applied to "elders" and "young people" in their peculiar roles in the governance of the community. Elders are to rule, but to do so with gentleness. Young people are to submit. Finally, everyone is to serve one another with the humility of a slave. All of this is done in the context of abuse by outsiders and the promise of a crown of glory, to be given by God to all who live the holy life.

These verses give evidence of communities that are, on the one hand, conscious of their need for order and hierarchy and, on the other hand, equally conscious of serving a God "who judges without partiality" (1:17). All may be equal in God's sight in the sense that each person will be judged solely by their deeds, but communities need order. It has long been noted that Christianity did not invent any new form of social organization. Most of its standards and patterns are found elsewhere. Such is the case here. Everyone in the Greco-Roman world knows the standard social expectations concerning elders and young people. First Peter assumes the validity of that social order but colors that order with some peculiar Christian hues. The admonition not only to gentleness but also to slavelike behavior is unusual, as is the notion that recompense for righteous living lies not in the present but in a future ordered by God's judgment.

1 Peter 5:6–11 Concluding Call to Suffering

Ancient letters, including those in the NT, tend to conclude either with brief summaries of the themes of the letter or with a series of general exhortations on those themes. First Peter takes the latter course: these verses do not pretend to summarize but instead offer a final set of exhortations and encouragements to these persecuted communities. These verses are filled with echoes of other biblical texts. For instance, readers have noticed that both Jas 4:6–10 and 1 Pet 5:5–9 combine Prov 3:34 with calls to be humble before God and to resist the devil. The imagery of casting your cares upon God recalls Ps 55:22 (54:23 LXX) and Matt 6:25. The call to be sober and watchful also occurs in 1 Thess 5:6. Other examples could be noted. That said, it does not appear that 1 Peter is quoting any of these texts or even drawing upon a fixed tradition. This passage reads more like a felicitous gathering of early Christian imagery than a series of quotations.

These verses also echo the language and theology of the rest of 1 Peter. In the usual stye of the letter, they combine imperatives with theological affirmations. They repeat the constant call throughout the letter to resist the temptations inherent in persecution and to trust God in spite of these persecutions. The face of persecution is no longer that of the offended Roman neighbor but of the devil himself. God is portrayed, not as the judge or even as the one who permits persecution, but as the one who will at the proper time "lift you up, ... restore, support, strengthen, establish you." In the persistent pattern of 1 Peter, these verses challenge and comfort one last time.

5:6 Therefore, be humbled[a] under the mighty hand of God, in order that he might lift you up at the proper time,[b] **7** casting[c] all your anxieties[d] upon him, because he cares about you.[e] **8** Be sober. Be watchful. Your adversary,[f] the devil,[g] like a roaring lion, is walking about, seeking someone[h] to devour. **9** Resist him, being firm[i] in the faith, knowing that the same kind[j] of sufferings are being completed[k] by your community[l] throughout the world. **10** But the God of all grace, who has called you into his eternal glory in[m] Christ, will himself, after you have suffered a short time, restore,[n] support, strengthen, establish you. **11** To him be the power forever. Amen.

a. The passive imperative *tapeinōthēte* means "be humbled" not "humble yourselves," which would require a conjugation in the Greek middle voice.

b. Some texts (A, P) read "at the time of visitation" in order to clarify that the proper time is at the Parousia.

c. A few late manuscripts replace the participle *epiripsantes* with the imperative *epiripsate* (cast), others ($\mathfrak{P}^{72}$) with the participle *aporipsantes* (cast away). The participle derives its imperatival force from the preceding imperative *tapeinōthēte*. It probably carries more the sense of attendant circumstance than cause.

d. The noun *merimna* has more the negative sense of "anxiety" than that of the neutral "care."

e. The rather idiomatic Greek reads, literally, "It matters [*melei*] to him about you."

f. The basic meaning of the noun *antidikos* is "legal adversary." However, it is often used for an opponent of any kind, not just one in a court of law.

g. The noun *diabolos* means "slanderer." In the NT and in early Christianity, *diabolos* becomes a common name for the cosmic opponent to God's kingdom.

h. The pronoun *tina* could be interrogative or indefinite, depending on the accent (which would have been missing from most ancient manuscripts). Several texts omit *tina* so that "you" becomes the implied object of "devour." It is best to include *tina* and to read it as an indefinite pronoun.

i. The Bodmer papyrus ($\mathfrak{P}^{72}$) replaces the better supported *stereoi* with *hedraioi*, probably to avoid the connotations of stubbornness in *stereoi*.

j. The phrase *ta auta tōn pathēmatōn* (lit., "the same of sufferings") is awkward at best. While this could mean "the same sufferings," it is grammatically more likely that the genitive is partitive, with the meaning "the same kind of sufferings."

Concluding Call to Suffering

k. Uncertainty over whether to read the infinitive *epiteleisthai* as middle or passive probably inspired textual variants that replaced the infinitive with indicatives (ℵ, A, B). If *epiteleisthai* is read in the middle voice, the sentence would read "knowing how to complete the same kind of sufferings . . ." If it is passive, it would be translated as above. The choice between these translations depends not on grammar but on which makes the best sense in 1 Peter.

l. The dative *adelphotēti* (lit., "brotherhood") could be translated "against," "in regard to," or "by." Thus it is not perfectly clear whether the suffering is being completed "against" the community either by God (or even by the devil) or "by" the community itself. The ambiguity in 1 Peter over the proper author of suffering permits all these readings, although a syntax of God or the devil as the one completing suffering sounds awkward. Hence it is best to read the suffering as being completed by the community.

m. While the prepositional phrase *en Christō* could be taken instrumentally ("through"), it more likely has the usual sense of "in" or "with."

n. The verb *katartizō* can mean "supply" or "complete," but in the NT most often means "mend" or "restore."

[6–7] The use of the passive "be humbled" reflects the ongoing social and ethical tension in the life of these Christians. On the one hand, they have no choice about their humble status. It is imposed on them by outsiders who abuse them for their Christian behavior. Their only choice is in how they respond. They can live the holy life within that persecution, or they can abandon their Christian behavior and reacquire their lost social status. The passive "be humbled" comes as a call to accept the humble status imposed upon them. On the other hand, they seem to have more choice in how they treat other members of the community. The imperatives in 5:5 assume a freedom either to serve or not serve others. A humble status within the community seems to be a matter of choice. Thus the imperative force of the passive verb remains in force.

In the theology of 1 Peter, submission to and acceptance of the social status of a slave is not the final accounting of a person's status. To "be humbled" is to cast one's future into the hand of God. Thus the note that this act of being humbled is done "under the mighty hand of God" asserts the ongoing presence of God's power in humble acts of service. In this language there is no hint whether God is enforcing the humility and abuse or offering comfort and encouragement in their midst. Both are possible in the theology of 1 Peter, although 5:7 assumes that God is offering comfort. In any case, the standard theological sequence of 1 Peter is repeated here. The imperative to "be humbled" is not done for the sake of humility itself: it is done in order that God "might lift you up at the proper time." At the proper time does not mean at some propitious moment but "at the last time" (1:5). First Peter offers no respite from abuse and humble status within the normal sequences of history. God will lift up these Christians only on the last day.

The image of casting anxieties upon God recalls the sayings of Jesus about anxiety in Matt 6:25–34 and Luke 12:22–32, where the same Greek root (*merimn-*) is used. A more likely direct source is Ps 54:23 LXX (55:22 NRSV), which has nearly identical wording. The anxieties are not specifically limited to those associated with persecution and loss of status, although those are certainly included. The citation reads as a general theological truth about all anxieties, which is applied to the peculiar anxieties of these communities. The capacity to cast anxieties upon God depends on decisions about God's character. The simple assertion that these Christians matter to God calls forth the large fund of biblical images of God's reliability. There is no call here, as in the Jesus sayings, that they should not be anxious. The life of persecution and humility produces anxiety. However, those anxieties can be cast away before the God who cares about these abused Christians.

[8] The opening imperatives "Be sober" and "Be watchful" are used elsewhere in the NT as eschatological warnings (e.g., Matt 24:42; Mark 13:35, 37; 1 Thess 5:6, 8). The verb *nēphō* (be sober) is used in participial form in 1:13 in the context of hoping for the "revelation of Jesus Christ" and as an imperative in 4:7 in preparation for prayer. The force of the imperatives in this verse is that of a summons to alertness and attention to the dangers at hand. The call to be watchful in the NT does not mean for believers to watch the heavens for signs of the end, but for them to prepare their lives for the arrival of the one who judges. Thus these imperatives serve not as a call to look away from the duties of life to a heavenly future; on the contrary, they call for a focus on the duties of life in preparation for the future.

This need for alertness and watchfulness is intensified with the brief and threatening narration of the activity of the devil. Though the NT and early Christianity do not offer the elaborate portraits and narratives of the devil that will emerge in later Christianity, the devil does emerge in these texts as the face of ultimate evil, rebellion, and temptation. There is nothing said in 1 Peter about the cosmic status or role of this devil. Calling the devil a "roaring lion" is unique to 1 Peter, although the enemies of Israel are often named as lions (see, e.g., Ps 22:13, 21; Jer 2:15). In any case, 1 Peter seems to assume its readers' familiarity with the devil as their great enemy. The context in 1 Peter suggests that the devil "devours someone" by tempting them away from their Christian lives. In the face of persecution and abuse, there are two choices for the readers. First, they can continue to live the Christian life, thereby entrusting their destiny to God. Second, they can avoid abuse by returning to their old lives, thereby becoming devoured by the devil.

[9] The call to resist the devil builds on the preceding imperatives to "be alert" and "watchful." Resistance is obviously not accomplished by a personal attack on an embodied devil. Resistance is indirect. It is accomplished by "being firm in the faith." Again, in the theology of 1 Peter, "being firm in the faith" carries less the sense of being adamant about doctrine and more the sense of continuing to live the Christian virtues in the face of abuse. Thus it is fitting that the verse points next to the challenges of suffering.

Concluding Call to Suffering

This verse adds more pieces to 1 Peter's ongoing argument that the capacity to stand firm in the face of abuse depends on understanding the true character of suffering. Two assertions, occurring here for the first time in the letter, recall the challenge in 4:12 not to be surprised at the burning. They should not be surprised at their own suffering, because similar suffering is occurring "throughout the world." The universality of this suffering does not result simply from pervasive social tensions between Christians and non-Christians, but also from the energy and activity of the devil, who wishes to devour them. Suffering is, therefore, unavoidable and inevitable for a Christian. Furthermore, this verse calls these Christians to understand that their brothers and sisters everywhere are indeed resisting the devil and completing the sufferings that come to them. If this suffering is universal and if their brothers and sisters can resist the devil, then they too should be able to resist.

[10–11] In the familiar pattern of 1 Peter, the letter turns from warning and exhortation to assertions of God's care and power. The imagery of verse 10 recalls that of the opening blessing in 1:3–7. In fact, these verses are composed almost entirely of terms that are central to the theology of 1 Peter. The word "grace" (*charis*) is perhaps the most common word in 1 Peter for summarizing the blessings God bestows on these Christians (1:2, 10, 13; 2:19, 20; 3:7; 4:10; 5:12). The diversity of the usages of this term in 1 Peter is typical of how the word is used throughout the NT. A phrase like "God of all grace" works in part by its lack of specificity. All graces in the Christian life and in the Christian story are included. The naming of God as the one "who has called [*kalesas*] you" repeats the familiar call imagery from throughout the letter (1:15; 2:9, 21; 3:9). The language of calling is used both for God's calling into salvation (2:9; 5:10) and for God's calling into suffering (2:21; 3:9). Finally, the language of glory can refer to Jesus' glory (1:11, 21; 4:13) or to the glory given to Christians (1:7; 4:14; 5:1, 4, 10). All of this repetition enhances the doxological feel of these verses.

Given the ongoing insistence on the necessity of suffering, it is not surprising that this verse again affirms its inevitability. The blessing in 1:3–7 includes the same warning in 1:6 about the necessity of suffering "for a short time" (*oligon*). Thus, this evocative blessing of 5:10 rearticulates the core theology of the letter. God is the God of grace, who calls these Christians into eschatological glory, a glory of which Christ already partakes. This God of grace also calls Christians into suffering, a suffering that Christ has already endured and that is the necessary prelude to glory. This suffering is, thankfully, "for a short time," whereas the "crown of glory" is "unfading" (5:4).

The four verbs that end verse 10 build upon one another to affirm the idea that God will work to save these people. All the terms convey a sense of strength: "restore, support, strengthen, establish." Since all the verbs are in the future tense, the explicit rhetoric is that of promise. Given the fact that in 1:5 God is affirmed as "guarding" in the present, there is probably no intention of limiting this active strengthening to the future. The tense derives more from the style of ascription to God.

The concluding ascription in 5:11 reaffirms the focus on power. The theological question is not simply whether God is willing to offer comfort to abused Christians, but whether God is able to do so. This affirmation of God's power leads to a concluding and fitting "amen."

Throughout the letter, the author of 1 Peter combines exhortation and encouragement in the face of persecution and abuse, using a rich variety of rhetorical forms. This section (5:6–11) once again combines exhortation and encouragement in one of the most appealing rhetorical pieces in the letter. For the most part, the imperatives in this passage depend on the letter's larger arguments. The content of "Be sober" and "Be watchful" derives from what precedes. In the same way, the affirmations of God's care and power emerge from the overall portrait of God in the letter. Thus this passage, while it does not try to summarize, offers a fitting conclusion to the letter.

The appearance of the devil adds a different dynamic to 1 Peter's account of suffering. Behind all the abuse and ridicule from their neighbors prowls the devil himself, who is seeking to swallow them whole. The presence of the devil adds a sense of potency and inevitability to suffering. The face of abuse is no longer that of the "surprised" Gentile. The origin of abuse is no longer simply the animosity of the neighbor. Suffering loses its occasional character. Instead, the devil, who is everywhere and whose animosity is cosmic, is prowling like a lion. Thus there will be suffering until the devil is finally overthrown.

To this point 1 Peter has asserted that the suffering of the individual Christian is the suffering of Christ. Suffering as a Christian unites one to the story of Jesus. It is a sign of unity with Christ. These verses increase the range of this unity. Suffering unites one not just to Christ but also to all Christians who suffer. This rather striking sense of Christian unity based on suffering is not unique to 1 Peter (cf. 2 Cor 1:3–7; 1 Thess 2:14). As both Paul and 1 Peter assert, each Christian who suffers is enduring the same suffering that Christ and all Christians endure. In this affirmation, the dual aspect of suffering is reinforced. Suffering is, on the one hand, negative. There is nothing in itself good in being abused. On the other hand, suffering is positive because it connects the one who suffers to all other Christians and to Christ.

It is fitting that the body of the letter ends with this wonderful ascription to God. The real terror of abuse and persecution is that it can undermine a person's faith and virtue. The reality of abuse overwhelms the promise of glory. If God has called these people to glory, then abuse seems to contradict that. Thus 1 Peter changes the language of call. God also calls each Christian to unjust suffering (2:21; 3:9). This unjust suffering unites them to one another and to the story of Christ. Because the story of Christ ends in glory, the story of these abused Christians will also end in glory. Given this context, the affirmations in 5:10–11 are an ideal closing. It calls the readers to affirm that God, in spite of the evidence of this suffering, is able to save. God will strengthen now and give glory in the end.

1 Peter 5:12–14 Epistolary Postscript

Ancient letters display considerable variety in their conclusions, ranging from a simple "Be strong" or "Be well" to rather lengthy greetings and blessings. Romans 16 offers a good example of how elaborate letter closings can become. The postscript of 1 Peter falls somewhere between a clean farewell and a full, Pauline-style closing. Its imagery is most reminiscent of the closings of Paul's Letters and is typical of other early Christian letters. As here, closings often include brief allusions to the preceding content of the letter. Particularly in early Christian letters, which passed from community to community, greetings from and to others are common, as is a liturgical blessing. These verses offer a brief form of the common elements of the conclusions of an early Christian letter.

For all the rhetorical ordinariness of this postscript, there are considerable difficulties in the details. Most of the problems emerge from uncertainty over who actually wrote this letter and to whom. If the apostle Peter wrote this letter from Rome and sent it to the communities named in 1:1, then this postscript is fairly straightforward. However, if the letter is pseudepigraphical, as this commentary assumes, then it is much less clear how to understand these final remarks. Pseudepigraphical letters typically had all the trappings of regular letters, including the kind of personal remarks seen here. The problem is that names and persons in pseudepigraphical letters function in so many different ways. Sometimes the names are of famous people, adding credibility and weight to the letter. Sometimes the names seem to do little beyond adding a certain verisimilitude. Sometimes the names are those of people contemporary with the real author. Thus, in itself the presence of these names does not determine how they should be understood. It is not clear, for instance, who Silvanus was or is supposed to have been. Nor is it clear what the phrase means "through Silvanus." In the same way, it is uncertain who Mark is supposed to be or who is "she who is the coelect in Babylon." What we have are greetings typical of an early Christian letter that lead into a command for the "kiss of love" and concluding blessing of peace.

5:12 Through[a] Silvanus, the faithful brother, as I consider him,[b] I have written to you briefly,[c] exhorting and testifying that this[d] is the true grace of God. Stand in it. **13** She[e] who is the coelect in Babylon[f] greets you, and so does Mark my son. 14 Greet one another with a kiss of love. Peace to all of you who are in Christ.[g]

a. The preposition *dia* (through) in epistolary closings often designates the carrier of the letter.

b. The Greek phrase *hōs logizomai* lacks the implied pronoun and literally means "as I think" or "as I reckon."

c. The declaration of having written "briefly" (*di' holigōn*) is standard language in ancient letters, whether the letter is brief or not.

d. The antecedent of "this" (*tautēn*) is probably the letter in its entirety. Some readers suggest that "this" refers back to the "grace" in 5:10, which is here affirmed as "true." While grammatically possible, the purpose of such an affirmation is a bit mysterious. Grace in the phrase "God of all grace" scarcely needs reinforcement.

e. The feminine gender of the noun *syneklektē* (coelect) has occasioned much discussion. The word could refer not only to a person but also to any other Greek word of the feminine gender. Some texts (א) insert *ekklēsia* (church), suggesting thereby that the reference is to the church. Most texts leave the reference ambiguous.

f. A few minor texts replace "Babylon" with "Rome."

g. As is typically the case with concluding blessings of NT letters, there are numerous textual variants, ranging from the omission of the entire blessing ($\mathfrak{P}^{72}$) to additions of the name Jesus and a final "amen" (א, P, 𝔐).

[12] The most difficult phrase in the entire closing is the opening "through Silvanus." On a few occasions the preposition *dia* (through) can refer to the secretary or amanuensis of the letter. Several readers have suggested that Silvanus was the actual author of the letter and is signaling that fact here. In the NT we have one such example in Rom 16:22, where Tertius identifies himself as the amanuensis. The syntax there is quite different from what we have here. There are also instances in which Paul notes that he is adding a postscript in his own hand (1 Cor 16:21; Gal 6:11; see also Col 4:18; 2 Thess 3:17). Such notes were common in antiquity, when most letters of any length were dictated to professional scribes. None of this, however, fits the syntax of this phrase. Instead, in both Christian and non-Christian letters, we find this exact phrase to be a standard way of designating the carrier of the letter. The conceit of the letter is that Peter is the author and sends the letter to these communities by way of Silvanus. Silvanus is presented as having the same role as Timothy with 1 Corinthians (4:17), Titus with 2 Corinthians (8:16–19), Tychicus and Onesimus with Colossians (4:7–9), and Tychicus with Ephesians (6:21–22). They all carry the letter and bring further instructions and greetings.

While the intent seems fairly clear that Silvanus is to be understood as the letter's carrier, it is less clear who Silvanus is. Readers have traditionally equated Silas of Acts with Silvanus of Paul's Letters. In Acts 15:22 Silas is introduced as one of the leaders of the church in Jerusalem. He is sent along with Judas as carrier of the letter from Jerusalem to Antioch (15:27). He is also called a prophet (15:32) and accompanies Paul on some of his journeys (15:40; 16:19; 17:4; 18:5). Paul names Silvanus, along with Timothy, as cosender of the letters to the Thessalonians (1 Thess 1:1; 2 Thess 1:1). In 2 Cor 1:19 Paul reminds the Corinthians that it was Silvanus, Timothy, and Paul himself who proclaimed the gospel to them. The name "Silvanus" could be a Latin version of the Greek "Silas." Both names are used for a companion of Paul. Thus identifying Silas with Silvanus is reasonable. However, many interpreters have pointed out that Silvanus is a common name in the Roman world. It is certainly possible that Silas and Silvanus are two different people. Furthermore, none of this really answers the question of who Silvanus in 1 Pet 5:12 is supposed to be.

Although the possible readings here are numerous, the most likely reading is that "Silvanus" is intended to refer to the Silvanus/Silas who was Paul's companion and who was also one of the leaders of the church in Jerusalem. His name occurs here because of his connections with Jerusalem, Peter, and Paul. The name "Silvanus" lends authority to the letter. This authority is reinforced by Peter's assertion that he considers Silvanus to be a "faithful brother." Such affirmations about the bearers of ancient letters are common, since the reliability and credibility of the bearer of the letter was crucial to its success. There is nothing in the NT itself about the relationship between the historical Peter and the historical Silvanus/Silas, but rhetorically this affirmation reinforces the credibility of the letter.

Readers have often noted the effectiveness of the two participles "exhorting" and "testifying" in summarizing the contents of the letter. In fact, this verse itself repeats this pattern of testimony and exhortation. First, the verse affirms that the accounts of God, Jesus, and the Christian life that are detailed in the letter are "the true grace of God." The sequence of suffering and glory, manifested in Jesus' life and in the lives of these Christians, is not an unfortunate accident caused by evil neighbors. This sequence establishes the essential character of the Christian life. As 1 Peter keeps insisting, suffering is part of the story of God's grace. Second, this verse calls the readers to "stand" in this story of suffering and glory. The substance of this imperative comes from the larger arguments of the letter.

[13] The feminine sense of the noun "coelect" has been rendered in a variety of ways. It could refer to a woman who is unnamed. The reference to Mark my son has occasioned the suggestion that the wife of Peter is intended here. Peter is known to have been married (Mark 1:30; 1 Cor 9:5). Clement of Alexandria reports (*Strom.* 7.11) that Peter's wife was martyred before Peter was. However, the phrase "she who is the coelect in Babylon" would be an odd way to refer to the wife of Peter. In any case, there is a much more obvious reading. The texts that add the noun *ekklēsia* probably indicate how the reference was normally understood. The elect is the Christian community. In 2 John 13 the phrase "elect sister" (*adelphēs . . . eklektēs*) is probably used the same way.

This reading also coheres with the normal usage of the term "elect" in 1 Peter (see 1:1 [1:2 NRSV]; 2:9). Thus the greeting is from the church "in Babylon."

It is unlikely that the historical Babylon is intended here. At the end of the first century, Babylon was mostly ruins, although it is possible that small groups of people lived there. However, there is no tradition linking Peter with Babylon. On the other hand, Peter is famously connected with Rome (Irenaeus, *Haer.* 3.3.2–3). Jewish tradition had developed the pattern of calling Rome by the name Babylon. This tradition is probably reflected here, as it is in the book of Revelation (14:8; 17:5; 18:2, 10, 21). The use of the name "Babylon" for Rome is an insult and a threat since it equates the historical fall of Babylon with a still-future fall of Rome. There is probably no attempt to be secretive in this renaming, since almost any Roman would recognize the insult.

Although the name "Mark" is common in the Greco-Roman world, the reference to "Mark my son" has traditionally been understood as referring to the John Mark of Acts. This Mark was part of the early Jerusalem community (Acts 12:12) and accompanied Paul and Barnabas on early missionary journeys (12:25; 15:37, 39). He is also mentioned several times (Col 4:10; 2 Tim 4:11; Phlm 24) as part of the Pauline entourage. In later tradition Papias names him as the interpreter of Peter and, in that role, the immediate author of the Gospel of Mark. The Mark named in 1 Peter as "my son" fits nicely in that tradition. Familial language is common in the NT and early Christianity among Christians working together (e.g., 1 Cor 4:17; Phil 2:22; 1 Tim 1:2, 18; 2 Tim 1:2; Titus 1:4). As far as we know, this reference is the first in early Christianity to an intimate working relationship between Peter and Mark. It is possible that this brief reference contributed to the later tradition that Papias cites.[32]

[14] Paul concludes several of his letters with the encouragement to greet one another with the "holy kiss" (Rom 16:16; 1 Cor 16:20; 2 Cor 13:12; 1 Thess 5:26). There is probably no distinction to be made between the Pauline "holy kiss" and the phrase "kiss of love" that is used here. It is not clear from the word "kiss" (*philēma*) itself or from early Christian literature precisely what the act involved. In the Greco-Roman world a "kiss" could be on the lips or on the cheek. In fact, the word *philēma* could even refer to a hug. The form of the kiss would depend on the character of the relationship. It is generally assumed that the early Christian kiss was either a kiss on the cheek or a hug.

The placement of this call for a kiss in both Paul's Letters and 1 Peter is significant. While the imperative to "greet one another with a kiss of love" may refer to greetings in all moments and places, it is more likely that this is a liturgical moment. The letter is being read during the gathering of the community, perhaps in worship itself. The call for the kiss of love is a call to end the reading and to greet one another. As is usually the case, the text of the Bible points away

---

32. On the various traditions about Mark, see Black, *Mark: Images of an Apostolic Interpreter.*

from itself to the lives of the people named in the text. This call for a real kiss among real people gathered for the reading is another reminder that holiness is found in life, in relationship, and not just in the act of reading.

The final wish for peace is typical of early Christian letters. There is probably little at stake in the use of the word "peace" instead of the somewhat more common term "grace." Both terms are central to the theology of 1 Peter. Both are used in the opening greeting of the letter (1:2). Grace is highlighted in 5:12, and peace in 5:14. Many readers have also noted that the context of persecution gives urgency to this wish for peace. The naming of the recipients of peace as "all of you who are in Christ" may hint at the exclusion of peace from those who are not "in Christ." More likely it is an attempt to include all who are reading or hearing the reading of the letter.

While epistolary conclusions are highly formulaic, they typically highlight in the midst of those formulas the letter's key ideas. Such is the case here. The classic greeting between communities is couched in a way that emphasizes the authority and influence of Peter the author. The naming of Silvanus and Mark reinforces the apostolic status of the letter. The metaphor of Babylon somewhat ironically invokes both the political status of the city of Rome and its coming destruction. Furthermore, almost every single term used in this conclusion echoes larger arguments in 1 Peter. Without explicitly rehearsing the letter's full theology, the careful choice of language puts that theology in place once again. This brief conclusion is full of echoes.

Finally, in that pattern familiar from the Letters of Paul, the call for a kiss of love turns the attention of the readers from the syntax of the letter to the faces of those around them. The purpose of the letter is not to produce a rich reading experience, even if it does manage to do that. The purpose of the letter is to guide the behavior of these Christians in their relationships with one another and with their non-Christian neighbors.

THE LETTER OF JUDE

INTRODUCTION TO JUDE

Authorship

As with the other letters in this volume, the question of authorship has proved to be both controversial and persistent. The difficulties begin with the curious attribution of the letter to "Jude [*Ioudas*], servant of Jesus Christ, brother of James." It is unusual, although not unheard of, to identify someone by their brother and not their father. Unless such a move is an attempt to avoid confusion, this pattern depends on the renown of the brother. In early Christianity, there was one Jude who had a well-known brother named James. A "Judas" is mentioned in both Mark 6:3 and Matt 13:55 as one of the brothers of Jesus, along with James, Joses (or Joseph), and Simon. The absence of any other identifying information in the letter on either "Jude" or "James" indicates that the brother "James" was well known. All of this points to "James" as James the brother of Jesus, who became head of the Jerusalem church and the figurative leader of much of Jewish-Christianity. Most modern readers argue that only this James would have had the kind of status and renown to be identified in this way and to inspire Jude's identification with his brother. Thus "Jude" is the brother of Jesus, named in the Gospels, who is here identified by his famous brother James.

However, there is much disagreement with this reading. There are two common counterarguments. First, there are many other people called Jude or Judas in early Christianity who make good candidates as author. Second, if this Jude is indeed the brother of Jesus, then he would not need the fame of his brother James in order to be identified. Some readers argue that if this Jude were intended to be the brother of Jesus, then he would be identified as such, probably as "brother of the Lord."

In Luke's version of the Twelve (6:16; cf. Matt 10:1–4; Mark 3:16–19), one is named "Judas of James," meaning "Judas son of James." In fact, the tradition in English translations of rendering the Greek *Ioudas* of Jude 1 as "Jude" and not "Judas" is largely an attempt to distinguish the Judas of James, who was one of the Twelve, from the Judas, brother of James, who authored this letter. The *Apostolic Constitutions* (7.46) records the third bishop of Jerusalem as "Judas of James." Eusebius (*Hist. eccl.* 4.5.3) states that a certain "Judas" was the last Jewish bishop of Jerusalem. An otherwise unknown Judas Barsabbas is designated along with Silas to carry the letter from the council in Jerusalem to the church in Antioch (Acts 15:22, 27, 32). Perhaps the best-known Judas in early Christianity was Judas Thomas (*Gospel of Thomas*; *Acts of Thomas*; Eusebius, *Hist. eccl.* 1.13.11). The name Thomas in Aramaic means "twin" (Didymus in Greek). A complicated and diverse tradition about Judas the twin develops in early Christianity, although these traditions clearly postdate the writing of Jude. This Judas was portrayed in some of these traditions as the twin brother of Jesus (e.g., *Acts of Thom.* 31, 39). All of these people have been proposed as the Jude of this letter. However, almost all modern readers think that difficulties with any of these other Judes as the author are insurmountable.

Although a few readers have suggested that, in light of all these problems, this Jude and this James are perhaps persons known to the original recipients but unknown to modern readers, most readers conclude that this Jude is Jude the brother of Jesus and James. Unfortunately, there is little known about this Jude. Later and mostly legendary stories about Jesus' family provide little narrative about Jude. Paul includes "the brothers of the Lord" among his list of people (or apostles) who travel with a woman (1 Cor 9:5). Perhaps this means that Jude, the brother of the Lord, was a traveling evangelist. However, there is really no information about Jude that would offer direction to the reading of the present letter. If Jude did actually write this letter, then the letter provides data about the author and not vice versa.

The question then becomes whether the historical Jude actually wrote the letter or the letter was attributed to him pseudonymously. Some readers have argued that the historical Jude makes an excellent candidate as the author. The refusal to name himself "brother of the Lord," choosing the more modest "brother of James," suggests sensitivity more likely to belong to the historical Jude than to later tradition. The letter's fondness for Jewish texts, the apocalyptic theology, the absence of classic Greek imagery, and the lack of concern for the usual issues surrounding Gentile Christianity fit perfectly with a Jewish brother of Jesus living in Palestine.

Most readers, however, conclude that the letter is pseudepigraphical. They point out that fondness for Jewish texts, apocalyptic theology, and so on fit perfectly with almost any Jewish Christian or even with Gentile Christians who had affection for sacred texts. Furthermore, it is difficult to understand how the historical Jude would have used the phrases "the faith that was once and for all handed over to the saints" (v. 3) and "the words spoken beforehand by the apostles of our Lord Jesus Christ" (v. 17). It is also much easier to place both the theology and the controversy of the letter into the end of the first century or even the beginning of the second. Jude would have to have been much younger than his brothers to live so long. As for the avoiding of the epithet "brother of the Lord," in truth it is impossible to know much about the history of the theological sensitivities surrounding the phrase. It is pertinent that, in the letter of James, James is identified as "a servant of God and the Lord Jesus Christ" and not as "brother of the Lord." No one really knows why. Thus the best guess is that the letter is pseudepigraphical and that Jude was named as author mostly for the authority of his brother James.[33]

The Opponents

The dominating face in the letter is that of "certain people" who "have slipped in" (v. 4). Almost the entire letter, except for the concluding benediction and parts of verses 17–23, describes and attacks these people. Much of this is done by way of textual citation. These people are connected to the rebellions after the flight from Egypt, Sodom and Gomorrah, Cain, Korah's rebellion, and the impious in *1 Enoch*. They are described with classic negative images from Jewish texts: they are the impious; they practice sexual immorality; they are grumblers; they reject authority; they are dreamers; they slander the glorious ones; they are irrational animals; they live according to their own desires; they show partiality for the sake of gain. They are also described with an array of other images: they "change the grace of our God into licentiousness and deny our only Master and Lord, Jesus Christ" (v. 4); they are dangerous reefs at love feasts; they shepherd only themselves; they are waterless clouds, wild waves, and wandering stars; they do not have the spirit.

In all of this (and more), it is difficult to know what is classic religious invective and what is truly descriptive. Most readers assume that some of this attack must have something to do with the character of these intruders. But what? The accusations of creating divisions (v. 19) and attacking angels (v. 8) have led to the suggestion that the intruders were early gnostics. However, the more common suggestion is that these intruders are antinomians. Their attack on "the glorious ones" is an attack on the angels who traditionally gave the law and supervised its enforcement (v. 8). The appeal to James is an appeal to his support for the law. The persistent tethering of all argument to Jewish texts reflects loyalty to the "law" in the broad sense. The accusations of sexual immorality (vv. 7, 16) come from the opponents' neglect of its moral constraints. The various references to rebellion against authority and proper order reflect this rejection of the authority and ordering powers of the law. In fact, the antinomian suggestion works well. It fits nicely with the rhetoric of the letter.

---

33. For typical arguments for pseudepigraphical authorship, see Kraftchick 20–22; or Harrington 182–83. However, both Bauckham, *Jude, 2 Peter*, 14–16, and Davids 8–12, lean toward authorship by Jude, the brother of Jesus, simply because there is insufficient evidence not to do so.

However, there is nothing in Jude that explicitly suggests antinomianism. Certainly none of the accusations require such an explanation. Accusations of sexual immorality and rejection of authority are pervasive in ancient polemic.[34] Thus they may disclose nothing helpful about these intruders. All of the accusations in Jude can be read several ways and fit with a variety of theological profiles. Hence it is preferable to refrain from any confident description of these opponents. A summarizing adjective, such as gnostic or antinomian, should be avoided.

There are some things that can be concluded. The opponents participate in the love feasts and thus are part of the community. They are creating divisions and controversy. The letter itself attests to that. They appear to reject the traditional authorities in the community. However, it is hard to know what that means. The letter does not say who or which authorities in the community are being questioned. The accusation of denying Jesus Christ may not mean that they explicitly do so. Since they are accused of slipping in, they are portrayed as outsiders. Again, it is difficult to know what that means. Everyone in the community was at some point an outsider. Thus any attempt to reconstruct the face of the opponents is frustrated by the rhetoric of the letter. It is as though the letter assumes that its readers will know who these people are and what they believe. The task of the letter is not to rehearse all that but to bring these people under the righteous judgment of sacred texts.

Date and Setting

For all the difficulties in identifying both the sender and recipients of the letter, most readers still conclude that this letter is in some sense a real letter. The crisis is not simply a literary fiction that was created to give space to theological rhetoric. The community or communities of Jude are enduring a real controversy that is creating divisions. The Letter of Jude is a response to this.

The letter gives no explicit information about its place of origin, the location of the recipients, or the date of the writing. Jude has been dated anywhere from 50 to 120 C.E. It has been located from Egypt to Palestine to Asia Minor to Greece. The letter's early acceptance in Egypt and its dependence on *1 Enoch* suggest Egypt. Its Jewish apocalyptic theology, its mode of reading texts, and the high status it gives to James suggest Palestine. The antinomian feel of the controversy hints of similar controversies in Asia Minor and Greece. Dating has depended largely on trying to place the theological arguments of the letter into the historical narrative of early Christian theology. Thus a proposed date of Jude depends on how a reader configures the development of early Christian thought and the structure of Jude's theology. Since both of these can be done in numerous ways, numerous dates have been proposed.

---

34. On the stock character of these attacks, see Karris 549–64.

The letter assumes knowledge of a fairly long list of Jewish texts. Among canonical texts, Jude has particular fondness for Isaiah, but also evokes passages and images from the Psalms, Proverbs, Numbers, Ezekiel, Amos, Hosea, Zechariah, plus echoes from others. Among noncanonical literature, Jude probably evokes the *Testament of Moses*. However, its main text is *1 Enoch*. The only explicit quote of a text in Jude (vv. 14b–15) is from *1 Enoch* 1.9. There are also fairly obvious allusions to *1 Enoch* in verses 4, 6, 12–13, 16. Jude cites texts while assuming that the readers know the larger context of the citation. For instance, it refers to Sodom and Gomorrah, Korah's rebellion, the flight from Egypt, Cain, and Balaam without explaining any of them. Jude assumes that its readers know these stories and can fill in the details. Furthermore, the syntax of its allusions to these texts does not seem to favor the Greek text over the Hebrew. In fact, it often favors the Hebrew wording. All of this suggests a Jewish Christian audience. It does not necessitate it, since Gentiles could learn Hebrew texts. Nevertheless, Jude's selection of texts and method of citation makes it likely that the letter is from a Jewish Christian author to Jewish Christian communities.

Palestine is perhaps the least problematic guess for its location. The high status of James, the role of Jewish texts in the theology, and the apocalyptic framework of the theology fit nicely with Palestine. Of course, other places are possible.

The date is also a guess although a later date is easier to explain than an earlier one. The reference to faith as a fixed tradition (v. 3) and the apostles as a group that prophesied together (v. 17) suggest—but no more than suggest—a later date. Jude is presumably cited by 2 Peter, but 2 Peter is itself difficult to date. Perhaps the best guess is sometime in the 90s, although anytime from 80 to 110 C.E. seems possible.

Literary Structure

In some ways, the literary structure of Jude is both straightforward and obvious. Almost all readers of Jude detect a similar structure, although the precise division of verses 5–23 varies.

1–2 Opening Salutation
3–4 Statement of Purpose and Opening Accusation
5–16 Condemnation of the Impious
    5–7 Three Examples of Divine Punishment
    8–13 The Naming of the Impious
    14–16 Enoch's Prophecy of Judgment
17–23 Appeals to the Beloved
    17–19 The Prophecy of the Apostles
    20–23 Appeal for Mercy
24–25 Concluding Doxology

While this basic outline (or one close to it) seems fitting enough, the rhetorical dynamics of the letter are not clear. One way to frame the letter's debate is to observe that it has three pieces: a statement of purpose, a textual and theological condemnation of the impious, and appeals to the beloved. The question is how these pieces fit together or which is the center of the text. Jude 3 laments that the author wanted to write about "our common salvation" but is forced by the presence of people who have slipped in "to write, appealing to you to contend for the faith." This is exactly what the letter does. It is not an elaboration of the faith of the community but an appeal for the "beloved" to reject these impious people. This appeal has two parts: the condemnation of the impious and the appeal to the beloved to be merciful. It is not clear how these two pieces should be connected.

Most readers see condemnation as the heart of the letter. Furthermore, they see the quote from *1 Enoch* 1.9 as the heart of that condemnation. As verse 4 asserts, these people "long ago were written down for this judgment." The texts have named them as impious people and have promised them judgment. The core theology is that of *1 Enoch* 1.9, where the Lord comes to convict all people of their impious deeds. Yet a whole series of texts, not just *1 Enoch*, identifies the impiety of these people. Jude articulates that naming. At the conclusion of this textual condemnation, two appeals to the beloved are added. The first reinforces the judgment of the texts with the words of the apostles. The second softens the condemnation with an appeal for mercy.

However, a few interpreters see these appeals as the heart of the letter. For them, the textual condemnations provide a context, but they are not the main point. The main point was announced in verse 4. The letter is an appeal to the beloved to "contend for the faith." It is not until verses 20–23 that the letter describes how this is to be done. The readers contend for the faith by keeping themselves in the love of God and by showing mercy to those who are disputing with them. These verses have always struck readers as marking a change in tone. Such readers argue that this striking shift in tone results from the rhetorical centrality of the appeal.

Both of these readings, the condemnatory and the merciful, probably unbalance the rhetorical force of the letter. Ancient polemic, maybe all polemic, is filled with positives and negatives, condemnations and appeals. Effective polemic needs both. On the one hand, Jude has much more condemnation than appeal. On the other hand, the placing and syntax of the concluding appeals highlight their importance. Perhaps it is best to read neither aspect as dominating the other. If there is a controlling statement in Jude, it would be the announcement of purpose in verses 3–4. To accomplish that purpose, both condemnations and appeals are necessary.

Canonical Status

Jude is cited as authoritative by both Tertullian and Clement of Alexandria.[35] It is included in the Muratorian Canon and is well attested in the early manuscripts. Doubts about its status apparently arose because it quotes the noncanonical *1 Enoch* as authoritative. Origen, Eusebius, and Jerome all expressed doubts about Jude's canonicity. While both the Eastern and Western churches eventually treated Jude as canonical, its deep dependence on a noncanonical text has continued to trouble some readers.

Text and Translation

Jude has excellent representation among papyri ($\mathfrak{P}^{72}$, $\mathfrak{P}^{74}$, $\mathfrak{P}^{78}$) and in the major uncials (א, A, B, C). Apart from the textual mess of verses 22–23, the variants in Jude are mostly minor and easily understandable. As noted in the introduction to 1 Peter, two kinds of variants are cited in the commentary. When it is not possible to decide between possible versions, the various options will be noted. Other variants will be cited because they provide interesting glimpses into early Christian thought.

Again, as mentioned in the introduction to 1 Peter, the translations in this commentary try to convey the grammatical tensions in the Greek that are key to the meaning of the text. This means that the resulting English is, on occasion, a bit awkward.

---

35. See Kelly 223–24, for citations of Tertullian, Clement of Alexandria, Origen, Eusebius, and Jerome.

COMMENTARY

Jude 1–2 Opening Salutation

Jude begins with a fairly standard-looking Christian-style salutation. Christian salutations tend to follow the Jewish style with their added prayer or blessing (see Dan 4:1; 6:25), although the cleaner Greek form does occur in Christian letters (e.g., Acts 15:23; 23:26). Given the frequency of both the basic format and the minor deviations from it, it is always difficult to know how much importance to give to the particulars of such salutations. In Paul's Letters, we often detect a signaling of the larger issues of the letter in the wording of the salutation. But this is not the case with every salutation. Readers of Jude have most often wondered both about the unusual instance of identifying someone by the name of their brother rather than the name of their father and about the theological themes that surface in the naming of the recipients. Both shall be examined below.

1 Jude,[a] servant of Jesus Christ and brother of James, to those who are called, who are loved[b] in[c] God the Father and kept for[d] Jesus Christ.
2 May mercy, peace, and love be multiplied for you.

    a. The Greek is actually "Judas" (*Ioudas*). However, this "Judas" is traditionally rendered "Jude" in order to distinguish him from the "Judas [son] of James" in the list of the Twelve in Luke 6:16.
    b. Probably in an attempt to avoid the awkwardness of the phrase "loved in God," some later manuscripts (P, M) read "sanctified" (*hēgiasmenois*).
    c. The awkwardness of the phrase "loved in God" has led to various emendations, especially translating the *en* as the instrumental "by."
    d. Again, some translators prefer an instrumental "by" for the dative. However, the more common dative of interest fits nicely with the theology of the letter.

[1] As we noted in the introduction, it is simplest to understand this Jude as Jude the brother of Jesus. Jude the brother of Jesus is mentioned in Mark 6:3 and Matt 13:55, but little is known about him beyond his name and lineage. There is certainly nothing about the character, history, or beliefs of this Jude

that would assist in the reading of this letter. The author seems to employ this name not because of some peculiar tradition about him. What is needed is the name and the pedigree.

The designation "servant of Jesus Christ" is of course common in the NT. Forms of it are found in the self-designations of the writers of James and 2 Peter, and of Paul in Romans and Philippians. Furthermore, the term "servant of God" is a key designation in the OT for various leaders. And the term "servant" is used for Christians in general (e.g., 1 Pet 2:16). The question for readers of Jude is whether the term here means something beyond a simple naming of Jude as a Christian. Readers have often pointed to 1 Cor 7:22–23, with its notion of being bought by Christ and now being his slave. However, it is difficult to know how aggressively to import these larger theological arguments from different texts into a simple and common phrase such as this. More helpful is the idea that the term conveys an acknowledgment of responsibility for a particular task. Jude is not being called a servant of Jesus Christ simply to note that he is a good Christian but to suggest that in the particular task of writing this letter, he is doing service for Jesus Christ.

More puzzling is the designation "brother of James." People do not normally designate themselves by naming their brother. In so doing, the author highlights the status of James. There is little debate about which James is intended here. It is probably true that only James the brother of Jesus would be so named without further explanation. This awkwardness signals the peculiar nature of the claim being made here. The author does not name his father or even his brother Jesus but James. Thus it must be James's position as leader of the church in Jerusalem that is being evoked here. The author wants to speak from within that special authority. Hence the general claim to be acting on behalf of Jesus Christ as his servant is narrowed to a more special claim to be speaking from within the aegis of the church of Jerusalem.

The James tradition in the early church is complex, and little of it seems relevant to the arguments of Jude.[36] There is, for instance, no real evidence of a struggle with any developed form of antinomianism. However, there may be a connection with James's affection for the law. Much of the syntax of Jude is exegetical, resulting from readings of the OT. Thus, if the "law" is understood in the broad sense as being the ancient Jewish texts, then the claim to be brother of Jesus gives warrant and energy to the complex scriptural readings of Jude. As brother of James, Jude is committed to "what was written long ago" (cf. v. 4). It is this commitment to these texts that fuels the theological force and authority of the letter.

---

36. On the tradition of James, the brother of Jesus, see Bruce Chilton and Jacob Neusner, eds., *The Brother of Jesus: James the Just and His Mission* (Louisville, Ky.: Westminster John Knox Press, 2001).

Opening Salutation

The recipients are named by way of classic Jewish theological terms. To be named "those who are called" is, on the one hand, such a general Jewish and Christian self-designation that the peculiar sense of being called to a task or role or position is almost lost. On the other hand, it is this general sense that seems to matter most in Jude. The recipients are the ones who stand in this tradition of calling. The voices of both the ancient texts and the Christian apostles are in force in the lives of these Christians. The prophetic voices are speaking about them and their enemies. Thus the aggressive application of Scripture to the details of the contemporary debate is warranted because these people are, after all, "those who are called."

The force of this divine calling is perhaps best understood by means of the modifying participles "being loved" and "being kept." Few images are more pervasive and fundamental to both Jewish and Christian thought than that of "being loved" by God. The phrase in Jude is couched as being "loved in God the Father," not "by God." However, with this locative syntax the author is probably not denying that these called ones are loved by God; rather, the author is placing them in God's presence, in the location wherein God's blessings, promises, and warnings are and will take effect.

Furthermore, the classic imagery of being called and being loved finds a particular nuance in Jude. The calling and the loving include a keeping. These called ones are the ones who are "kept for Jesus Christ." God does a variety of keeping in Jude: keeping angels in chains awaiting punishment (v. 6), keeping darkness for the impious (v. 13), and keeping "you" from falling (v. 24). It is clearly this last that is in force here. God is keeping these called-ones safe. God loves them by protecting them from impious people and from impiety itself so that they will stand without blemish in the presence of God's glory at the very end (v. 24). Thus, as the letter of Jude opens upon the dangers of the Christian life in the arguments that follow, it does so with an evocation of God's love and keeping. Those same persons who are threatened by impiety are being kept safe by God for Jesus Christ. The syntax of keeping "for" Jesus Christ rather than "by" means that it is God who is the keeper. And God is keeping for Jesus because it is in Jesus where mercy lies (v. 21).

[2] The greeting itself takes the classic Jewish Christian form, although it deviates slightly from the most common form by having three elements rather than two. Mercy and peace are the most common terms in Jewish greetings. The addition of love is classically Christian. And the imagery of these gifts "being multiplied" is common to both traditions. The fact that this greeting is quite standard in syntax does not mean that it has no meaning or force. Certainly the letter itself, in its peculiar polemic, is hunting for mercy, peace, and love.

The salutation proves to be a fitting one for Jude. It names the author as someone who is performing a duty for Christ and who is speaking out of the authority of James, the head of the church in Jerusalem. The recipients are identified as standing in the great Jewish and Christian tradition of God's love and God's protection. They are the called ones. In being the called ones, God's words, spoken through texts and apostles, belong to them. And God's power to keep, both for blessing and punishment, is at work for them and their enemies. All of this will unfold in greater richness in what follows.

Reading this salutation through the lens of the larger arguments of Jude is perhaps appropriate, but it can be overdone. All the images here resist confinement to a precise theological agenda. The images are too pervasive and classical to disappear into any one theological argument. Instead, this salutation invokes such a richness of Jewish and Christian texts and teachings that it can be read almost liturgically. It creates echoes and memories of many other texts. Servant of God, called ones, loved in God, kept by God, love, peace, and mercy combine in these sentences less to create a precise argument and more to orient the reader and hearer to the greater theological world to which this text belongs.

Jude 3–4 Statement of Purpose and Opening Accusation

The opening of the body of this letter, while not following the common Jewish and Christian pattern of a prayer or blessing, shows the common Greek form of a petition. The petition itself is "to contend for the faith" (v. 3). However, the entire letter seems to be less a petition for others to contend and more an act in itself of contending for the faith. As an appeal the letter functions mostly as an example.

This petition also introduces two key rhetorical strategies that recur throughout the letter: those of naming and of appealing to the ancient text. The readers are named "beloved." The "certain people" who have entered the community are named the "impious." This naming will be greatly expanded in the following verses. And the distinction between these two groups drives the theology of the letter. Over them both will preside the notion of divine keeping. God is keeping one group for blessings and the other for punishment. The question of who is in which group and how firm is the line between them will haunt the letter. Furthermore, this naming receives warrant and force not simply from the peculiar authority of James. This act of naming emerges from the sacred text. Name-calling is, for Jude, largely an exegetical enterprise.

All of this illustrates the proper way to contend for the faith. Jude argues that Christians should contend by engaging in name-calling and by using the sacred texts to supply ancient names and stories with which to name the present.

Statement of Purpose and Opening Accusation 173

3 Beloved, being very eager[a] to write to you about our common salvation,[b] I find it necessary to write, appealing to you to contend for the faith that was once and for all handed over to the saints. 4 For certain people have slipped in, people who[c] long ago were written down for this judgment—impious people,[d] who change the grace[e] of our God into licentiousness and deny our only Master[f] and Lord, Jesus Christ.[g]

a. The circumstantial participle *poioumenos* has occasioned much debate. Many readers render the participle with a concessive sense: "although I was very eager." This reading suggests that the author changed his mind because of the pressing danger of the impious people. Thus Jude is not a letter about "our common salvation," but is instead an appeal to contend for the faith. Other readers see it as temporal ("when") or causal ("because"). The temporal reading given here suggests that writing about "our common salvation" includes an appeal to contend for the faith.

b. What is meant by "salvation" is not clear. Readers have pointed to both the common political meaning of the security of the state and the peculiarly Christian notion of eschatological deliverance. A few manuscripts (ℵ, Ψ) provide a helpful interpretation by adding the general term "life," so that the text reads "our common salvation and life." "Our common salvation" would mean "our life together," perhaps with both its communal securities and its eschatological forces.

c. The relative pronoun *hoi* (who) governs the three participles which follow: "were written down" (*progegrammenoi*), "change" (*metatithentes*), and "deny" (*arnoumenoi*).

d. Jude does a lot of naming or name-calling. This naming is crucial to the theological force of the letter. Attempting to capture the rhetorical effect of this naming in the Greek, as we have done here, leads to an occasional awkwardness in English.

e. The variants *charin* (ℵ, C. P, Ψ) and *charita* ($\mathfrak{P}^{72}$, A, B) are two alternate spellings of the accusative singular of *charis* (grace).

f. The term *despotēs* refers to the "master" of the house. It often implies the ownership of slaves. Judaism uses the term to refer to God, and early Christianity continues that usage. It is only rarely used to refer to Jesus.

g. The presence of the article *ton* before "Master" and the lack of one before "Lord" suggests that Jesus Christ is referred to as both Master and Lord. However, the fact that the title "Lord" often lacks an article in Christian texts means that "Master" and "Lord" could be referring to different persons. Some texts (P, Ψ, 𝔐) insert the name "God" with "Master" in order to guide the reading of the text. In spite of those emendations, Jude is probably addressing Jesus as both Master and Lord.

[3] The opening naming, "loved ones" or "beloved," serves as more than a polite address. This naming inaugurates the name-calling that forms much of the theology of the letter. Furthermore, the notion of being "loved in God" (v. 1) structures not only the character and task of the life of the recipients but also the character and task of the letter. The recipients are the ones who live in God's love. This place of God's love is formed not only by divine keeping for end-time blessings but also by a present keeping. This present keeping is

accomplished not only in unnameable ways by God (v. 24) but also by the rhetoric of the letter itself and the mercy and admonitions of the community (vv. 20–23). These loved ones are being loved in many ways, even by the admonitions of this letter.

The question of whether the participle *poioumenos* should be rendered as temporal or concessive is significant. Is contending for the faith, with its violent name-calling, an essential part of "our common salvation," or is such contending an aside, an interim, that distracts from the more proper tasks of living in God's love? The letter can clearly be read either way. The decision to render the participle as temporal means that the act of contending for the faith, all the aggressive name-calling in the letter, is understood as a proper moment in talking about salvation. The letter opens by saying that because certain people have come in among this community, the most pressing thing to address concerning the readers' "common salvation" is the danger that these persons pose. Reading this letter this way means, for instance, that we do not need to separate verses 17–19 from 20–23. In fact, the sequence of warnings and admonitions in 17–23 makes a concessive reading of *poioumenos* problematic. Living in God's love involves Christians in dealing with the impious in their midst.

The recipients are called "to contend for the faith that was once and for all handed over to the saints." A direct imperative for such contending seems to occur in verses 22–23, wherein the recipients are enjoined to practice mercy on the impious. But the letter itself also exemplifies what it means to contend for the faith. To contend means to read the sacred text, to learn where the line between being a loved one and an impious one is properly drawn, to apply the naming of the persons on each side of this line to their own community, and to seek themselves to remain or to return to the proper side of this line. To contend is to do exegesis.

What is meant by "the faith that was once and for all handed over to the saints" has long puzzled readers. The syntax suggests that faith must refer to a body of doctrine, a sequence of sentences. Something as slippery as "our life together" or "our common salvation" can hardly be handed down intact to the saints. However, it is not clear what this body of doctrines might be. There is certainly theological doctrine in the letter if the term "doctrine" is used loosely. But it does not seem to be of the kind of doctrine that provides a secure referent for this "faith." The doctrines that surface in the letter seem to be more the implications of such a body of faith than the body itself. Thus we must admit that we cannot be precise here. The letter suggests that this body includes the lordship of Christ (v. 4), grace (4), God's keeping (1, 6, 13, 24), final judgment (14–15), the mercy of the Lord Jesus Christ (21), and perhaps other notions implied by the letter. Beyond this it is difficult to know. In any case, this faith has been handed over to the saints, whose numbers must include the loved ones of the letter. They possess it and know what it is.

More striking is the notion of "once and for all." The notion of a fixed, complete, and inviolable deposit of doctrine is suggested here. Unless this "once and for all" is idle rhetoric, which seems unlikely, Jude adopts a position reminiscent of that in the Pastorals, wherein the image of a static body of traditions is evoked against the innovations of heretics (e.g., 1 Tim 6:20; 2 Tim 1:12–14). Yet in neither Jude nor the Pastorals is this body of tradition perfectly static. A perfectly static set of doctrines is not really conceivable. The meaning and force of every sentence changes as times, settings, and readers change, even if the words themselves do not. Nevertheless, in the rhetoric of Jude the origin of theological concepts lies in both the apostolic tradition (Jude 3, 17) and the sacred text (4, 5–11). In some ways the limitations on creativity and innovation implied in the language of "once and for all" are belied by the letter of Jude itself. It is itself an innovative text, composed not only of creative readings and applications of the sacred text but also of its own playful, if confrontational, rhetoric.

[4] Jude now moves to the heart of its argument. Most of Jude is a continuous name-calling of the impious. The particular structure of this name-calling is outlined here. With some irony, these impious people are never named by their own names. In this verse they are simply referred to as "certain people." The name-calling thus begins with a refusal to give proper names. The names of these people, it turns out, are properly derived by a reading of the sacred text. These people were written about long ago. Thus the name-calling is inaugurated and even warranted by the sacred text.

There is some debate about what books might be referenced here. The two real possibilities are either heavenly books, in which judgment is recorded, or the traditional Jewish texts. Although the language of judgment in Jude suggests the heavenly books where judgment is written down, the far simpler reading is that it is the prophetic books of the Old Testament and other Jewish texts, especially *1 Enoch*, that are being called upon here. This latter reading fits perfectly with the larger rhetorical structures of the letter. The names, the character, and the destiny of these impious people are discovered in the Jewish texts. There is no reason to imagine heavenly books. The books the readers have in hand are quite sufficient.

There is a further question of the precise reference of "this judgment." It is unlikely that "this judgment" refers back to general accusations of Jude 3; therefore, "this judgment" must refer forward. The question is how far the referent extends. It may be limited to the simple "impious people" or even to that phrase plus the immediately succeeding participial clause, "who change the grace. . . ." However, this pointing to judgment may simply be an opening upon the whole series of accusations from Jude 4 to 16. In either case, the bulk of the letter becomes, by way of this verse, a pronouncing of judgment. The geography of this judgment is complex. The final execution of it occurs at the final judgment, which hangs over the whole letter. This judgment is also already accomplished in that the texts have already named these people. Furthermore, these already-judged persons are being kept by God for their final judgment.

The name given them here is, in some ways, the perfect name for ancient polemic. *Asebeis* ("impious" or "ungodly") is a common word in Greek, Jewish, and Christian polemic. Although the term is perhaps the central one in Jude for the naming of these opponents (4, 15, 18), it is such a common term as to have little precise content. What makes someone "impious" is not clear in the word itself. The meaning and force of the word require explanation. To be impious means at least that one has fallen on the wrong side of God (or the gods). Beyond that, we must search the letter for hints as to what Jude might mean.

The first hint occurs in the phrase "who change the grace of our God into licentiousness and deny our only Master and Lord, Jesus Christ." The first part of this phrase contains the common Christian concern of libertine readings of Christian freedom. The immorality of *aselgeia* often includes sexual debauchery of some kind. Again, we cannot be precise. What kind of immorality the impious may be practicing is not clear. They are also accused of denying Jesus Christ. Again, there are questions. This denial could be an ethical denial of the sort attacked in Titus 1:16: "They profess to know God, but they deny him by their actions." Or we could have two separate accusations: these people practice immorality, and they deny that Jesus is our only Master and Lord. They will be accused of rejecting authority (6, 8), although this rejection is not christological. However, throughout Jude there is a persistent link between theological disobedience and immorality. This linkage is common in the New Testament. Bad theology and bad ethics go together, as do good theology and good ethics.

None of this brings us very close to any real insight into the character of these impious people. Perhaps the best hint lies in the verb at the beginning of the verse. These people "have slipped in." In the rhetoric of verse 4, these people are outsiders. In fact, the persistent negative naming in the letter constantly reinforces the outsider status of these impious persons. They belong to names, stories, and fates that are distinct from "you." Nevertheless, Jude conveys a danger beyond articulating the terrible judgment that awaits these impious: the readers themselves may become one of them if they are not careful.

The two verses form an effective introduction, not only to the purpose of the letter, but also to the whole rhetorical structure of the letter. The dual structure of naming, the authority and force of the sacred text, the promise of judgment, the idea of being kept, the struggle for orthodoxy and morality, and overall sense of polemic and warning—all these are etched in these two verses. Like all introductions, this one makes sense only when we see what follows.

Jude 5–16 Condemnation of the Impious

Jude 5–7 Three Examples of Divine Punishment

The denunciation of the impious (vv. 5–16) alternates between textual naming and contemporary naming. These two voices, those of the text and of the author, combine to produce a rather intense denunciation of these impious people who are living among them. The naming consists mostly of two types. The first, which is displayed in these three verses (vv. 5–7), but also in 9, 11, 14, and 15, consists in loose evocations of classic biblical persons and their fate. The second, which we see in verses 8, 10, 12, 13, and 16, seems to be a naming created by the author himself.

The exegesis that drives this section resists any neat categorization. Jude's reading of texts recalls rabbinic midrash, Qumran-style pesher, and Christian typology, but it does not coincide precisely with any of these.[37] In Jude the ancient text determines and names the present. In some ways, Jude's own time gains its structure through its invasion by the textual past. Herein lies a key dynamic in Jude's theology. To be a Christian is to be defined by times, both past and future, that are not this present time. To be a Christian is to live in the sacred texts. Christian theology occurs by way of unstructured and unprogrammed readings.

These verses use three examples from Jewish texts to warn the readers that God will judge and punish everyone, even God's own people. While verses 8–16 clearly focus the threat of God's judgment on the intruders, the examples in 5–7 seem to include the members of the community who have welcomed these intruders. This welcoming endangers all the members of the community.

> 5 I wish to remind you, even though you know everything, that the Lord,[a] having once and for all[b] saved a people out of the land of Egypt, on a second occasion[c] destroyed those who did not believe. 6 And the angels who did not keep their own position of authority,[d] but left their proper dwelling, he has kept under darkness in eternal chains for the judgment of the great day. 7 Likewise Sodom and Gomorrah and the cities around them, which, in the same manner as these,[e] practiced sexual immorality and went after the flesh of others,[f] are set forth as an example by undergoing a punishment of eternal fire.[g]

---

37. On midrash, see Jacob Neusner, *Judaism and the Interpretation of Scripture: Introduction to the Rabbinic Midrash* (Peabody, Mass.: Hendrickson, 2004). On Jewish hermeutics in general, see Michael Fishbane, *The Garments of Torah: Essays in Biblical Hermeneutics* (Bloomington: Indiana University Press, 1992).

a. Some texts (A, B) read "Jesus," some (C²) read "God," some (𝔓⁷²)read "God Christ," and still others (ℵ, C, Ψ, 𝔐) read "Lord." The best proposal for this confusion is that the text originally read "Lord," meaning God. Christian readers heard "Lord" as "Jesus." Textual variants emerged from this confusion.

b. Several texts (𝔓⁷², A, B, 𝔐) place *hapax* (once and for all) with the opening phrase, so that the text reads "you who know everything once and for all." However, its placement with "Lord" better reinforces the contrast in the Lord's behavior "on a second occasion," which is essential to the argument of these verses.

c. Uncertainty over the referent of the phrase "on a second occasion" has led many translators to suggest "later." This is a possible clarification but not necessary to the logic of the verse.

d. *Archē* can mean "beginning," "ruler," "rank," "dominion," or "authority." However, the context suggests that the proper rendering is "dominion" or "position of authority." In Jewish tradition, the angels are given authority to rule over the earth in God's behalf.

e. The pronoun "these" could refer to either the angels or the impious. The comparison in v. 8 might suggest the impious. However, a more natural reading understands the angels as the antecedent. Thus, both angels and the cities of Sodom and Gomorrah share a sexual sin.

f. "The flesh of others" probably does not mean simply "the flesh of other people." The phrase more likely has the sense of "strange or different flesh."

g. The Greek could be translated "an example of eternal fire when they underwent punishment."

[5] The rhetoric of reminding is significant, not because it expresses a politeness about the competency of the recipients, but because it reveals the open character of the exegesis. The author is evoking stories that he assumes his readers already know. Their knowledge is crucial to the force of the citations. He is not writing down everything he wants his readers to think. He is recalling rich stories with complex characters, and he is inviting his readers to read and remember with him. It is not, of course, literally true that the readers "know everything." Rather, they already know these stories and are being invited here to recall these stories in a particular way. They are to remember and rethink these stories in light of the impious people in their midst.

Each of these texts, when read a certain way, contains a warning to the readers. The first time Jude uses "once and for all" (v. 3), it calls forth images of surety and security in God's keeping. But in this verse the surety of the "once and for all" is compromised. God can save a people "once and for all" and later destroy them. A warning is hereby put in place. The recipients of the letter were also saved once and for all, but this "once and for all" comes with conditions. A person cannot, for instance, pervert God's grace into licentiousness (v. 4). The implied point seems to be that God destroyed these ancient people and might destroy the recipients of the letter.

On closer inspection, the point seems less clear. It is not clear what is meant by God's act of either saving or destroying. We might assume that the reference

Three Examples of Divine Punishment

to saving is not to one specific moment in the exodus story but to the whole thing. The readers need to rethink the whole story in order to hear this sentence well. God did lots of saving then, just as God does now.

Even more allusive is the referent about destroying those who do not believe. The curious expression "on a second occasion" suggests a specific event. Most readers of Jude have pointed to Num 14, which contains the story of Israel's "disbelief" following the report of the spies sent into Canaan and of God's reaction to their disbelief. The language of Jude 5 recalls especially the language of Num 14:11–12. However, the open imagery of Jude 4 should not be confined to the specifics of Num 14. Such texts as Ps 106 demonstrate that many kinds of disbelief and many instances of punishment by God can be found in the exodus story. The fuzziness of the referent here is functional. The rich variety of stories in the exodus complex shows that there are many ways that people can disbelieve and many ways that God might punish them.

[6] The second biblical allusion is to the angels (or the "Watchers," as they are known in tradition, see, e.g., Dan 4:13, 17, 23) of Gen 6:1–4. These watchers become key figures in Jewish tradition as corrupters of the human race. Jude, however, seems less dependent on this general tradition than on the specific version found in *1 Enoch*.

Jude's treatment of *1 Enoch* has long troubled Christian readers since he cites this book as though it had all the authority of a canonical text. In fact, *1 Enoch* is not simply treated as having authority; it is the key text for Jude. The basic theology of *1 Enoch* is the basic theology of Jude. Jude does not simply cite *1 Enoch* as authoritative; Jude sees the world through the theology of *1 Enoch*. The story of the watchers, which is perhaps the fundamental story in *1 Enoch*, serves for Jude as more than an example. The story of the watchers, as narrated in *1 Enoch*, articulates for Jude the truth about both people and God. People are ready to abandon their calling and pollute the world; God is ready to punish. (For further consideration of Jude's theological framework, see the excursus "The Tradition of Enoch and the Fallen Angels" pp. 116–17, after the comments on 1 Pet 3:18–22).

The misdeed of the angels seems to be in abandoning both their responsibility ("their own position of authority") and their home ("their proper dwelling"). In *1 Enoch*, as in most other texts, the disaster of the watchers lies less in some neglect of the world and more in the devastations that their arrival on earth produces. Their lust for human women leads to the issuing of a race of giants that inflicts evil on the world. Though this lust is recalled in the next verse, here the problem seems to be that of disorder. This is a prevalent accusation in the ancient world. Things and people should stay in their proper place.

The description of punishment given in this verse provides a wonderful summary of Jude's overall imagery of divine punishment. As in *1 Enoch*, not only will God punish at the very end; God also is already beginning that punishment.

Punishment in Jude is twofold: it is occurring now through God's power to keep, and it shall occur in full at the very end. In Jude, as in *1 Enoch*, God keeps. God keeps the angels "under darkness in eternal chains." And this keeping awaits the "judgment of the great day." God's power to keep is key to Jude's theology. Perhaps this is why the angels are named as ones "who did not keep their own position of authority." God keeps all creatures in their proper place. These angels do not even keep themselves thus.

Finally, there is the puzzle of how to connect the angels of this verse to the cosmic powers mentioned in the following verses. In 8 the intruders are accused of slandering the glorious ones. These "glorious ones" cannot be identical to the disobedient angels of verse 6 because the author of Jude would be guilty of the same slandering as the intruders are. It is not possible to identify with any precision what the approved cosmic hierarchy is for the author. The orders of the heavens include both disobedient angels and glorious figures that deserve respect. Given the ambiguities of all of this, it is also not possible to detail the precise theological errors of the intruders.

[7] There seem to be two comparisons accomplished in the example of Sodom and Gomorrah. The first comparison ("likewise") hinges on the similarity of punishment. The second ("in the same manner as these") turns on the similarity of sexual immorality. Finally, the whole story is affirmed as an example (*deigma*) of how God punishes. Jude has a wonderfully fluid use of ancient texts. In these verses, the ancient text does not provide names for the present (vv. 4, 11) but examples. This requires a different kind of reading. Apparently Jude is not working out of a formal exegetical theory: the text speaks in many ways.

Sodom and Gomorrah (and the cities around them) are declared to be examples of how God punishes. God's capacity to punish the impious, which is absolutely essential to the argument of Jude, here finds textual proof. The story of Sodom and Gomorrah proves that God can and will punish.

The sexual sin of the cities is not homosexuality. Neither the syntax of going after "the flesh of others" nor the comparison with the sins of the angels suggests homosexuality. In place here is the tradition that the visitors to Sodom and Gomorrah were angels. Just as the angels in verse 6 desired the flesh of human women, the men of Sodom and Gomorrah in verse 7 desired the flesh of angels. The problem then is sexual disorder.

The reference to "the cities around them" may be an oblique warning to the readers. Perhaps the recipients themselves are not Sodom and Gomorrah, but they are the surrounding cities. Thus they are in danger of suffering the same punishment as the impious.

It is not adequate to see these three examples simply as proof that God punishes sins. Though these stories do serve as proofs or examples or illustrations of how God punishes, they do more than that. The specifics of the story cannot be discarded too easily. The sins of disbelief, disorder, and fornication are highlighted here. While in verse 8 the impious intruders will be specifically attached to these sins, these verses also serve as a warning to everyone in the community.

The question remains as to what dangers for the community are being highlighted in these three examples. Fornication, disorder, and disbelief are so common in the rhetoric of ancient polemic as to become, at least at times, nothing more than cliches. However, most readers of Jude detect something substantive and specific in these three charges. The accusations of disorder and disbelief fit with other accusations in Jude. For instance, the intruders are accused of denying "our only Master and Lord, Jesus Christ" (v. 4) and of rejecting authority (v. 8). Sexual immorality is also suggested in the imagery of defiling the flesh (v. 8) and turning grace into licentiousness (*aselgeia*, v. 4). Thus we should probably conclude that the author of Jude sees bad belief, disorder in the community (and perhaps the heavens), and sexual immorality as serious threats. Furthermore, the intruders are perceived as embodiments of these threats. It is not possible to be precise about what the wrong belief is, what the disorder might be, or what sexual practices are envisioned. Jude provides no specifics, and each of these threats could take many forms.

Jude 8–13 The Naming of the Impious

The unmasking of the impious is taken up directly in these verses. The blending of textual voice and the author's voice produces an intense and complex denunciation of these impious ones. The volume of the author's own voice increases here. Nevertheless in verses 9 and 11 (and even 12–13) the voice of the ancient text returns, reinforcing and giving warrant to the personal polemics of the author. Some readers connect verse 8 with 5–7 and read the three accusations of 8 as the concluding application of the three examples of impiety. However, most readers read the explicit accusations of 8 as introducing the explicit accusations of 9–13.

It is not possible to settle upon a neat outline for these polemics. They seem to work mostly by way of accumulation. The author piles accusation upon accusation, bad name upon bad name. It is the growing weight of it all that produces the rhetorical force of these verses.

> 8 Yet in the same way, these people,[a] in their dreaming,[b] defile the flesh, reject authority,[c] and slander the glorious ones.[d] 9 But when the archangel Michael, while disputing[e] with the devil, argued over the body of Moses, he did not dare to bring a judgment of slander[f] but said, "May the Lord rebuke you." 10 But these people slander whatever they do not know, and whatever they do understand instinctively,[g] like irrational[h] animals, by these things they are destroyed. 11 Woe to them! For they walked in the way of Cain, they poured themselves into the error of Balaam for the

sake of profit, and they were destroyed in the rebellion of Korah. 12 These people are dangerous reefs[i] at your love feasts,[j] feasting[k] with you without reverence, shepherding themselves; clouds,[l] waterless, blown along by the winds; trees,[l] autumnal,[m] fruitless, twice dead, uprooted; 13 waves[l] of the sea, wild, foaming up their own shame; stars,[l] wandering, for whom the gloom of darkness is kept forever.

a. Jude uses the demonstrative pronoun *houtoi* (these) to organize the naming sequences of the verses that follow. It is the opening word of vv. 10, 12, 16, 19. By using the demonstrative in this way, the text points precisely at "these people" without giving their names.

b. The circumstantial participle *enypniazomenoi* could be temporal ("while dreaming") but is more likely causative ("based on their dreaming").

c. Some texts (א, Ψ) have the plural *kyriotētas* (authorities) instead of the singular *kyriotēta*, thereby suggesting that "these people" reject specific humans or specific heavenly figures. The singular suggests that they reject either the Lord himself or the proper structure of cosmic and communal authority.

d. Given the ambiguity of the meaning of "the glorious ones," it is not surprising that some texts have the singular *doxan* (the glorious one).

e. The verb *diakrinō* often refers not just to argument but specifically to legal argument.

f. While the phrase *krisin blasphēmias* means literally "the judgment of slander," many readers have suggested a genitive of quality ("a slanderous judgment") so that this phrase would balance the slandering of the glorious ones in v. 8. However, if Jude is referring to the version of the conflict story proposed in the excursus "Michael and the Body of Moses" (pp. 184–85, after comments on Jude 9), then "judgment of slander" would balance the slander of the devil against Moses for being a murderer.

g. The adverb *physikōs* means "naturally" or "in accordance with nature."

h. The expression *ta aloga zōa* (irrational animals) evokes the common distinction in the ancient Mediterranean world between animals and humans. Humans are driven by reason (*logos*), while animals are not.

i. The feminine plural noun *spilades* is often translated as "spots" or "blemishes." This translation assumes that the word is a feminine form of the common masculine noun *spilos* (spot). The fact that 2 Pet 2:13 seems to replace the *spilades* of Jude with *spiloi* and that Jude 23 uses the verb *spiloō* gives credence to this translation. However, the feminine noun *spilas* is a common Greek word used mostly for large rocks hidden under the water near the shore. Furthermore, the translation "dangerous reefs" fits with the nature imagery that dominates these verses.

j. A few texts (A) read "in your deceptions" or "in their deceptions," replacing *agapais* with *apatais*. This is the earliest known usage of *agapē* to refer to the early Christian communal meal.

k. While the verb *syneuōcheomai* can have the negative connotation of "carousing," its normal meaning is "feasting together."

l. The force of vv. 12–13 derives in part from a Greek syntax that collocates four nouns in the nominative case, with each being followed by a series of modifiers. The

The Naming of the Impious

rather awkward English syntax offered here is an attempt to reflect the rhetorical impact of this repetitive naming.

m. The adjective *phthinopōrinos*, composed of *phthinas* (decay) and *opōra* (end of summer), normally refers to the late autumn. This is normally the time after the harvest.

[8] The persistent uncertainty in Jude over the relationship between the details of the rhetorical attack and the true character of the intruders surfaces again in this verse. The three accusations against "these people" explicitly echo the three exegetical examples in verses 5–7. Thus some readers see this verse more as exegesis than as description. It is more likely that this verse, like most of Jude, is a bit of both. It uses traditional polemics, but the accusations are not nonsense.

The force of the opening reference to dreaming as the foundation for these behaviors is not clear. In antiquity dreams are a well-known source of visions and revelations. However, revelations based solely on dreams were often suspect. This is apparently the sense here. Nevertheless, it is not clear what these people were dreaming or what they were claiming because of those dreams. Readers have often speculated that this dreaming is the source of the problem. The intruders are basing their theology and their behavior on suspect dreams and not on reliable traditions and accepted authorities. This scenario is possible but uncertain.

The accusation of sexual impropriety is so common in antiquity that it is always difficult to know how to hear it. It is possible that we have intentional flouting of sexual mores by the impious. It is perhaps more likely that the author assumes, as did many in antiquity, that sexual deviation underlies many other vices. Disordered sexual passion is at the root of much evil. Thus the author may not be accusing the impious of specific acts of sexual immorality. Instead, in accusing them of abuse of the flesh, he is signaling their general unrighteousness.

The accusation of rejecting authority (*kyriotēta*) should probably be connected to the denial of "our only Master and Lord [*kyrion*], Jesus Christ" in verse 4. These impious deny the Lord. This assertion begs the question. Jude gives no direct comment on exactly how they are denying the Lord.

What Jude might mean by accusing them of slandering of the glorious ones (*doxas*) is even less clear. Although humans can occasionally be called "glorious ones," it is much more likely that the common referent of angels is intended here, especially since there are so many angels surfacing in Jude. But it is once again difficult to know precisely what the impious are doing. Of the many suggestions, two seem somewhat plausible. Christians were wont to assert their superiority to angels (1 Cor 6:3; perhaps even Heb 2:7). Perhaps these impious persons, out of a sense of sharing Christ's superiority to angels, place themselves above the angels in the cosmic order. Or perhaps the impious are rejecting the role of angels in the giving and administering of the law. We do not need to imagine a full-blown antinomian position in this rejection. We might imagine instead that God is speaking to these persons in dreams and that those encounters provide the impious with their primary moral and social directives. Such a private moral compass would also help to explain the accusation of sexual immorality.

[9] The reference to the debate between Michael and the devil is notoriously obscure. It is not clear what version of the story Jude might be recalling. It is also not clear what point Jude is trying to make.

As noted in the excursus "Michael and the Body of Moses" (below), the story of the conflict between Michael and the devil over the body of Moses circulates in several versions. The version most likely suggested in Jude is the devil's dispute of Moses' right to a proper burial because Moses killed the Egyptian. Michael argues with the devil, eventually calling upon the Lord to rebuke the devil. The initial force of the citation is to affirm Michael as exemplary in his refusal to presume the right to judge the devil for slandering Moses. Such judgment apparently belongs to God. However, it is not clear what the function of this example is in the argument of Jude. Most readers hear an echo of the slandering in verse 8. The impious slander angels, while Michael refused to slander even the devil who himself was slandering Moses. This reading suggests that the example of Michael's reserve functions as a further rebuke of the impious. In this reading, Michael's refusal to judge serves also as a model for the readers, who should leave final judgment to God. Perhaps in this reserve there is an anticipation of the solicitude for the opponents in verses 22–23. Finally, readers who detect a debate in Jude over the status of the law hear a warning to those who follow the law. While loyalty to the law is a good thing, it does not give anyone the right to judge others based on that law. In all of these readings, the quote from Zech 3:2 forms a fitting conclusion. May the Lord, and not anyone else, rebuke the impious.

Excursus: Michael and the Body of Moses

The reference in Jude 9 to a dispute between Michael and the devil (*diabolos*) over the body of Moses is couched, as are most textual citations in Jude, as if the readers are familiar with the story. The difficulty for the modern reader is that, although the canon contains no reference to such a conflict, in extracanonical Jewish literature are many versions of this story. Early Christian literature typically attributes the citation in Jude to the *Assumption* [*analēpsis*] *of Moses* (e.g., Clement of Alexandria, *Fragment in Epistula Judae*; Didymus the Blind, *Epistula Judae enarratio*; Origen, *De princ.* 3.2.1). This attribution creates its own problem, because the fragment of the so-called *Assumption of Moses* that we possess does not contain this story nor does it make any reference to a coming assumption. We cannot, therefore, either confirm the attribution or discover what version of the story might have been provided in the text.

Among the many accounts with their numerous variations, there are three basic versions of the story. First, the devil wants to return the body of Moses to the Israelites so that they can bury him in a prominent place and make a god of him. Michael fights with the devil and wins the body. Michael then removes the body to an unknown place. Second, the devil denies Moses the rights to an honorable burial because Moses killed the Egyptian. This conflict is more legal than spiritual. Michael calls on the authority of the Lord in order to take possession of the body. Third, the devil does not accuse Moses but rather asserts his own authority as master of the material world. The devil insists that all bodies, including that of Moses, belong to him. Michael again calls on the authority of the Lord to claim the body.

Mixed in with these accounts are references to the rebuke of Satan in Zech 3:2. Zechariah's fourth vision contains a dispute between "the angel of the LORD" and "Satan." In this dispute, the Lord rebukes Satan with the words quoted in Jude 9: "May the Lord rebuke you." Jude cites the text as if the angel of the Lord and not the Lord states the rebuke. It is possible that the text Jude was citing read thus. There is nothing about the body of Moses in Zechariah's vision. However, this rebuke surfaces in various forms throughout the accounts of the conflict over the body of Moses. The author of Jude is not the first one to combine the two accounts.

The question remains: What version of the story was Jude citing? We can assume that early Christian writers are reliable in their attribution to the *Assumption of Moses*. Yet this does not help much since we only possess a fragment of the text and that fragment does not contain this story. In the various versions of the story, language of blasphemy and slander occurs most often in accounts where the devil accuses Moses of murder. Michael does not return the slander of the devil with a slander of his own but calls upon the Lord. Given Jude's use of the semilegal term *diakrinō* and its inclusion of the rebuke from Zech 3:2, this version seems to fit best with the imagery of Jude 9.

[10] This verse opens with the demonstrative pronoun *houtoi* (these people). This is the second of four instances in Jude (vv. 10, 12, 16, 19) of this rather effective rhetorical move where the demonstrative pronoun points to the impious opponents without having to provide a name for them. This verse builds upon the classic ancient contrast between humans and animals. As this verse points out, animals act by instinct and not by reason. "These people" are accused of acting the same way. They lack understanding based on reason. Furthermore, what they do understand, they understand "instinctively," as animals do.

While the accusation of only having animal-like understanding is straightforward, the force of the other images in the verse is less clear. First of all, the usual accusation by Christians against Christian opponents is that they lack the spirit (e.g., 1 Cor 2:7–16), not that they lack reason. Second, while the accusation that they "slander whatever they do not know" obviously echoes the accusation in verse 8 that they "slander the glorious ones," the point of neither reference is clear. As noted above, these impious people seem to have some disagreement with the traditional view of angels. However, it is not apparent what that difficulty is. Finally, the text does not detail precisely what these people understand on the basis of nature and why this instinctual understanding leads to their destruction. Most readers point to the suggestions of sexual immorality in imagery of licentiousness (v. 4) and the defiling of the flesh (v. 8). Sexual immorality was often attributed to absence of reason. Given all of this, the exact force of this verse is difficult to determine. These people are animals in the sense that they live according to instincts and not according to reason. In this less-than-human life, apparently they slander heavenly beings and defile themselves with sexual immorality. In consequence for living this way, they will be destroyed. Their destruction probably does not come from forces inherent to these vices but from God's judgment.

[11] This traditionally couched woe changes the format of the attack back to the pattern of using the ancient text to provide the naming. Biblical woes tend to enumerate either the sins of the people or their coming punishments. Some woes contain both. This woe is unusual in that it invokes three biblical stories, each of which contains sins and their punishments. Each of these stories is further developed in extracanonical Jewish literature, and each is frequently cited in both Jewish and Christian literature as exemplifying certain kinds of sins and their punishments. The different forms these stories take in extracanonical literature makes it difficult to know what version is referred to here and thus what sins and punishments are being evoked.

Cain is cited in this literature not only as a murderer who pollutes the land with innocent blood (Gen 4:1–16) but also as the archetypical sinner and even the first heretic. Balaam is narrated mostly as a hero in the older version of his story (Num 22–24). He resists the request of King Balak to curse Israel because doing so was contrary to the command of God. It is possible that Jude is recalling suggestions of bestiality that later texts imply as having occurred between Balaam and his donkey. However, this fits poorly with the accusation of sinning for the sake of profit. It is more likely that Jude is referring to versions of the story in which Balaam, perhaps out of desire for financial gain, gives in to Balak's request (e.g., Deut 23:4–5; Neh 13:2; Philo, *Mos.* 1.264–300). Korah's rebellion (Num 16:1–50) centers on the question of the rights of the priesthood. Korah, a Levite, objects to the exclusive rights of the sons of Aaron. Korah joins forces with Dathan and Abiram to oppose the authority of Moses and Aaron. They and their families are swallowed up by the earth. A fire comes from the Lord, which begins to consume the people of Israel. Moses stands between the Lord and the people in order to save them. In later Jewish tradition, Korah objects not only to the rights of the priesthood but also to other aspects of the law (*Tg. Ps.-J*, Num 16:1–2; *Num. Rab.* 18.3). He accuses Moses of making things up. Korah thereby becomes the epitome of the antinomian heretic.

The question for readers of Jude concerns how any of these stories connect to the opponents of the author. In some ways, these references can be read simply as an exercise in name-calling. Three famous, or infamous, figures in

Jewish history are connected to the opponents, thereby placing "these people" on the wrong side of the story of Israel. However, it is also possible that these examples were chosen because the specifics of the story connected to the specifics of the author's debate with his opponents. Cain as the murderer is probably not relevant, but Cain as the original heretic might be. Balaam's disobedience to the commands of the Lord for the sake of money may signal a problem with greed or money that the author perceives in his opponents. Finally, the story of Korah is applicable not just for its illustration of rebellion against proper authorities but also for the terrible fate of Korah, his friends, and his family.

[12–13] The opening demonstrative *houtoi* (these people) introduces a quite different set of images. Five negative images drawn from nature are interspersed with two accusations of impiety. The author appears to draw on *1 Enoch* for four of the nature images and for the language of the "gloom of darkness" being kept forever. These verses are classic examples of how Jude gathers and accumulates diverse imagery from diverse sources that together produce a rather effective rhetorical attack.

Although we cannot reconstruct many details about early Christian communal meals, in Jude's time "love feasts" (*agapai*) probably included both a celebration of the Eucharist and a communal meal. The image of "dangerous reefs" (*spilades*) is a natural one for the world gathered around the Mediterranean Sea, where there were many submerged rocks. The image also fits with the accusation that heretics are in the midst of the community. These impious people are hidden beneath the water or beneath the facade of being a good member of the community; thus they can inflict great damage. The imagery of a lurking danger within the community issues in the only direct statement in these verses. These hidden reefs feast with the community, but they do so without proper reverence. Though no details of either the feasts or the irreverent behavior of these people is given, this imagery assumes that these people are members of the community. They participate in the communal meals. What distinguishes them is that they do so improperly. The images that follow build an evocative, if allusive, picture of their behavior.

In a rather imprecise echo of Ezek 34:2–3, the initial accusation is that they shepherd themselves. In early Christian literature, shepherding language typically refers to leadership within the community (e.g., John 21:16; 1 Cor 9:7; Eph 4:11; 1 Pet 5:2). Apparently these people aspire to leadership; they play the role of shepherd. However, they do so in a way that denies the core duty of shepherds. They do not shepherd the flock but themselves. While we cannot reconstruct what these people were or were not doing that evoked this accusation, this charge seems to articulate the fundamental problem that governs the ensuing images. These people are worthless to the community.

The grammatical structure of the next four images is striking and difficult to reproduce in English. Four nouns are given in sequence, each in the nominative case, each followed by a series of negative adjectives. Each is a common image from nature. In fact, the sequence of clouds, trees, waves, and stars seems to include every domain of the ancient universe. The entire sequence provides an account of nature that is neither productive nor orderly.

Clouds that are waterless are useless to others. People that are driven by the wind are unreliable, unanchored in orthodoxy, and thus unfit for leadership. These people are also trees that are so dead and useless that they are uprooted. "Autumnal" could refer to harvest time or more likely to postharvest time. The accusation of being fruitless normally means that one lacks righteous deeds. The precise botanical condition of trees that are "twice dead" is hard to reconstruct, even if the point is clear enough. The accusation of being disconnected from tradition and lacking in righteousness is reinforced in the description of waves that are wild, foaming up their shame, and in the final image of wandering stars. Stars should stay in their assigned positions. Wandering stars are rebelling against cosmic order. For these stars and thus for these impious people, the "gloom of darkness" is waiting.

All of these images appear to be derived from the key textual traditions of Jude. The imagery of waterless clouds probably comes from Prov 25:14 or *1 Enoch* 80.2–8. The image of trees and their fruits could come from anywhere since Jewish and Christian texts are filled with that imagery (e.g., Ps 1:3; Matt 7:16–20; Luke 3:9; 13:9). The imagery of wild waves and their foam probably depends on Isa 57:20. The language of wandering stars probably comes from *1 Enoch* (e.g., 18.13–16; 21.3–6), as does the language of the waiting darkness (e.g., 46.6; 63.6; 88.1). In fact, the sequence of clouds, trees, waves, and stars also occurs in *1 Enoch* 2.1–5.4 and 80.2–8. These traditional images are used rather effectively to make an interesting argument. The disorder of these impious, would-be leaders is equal to the infamous disorder and rebellion of cosmic beings. Furthermore, as the textual tradition affirms, all disorderly beings, whether of heaven or earth, will be punished.

This wonderful agglomeration of images paints a rich and condemning portrait of the impious opponents of the author. Apart from the sheer piling up of negative images, the main impact of this passage (8–13) derives from using classic textual images to name these people. Explicitly this passage connects the impious to well-known stories and persons in Jewish texts, characters who are always on the wrong side of the story. They are connected, for instance, to murderous Cain, greedy Balaam, and rebellious Korah. They are also connected to a disordered and rebellious natural world. They are dangerous reefs, waterless clouds, dead trees, and wandering stars.

In all of this, they are portrayed as people who aspire to leadership but lack all the qualities needed. Unlike the readers of the letter, who are admonished in verse 20 to build each other up, these people shepherd themselves, have no

Enoch's Prophecy of Judgment

loyalty to tradition or order, practice shameful deeds, and endanger the community. In doing this, they join a long line of unrighteous and rebellious people. The ancient texts describe them perfectly. This passage uses the language of those sacred texts to identify, unmask, and condemn these impious people.

The intensity and repetitiveness of this attack suggests that these opponents were enjoying some success. This passage attempts an unmasking. It gives unfavorable names to people enjoying favor. The persuasiveness of this attack depends on whether the naming sticks. Appealing to the authority of the ancient texts is not enough. These people must fit the profile. It is not possible to know for certain how the readers of Jude responded to this textual naming. However, the presence of Jude in the canon suggests that this attack worked.

Jude 14–16 Enoch's Prophecy of Judgment

Jude's extensive reliance on *1 Enoch* is clearly displayed in this passage. A quote from *1 Enoch* 1.9 forms the heart of the passage (Jude 14b–15). This quote is followed by the familiar rhetoric of "these people," who are denounced with a combination of biblical images. The style is typical of Jude. More to the point, the theology of *1 Enoch* 1.9 becomes the theology of Jude. *First Enoch*'s announcement of judgment on the impious, not just in this verse but throughout *1 Enoch*, is central and formative to Jude. Much of the Letter of Jude is announcement of judgment on the impious who have slipped in. This announcement comes from a combination of identifying these impious people with the impious people in the sacred texts and of affirming the promise of judgment in these same texts.

Jude's quotation seems to be a combination of Ethiopic and Greek versions of *1 Enoch* 1.9. We do not know, of course, what versions were known by the author of Jude. Thus it is not possible to say whether this is a loose quote from memory, an intentional combination, or a precise quotation from a version we do not possess. The further naming in verse 16 is also filled with familiar textual images.

> 14 It was also about these that Enoch, who was seventh[a] from Adam, prophesied, saying, "See, the Lord has come with his tens of thousands of holy ones[b] 15 to execute judgment on all and to convict every life[c] for all their impious[d] deeds which they have impiously done[e] and for all the hard things which these impious sinners[f] have said against him." 16 These people are grumblers, complainers,[g] walking according to their own desires. And their mouths speak arrogant things,[h] showing partiality[i] for the sake of gain.

a. While Enoch is seventh only if Adam is counted, this is the traditional counting (see *1 En.* 60.8; 93.3). The designation as the seventh obviously enhances Enoch's status as a prophet.

b. Some texts ($\mathfrak{P}^{72}$, ℵ) add the clarification that these tens of thousands are "angels." The Greek literally reads, "holy tens of thousands."

c. Texts are divided between *pasan psychēn* (every life or self or soul) and *pantas tous asebeis* (all the impious). The latter reading is supported by more texts (A, B, C, Ψ, 𝔐), and the Greek version of *1 En.* 1.9 reads *asebeis*. However, the former is the more difficult reading and has excellent early support ($\mathfrak{P}^{72}$, ℵ). There is no completely satisfactory English translation of *psychē* in this context. Whether the term is rendered as "life" or "person" or "soul," the point of the phrase seems clear enough. The Lord has come to judge every single person, living and dead.

d. The Greek version of *1 En.* 1.9 includes four usages of the root *aseb-* (impious, ungodly). Jude repeats them all, with the possible exception, noted above, of reading *psychēn* instead of *asebeis*.

e. The verb *asebeō* means "to act impiously." It is used to describe sins against the gods or abuse of religious duties.

f. While the words "impious sinners" can and probably should be read as the subject of the verb "have said" (*elalēsan*), they stand somewhat strikingly at the end of the sentence as though they begin a new naming sequence. There are parallels with the terminology and syntax of v. 4a, where the name "impious people" is highlighted in a similar way. In fact, v. 4a may ultimately depend for its general theology on *1 En.* 1.9.

g. The compound noun *mempsimoiroi* means, literally, "complainers against fate."

h. The compound *hyperonka* comes from *onkos*, which means "bulk" or "size." When combined with *hyper*, the word means something like "superbig" or "too big." Its normal usage is to refer to arrogant speech.

i. The phrase *thaumazontes prosōpa* literally means to "admire or flatter faces." It is a common Greek translation (along with *lambanō prosōpon*) for the Hebrew idiom "receive a face," which can be positive or negative. The image becomes the common one in the OT for showing partiality to the rich (e.g., Lev 19:15; Deut 10:17).

[14–15] While the letter of Jude is filled with partial quotes and allusions to sacred texts, these verses introduce the only quotation identified as such. Furthermore, this citation is fundamental to the theology of the letter. Debates about whether Jude considered *1 Enoch* to be canonical are anachronistic. It is unlikely that Jude had a working notion of canon. What is clear is that *1 Enoch* is the most important and powerful text for the author of Jude. This does not mean it has more authority than the Pentateuch or Isaiah, all of which are treated as sacred by Jude. It simply means that *1 Enoch* is the text that Jude cites most frequently.

In *1 Enoch* 1.2 the prophet insists that his vision is not for his own time but for the future. This view of prophecy becomes the standard one in early Christianity and is explicitly announced here. Jude insists that Enoch was speaking "about these." Jude seems to give Enoch special status among the prophets by noting that he is "seventh from Adam." The absence of a noun with the adjective "seventh" indicates that it is the number, not the just the antiquity of Enoch, that demonstrates this status.

The quotation itself is, as noted above, a combination of our Ethiopic and Greek versions. In *1 Enoch* the opening judgment begins with blessings for the elect (1.8) and issues in the condemnations of this verse. In all extant versions of the text, God is clearly the one who comes. Thus the introduction of the subject "the Lord" raises the question of the identity of the Lord and the origin of Christian imagery of final judgment. Language of the Lord coming with his angels certainly becomes one of the most common ways that early Christians will refer to the return of Jesus as judge (e.g., Matt 16:27; 25:31; 2 Thess 1:7). Though it is therefore likely that most Christian readers would have heard "the Lord" as a reference to Jesus, it is not clear what the author of Jude intended. Uncertainty over the meaning of "Lord" in Jude 4 (and the variants that the word "Lord" inspired) suggests a similar uncertainty here. In Jude, it is God who seems to keep people safe for final glory (vv. 1, 24–25). Furthermore, it is likely that the author of Jude intended "Lord" in verse 4 to refer to God. Thus the naming of the one who comes as "the Lord" may not be an attempt to affirm Jesus and not God as judge. In the theology of Jude, it does not seem to matter whether it is God or Jesus who acts as judge. What matters is that judgment occurs.

In *1 Enoch* "judgment on all" includes blessings on the elect. When Jude cites texts, it usually does so in a way that assumes some knowledge of the text. The reader is expected to recall things that are not explicitly said. In this case, however, Jude seems to focus judgment upon the specific condemnation of the impious that is quoted in the text. Various forms of *aseb-* build an account of impious people doing impious things. To this account of deeds is added that of "hard" words spoken "against him." Imagery of God as judging deeds and words is common not only to *1 Enoch* but also to Judaism and early Christianity. This imagery thus provides little in terms of a description of the behavior of these "impious sinners." Again, what matters is the reality of the coming judgment.

[16] In the usual rhetorical pattern of Jude, a textual reference gives way to a direct naming, which itself often has textual echoes. Grumblers and their grumbling are an essential part of the wilderness narratives (e.g., Exod 15:24; 16:2–12; Num 14:27–29). The word "grumbler" may even recall the grumbling that was part of Korah's rebellion mentioned in Jude 11 (Num 16:11) or the disbelief in the wilderness mentioned in Jude 5. "Complainers" (*mempsimoiroi*), with its etymological meaning of "complainers against fate," has more Greco-Roman echoes than Jewish, although Philo uses a form of the word in his *Life of Moses* to refer to wilderness grumbling (1.118). Together they create the image of people who, in parallel perhaps to the rebellious angels in Jude 6 and the wandering stars in 13, refuse to submit to proper order. The accusation of "walking according to their own desires" reinforces this portrait. It is possible that antinomian attitudes on the part of the "impious" are implied in all of these terms.

The accusation of speaking arrogant or boastful things is common in Jewish literature of this period (e.g., Dan 7:8, 20; *T. Mos.* 7.9). The Aramaic version of

1 Enoch 1.9 declares that the impious said "great and hard things." This arrogant speech is usually depicted as part of a person's rejection of the authority of God. Speaking arrogant things is a stereotypical act of impiety. The accusation of "showing partiality for the sake of gain" sounds almost exactly like the *Testament of Moses* 5.5. Of course, Jewish and early Christian literature is filled with this terminology (Lev 19:15; Deut 10:17; Prov 24:23; 28:21; Mal 2:9; Luke 20:21; *Did.* 4.3; *Barn.* 19.4). Unjust judges show partiality, while just ones do not. God certainly does not (e.g., 1 Pet 1:17). James 2:1–9 gives a classic early Christian account of such favoritism. The additional charge of showing this partiality "for the sake of gain" is a natural part of the traditional charge. People show partiality to the rich and powerful in order to be rewarded by them. Little can be said about the actual behavior of the impious in these communities based on this language alone. Nevertheless, all the charges in Jude create a powerful portrait of these would-be leaders who shepherd themselves and not the community.

The key affirmation of these verses (14–16) is that the Lord is coming to execute judgment. Jude does not give an account of the cosmic and historical events of God's judgment, although we might assume that the author would agree with the visions and narratives of *1 Enoch*. Furthermore, the author of Jude does not appear to be interested in giving a new account of the divine narrative. Instead, he tries to place his community into a narrative that is already known.

Finally, the crucial role of *1 Enoch* in the theology of the letter of Jude is displayed in these verses. Even if it never quite makes it into a Jewish or Christian canon, *1 Enoch* was a central text for the communities at Qumran and for much of early Christianity and early Judaism. Although its role in these communities is as diverse as is the text itself, its most common voice is the one it has here. *First Enoch* announces God's judgment. It does not say when it will happen, but it affirms that it will. This affirmation is fundamental to the theology of Jude.

Jude 17–23 Appeals to the Beloved

Jude 17–19 The Prophecy of the Apostles

These verses begin a transition that will be completed in verses 20–23. Ancient letters typically included direct appeals to the readers at the end of the letter. Following that classic pattern, the direct address "but you, beloved" signals a shift from focusing on the destiny of the impious to the proper response of the "beloved" to these impious. If it is true that impious people have slipped in, people who are to be identified with various negative characters in the sacred

The Prophecy of the Apostles

story, then the question remains as to what should be done. These verses begin to address that question.

They begin in a tone similar to that of verse 5. This is reminder. However, this reminder appeals to an authority not yet mentioned in Jude, that of "the apostles of our Lord Jesus Christ." These apostles have predicted that there will be "mockers" who "create divisions." There is no precise parallel in early Christian literature to the words of the apostles that are cited here, although the extensive predictions of 2 Tim 3:1–9 sound somewhat similar. Nevertheless, the rhetoric assumes that the readers would recognize this prediction, in some form at least.

The prediction itself contains such standard accusations that it is difficult to know if any real description of the impious is being offered. If these verses do contain information about the author's opponents, it is probably in verse 19, which offers three intriguing images that are new to the letter.

17 But you, beloved, remember the words[a] spoken beforehand[b] by the apostles of our Lord Jesus Christ, 18 that they said to you, in the last time[c] there will be mockers walking according to their own impious desires.[d] 19 These people are the ones who create divisions,[e] who follow natural instincts,[f] not having the spirit.

    a. Unlike *logos,* which has its etymological roots in "reason," the noun *rhēma* has its roots in "speech." Thus, *rhēmata* means something like "the things said."

    b. The participle *proeirēmenōn* (spoken beforehand) comes from the same root (*erō*) as *rhēmata.*

    c. In some texts ($\mathfrak{P}^{72}$, B, C, Ψ) the awkward *eschatou tou chronou* is improved with the omission of *tou.* Although forms of this phrase are common in early Christian literature, most instances read *hēmera* or *kairos* instead of *chronos.* In the OT the expression can refer to the future or, as it usually does in later literature, to final days of judgment. While early Christianity continues the pattern of using the phrase to refer to the days of judgment, the coming of Jesus as messiah constituted the beginning of "the last days." Thus the phrase is not confined to final days of judgment.

    d. The genitive *tōn asebeiōn* could be an objective genitive ("desires for impious deeds") or a genitive of quality ("impious desires"). The latter better preserves the feel of the common idiom of "walking according to desires."

    e. The rare verb *apodiorizō* and its more common form *diorizō* have the general meaning of "define," "classify," or "separate." There is nothing inherently negative about the word. Since the word is obviously intended to be negative in context here, most translations build on the sense of "separate" within the context of the community. Thus *apodiorizontes* is normally rendered as "the ones who create divisions."

    f. The adjective *psychikos* means "of the soul or life." In Stoic literature it means "natural" or "according to nature." Whether the word is positive or negative depends on context. In Greek philosophical literature, *psychē* is occasionally ranked beneath *nous* (mind) in the anthropological hierarchy. Probably in dependence on 1 Cor 2:14–15, in

Christian literature *psychikos* is often contrasted with *pneumatikos* (spiritual). Given the phrase that follows, a somewhat similar contrast seems to be in place here. In fact, *psychikoi* in Jude 19 seems to have much the same force as the adverb *physikōs* does in verse 10. Both terms separate these people from the realm of the Spirit and the understanding that goes with it. Thus most translators try to render *psychikoi* as meaning that these people have "soul" or "life" but not spirit. The rather awkward "who follow natural instincts" is an attempt to capture this distinction. These are people who are not led by the spirit of God but by their own human resources.

[17] The change in subject matter is signaled by the direct address to the readers: "but you, beloved." While in some sense all of the letter is addressed to "you," these verses and 20–22 (v. 20 repeats the phrase "but you, beloved") focus less on identifying the impious character of "these people" and more on what the "beloved" should do about them. As noted above, direct appeals to the readers were often included in ancient letters, and those appeals often rehearsed the main theme or themes of the letter. Such is the case here.

The readers are challenged to remember what the apostles said beforehand. Several uncertainties emerge from this challenge. Most readers see the combination of referring to the apostles as an established authoritative group and the appeal to remember their sayings as evidence of the postapostolic origin of the letter. It is possible that the apostles, or some of them, really did warn these readers, perhaps in person, about coming mockers. In such a reading the term "apostles" could refer to any and all apostles sent by Christian communities and not just to the Twelve. However, such a reading seems contrary to the usual sense of such appeals in early Christianity. It is easier to read the phrase "apostles of our Lord Jesus Christ" as referring, as it normally does in early Christianity, to the Twelve and perhaps Paul. Thus the question remains as to how and where these apostles said these things to these readers. As noted above, there is no known text that seems to be the obvious source for the content of what was said. However, there are many warnings in early Christian literature that sound similar to this (e.g., Acts 20:29–30; 1 Tim 4:1–3; 2 Tim 3:1–9). Jesus himself predicts false messiahs (Mark 13:5–6, 21–22). Jude, then, seems to be appealing to the broad range of apostolic tradition and not to specific texts or to a specific event in the community.

[18] The general force of the argument requires that the phrase "in the last time" means the present time of the readers. Furthermore, there is no indication other than this text that the author of Jude expected the Lord to come and judge in the immediate future. Thus, the argument must be that the presence of these impious mockers is evidence that the last times are drawing near. The argument is not that these are the last times and thus the beloved should be alert for mockers but its reverse. These mockers are a sign of the end.

Although the term "mockers" occurs in the NT only here and in 2 Pet 3:3, which is probably quoting this text, the figure is common in Jewish literature. In

The Prophecy of the Apostles

this literature, mockers are either people who reject religion and public morality (e.g., Ps 1:1; Prov 1:22; 9:7–8) or people who reject the claims of a particular religious group (CD 1.14). The latter seems the more likely nuance in Jude. These are people who obviously think of themselves as Christian but do not, in the opinion of the author of Jude, submit to the proper religious orders. The accusation that these people walk according to their own impious desires fits with the general sense of the term "mockers." These are people whose lives are ordered not by the proper religious powers but by their own desires. In Jewish, Christian, Greek, and Roman literature, it is agreed that to live driven by one's own desires is to live a terrible life.

[19] The three images of this verse have created considerable debate among readers. Many readers detect each of these accusations as evidence of the gnostic leaning of the impious in Jude's community. There are good reasons for this. Irenaeus (*Haer.* 1.6.1ff.) and Epiphanius (*Pan.* 31.7) accuse the Valentinians of dividing humans into three categories. The bulk of humanity are people of the earth (*choikos*). Most Christians are people of the soul (*psychikoi*). The true gnostics are people of the spirit (*pneuma*). These terms obviously fit nicely with this verse. The argument of Jude becomes a nice bit of irony. These are people who create divisions. They, we assume, would agree with this charge. However, Jude ironically asserts that these mockers are people of the soul, not people of the spirit. The author of Jude turns their divisions against them. This reading explains the accusations of creating divisions and not having the spirit. It also explains the negative use of *psychikoi*.

However, there are problems with this reading. These second-century gnostic distinctions probably came from reading 1 Cor 2:14–15, where Paul makes a distinction between the *psychikos* person, who does not understand the gifts of the spirit, and the *pneumatikos* person, who discerns all things. Many readers of 1 Corinthians think Paul is employing the terminology of his opponents against them. If so, this would indicate that these distinctions were not only current in early Christian communities but were also part of divisive rhetoric in those communities. However, few readers see the later gnostic distinctions in this debate between Paul and his opponents in Corinth. Instead, the terminology simply seems to be a convenient way to distinguish those who have the spirit and those who do not. Thus the accusation of creating divisions must be separated from that of being *psychikoi* and not having the spirit. It is possible that the impious of Jude are claiming that they have the spirit and that this claim creates divisions. However, it is also possible that Jude is simply employing a common early Christian accusation against these people and that nothing is divulged thereby about their true behavior. The similarity between this charge and that in Jude 10, which claims that these people only know things "instinctively [*physikōs*], like irrational animals," suggests that the point of all this is the accusation that they lack the spirit.

The most obvious new dimension of these verses (17–19) lies in calling upon the authority of "the apostles of our Lord Jesus Christ." This authority is employed in a quite general way. There is nothing specific reported about the lives of the apostles that warrants the particular prediction credited to them in these verses. For instance, the special relationship that these apostles had with Jesus is not evoked. The apostles function simply as prophets. Their prophecy also seems to add nothing really new or surprising in Jude's account. Thus it appears that the apostles are named at this point in order to assert that all accepted authorities agree with Jude's account of these impious people.

As is persistently the case in this letter, it is difficult to determine whether the accusations are disclosing any real data about the author's opponents. For these attacks to have any persuasiveness, there must be some overlap between rhetoric and reality. Though the accusations must have something true about them, it is not clear where the line is between rhetoric and reality. Certainly the author thinks that these people create divisions. The author also thinks that they are operating outside the proper orders and empowerments. The similarities with verse 10 are instructive. The charge is clear enough. These people do not have the spirit. This means that they live based on their own resources, which makes them inadequate guides for the community. They create divisions. They shepherd themselves. The contrast between this pattern and that imposed on the beloved in verses 20–23 is striking.

Jude 20–23 Appeal for Mercy

Given the intensity of the condemnations of the impious in the preceding verses, the pastoral tone of verses 22–23 comes as a surprise. Many readers actually feel that these verses change the entire tenor of the letter.[38] It turns out that the condemnations are not the last word. These verses counsel the beloved to rescue the impious from being the condemned people they have become. Thus the Letter of Jude first carefully and forcefully names these impious people with the names of the most infamous sinners of the history of Israel. But now, this same letter exhorts their rescue from these names.

The opening exhortation in Jude 20–21 provides an evocative summary of the Christian life. The four injunctions have a liturgical feel. The first, third, and fourth use the pervasive triad of faith, love, and hope. The second, third, and fourth follow the Trinitarian pattern of Spirit, God, and Christ. These patterns suggest the possibility of these verses coming from an unknown liturgical source. The author of Jude might well have penned the verses himself, using a liturgical style.

---

38. See, e.g., Bauckham, *Jude, 2 Peter*, 3–11. More typical is Kelly 228, who sees Jude as "a straightforward polemical tract."

Appeal for Mercy 197

The textual traditions behind the exhortations in verses 22–23 are as confused and uncertain as any passage in the NT. It is not possible to know with any certainty what the earliest text might have been. But for all the confusion and disagreement among the early texts about the precise wording of these verses, the main point is consistent. The beloved should try to save the impious from their impending punishment.

20 But you, beloved, building[a] yourselves up on[b] your most holy faith, praying[a] in[b] the Holy Spirit, **21** keep[a] yourselves in[b] the love of[c] God, waiting[a] for the mercy[d] of our Lord Jesus Christ into eternal life. **22** And[e] some who are disputing[f] have mercy on; **23** some save, seizing them from fire; some have mercy on in fear, hating even the garment stained by the flesh.

    a. These verses contain three circumstantial participles ("building ... up," "praying," and "waiting") that depend on the single imperative "keep." Some translations, in an attempt to capture the governing imperatival mood of the sentence, render the participles as imperatives, so that the verses read "build up ... , pray ... , keep ... , wait. ..." However, in order to maintain the centrality of the imperative "keep yourselves," it is preferable to render the participles as participles. From the syntax or context, it is not clear whether the participles are temporal ("while") or causative ("by"). This translation maintains that uncertainty.

    b. It is not clear how to translate these three dative locutions. Most translations render each dative in a way that makes sense for the content of each phrase. Thus the image of building suggests "building ... on," the image of praying suggests "praying in the Holy Spirit," and the command to "keep yourselves" suggests keeping "in the love of God."

    c. Grammatically the genitive could be objective, thus translated "love for God." However, the larger context fits better with "love of God" in the sense of God's love for the beloved.

    d. While the noun *eleos* normally means "mercy" in the sense of "pity," when it is used in Jewish and Christian literature in the context of final judgment, it has more the sense of compassion, kindness, and forgiveness.

    e. As noted above, the textual problems with these verses are notorious and unsolvable. Among the many variations in the ancient text, which cannot be explored here, two main options emerge. The first is the so-called two-clause text ($\mathfrak{P}^{72}$, C), which has various forms, with the oldest reading "some you seize from fire, some who dispute you have mercy on in fear." One of the ancient uncials (B), which supports the two-clause texts, reads "some who are disputing have mercy on, save them by seizing them from fire, but some have mercy on in fear." The three-clause reading is either as translated above or "some who dispute you convict; some you save, seizing from fire; some you have mercy on in fear." A good case can be made for all these readings. A decision in favor of one is mostly a guess. The three-clause version translated here has the virtue of good textual support (ℵ, A) and the fact that it includes much of the imagery that floats among the various versions.

    f. The participle *diakrinomenous* could refer to people who are disputing, doubting, wavering, or even judged. Disputing is perhaps the preferable translation because there is clearly dispute in Jude's community and because the same verb means "dispute" in verse 9.

[20–21] The repetition of the phrase "but you, beloved" introduces a new exhortation. The abbreviated style of these four traditional images suggests that the author of the letter is drawing on language and imagery familiar to the readers. Thus the full content of these verses probably depends on knowledge of the common traditions of the community. The liturgical feel, noted above, may indicate a source, although it is more likely that the author penned these liturgical-sounding images himself.

Imagery of buildings is common and diverse in early Christianity. It is typically used as an image of the community and especially for the need for the community to grow and be strong (e.g., 1 Cor 3:10–14; 1 Thess 5:11; 1 Pet 2:5). The imagery of buildings often includes that of a foundation, which varies from being the apostles (Eph 2:20) to Jesus Christ (1 Cor 3:11). Here the foundation is "your most holy faith." In this context, faith refers not to the act of belief but to its content. The beloved are to build themselves up by relying on the theological traditions of the community.

The commands, in participial form, to pray in the Holy Spirit and to wait for the mercy of "our Lord Jesus Christ" are also common in early Christianity. Though these are standard phrases, they are not without content. Prayer in the Spirit is probably to be distinguished from prayer not guided by the Spirit. The necessity for prayer being guided by the Spirit recalls the accusation that the impious lack the Spirit (v. 19). Waiting for the Lord is a common theme throughout the Bible. Here the emphasis is on a waiting for mercy that leads to eternal life. This hopeful waiting contrasts with the coming punishment for the impious. The tension between mercy and justice is fundamental to Jewish and early Christian notions of final judgment. Even the punishments of the impious narrated in *1 Enoch* 1.9 are combined with images of blessings and mercy for the elect (as in 1.8).

All three of these participles are anchored in the imperative to "keep yourselves in the love of God." The first two participles ("building" and "praying") probably have sense of accompaniment, while the last ("waiting") probably has the sense of result. In any case, these verses insist that all of this happens only if the beloved keep themselves in the love of God. Jude 1 named the recipients of the letter those "who are loved in God the Father and kept for Jesus Christ." Both verses 17 and 20 called the readers "beloved." Though we do not have access to the full theological thinking of the author of Jude, it seems that God's love for those who are called is the primary ordering force in that theology. God's love involves salvation (vv. 3, 21). Perhaps if the author had written about "our common salvation" (v. 3) instead of focusing on the impious intruders, this would have primarily involved articulating the character of God's love. It is striking that the author insists that people can keep themselves in that love. By implication, this means that people can exchange that love for punishment. These verses insist that the way they keep themselves in this realm of God's love is by building each other up on the foundation of the good tradition, by praying under the guidance and control of the Spirit and under the power of one's own desires, and by waiting for the mercy of Jesus Christ, which leads to eternal life.

[22–23] These verses have echoes of Zech 3:1–5, where Joshua is standing before Satan and the angel of the Lord. The Lord not only announces that Joshua is not condemned but also refers to Joshua as a burning stick snatched from fire and orders Joshua's filthy garment replaced with clean, rich ones. The context of judgment, the imagery of being saved from fire, the uncleanness of filthy clothes, and the ultimate salvation of the one threatened—these are all repeated in some form in Jude 22–23. There is no obvious reason that the letter invokes Zechariah. Perhaps the declaration in Zech 3:2, "The LORD rebuke you, O Satan!" connects with Satan's rebuke by Michael in Jude 9. In any case, these verses seem to employ only the imagery of Zechariah and not the larger theological themes.

The general purpose of these verses is clear enough. They call on the beloved to be merciful and to save those who are in theological danger. However, there is considerable debate concerning the identity of these people who are in danger and the force of the commands to be merciful and to save. In the longer textual tradition that is used here, three different responses are exhorted for three different groups. There are many attempts to determine the identity of these groups. For instance, if the participle *diakrinomenous* is translated as "wavering" or "doubting," then the endangered people would be those who are not the impious but are in danger of becoming so. The first imperative (and perhaps all three) would be a call to save the members of the community who are tempted to follow the impious sinners who have slipped in. The author's writing of this letter would be an example of how the beloved might do that.

Most readers, however, think these verses call on the beloved to have mercy on and to save the impious. These verses are addressed to the beloved, who are to have mercy on others. It is a bit awkward to call on the beloved to have mercy on themselves. Furthermore, the assumed topic in Jude is the impious and how to live with them. If at this point the driving issue were to shift to the question of wavering elect, then the text would need to signal such in a much clearer way than this. It is simplest to read the *diakrinomenous* as "those who dispute" and to understand the verses as advising the loyal beloved to show mercy on these impious people. The question remains as to whether there are three different groups or just three different ways of responding to one somewhat mixed group. Since the lack of explanation and description of these groups suggests that clear lines are not being drawn, these verses are probably discussing one large group who are caught up in the disputes in various ways.

The first command, to show mercy on those who are disputing, summarizes the intent of the verses. This is a basic norm that should drive all relationships with the impious and their followers. The beloved should be merciful toward them all. The second and third commands can be read as examples of two different ways this mercy might be displayed. The beloved will save some of these people from fire. Given the prevalence of fire imagery in early Christian accounts of judgment (e.g., Matt 3:10; 5:22; 18:9; 25:41; Rev 20:15) and its occurrence in Jude 7, the language of saving from fire must refer to the fire of judgment. Thus this command affirms that by being merciful on those who are caught in these disputes, the beloved will actually save some of them from eternal fire. The third command assumes that some of these people will be more resistant to this saving. Since the call to hate garments stained by the flesh is connected to Zech 3:3–5 and given the general use of clothing imagery and the staining power of the flesh, the imagery here must refer to people who have sins to which they are powerfully attached. These people are dangerous because their sins can stain others. Thus, while the call to have mercy on them remains, this mercy must be done "in fear." Some of the impious people will not be saved from fire. Their garments remain stained by the desires of the flesh. They are dangerous to the beloved. Nevertheless, the beloved should show mercy to them.

The direct address to "you, the beloved" continues and intensifies the shift in tone that began in Jude 17. These verses (20–23) contain two striking and somewhat surprising exhortations. First is a call to "keep yourselves in the love of God." This call is couched in liturgical rhythms and offers a concise and balanced summary of "the most holy faith." Second is a call to have mercy on those who are disputing. This call announces a noticeable change in the rhetoric of the letter from one of condemnation of the impious to that of mercy for these same impious. This call assumes the possibility that some of the impious will return to the folds of the beloved and that some will not.

Early Christianity was fond of brief faith summaries. All of Christianity has shown such fondness. While such summaries have many purposes, they all assume larger discussions. As summaries, they serve not only as pointers to these larger discussions but also as outlines of the main points. In this way, they serve as reminders of what is most central. With its treatment of "the most holy faith" as a reliable foundation for the community, this summary evokes the presence of a core set of traditions, much like the entrusted traditions of the Pastorals (1 Tim 6:20; 2 Tim 1:12, 14). Its reference to the four key themes of faith, prayer, love, and hope ("waiting for . . . mercy") parallels the Pauline triad of faith, hope, and love (1 Cor 13:13; 1 Thess 1:3). By way of these traditional terms, this summary makes two key points. First, God's love is the foundation of the life of the beloved, and this love is intended for salvation. Second, the beloved must participate in this love by means of faith, prayer, and hope.

Instructions for the treatment of heretics and their potential followers are also common in early Christianity. The tolerant tone of Jude is actually the usual one in early Christianity. There are exceptions. The book of Revelation, for instance, shows no mercy whatsoever to Christians who traffic with Rome. The surprising aspect of Jude is not that it would recommend mercy toward the impious but that the recommendation for mercy would be preceded by such thorough denunciation. There are, however, parallels to such combinations. For instance, after an intense condemnation, Paul pleads for the restoration to the community of the one who caused him pain (2 Cor 2:5–8). The similarly intense debates of the Pastorals are balanced with a reminder that Christ came to save sinners, of whom Paul himself is the foremost (1 Tim 1:15). Though the combination of strong condemnation and overriding mercy is not unique, it is still difficult to strike the proper balance. Jude condemns the impious with some of the most aggressive naming in the NT. We must assume that the author believed the danger to the community required such. However, Jude also remembers that mercy and love are key to the story of salvation. Even over these impious people, these children of Sodom and Gomorrah, these descendents of Cain and Korah's rebellion, these waterless clouds and wandering stars, God's mercy and love still hover.

Jude 24–25 Concluding Doxology

This well-known closing doxology has enjoyed rich usage in Christian tradition. Most Christian letters, including those in the NT, end with personal greetings and a blessing and not with a doxology. While doxologies are fairly common in the NT, they usually occur to mark a transition (e.g., Eph 3:20–21; 1 Pet 4:11). The most common location in a Christian letter is between the main body and the closing greetings (Phil 4:20: 2 Tim 4:18; Heb 13:20–21; 1 Pet 5:11). While many post-NT Christian letters close with doxologies (e.g., *1 Clem.* 65.2; *Mart. Pol.* 21), in the NT only Romans (16:25–27), 2 Peter (3:18), and Jude have concluding doxologies.

Although doxologies are more common in early Christian literature than in Jewish writings, they have similar forms in both. There is the naming of the addressee, usually in the dative; an ascription of praise, usually "glory"; a reference to time; and a concluding affirmation, usually "amen." This doxology has all of those pieces, with the first three being greatly expanded. The closest parallel to this particular doxology is the one in Rom 16:25–27, although there is probably no direct connection.

The formulaic and repetitive style of this doxology (and of all doxologies) raises the possibility that it originated from the dynamics of liturgy and not from the hand of the author of Jude. In particular, the expansiveness of this doxology seems to reflect the elaborating forces of worship. Thus some readers prefer to see this doxology more as a reflection of early Christian worship than as a final articulation of the theology of the author of the letter. However, even if this doxology was taken in its entirety from the worship tradition of the author or the readers, its themes and images cohere nicely with the rest of the letter.

> 24 Now[a] to the one who is able to keep[b] you from falling[c] and to present[d] you blameless[e] in the presence of his glory with rejoicing,[f] 25 to the only[g] God our Savior through Jesus Christ our Lord belong[h] glory, majesty, power, and authority,[i] before all time[j] and now and for all ages.[j] Amen.

a. The doxology begins with *tō de* and not with "now." Most translations attempt to render the adversative force of the conjunctive particle *de* with some adverb that evokes a transition.

b. The frequent biblical references to God keeping people safe employ a variety of terms for that keeping. In v. 1 Jude uses *tēreō*, which is the most common Greek term for divine keeping. Jude also uses forms of *tēreō* for angels who do not keep their proper positions (v. 6), for God keeping those angels under darkness (v. 6), and for the beloved to keep themselves in the love of God (v. 21). Here Jude uses *phylassō*, which has more the sense of "guarding."

c. The adjective *aptaistos* can mean "not stumbling" or "not falling." Stumbling expresses nicely the early Christian and Jewish sense of stumbling before the law or God's will. However, "falling" is the traditional translation.

d. The infinitive *stēsai*, which means "to stand," in the transitive has the sense of "cause to stand" or "present." There is an obvious contrast between the image of falling and that of standing.

e. The adjective *amōmos* is sometimes translated "without blemish." However, it literally means "blameless." The common translation "without blemish" comes from the use of *amōmos* to describe sacrificial animals found blameless by the priests because they are without blemish.

f. The noun *agalliasis* occurs only in Jewish and Christian literature. It comes from the verb *agallō*, which in the active means to "glorify" or "exalt," but in the passive means "to take delight." In Jewish and Christian literature the noun means something like "excessive joy" or "great exultation."

g. Most late manuscripts (P, 𝔐) add "wise," reflecting the syntax of Rom 16:27.

h. Almost all doxologies, including this one, lack the copulative, having simply the nominative "glory, majesty . . ." and the dative "to the one," with no verb connecting them. The question for translators is whether the verb should be construed as optative, expressing wish (with the doxology becoming a prayer of petition), or as indicative, expressing reality (with the doxology becoming praise and celebration). Most traditional translations prefer the optative, while most students of ancient doxologies prefer the indicative. The indicative translation given above reflects the sense that early Christian doxologies, including this one, were celebrations of God's glory and power.

i. There is some disagreement in the ancient texts on the exact terms and sequence of these divine attributes. However, this ordering has the best textual support (ℵ, A, B, C).

Concluding Doxology

j. While both expressions have the noun *aiōn*, which means "a period of time," "an age," or even "a generation," the first has the singular form and the second has the plural. The translation "before all time" (*pro pantos tou aiōnos*) attempts to distinguish the force of the singular from the plural "for all ages" (*eis pantas tous aiōnas*).

[24] The opening designation of God as the "one who is able" announces the core assumption of all doxologies. They are celebrations of God's power. The power celebrated here and in most doxologies is the power to bless and save human beings. Two traditional Jewish images are employed. The Psalter is filled with images of God's capacity to keep the righteous from tripping, stumbling, or falling (e.g., Pss 56:13; 66:9; 116:8; 121:3–8). This imagery is employed by early Christianity in a variety of ways (e.g., John 17:11; 2 Thess 3:3; 1 Pet 1:5; Rev 3:10). Given the context of judgment in these verses of Jude, "falling" or "stumbling" probably means falling into sin. Thus the opening affirmation is that God is able to keep the beloved safe from the temptation of sin, including that presented by the impious in the community.

The second affirmation is the positive side of the first. This God who is able to keep people from the dangers of sin is also (or thereby) able to present these people "blameless in the presence of his glory." Thus God presents people to God. The background of this imagery is the presentation of the sacrificial animal before the altar. Only an animal determined by the priests to be without blemish can be an offering (e.g., Exod 29:1; Lev 1:3, 10; Ps 15:2). In early Christian literature this imagery is not used to discuss the cleanness of sacrificial animals but of humans about to be judged by God. Nearly identical sentences to this one occur in Eph 1:4; 5:27; Col 1:22; and 1 Thess 3:13. The force of this blamelessness is intensified by the imagery of God's "glory," which evokes the radical otherness and magnificence of God. The wonder of all this receives a final intensification with the assertion that this ends "with rejoicing." While early Christianity mostly avoids speculation about the details of final salvation, this verse and others affirm that the people who are saved will be joyful.

[25] The second part of the doxology addresses less who God is toward people and more who God is in God's own attributes. All the terms here are the usual ones in early Christian and Jewish literature. God is the "only" God (e.g., Neh 9:6; Pss 83:18; 86:10; John 17:3; Rom 16:27; 1 Tim 1:17). God is "Savior." Although in the NT the term "Savior" more often refers to Jesus than to God, the traditional OT designation of God as Savior continues to some degree in the NT (e.g., Pss 65:5; 79:9; Isa 17:10; 43:3; Luke 1:47; 1 Tim 1:1; 2:3; 4:10). Given the centrality of the role of Jesus in salvation narratives in early Christianity, it is not surprising when Jude insists that God saves "through Jesus Christ our Lord." There is no need to detail the specific roles of God and Jesus. The point is not to lay out the full narrative of salvation but to gather, in a moment of praise, the key faces and forces.

As noted above, the form of the doxology is more likely that of praise and affirmation than that of prayer and petition. The point is to name the wonders of God. Thus the doxology does not pray that certain powers might belong to God; it asserts that certain powers already do. All the terms in the sequence of "glory, majesty, power, and authority" are both traditional and common. While the point of these terms is not to make careful theological arguments about the character of God but rather to celebrate the wonders of God, each term does carry its own nuance. "Glory" is the most common divine attribute in doxologies. Doxologies, after all, derive their name from glory (*doxa*). In Greek literature, *doxa* means "appearance" or "reputation." When Jews and Christians used the term about God, it acquired two nuances. God's appearance is beyond description, hidden in God's holiness and otherness. Thus glory, when applied to God, conveys a sense of splendor and mystery. Second, since God's reputation is beyond all reputations, glory conveys God's exalted and incomparable status. The second attribute, *megalōsynē*, comes from *megas*, which means "big" or "great." The term *megalōsynē* itself was used to describe the status and power of both human kings and God. The third term, *kratos*, usually means "strength," although it can have a sense of "sovereignty" or "authority." In this latter sense it overlaps with the fourth term, *exousia*, which usually means "authority" but can also have the sense of "power." Together *kratos* and *exousia* convey the right to do something and the capacity to do it.

The affirmation that these powers belong to God "before all time and now and for all ages" simply affirms, in a rather traditional way, the eternity of God's power and glory. The threefold division of time is a bit unusual for a doxology but not for Jewish or Christian thought (cf. Rev 1:4, 8; 4:8; 11:17). The final "amen" is both standard and effective. It is a nice liturgical way to assert that what was just said to be true is indeed true.

For all the controversy and dispute in the Letter of Jude, it ends with a celebration of God's glory that in some ways changes the tone of the letter. The shift from condemnation to mercy that began in verse 22 and the shift from attacking the impious to exhorting the beloved that began in verse 20 culminate in this rather eloquent doxology. For all the dangers of the impious and the temptations to sin that come with them, these verses affirm that God can protect the beloved from sin and present them blameless before God's glory. This doxology gathers traditional and familiar imagery from Jewish and Christian theology into a doxology that forms a fitting and transforming conclusion to the letter.

THE SECOND LETTER OF PETER

INTRODUCTION TO 2 PETER

Despite the richness of its theological imagery and the intriguing window it opens onto early Christianity, the Second Letter of Peter has occupied a somewhat secondary status in Christian discussions. This secondary status was probably foreshadowed by its awkward entry into the canon. From the beginning there have been questions about the origin and authorship of the letter. Jerome, for instance, noted the striking differences in style between 1 Peter and 2 Peter, concluding thereby that the apostle Peter did not write 2 Peter (*Ep.* 120.11). There is infrequent mention of the letter in early Christian documents. There are possible but uncertain allusions to it by Clement, Cyprian, Irenaeus, and a few others. But it is mostly ignored. However, it is included in the Bodmer papyri in the third century. Origen cites it, but as disputed (*Comm. Jo.* 5.3), and Eusebius lists it among the "Antilegomena" (*Hist. eccl.* 3.3.1–4; 3.25.3). It does not really claim any canonical status until it is cited in the festal letter of Athanasius in the late fourth century. Questions have haunted it ever since.

In fact, the observations of Jerome have proved to be convincing. Readers have long noted the striking differences in language, literary style, and theology between 1 Peter and 2 Peter. It seems unlikely that the same author could have written both letters. Calvin's response is in some ways typical. He admits that Jerome might be correct but argues that we must accept Petrine authorship since the letter is included in the canon (*Catholic Epistles*). However, modern discussions of the authorship and origin of the letter begin not with its relationship to 1 Peter but with its relationship to Jude.

Relationship to Jude

The extensive similarities between Jude 4–13, 16–18 and 2 Peter 2:1–18; 3:1–3 suggest a literary relationship of some kind. Four explanations have been offered.[39] (1) The same author wrote both letters. This theory has received

---

39. For a good survey of the possibilities, see Lauri Thurén, "The Relationship between 2 Peter and Jude—A Classical Problem Resolved?" in *The Catholic Epistles and the Tradition* (ed. Jacques Schlosser; BETL 176; Leuven: Peeters, 2004), 451–60.

little support, given the striking differences in literary style and theology of the two letters. (2) The letters are using a common source. This is certainly possible, although most readers find too many agreements in wording for both to be using a common source. It is more likely that the agreement in linguistic details results from one letter's copying of the other. This leaves two possibilities. (3) Jude is using 2 Peter. (4) Second Peter is using Jude.

In literary agreements of this kind, it is always difficult to determine who is copying whom unless there is other, more directive evidence. It is possible that Jude used scattered polemics in 2 Peter along with stories about Enoch to compose its carefully ordered and tightly managed attack on the impious. However, it has proved difficult to provide redactional explanations for the changes, omissions, and additions that Jude would have made if it were using 2 Peter. As the commentary will show, it is relatively easy to explain the redactional motives of an author starting with Jude and composing 2 Peter. Both the expansions of the imagery and the omission of reference to the noncanonical *1 Enoch* fit readily into the theology and rhetorical style of 2 Peter. Thus almost all modern commentaries assume that 2 Peter is redacting Jude.

Nevertheless, it must be admitted that there are several plausible options for the agreements between the two letters. The most likely explanation is that 2 Peter is using Jude. However, nothing can be proved here. In any case, since the date and provenance of neither letter is secure, little is learned about the historical origins of 2 Peter beyond the fact that it probably used Jude as a source.

Authorship and Date

Although 2 Peter claims to be written by Simon Peter, there are few commentaries that admit such to be the case. The continuing debate about possible Petrine authorship of 1 Peter is not mirrored for 2 Peter. In part, this is due to the unlikelihood that one author could have written both 1 Peter and 2 Peter. More to the point is the peculiar character of 2 Peter itself. Its obscurity in the early church, its terminology and rhetorical style, the Gentile setting of the letter, the difficulty in imagining the apostle Peter espousing the theology of 2 Peter—these all combine to make rejection of Petrine authorship convincing and pervasive. Yet this leaves the questions of who wrote it, to whom it was written, and when. None of these can be easily answered.

The letter provides few hints about the author. The Greek style is elaborate.[40] In fact, some readers find the Greek syntax a bit labored. In any case, the style shows facility with that language. The author seems to know a variety of OT stories but does not quote the text directly. The use of Greek rhetorical patterns suggests someone at home not just in the Greek language but also in

---

40. For a discussion of Greek style in 2 Peter, see Watson, *Invention, Arrangement, and Style*.

The False Teachers and Mockers

Greek rhetoric. All of this says very little about the author. It could be almost any educated Christian.

The date and location are equally uncertain. The Bodmer papyri, which date from the early third century, are the first absolutely certain evidence of 2 Peter. All earlier references are debatable. The closest parallels in both issues and terminology are with other Christian texts in the second century. Thus there is very little data to help with dating. It could have been written anytime in the second century. Most commentators think the first half of that century would be more likely than the second half. Sometime between 120 and 150 C.E. would be a good guess, but it is only a guess. There is also no good evidence for its location. The reference to Peter suggests Rome. However, the Petrine traditions also had coinage in Asia.[41]

These uncertainties about authorship, date, and provenance mean that the historical context of the letter cannot be predetermined. The imagery and arguments of 2 Peter have many parallels in the ancient Roman world. Consequently, readings of 2 Peter, including those in this commentary, tend to wander all over the ancient world, drawing from a wide variety of Jewish, Greek, Roman, and Christian texts.

The False Teachers and Mockers

The most specific contextual reference in 2 Peter is to the presence of "false teachers" and "mockers" in the community. All of chapter 2 is devoted to an attack on false teachers, and much of chapter 3 is devoted to an attack upon mockers. As noted above, much of the imagery of that attack is probably drawn from Jude. However, the portrait of these opponents in 2 Peter is different from that of the "impious" in Jude. In particular, 2 Peter addresses doctrinal errors in a way that Jude does not.

The "false teachers" in 2 Peter are painted with the same linguistic brush as the impious in Jude. They both are part of the community; they both invite divine punishment in the pattern of rebellious angels and Sodom and Gomorrah. They both reject authorities and engage in immorality, especially sexual immorality. They both are waterless clouds. As noted in the commentary on these passages, it is difficult to know how to attach such metaphorical attacks to real behavior. The false teachers have some of their own characteristics. They deny their master. They revel in the daytime like animals. In fact, they practice all kinds of immorality. They are also successful as teachers. They entice others to follow them, but at the same time they pollute the community. Finally, even though they are slaves themselves, they promise freedom. This last comment

---

41. The expressed destination of 1 Peter (1:1) suggests that Petrine traditions were current in much of Anatolia.

is often read as an indication of the real problem. The accusation of immorality is so standard in ancient (and modern) polemics that such attacks in themselves cannot be used for historical reconstruction. However, there is nothing quite so standard about the promise of freedom.

There is much debate about the foundations and purposes of this promise of freedom. Most commentators connect the promise of freedom by the false teachers in 2 Pet 2 to the skepticism and ridicule of the idea of the Parousia by the mockers in chapter 3. This certainly makes sense. These mockers reject the coming Parousia, citing the steadfastness of creation. This is read as a rejection of final judgment. Thus freedom would be freedom from the constraints of divine punishment. A person becomes free to do whatever their passions dictate. Modern commentaries often point to the Greco-Roman debate about Epicureanism, which argued against the involvement of the gods in morality.[42] Most ancient people assumed an intense interest by the gods in the propriety and morality of human behavior. This interest would include punishment and rewards. Thus they would see little new in Christian notions of divine rewards and punishments, although Christian apocalyptic scenarios might seem peculiar. Given the pervasiveness of notions of divine justice, it is hard to know why some early Christians would reject Christian notions of the Parousia and final judgment. Epicurean skepticism is a possible explanation, although there may well have been specific issues with the Christian version of judgment that are not stated here.

All of this assumes that the "false teachers" in 2 Pet 2 are the same as the "mockers" in 2 Pet 3. This is not perfectly clear. What we know for certain is that there is doctrinal and ethical controversy in the communities of 2 Peter. Much of the letter is an attempt to address these controversies. There are disagreements about the Parousia and disagreements about the ethical norms of the Christian life. Second Peter offers a classic and orthodox response.

Literary Structure

In some ways, the literary structure of 2 Peter is straightforward. It is rather easy to outline, and there is little debate about its basic divisions.

1:1–2 Opening Salutation
1:3–11 Exordium
1:12–15 Testamentary Reminder
1:16–21 Apostolic and Prophetic Witnesses
2:1–22 False Teachers and Their Punishment
    2:1–3 The Prediction of False Teachers
    2:4–10a Examples of God's Judgment

---

42. See Neyrey, "Form and Background of the Polemic," 407–31.

Theology

    2:10b–16 The Immorality of the False Teachers
    2:17–22 The Slavery of the False Teachers
3:1–13 The Promise of His Coming
    3:1–7 The Coming of Mockers
    3:8–13 God's Patience
3:14–18 Final Exhortation and Doxology

What is debated is the rhetorical and theological narrative that holds these pieces together. Most commentaries detect a loose form of deliberative rhetoric with an opening exordium (1:3–11), various proofs (1:16–3:13), and concluding *peroratio* (3:14–18). The problem with this structure is that only the exordium fits the standard profile. It is difficult to read the various arguments of 1:16–3:13 as proofs of the exordium. The final exhortations and doxology in 3:14–18 do not have the usual summarizing characteristics of a *peroratio*. Within the letter there are rhetorical parallels to both ancient testaments and farewell speeches. Some readers even classify 2 Peter as a testament. While there are similarities in themes and rhetoric between 2 Peter and testaments, the formal arrangement of each is quite different. The same must be said about 2 Peter and farewell speeches. Furthermore, it may be misleading to speak of either testaments or farewell speeches as distinct genres. Second Peter is a letter. In fact, its closest rhetorical parallels are with other NT letters. Most NT letters combine rhetorical norms and patterns with epistolary norms and patterns. This is usually done in a flexible and unforced way. It is best to see 2 Peter in this style. It is formally a letter that uses some classic rhetorical norms. In the end, its argumentative structure is loose and is not managed by any single rhetorical format. If there is anything that anchors the various arguments of the letter, it is its theology.

Theology

There is nothing particularly surprising about the theology of 2 Peter. Its theological images, sentences, and point of view fall within the common theological parameters of early Christianity. The energy and vitriol of the attack on the false teachers has often disturbed Christian readers. However, it is the tone of that attack that is bothersome, not its content. The opening exordium (1:3–11) provides an effective summary of the letter's theology. God's divine power has given what is needed for life. This enables escape from the passions of the flesh and the corruptions of the world. This same power articulates classic Christian virtues, which the readers are called to pursue. Such virtues effect entry into God's kingdom. These divine powers with their ethical destinations find support in the traditions of the apostles, especially that of Peter himself, and the prophets. The centrality of ethics leads to the intense condemnation of certain Christian teachers who are perceived as living like animals and enticing others to vice.

The letter's intense and intriguing defense of the second coming of Christ reinforces the necessity of the righteous life. In some ways, the account is quite traditional. The second coming is depicted as it is usually is, as necessary for the victory of God's righteousness. People who live the life of vice will be punished in the usual way. People who live a virtuous life will be rewarded in what is also probably the usual way. The promise of new heavens and a new earth, in which righteousness dwells, is a nice summary of standard early Christian eschatology. In the midst of this account, however, two somewhat more unusual ideas are included. The delay, which is not a delay, results not simply from the differences between human and divine time but also from the character of God. God is described as "not wishing anyone to be destroyed but for all to come into repentance" (3:9). God's mercy seems to control and limit God's justice. The end does not come because God does not want to punish the unrighteous. Second, the suggested response by people to this delay goes beyond the usual pursuit of virtue to the suggestion that people can influence the timing of judgment. People should not only wait patiently for the day of the Lord to come; they also should hasten it. This hastening is done by living the righteous life. While this imagery may not be beyond the bounds of classic Christian eschatology, it is an unusual and powerful response to the delay of the day of the Lord.

Text and Translation

Given the lack of attention to 2 Peter in early Christian documents, the letter has surprisingly good representation in the early Greek manuscripts. For instance, a partial text is included in the Bodmer papyri ($\mathfrak{P}^{72}$, $\mathfrak{P}^{74}$), and nearly complete texts are included in all the major uncials. As noted in the introduction to 1 Peter, two kinds of variants are cited in the commentary. When it is not possible to decide between possible versions, the various options will be noted. Other variants will be cited because they provide interesting glimpses into early Christian thought.

Again, as was noted in the introduction to 1 Peter, the translations in this commentary try to convey the grammatical tensions in the Greek that are key to the meaning of the text. This means that the resulting English is, on occasion, a bit awkward.

COMMENTARY

2 Peter 1:1–2 Opening Salutation

The opening salutation follows the typical NT form. It begins with the name and identification of the sender (in the nominative case), then identifies the recipients (in the dative case), and concludes with the usual invocation of grace (and peace). Each piece uses theological imagery common in early Christianity. Apart from the claim in 3:1 that this is "the second letter," this salutation is the only explicit sign that this document is a letter. Second Peter lacks the usual greetings, the typical postscript, the opening prayer or blessing, and any direct appeals to the readers that suggest the context of reading a letter. As readers have long noted, 2 Peter seems to combine the genres of letter and testament, using the rhetorical appeals of both. The lack of specificity in the profile of the recipients reinforces the sense that this salutation is mostly a literary exercise. The recipients are simply people who have faith of "equal honor as ours." This could refer to any Christian anywhere.

Two curiosities have long attracted the attention of readers. First, the name of the apostle Peter is given in the Hebrew form of "Simeon" and not in the more common Greek form of "Simon." In a letter that shows as much fondness for Greek terms and images as it does for Jewish, this Hebraic naming is puzzling. Second, the phrase "our God and Savior Jesus Christ" is most naturally read as calling Jesus "God." This is unusual in early Christianity. Apart from these two minor curiosities, this salutation sounds much like most other early Christian salutations.

> 1:1 Simeon[a] Peter, slave and apostle of Jesus Christ, to those who have received[b] a faith of equal honor[c] as ours through the justice[d] of our God[e] and Savior Jesus Christ. 2 May grace and peace be multiplied to you in the knowledge[f] of God and Jesus our Lord.

a. The Hebrew spelling *Symeōn*, instead of the usual Greek spelling *Simōn*, is used for Simon Peter only here and in Acts 15:14. While "Simeon" is a quite common Jewish name of this period, it is typically changed to "Simon" when it occurs in the Greek language or in non-Jewish contexts. In light of this, it is not surprising that some texts replace this spelling with the more common *Simōn*.

b. The verb *lanchanō* means "to obtain by lot" or "to receive by the will of the gods." There is no English word that adequately evokes the religious dimensions of the term. The use of the verb to describe the acquisition of faith recalls the persistent early Christian notion that faith is a gift given by God and not something acquired solely or even primarily by human effort.

c. The adjective *isotimos* means "of equal value," "of equal privilege," or "of equal honor." Although all three meanings fit here well enough, "honor" with its sense of public status fits somewhat better than the others.

d. Translations are divided between rendering *dikaiosynē* as "justice" or "righteousness." The somewhat more traditional translation of "righteousness" suggests that the gift of faith is part of the redemptive righteousness of Christ. However, all other occurrences of *dikaiosynē* or *dikaios* in 2 Peter (1:13; 2:5, 7, 8, 21; 3:13) have an ethical or moral sense. The translation "justice" conveys somewhat better the ethical dimensions of *dikaiosynē* and fits nicely with the imagery of receiving a faith that is "of equal honor" to that of the apostles.

e. The absence of the definite article before "Savior" grammatically means that "God" and "Jesus" are one person. The phrase would then mean that Jesus Christ is both God and Savior. However, there is a general tendency for articles to be omitted in common formulas, and the very next verse clearly distinguishes God from Jesus. Nevertheless, most readers think the grammatical structure of the phrase requires that God and Jesus be one person in this verse (cf. 3:18).

f. Many readers have argued that 2 Peter makes a careful distinction between *epignōsis*, which it uses here and in 1:3, 8; 2:20, and *gnōsis*, which it uses in 1:5, 6; 3:18. The inceptive force of *epi* means that, while *gnōsis* refers to "knowledge" of any kind, *epignōsis* refers to the core knowledge that is acquired at the moment of conversion. These readers point out that *epignōsis* in 2 Peter always has God or Jesus as the genitive object. Other readers think that the shift in terms simply reflects normal Greek style, which resists repetition of the same word.

[1:1] While the use of the Hebrew spelling "Simeon" is, as noted above, unusual, there is no doubt who "Simeon Peter" is supposed to be. Both the designation "apostle" and the reference to his being an eyewitness to the transfiguration (1:16–18) make it clear that Simeon Peter is Simon Peter. The use of the Hebrew spelling has been explained variously as proof that the letter was written by Peter himself, as evidence that the author may have known Peter personally, as evidence that the author was Jewish, and as an attempt by a pseudepigraphical writer to make the letter seem genuine. Readers have even wondered why the Semitic "Cephas" was not used in place of the Greek "Peter." The multitude of possibilities, coupled with the lack of any hints in the letter, means that no real conclusion can be drawn. The use of the Hebrew spelling remains an interesting curiosity.

Opening Salutation

The designation of Peter as "slave and apostle of Jesus Christ" mirrors the designations of Paul in Rom 1:1 and Titus 1:1, although there is no evidence that 2 Peter knew either. Both epithets are common in early Christianity. It is hard to know whether the full theological possibilities of the term "slave" (*doulos*) are in place or whether this is simply a traditional naming. In any case, the letter does not develop the sense of radical ownership and obedience implied in the term. The crucial term is "apostle." The numerous permutations among the terms "the Twelve," "the disciples," and "the apostles," do not seem to be relevant here. The term "apostle" is being used in its traditional way in early Christianity. Apostles are the first-generation Christians who had a special relationship to Jesus. Though there may be echoes of the etymological force of "apostle" as one who is sent, the word is used here for the authority it conveys.

As noted above, the description of the recipients gives no hint as to who these Christians were or where they lived. They could be any Christians anywhere. They are described as people who have received from God a faith of equal honor to that of the apostles. It is not clear whether the term "faith" refers to the act of belief or to the theological traditions of the gospel. The attention that 2 Peter devotes to knowledge (1:3, 5, 6, 8; 2:20; 3:18) and to the reliability of the prophetic message (1:16, 19–21) indicates that "faith" probably refers to the content of the gospel. In any case, the central affirmation is that the faith of this later generation is of the same order, honor, status, and value as that of the first apostles. Such assertions are common in early Christianity in the postapostolic age. Early Christians professed the unity of faith through time. This giving of this faith is accomplished by the justice or righteousness of Jesus Christ. The ethical force of *dikaiosynē*, as noted above, means that Jesus Christ has justly and fairly dispensed faith of equal honor to the next generation.

Jesus is curiously called "God" and "Savior." There are a few other instances in the NT where Jesus appears to be called God (John 1:1; 20:28; Heb 1:8–9; cf. also Rom 9:5; 2 Thess 1:12; Titus 2:13; 1 John 5:20). The extreme care that Christianity will develop in the naming of the persons of the Trinity is not in place in the NT. Using the name "God" for Jesus is probably nothing more than an attempt to assert Jesus' divinity. The looseness of the terminology seems to be a bit more at home in the Greco-Roman world than the Jewish.

[2] The "grace and peace" blessing on the recipients parallels many other such blessings in NT Letters (see esp. 1 Pet 1:2). Though the blessing is important to the rhetoric of the letter and is real enough, it does not have any apparent impact on the theology of the letter. However, the reference to "knowledge of God and Jesus our Lord" signals a major theme of the letter. Knowledge, both here and in the rest of the letter, is both personal and theoretical. Second Peter affirms the centrality of personal knowledge of God and Jesus. However, that

knowledge includes the traditions about them. These recipients know the true story of salvation.

This rather standard salutation highlights two of the central themes of the letter. First, the faith of the postapostolic readers is of the same honor and value as the faith of the apostles themselves. The entirety of 2 Peter assumes and affirms the unity of faith through time. Simon Peter may have been unique in being an eyewitness to the transfiguration, but this apostolic uniqueness serves to unite the apostles and the postapostolic readers in a common faith. The unimpeachable authority of the apostles means that the traditions in the later church are reliable.

Second, knowledge is key to the life of faith. This knowledge is of many kinds. As the syntax of this salutation affirms, this knowledge includes personal knowledge of God and Jesus. As the letter unfolds, it is clear that this personal knowledge is not simply relational; it is also knowledge of the gospel narrative, knowledge of the true character of God and Jesus. Second Peter will rehearse some of that narrative. Finally, this knowledge is ethical. It issues in the classic Christian virtues.

2 Peter 1:3–11 Exordium

The core structure of 1:3–11 follows a pattern common to Jewish and early Christian literature, especially homiletical literature. A historical, theological section (1:3–4) enumerates divine acts of salvation. These theological affirmations are followed by a set of ethical exhortations (1:5–10) that emerge from these affirmations and anticipate the concluding images of judgment. The sequence concludes with eschatological promises of reward (1:11) and/or judgment. Thus most readers distinguish this section as a familiar and self-contained rhetorical piece. This piece seems to replace the blessing or prayer that most early Christian letters have immediately following the salutation. Some readers also maintain that these verses come closest in form to the classic exordium that opens ancient argument by introducing the main points and gaining the favor of the hearers. However, for all the similarities, this section is not a typical exordium because the theological and ethical issues of these verses do not identify the main themes of the letter in a formal and precise way.

For all the internal coherence of this section, its borders are not certain. The passage opens with a grammatically uncertain particle *hōs*, which suggests to most readers a necessary syntactical connection to what precedes (see below for discussion). The verses (1:12–15, perhaps even 1:16–21) that follow this section appear to many as a personal affirmation of the reliability of this section. Thus some readers stress the rhetorical unity of the entire first chapter.

Exordium

All of this means that no familiar rhetorical pattern, from either speeches or letters, precisely explains the format and function of this section. By all accounts, it is a rhetorically and theologically coherent piece. In fact, this section may be the most cleanly composed of any section in the letter. Though it does not formally name the dominant issues of the letter—the problems of "false prophets" who malign the truth and "mockers" who question the day of the Lord—this section does provide an effective summary of the theological framework on which the letter depends.

Finally, this section contains a form of virtue list unique to the NT. While there are virtue lists of various lengths and forms in the NT (cf., Rom 5:3–5; Gal 5:22–23; 1 Tim 3:1–7), none is composed in a rhetorical form like this one in 2 Peter. The readers are called to build, in a particular sequence, each virtue upon the preceding virtue. However, apart from the opening "faith" and concluding "love," the logic of the sequence of virtues is not obvious. The closest parallel is Rom 5:3–5, where one virtue leads to another. However, outside the NT, this form is relatively common (see esp. Wis 6:17–20; Herm. *Vis.* 3.8.7). Furthermore, the set of virtues in this list has closer parallels to Christian lists from the second and third century (e.g., *1 Clem.* 1.2; 62.2; 64.1; Herm., *Mand.* 6.1.1; 8.9; *Barn.* 2.2–3) and to Hellenistic Jewish lists (e.g., Philo, *Sacr.* 27; *Leg.* 1.64) than to other NT lists. Both the format and content of this list evidence close affinity with Hellenistic moral philosophy. All of this suggests a second-century origin.

1:3 Inasmuch as[a] his divine power has given us everything that leads to life and piety through the knowledge of the one who called us by[b] his own glory and virtue,[c] 4 through which he has given to us the precious[d] and very great promises, so that through these[e] we might become sharers of the divine nature, having escaped from the corruption that is in the world because of desire, 5 for this very reason, using all eagerness,[f] to[g] your faith supply[h] virtue,[c] to virtue knowledge, 6 to knowledge self-control, to self-control endurance, to endurance piety, 7 to piety family affection,[i] to family affection love. 8 For if these things belong to you and are abundant, they establish[j] you as neither idle nor fruitless in[k] the knowledge[l] of our Lord Jesus Christ. 9 The one to whom these things are not present is blind, nearsighted, forgetful of the cleansing of past sins. 10 Therefore, brothers and sisters,[m] be all the more eager[n] to make[o] your call and election firm, for if you do this, you will never stumble. 11 For in this way entry will be richly supplied[p] to you into the eternal kingdom of our Lord and Savior Jesus Christ.

a. While the particle *hōs* can have a considerable variety of meanings, here it probably has the causal sense of "since," "seeing that," "inasmuch as." However it is rendered, it creates grammatical problems. In fact, most modern translations simply ignore it. The *hōs* requires a causal connection between 1:3–4 and either what precedes or what follows. If these verses connect to the preceding, the sense would be that the blessing of 1:2 is evoked because of the divine gifts enumerated in 1:3–4. This would unravel the rhetorical unity of both the salutation and the affirmations of 1:3–11. If these verses connect to what follows, this creates an anacoluthon at 1:5 with "for this very reason" repeating the force of "inasmuch as." A good case can be made for either option. However, since anacolutha are common in Greek rhetoric and both 1:1–2 and 1:3–11 function so nicely as complete rhetorical pieces, it is preferable to read the *hōs* as connecting 1:3–4 to what follows.

b. While it is grammatically possible that the dative could be rendered as locative ("to"), an instrumental reading ("by") is grammatically more natural.

c. The common Greek noun *aretē* is difficult to translate into English. The usual translation of "virtue" does not convey the sense of power, capacity, and ability that the Greek word contains. "Virtue" also does not convey the overall sense of moral excellence that the Greek word also contains. However, the various alternative translations of "might," "excellence," or "goodness" all have their own problems.

d. Although *isotimos* was translated in 1:1 as "equal honor," *timia* probably has the sense here of "costly," "valuable," or "precious."

e. The antecedent of *toutōn* is probably "promises" and not "glory and virtue."

f. This translation mirrors the Greek syntax of the participle *pareisenenkantes* and finite verb *epichorēgēsate* with a corresponding English participle and finite verb. In an attempt to capture the circumstantial force of the Greek participle in proper English, many translations render the Greek participle with a finite verb and the Greek finite verb as a supplementary infinitive. Doing so would change the translation to "use all eagerness to supply to your faith virtue. . . ."

g. The dative could indicate an indirect object, as it is here translated, or agency ("by means of faith supply virtue").

h. The root verb *chorēgeō* meant originally to "pay the expenses of a chorus" but came to mean to "supply" or "furnish" anything for any reason. The compound *epichorēgeō* means to "supply in addition."

i. The term *philadelphia* is widely used in early Christian literature. It does not mean, as its etymology might suggest, "affection [just] between brothers." Rather, it has the sense of "affection within a family group or household."

j. Most modern translations reject as excessively awkward the literal rendition given here. Typically they move the negative from the predicate adjectives and place it with the main verb: "they keep you from being idle or unfruitful. . . ." However, this changes the feel of the Greek syntax and the logic of the main verb.

k. Some translations render *eis* in its common meaning of purpose or result, so that the sentence is asserting that virtues lead to increased knowledge of Jesus Christ. However, *eis* often means "in regard to" or "with reference to," which fits much better in the general sense of the passage.

l. As is typically the case in 2 Peter, when the object of knowledge is God or Jesus, the author uses *epignōsis* instead of the more common *gnōsis*.

m. The Greek reads just "brothers."

n. The verb *spoudazō* (to be zealous or eager) repeats the root of the noun *spoudē* in 1:5.

Exordium

o. The phrase *bebaion poieisthai* (to make firm, to confirm) can have the legal connotation of "guarantee." Some texts add the explanatory phrase "through good works."

p. The same verb *epichorēgeō* is used here as in 1:5, creating the explicit connection that entry into the kingdom is "supplied" to those who "supply" virtues.

[1:3–4] These verses offer a compact and dense account of what the "divine power" has given. The two causal phrases, "inasmuch as" (1:3) and "for this very reason" (1:5), connect these gifts to the exhortation to build up the virtues in 1:5–7. The density of this theological narrative makes it difficult to determine precisely the force of the various images. Nevertheless, the basic narrative is clear enough. God (or Jesus) has given gifts and bestowed promises that enable the recipients to have life, to partake of the divine nature, and to flee from the world's corruption.

The phrases "his divine power" and "the one who called us" could refer to Jesus. However, since they are such common attributes of God, it likely that God is the giver of these gifts. While the adjective "divine" (*theios*) is more common in Greek literature than in Jewish or Christian, it occurs with some frequency in Hellenistic Jewish literature. In Jewish and Christian literature, this phrase, like the similar "the power of God," serves almost as a circumlocution for the word "God" while emphasizing God's capacity to accomplish things. The initial affirmation is that God has given "everything" necessary for "life and piety." Similar affirmations are standard in Christian theology. Second Peter adds its own touch with assertion that these gifts work through knowledge of the God who called. As noted in 1:2, knowledge of God, Jesus, and the gospel is key to the theology of 2 Peter. It is also particular to 2 Peter that these gifts are given "by his own glory and virtue." While "glory" is the common word for such affirmations, the choice of "virtue" ("might," "excellence") connects the virtue of God, which gives these gifts, to the virtues that these Christians are to pursue (1:5–7).

The second affirmation repeats the sequence of the first but adds several interesting images. God gives "the precious and very great promises." There is no hint in 2 Peter as to which promises are meant here unless they refer to the other two images in this verse. The sequence ends with the common promise of fleeing from the world's corruption, which is built on the passions. This imagery recalls the story of the fall, wherein passions lead to corruption and death for humans and all of creation. However, with equal intensity the Greco-Roman world pursued escape from the power of the passions and their capacity to destroy. Greeks would probably hear this promise as the fulfillment of virtuous life. Virtue overcomes passions. Jews would probably hear this promise as the undoing of the fall. These Christians may have heard it both ways.

The most striking and controversial image is that these Christians will become "sharers of the divine nature." While this language is fairly rare in

Jewish and Christian thought, it is common in Greek philosophy and religion.[43] It is used in a variety of ways, depending on the system of thought in which it occurs. The most common sense of the phrase concerns the immortality of the gods and the mortality of humans. To partake of the divine nature means, first of all, to partake of immortality. Second Peter's promise of escape from "the corruption that is in the world" reflects this usage. Probably the other divine attribute most often evoked in this imagery is escape from the polluting power of the passions. Immortality includes being cleansed from desires and the vice that results from desire. Thus 2 Peter fits nicely in the standard usage of the image. It also asserts that the corruption of the world is caused by the passions and that acquiring the divine nature will lead to virtue.

Finally, some readers have suggested that "us" and "we" in these verses refer only to Peter and the apostles and not to the recipients of the letter. However, this is unlikely. No other Christian text suggests that only the apostles receive the gift of immortality. Furthermore, the exhortations to virtue in 1:5–7 make much less sense if the readers are not included in this divine empowerment.

[5–7] This call to build up virtues is explicitly dependent on the divine giving enumerated in the preceding verses.[44] The logic is that God has given everything that leads to life; therefore, these people must respond by living the life of virtue. Theology not only leads to ethics; it also requires it. There is an obvious linkage between God's virtue, which empowers the calling of people (1:3), and the virtues enjoined here.

As noted above, the format of this listing of virtues is somewhat distinctive in that one virtue is explicitly linked to the next. Some readers construe the datives as indicative of agency, so that each virtue directly empowers the arrival of the next ("by means of your faith supply virtue . . ."). This reading is grammatically possible but unnecessarily complex. Furthermore it is unclear how each virtue does this. Instead, the simpler reading is that these virtues are built up, one after the other, by the effort of those who have been called. Thus virtue does not emerge from faith or knowledge from virtue. Each emerges on its own from the combination of the divine calling and intense human effort. Although there is no satisfactory account of the precise order of these virtues, the terms fit together nicely. Most readers note that the series begins in classic Christian fashion with "faith" and ends with "love." There is familiar logic in the groupings of "virtue," "knowledge," and "self-control," as there is with "piety," "family affection," and "love." However, to some extent each term stands on its own.

---

43. James M. Starr, *Sharers in Divine Nature: 2 Peter 1:4 in Its Hellenistic Context* (ConBNT 33; Stockholm: Almqvist & Wiksell, 2000).

44. For a good summary of virtue lists in early Christianity and the Greco-Roman world, see Hans Dieter Betz, *Galatians* (Hermeneia; Philadelphia: Fortress Press, 1979), 278–90.

In most virtue lists, *pistis* would mean "faithfulness" and not "faith." At the beginning of a Christian list, the more specialized meaning of "faith" is more likely, although the sense of "faithfulness" is probably still in place as well. While *aretē* can have general sense of "virtue," as it is translated here (in order to make explicit the connection between its use here and in 1:3), in virtue lists it often has sense of "goodness" or "excellence." Originally the term apparently had the sense of "power" or "prowess." A virtue is not simply something good; it is also a capacity to do that good.

"Knowledge" was also seen as a necessary aspect of the virtuous life. In Greek tradition, a person cannot do the good without knowing the good. This tradition is transformed a bit in Christian thought, including 2 Peter, since knowledge is knowledge of the gospel. Furthermore, in 2 Peter, knowledge is also personal knowledge of God and Jesus, although the letter uses *epignōsis* instead of *gnōsis* in such contexts (1:2, 3, 8; 2:20). "Self-control" (*enkrateia*) was a fundamental virtue in Greco-Roman ethical thought. In some ways the role of "self-control" is negative; it resists the power of the passions to seduce and drive a person from the ethical life. Without it, the door is opened to the seductions of the passions. "Endurance" is more typically Christian. In Greek contexts *hypomonē* has the sense of "steadfastness" or "perseverance" in the face of danger. This sense is tweaked a bit in Christian contexts to refer to "endurance" in the face of suffering and persecution. Though the term *eusebeia* (piety, godliness) occasionally appears in Christian circles, it is common in Greco-Roman literature. The term is often used as the summary term for the fulfillment of religious duties. These duties are to both the gods and people. Christian literature tends to use it in the same way. This sense of duties to others may form a link to the final two terms.

As noted above, the term *philadelphia* is not confined to male-to-male brotherly affection; it refers to the love that binds families and households together. When Christians use the term to refer to love within the community, they import the family context. Despite the extensive literature detailing the difference between *philia* and *agapē*, it is impossible to maintain clean distinctions in early Christian literature. The terms overlap more than they diverge. It is probably fair to assert that in this context *philadelphia* evokes the sense of family and mutual affection to which Christian communities aspired. The place of *agapē* at the end of the list is almost certainly intentional. The term becomes the umbrella for the Christian life in much of early Christianity. The frequency and diversity of its use makes it nearly impossible to say with any precision what *agapē* might mean in 2 Peter. In some ways, it functions much like the word "love" does in modern Christian thought. All Christians claim it and aspire to it, but they often mean quite different things by it. Its general usage in early Christianity suggests that the term *agapē* highlights the sense of gentleness and self-sacrifice that the English word "love" might also include.

[8–9] These verses (and 1:10–11) reinforce the centrality of the virtuous life. Knowledge of Jesus Christ is not an end in itself. As this passage has already affirmed, knowledge of the one who called effects escape from the passions (1:4) and the acquisition of the many virtues of the Christian life (1:5–7). These verses restate that logic positively and negatively.

Based on the combined power of the divine gifts and intense human effort, these virtues must not only be present but should be so in abundance. If (or when) they are present, these virtues will themselves establish these Christians as being neither idle nor fruitless. The terms "idle" (*argos*, which literally means "without work") and "fruitless" are common early Christian terms for the immoral and unrighteous life. Virtues seem to function almost as proof. They are evidence that personal knowledge of Jesus Christ has not been fruitless. As is typically the case in early Christianity, a relationship with God should result in righteousness. If it does not, then something is broken in that relationship.

The negative image draws on the imagery of sight. When these virtues are not present, it is a sign that these people cannot see properly. Though the language of being "nearsighted" is unusual, language of blindness toward the truth is common in the NT and early Christianity (e.g., Matt 15:14; 23:16; John 9:40–41; Rom 2:19; Rev 3:17). The pervasiveness of the imagery and the multiplicity of contexts in which it is used means that it is difficult to determine the full force of the imagery in 2 Peter. Blindness is a sign of resistance to the truth of the gospel. However, there is no evidence about the precise character of that blindness. The further accusation that these people have forgotten the cleansing of their sins suggests to most readers a problem with baptism. Although the theological narratives surrounding baptism are diverse, the connection between baptism and the cleansing of sins is standard and nearly ubiquitous. The theology of baptism in force here seems to be not only that baptism cleanses from sin but also that this cleansing must issue in the righteous life. The Greek phrase translated as "forgetful of the cleansing of past sins" reads literally as "receiving forgetfulness" (*lēthēn labōn*). It as though forgetfulness of the ethical force of baptism overtakes certain people, with the result that the virtuous life abandons them.

[10–11] These concluding verses offer a final plea to the virtuous life and an eschatological promise to those who heed that call. In this way, they complete the theological logic of the section. Knowledge of God and the divine gifts that come from being called lead, with the help of human effort, to the righteous life, which in turn leads to eternal rewards from God.

The plea itself uses classic early Christian imagery. There is little theological distinction between calling and election. In fact, the terms seem almost interchangeable in the NT. In this context, they obviously refer back to the calling in 1:3 that formed the theological foundation of this passage. The term *bebaios* (firm) and its cognates are fairly frequent in the NT. It is used almost identically

Exordium

by Paul and 2 Peter as confirmation of the promises (Rom 4:16; 15:8) or the prophetic word (2 Pet 1:19). Furthermore, 1 Cor 1:8 uses the verbal form in almost exactly the same context as it is used here: "He will also strengthen [*bebaiōsei*] you to the end, so that you may be blameless on the day of our Lord Jesus Christ." The language of "stumbling" (*ptaiō*) is common imagery for sinning (e.g., Jas 2:10; 3:2). Finally, the content of the plea is itself typical of early Christianity. Eternal rewards depend in part on the zealousness, the eagerness, and even the success of the individual's pursuit of the ethical life. Within the contexts of divine calling and gifts, only strenuous effort for the virtues can confirm God's calling and result in eternal rewards.

The imagery of the coming rewards is in some ways traditional and in some ways not. The language of entry in the kingdom recalls that of the Gospels (e.g., Matt 5:20; 18:3; Mark 10:23; Luke 18:17; John 3:5). The phrase "eternal kingdom," while theologically logical, does not occur elsewhere in the NT and rarely in early Christianity. While the NT occasionally attributes the kingdom to Christ (e.g., Luke 1:33; 23:42; Col 1:13), normally it belongs to God. The language of being "supplied" entry into the kingdom is also unusual, although the term "supply" is an obvious echo of 1:5. As noted above, the repetition of the term creates the theological narrative that God supplies the kingdom to people who supply their lives with virtues. In any case, the theological claim of the verse is typical of early Christian thought. Living the righteous life leads to participation in eternal rewards. The NT uses a variety of imagery to describe the character of divine rewards, but it does so in the context of great consistency. People are given the powers by God necessary to live the righteous life. When they do so, they will be rewarded.

This passage (1:3–11) provides the theological framework for the rest of the letter. It articulates the theological assumptions that drive the arguments in the subsequent chapters. Consequently, this passage governs the force of what follows. A comparison with Jude is instructive. Readers have long noted that, despite considerable shared material, the attack on the false prophets in 2:1–22 reads differently than the attack on the impious in Jude. It is not just that 2 Peter softens some of the edginess of Jude or amplifies the scriptural references; it is also that 2 Peter focuses more on the positive role of virtue. These verses insist that living the righteous life is central to the narrative of salvation. Without the presence of virtues, there is no promise of final blessing. In Jude the attack comes without explanation of the theological seriousness of the problem of impiety. In 2 Peter the announced necessity of virtues explains the dangers of the immoral life that the false prophets lead and promote.

A similar influence of these verses shapes the reading of 2 Pet 3. The danger of people who scoff at the coming of the Lord is that they undermine an essential tenet in the story of salvation. Virtue is not its own reward. Virtue leads to entry into the eternal kingdom. This means that Jesus must return and establish this kingdom where "righteousness dwells" (3:13). Thus the debate is not over an issue that could reasonably be decided either way. Perhaps Jesus is soon returning; perhaps not. Instead, to question the arrival of the eternal kingdom is to question the coherence of the entire story of salvation.

For all the centrality and potency of this passage, it remains a sketch. Each theological affirmation could be expanded. The imagery seems to assume larger theological discussions. For instance, nothing is said about how or when "the divine power" gives everything necessary for piety. The virtues themselves are evoked without explanation or illustration. The care with which most ancient ethical accounts, including Christian ones, detail the powers that enable someone to the live the virtuous life is lacking here. There is no account of the anthropological or theological forces that enable the virtues. Such an explanation does not seem to be of concern. What matters is the basic affirmation of the necessity of the virtuous life. The larger ethical and theological narratives that might support that affirmation are not recounted.

2 Peter 1:12–15 Testamentary Reminder

This passage is the primary reason that 2 Peter is often compared to ancient Jewish testaments. There are similarities and dissimilarities between 2 Peter and the typical Jewish testament.[45] Second Peter lacks the usual gathering of the family around the patriarch, who is often on his deathbed. It also lacks the final familial blessing, the rehearsal of the patriarch's life, and an account of the death itself. In general, the rhetorical atmosphere of 2 Peter is different from the feel of testaments that focus on the death of a patriarch in a way that 2 Peter does not. However, the announcement of impending death, the prophecies about the future, the exhortations to the righteous life, and the attempt by the patriarch to leave the words of his farewell speech in the place of his ongoing presence are all typical of testaments. Thus, while it is probably not helpful to define 2 Peter exactly as a testament, some of the patterns of testamentary literature are present.

This passage is also typical of letters, including pseudepigraphical ones, in that personal stories and details from the author's life are not only common but often central to the argument of the letter. In pseudepigraphical letters these personal details not only make the letter seem more genuine; they also reinforce the authority of the letter. In this role, this passage connects with the passage

---

45. The classic model of the testament can be found in the pseudepigraphical *Testaments of the Twelve Patriarchs* and the *Testament of Moses*.

that follows. The authority of Peter and the letter itself is established, first of all, by this death reference, which echoes the patriarchal testament; and second, by the appeal to the unique empowerment and authorization that comes from Peter's presence at the transfiguration (1:16–21).

> 1:12 Therefore I am going to be[a] always reminding you of these things, although[b] you know them and are firmly established in the truth that is present. 13 I think it is right, as long as I am in this tent, to awaken[c] you with[d] a reminder, 14 since I know that the putting off of my tent is soon, just as our Lord Jesus Christ has disclosed to me. 15 And I shall be eager[e] that even after my departure you are always able to remember these things.

a. The verb form *mellēsō*, the future of *mellō*, poses considerable difficulties. The basic meaning of the verb *mellō* is "to intend to do something" or "to be about to do something." It can also express certainty or probability. However, the translations "I shall intend to remind you" and "I shall be about to remind you" make little sense. Some manuscripts (𝔐) amend the text to *ouk amelēsō* (I shall not neglect) in an obvious attempt to solve this difficulty. No completely satisfactory translation has been offered. The word *mellō*, especially in participle form, can simply refer to the future. Thus the future form of the verb could be a way of combining the word's two senses of future action and intention.

b. The conjunction *kaiper* gives a concessive force to the circumstantial participles *eidotas* and *estērigmenous*.

c. The verb *diegeirō* means to "awaken," "rouse," or even "disturb."

d. The dative could be a dative of manner or of respect ("awaken you by way of reminder") but is more likely one of agency.

e. The translation given above preserves the awkwardness of the future form *spoudasō*. The root is common in 2 Peter (1:5, 10, 15; 3:14) and is used to express eagerness or zealousness.

[12] This passage opens with the common epistolary and paraenetic rhetoric of reminder (Rom 15:15; 1 Cor 15:1; Jude 5). Rhetoric of reminder was not only considered polite, since it did not assume negatives about the hearers or impute higher moral ground to the author; it was also considered to be a good tactic for persuasion. A reminder implies that the readers already think what they are being asked to think. By assuming the lack of conflict and presence of agreement, this rhetoric of reminder actually creates rhetorical space for extensive exhortation.

However, for modern readers this rhetoric makes it difficult to determine where the ethical controversy might lie. It is not clear what the readers are supposed to already know. The assertion that the readers already know these things and are firmly grounded in them suggests larger content than the specifics of 1:3–11. In fact, it would be difficult to read the phrase "the truth that is present" as referring only to what is named in the letter. The truth that is present in the community probably includes the full content of the gospel and the full realities of the Christian life. Thus "these things" certainly includes 1:3–11; it may include all that follows; and it probably assumes larger discussions not explicitly mentioned.

As noted above, the unusual and somewhat awkward use of the future of *mellō* creates a sense of ongoing reminder. Since Peter's death is assumed to be soon (1:14), this future reminder cannot be done in person. Hence the letter itself must function in this way. Ancient letters were often imagined as accomplishing an act of presence. In the absence of the author, a letter could convey something of the author's person. The claims of 2 Peter are modest in comparison. The letter does not claim to manifest the real presence of Peter into the community but to serve only as an ongoing reminder. In this way, 2 Peter reads more like a Jewish testament, which does not preserve the presence of the patriarch but does preserve his example and his teachings.

[13–14] The language of a letter begins to give way to language of a testament. This letter is written in expectation of Peter's death. The use of the image "tent" for body is common in Greek literature. While the language of "tent" may suggest a dualism of real self and unreal body, it is actually used to evoke the temporary character of life. Paul himself uses the image in 2 Cor 5:1–4 to discuss the death that awaits everyone. Thus no anthropological or cosmic dualisms are necessarily implied in the use of the term "tent." Furthermore, the language of "putting off" should not be read as a dualistic putting off the mortal flesh by the immortal soul. While in Greek literature such imagery can signal various dualisms, in the NT the image of "putting off" is used for transitions between an old self and a new self (see 1 Cor 15:53–54; 2 Cor 5:3–4; Col 2:11; 3:9–10). Thus putting off the tent refers to death and the transitions that accompany it.

The letter declares that "Peter" knows that his death is soon because Jesus Christ has disclosed this to him. Though the notion that death is soon or imminent is common and even standard in testamentary literature, it is not clear what event underlies the claim that Jesus Christ has revealed that Peter's death is soon. The announcements of Jesus to Peter in the Gospel of John stress the character of Peter's death and not its time frame (John 13:36; 21:18–19). There is nothing in extracanonical Christian literature that quite matches the imagery of 2 Peter. It is possible that there was a saying of Jesus about Peter's death that was known to these Christians but disappeared from the tradition. The traditions about Peter are notoriously fragmented. For instance, the resurrection appearance of Jesus to Peter, which is crucial to early Christian resurrection traditions (cf. Luke 24:34; 1 Cor 15:5), is never narrated in the NT. However, most readers think that the comments of Jesus in John 21:18–19 are ambiguous enough to fund the claims of 2 Peter.

In any case, the nearness of death leads to the writing of the letter. Its expressed purpose is to "awaken" the readers "with a reminder." There seem to be two assumptions about the readers. First, they already know, have already heard and believed, the truths of the gospel. Second, they have a tendency to forget these truths and perhaps to fall into immorality. Thus they need to hear them again. They need to be awakened from their forgetfulness. The letter not only reminds them of what they know; it also awakens them from the sleep of forgetfulness. In early Christian circles, Christians assumed that everyone needs to hear the gospel over and over again.

[15] Most readers understand this verse as the articulation of the ultimate purpose of the letter. The letter is to serve as a permanent reminder. The future tense of Peter's eagerness for the ongoing memory of these things creates a puzzle. The grammar suggests that this eagerness goes beyond the moment of writing the letter. Thus many readers suggest that this is an oblique reference to the high regard for the Petrine traditions in early Christianity. The future attempt to assure proper memory could refer to the Gospel of Mark. Eusebius, reporting the second-century comments of Papias on the origin of the Gospel of Mark, says that John Mark wrote down accurately but not in order the teachings of Peter on the story of Jesus (*Hist. eccl.* 3.39.15–16). Irenaeus records the same tradition, adding the note that Mark did this "after their departure" (*Haer.* 3.1.1). Both 2 Peter and Irenaeus refer to Peter's departure and use the same Greek word (*exodos*). It is entirely possible that Irenaeus is not only recalling this verse of 2 Peter but also understands the reference as being to the Gospel of Mark. However, it is unlikely that the author of 2 Peter intends a reference to the Gospel of Mark. The author wants the readers to remember "these things." As noted above, "these things" probably refers to the letter of 2 Peter itself and especially to 1:3–11. It is difficult to image how "these things" could include the Gospel of Mark.

The future eagerness of Peter concerns the readers' memory of the letter itself. It is not clear how this eagerness has an aspect of the future. Several suggestions have been offered, although none is completely satisfactory. Some readers suggest that Peter's eagerness involves taking steps to ensure the arrival and preservation of the letter. The existence of the letter indicates his success. Others suggest, perhaps more plausibly, that this is an instance of the confusion of tenses that often occurs in ancient letter writing. For instance, present time can refer either to the moment of writing or the moment of reading. The use of the future tense could be an awkward nod to the distance created by a letter between the time of the author and the time of the readers. In this reading, "I shall be eager that . . . you are always able to remember . . ." really means "I am eager that . . . you will always be able to remember. . . ."

In any case, there is in this verse an acknowledgment or anticipation of the canonical role of apostolic texts in Christian circles. Texts themselves can serve in the role of the apostles. They can preserve the memories and teaching of these apostles. They can remind forgetful Christians of these apostolic teachings. Of all the texts in the NT, 2 Peter may be the only one that seems to be written in order to be part of a canon. Admittedly, in second-century Christianity the concept of canon is inchoate and changing. Nevertheless, in these verses 2 Peter anticipates the ordering force that apostolic texts might have.

The testamentary language of these verses (1:12–15) builds upon the narrative of salvation in 1:3–11. The author of the letter calls upon the credibility of Peter in order to offer a text that is a reliable reminder of the truths of the gospel. The apostolic authority assumed in these verses will be fully articulated in 1:16–21, where both the person of Peter and the traditions originating from him receive the unique authentication that only something like the transfiguration could provide. In the midst of this rather focused literary sequence, these verses announce the guiding purpose of the letter. It wants to place apostolic theology into the life of the community in such a way that these readers can always remember it.

While the rhetoric of reminder is commonplace in ancient paraenesis, it serves more than a formal purpose. The assumption in 2 Peter, as in many ancient texts, is that people do not always remember what they know. They forget and they think about other things. The false prophets and mockers have filled their heads with other ideas. The task of 2 Peter is to inscribe the truth of the gospel in a permanent text that can be turned to again and again.

The way to remember is to read. In this sense, 2 Peter anticipates the adoption of a canon. The only way to ensure sustained memory of the apostolic version of the gospel is to inscribe texts that can be preserved and read and reread. The ancient argument that the emergence of writing killed human memory is hereby reversed. Memory is already unreliable; texts come to the rescue. Memory cannot guarantee the ongoing presence of the truth in the lives of these Christians, but texts can. The text must have unimpeachable credentials. These credentials are explored in what follows.

2 Peter 1:16–21 Apostolic and Prophetic Witnesses

These six verses are the most controversial in 2 Peter. Two uncertainties dominate the discussion. First, it is not clear whether the account of the transfiguration intends to authenticate Jesus' Parousia, the authority of Peter as witness, or both. Second, it is not clear whether the reference to the "interpretation" of prophecy refers to the interpretive act of the prophet or of the later readers. The answers to those questions affect not only the force of these verses but also the

Apostolic and Prophetic Witnesses 229

structure of the letter itself. Some readers, for instance, decide that the topic of 1:16–18 is distinct from that of 1:19–21 and separate the two sections. Other readers decide that the governing topic of both sections is the credibility of the Parousia and see the entire passage as an introduction to the body of the letter and especially to the issues of chapter 3.

The uncertainty over whether the account of the transfiguration intends to reinforce the authority of Peter or of the predictions of the Parousia is complicated by the usual puzzlements created by the story of transfiguration. The transfiguration was understood in a variety of ways in early Christian literature. Furthermore, early Christianity develops a variety of accounts of the transfiguration. Since 2 Peter seems to draw exclusively on no single one of them, it is not possible to determine which traditions are in play in these verses.

The pronouncements about the character of prophecy seem, at first glance at least, to have two edges. Many readers understand the reference to the interpretation of prophecy not being of "one's own interpretation" (1:20) as referring to interpretation done by later readers and hearers of the prophecy. However, the very next verse (1:21) argues that prophets do not speak out of their own will but from God through the Holy Spirit. The awkwardness of such a shift in topic leads other readers to conclude that 1:20 is speaking about the interpretative role of prophets in their own prophecies.

Finally, the reading of these verses offered here suggests that the issue of the Parousia is indeed the governing issue but not the only issue in these verses. The verses address the reliability of many things, including Peter, the Parousia, the theological narrative in 1:3–11, Christian prophecies in general, and the coming attacks on false prophets and scoffers. Although the literary role of these verses seems transitional, the theological role is to affirm and demonstrate the apostolic authority of the diverse claims in the letter.

1:16 Not by following cleverly devised[a] myths did we make known to you the power and coming[b] of our Lord Jesus Christ but by being eyewitnesses of his majesty. 17 For having received honor and glory from God the Father, when such[c] a voice was carried to him by the majestic glory, "This is my beloved Son, in whom I am well pleased"[d]—[e] 18 this very voice we[f] heard carried from heaven, when we were with him on the holy mountain. 19 And we have the prophetic word more certain,[g] paying attention[h] to which you do well, as to a lamp shining in a murky[i] place, until the day shines[j] and the morning star[k] rises in your hearts, 20 first of all knowing this, that no prophecy of scripture happens[l] from one's own[l] interpretation,[m] 21 for no prophecy was ever carried by the will of a person, but people carried by the Holy Spirit spoke from God.

a. The verb *sophizō* usually has the positive meaning of "to make wise" or, in the passive, "to be skillful or clever." It can, however, have the negative connotation of trickery or deceit. The context here requires the negative sense of skillfully crafting something in order to deceive.

b. The *ousia* in compound word *parousia* can be based the root *es* (am, be), in which case it means "presence." In fact, the participle *parousē* is used that way in 1:12 ("the truth that is present"). If this is correct, the translation would be "the power and presence of our Lord Jesus Christ." On the other hand, *ousia* could be based on the root *i* (come, go). In this case, *parousia* would mean "coming" or "arrival." Most readers think the context requires "coming." Furthermore, the term is clearly used in 3:4 to refer to the second coming.

c. The demonstrative *toiosde*, a stronger form of *toios* (such, such as), can have the sense of "so great."

d. There are numerous variants of what the voice says. Most of them try to conform more closely to what is said in the Gospel accounts.

e. The sentence breaks off at this point, leaving these two participial phrases without an anchoring indicative. Such anacolutha are common in Greek syntax.

f. The unnecessary inclusion of the pronoun *hēmeis* (we) makes the subject emphatic. Thus some translations read "we ourselves."

g. The comparative *bebaioteron* means "more firm, steady, or certain." Since the comparative can often be used for emphasis in later Greek, more or less as an equivalent to the superlative, and since the verb *echō* (have) often assumes the content of its predicates, some translations combine the images into "we have confirmation" or "we have firmly." However, the Greek makes perfect sense without such nuances.

h. The participle *prosechontes* could be supplementary ("you do well to pay attention") or, as rendered above, circumstantial.

i. The adjective *auchmēros* comes from the root "to burn" and refers to droughts and the conditions of drought. Its basic meaning is "dry" or "dusty" but can mean "squalid" or "unwashed." Its combination with the shining of a lamp suggests murkiness or darkness.

j. The verb *diaugazō*, which means "shine through," comes from the noun *augē*, the basic meaning of which is "sunlight" but can refer to light of any kind. In some contexts, it can mean "dawn" or "daybreak." This use, plus the aorist tense of the verb, produces the popular translation "the day dawns" (NRSV).

k. The compound noun *phōsphoros* means "light-bringer." Though it can refer to any person or thing that brings light (e.g., in Latin *phōsphoros* becomes "Lucifer"), in the context of the heavens it normally refers to Venus, the so-called "morning star."

l. The verb *ginomai* with the genitive *epilyseōs* (interpretation) can mean "belongs to" or "arises or happens from." The translation depends on the decision as to the antecedent of "one's own." If "one's own" refers to the later interpreter, the translation would be "belongs to." If "one's own" refers to the prophets themselves, the translation would be, as it is given here, "happens from."

m. The noun *epilysis*, which occurs only here in the NT, is a common word elsewhere that is used for the explanation of riddles, dreams, or even difficult texts.

[1:16] The passage begins with a denial that issues in an affirmation. The denial of following "cleverly devised myths" raises two obvious questions of what these myths might be and why their use is denied. The term "myth" has a rich history in Greek thought, most of it negative. Greek philosophical literature, in particular, used the term negatively in contrast to "logos" to designate fables and stories which were not necessarily true.[46] This negative tradition came into Judaism as a way to contrast the true stories of the Bible with the false myths about the Greco-Roman gods. The only real positive use of "myths" came from Greek and early Christian ideas that certain fabulous stories about the gods or the heavens were riddles that contained hidden truths. However, the modifier "cleverly devised" indicates that these myths did not come from divine revelation but from human creativity. Humans could easily compose entertaining stories with hidden meanings. All of this means that this passage about the transfiguration begins somewhat curiously with a denial that the story of transfiguration was based on such myths.

Three suggestions have been offered for this denial of myths. First, the opponents themselves use myths. Certain Christian gnostic groups apparently did so in order to narrate theological truths that plain narrative could not convey.[47] The author would be claiming that, unlike our opponents, "we" do not follow myths. Second, the opponents have accused the apostolic tradition of being based on myths. The ridicule of the Parousia by the scoffers in 3:3–4 could include this charge of "myth." Third, the distinction is simply rhetorical, a way to underline the historical character of the eyewitness account of the transfiguration. The choice among those options depends on how the rest of this passage is read. When the credibility of the Parousia is perceived as the governing issue, the second option becomes the most likely.

The core affirmation is that "we" have made known "the power and coming of our Lord Jesus Christ." While the plural "we" probably refers to all the apostles and not just those who were eyewitnesses to the transfiguration, the credibility of all of them depends on the eyewitness status of the few who were there. On its own, this sentence reads as a classic Greco-Roman epiphany. In fact, if removed from the larger context of 2 Peter, the term *parousia* would be read in its more normal sense of "presence," and this account of the transfiguration would be an announcement of Jesus' divinity. This is the central force of the transfiguration stories in the NT. Thus some readers of 2 Peter see this account as a typical epiphany. They translate *parousia* as "presence" and distinguish these verses from the discussions of the second coming in chapter 3. However, even in the Gospels the transfiguration is connected to the second

---

46. For a discussion of the role of the term "myth" in Greek thought, see Richard Buxton, ed., *From Myth to Reason? Studies in the Development of Greek Thought* (Oxford: Oxford University Press, 1999).

47. C. K. Barrett, "Myth and the New Testament: The Greek Word μῦθος," *ExpTim* 68 (1957): 345–48.

coming. The announcement in Mark 9:1 of the nearness of the second coming is immediately followed by the story of the transfiguration in 9:2–8. The term *parousia* clearly means "coming" in 2 Pet 3:4. It is, furthermore, difficult to separate the imagery of these verses from the discussions in chapter 3. Thus it appears that 2 Peter interprets the story of transfiguration not just as an epiphany, which it certainly is, but also as a promise of Jesus' return.

The capacity for making known the power and coming of Jesus comes from being eyewitnesses who saw his majesty. Some readers argue that the point of the eyewitness claim is only to reinforce the authority of Peter and not the credibility of the second coming. Others argue the opposite, that Peter is not the issue and that the point is only to establish the second coming. However, both of these readings undo the logic of the verses and probably the logic of witnessing itself. The epiphanic power of the transfiguration gives status to those who witness it. The apostolic credibility of Peter bestows credibility to his account of the transfiguration. The language of "majesty" comes more from the dynamics of a traditional epiphany and not from eschatological judgment scenes. This reinforces the sense that 2 Peter is transforming epiphany imagery with early Christian theology of the second coming.

[17–18] This account of the transfiguration is interesting both for where it disagrees and where it agrees with the Synoptic accounts. In general the prophetic motifs that are central to the Synoptic stories are lacking in 2 Peter. There is no mention of Moses or Elijah. There is no cloud, no command to listen, and no talk of erecting tents. Second Peter focuses on the voice and the naming. In this way, the role of Ps 2:7 (and to some extent Isa 42:1) comes more to the fore.

The syntax of 2 Peter emphasizes the event character of the transfiguration. This is not an announcement of an eternal status; it is the giving of the status. Jesus receives honor and glory when the voice designates him son. Honor (*timē*) and glory (*doxa*) are frequently paired in Jewish and Christian literature, referring typically to status in the heavenly hierarchies. Beyond that, both terms can be used in a variety of contexts. For instance, the two terms are used for Jesus in Heb 2:9 to describe his status above the angels, and for humans in Heb 2:7 to describe their status of being slightly below that of angels. These honors can have eschatological significance but not necessarily so. In any case, 2 Peter indicates that Jesus first received this status at the transfiguration.

The choice of terms indicates considerable care in the composition of this narrative. God is called "Father" because the "Father" will name Jesus "Son." The imagery of a voice being "carried" to Jesus (1:17) from heaven (1:18) anticipates prophets "carried" by the Holy Spirit (1:21). Having the "majestic glory" carry the voice avoids the somewhat offensive image of having God do such duty and creates the nice parallel of God's glory giving glory to Jesus.

Despite the apparent avoidance of having God act directly, the voice speaks on behalf of God, who is Father and full of glory and honor. The announcement itself is a combination of Ps 2:7 and Isa 42:1 and comes closest to that in Matthew (17:5). The terms can be read in many ways. In Ps 2:7 the naming of the anointed as son does not imply the kind of special paternity that it conveys when applied by Christians to Jesus. Similarly, the designation "my beloved," which is probably a Greek rendition of "my chosen" in Isa 42:1, does not in itself suggest divine status. And the announcement that God is pleased, which is also from Isa 42:1, implies only God's favor. Thus the role this naming plays in 2 Peter depends on the presence of established messianic readings of the transfiguration. Second Peter assumes in its argument that readers will supply the traditional christological readings of these terms and will hear the term *parousia* not simply as an epiphany but as an announcement of the future "coming."

The breaking off from the expected syntax at the end of 1:17 highlights the importance of the claims of 1:18. The Greek syntax highlights the identity of both the voice and the people who hear it. Both emphases are necessary to the logic of witness. First of all, it is this voice, not some other, that was heard on the mountain, a voice carried from heaven itself by the very glory of God, a voice that spoke on God's behalf to Jesus himself. Second, the "we" who heard it are the same people who, in the singular presence of Peter, attest to the truth of both this voice and the content of 2 Peter. Once again, the authenticating power of the transfiguration and the credibility of the apostles reinforce one another. The designation of the mountain or hill (*oros*) as the "holy mountain" further highlights the sacred character of the event, the words, and the apostles.

Strikingly, the "eyewitnesses" (*epoptai*, 1:16) do not so much see as hear. Though the phrase "majestic glory" suggests some kind of visionary data, it is the voice and what was said that is highlighted. This focus on words enables the transfer and communication of the essential content of the event. A portrait of heavenly glory or an account of who was standing where is not necessary. The words spoken by the voice form the core of the story. Yet these words need proper messianic interpretation.

[19] The meaning of this verse depends to a great extent upon the referent of the phrase "prophetic word" (*prophētikos logos*). There are numerous proposals, of which three have the most influence. Some readers argue that, since this entire passage focuses upon the credibility of the second coming, the "prophetic word" refers to the announcement of the heavenly voice in the transfiguration. However, most readers think that the range of "prophetic word" cannot be confined so narrowly. Other readers argue that "prophetic word" refers to any prophecy done by anyone, whether ancient Jewish prophets or modern Christian ones. However, the parallel phrase "prophecy of scripture" in 1:20 suggests to most readers that "prophetic word" refers, as it normally does, to OT prophecy.

Reading this verse as a reference to OT prophecy creates the puzzle of how the transfiguration of Jesus could make OT prophecy "more certain." Some readers argue that it does not. They separate this passage into two distinct sections: one dealing with the transfiguration, the other dealing with prophecy. However, given the various literary interplays among these verses and the fact that 1:19 reads as a conclusion drawn from what precedes, most readers insist on the literary and thematic coherence of 1:16–21. This means that the account of the transfiguration makes OT prophecy more reliable. Second Peter does not detail why this is so, but the reasons are not difficult to imagine. As noted above, the account of the transfiguration depends for its logic upon unstated messianic readings of the story. Given the early Christian tendency to read the OT as prophecy and especially as messianic prophecy, "the prophetic word" (1:19) and "prophecy of scripture" (1:20) may refer to messianic interpretations similar to those attached to the transfiguration. Thus the giving of honor and glory to Jesus at the transfiguration reinforces the credibility of OT prophecies about the messiah. What holds the passage together is the assumed messianic status of Jesus.

The call to focus on these prophecies as a "lamp shining in a murky place" anticipates the light of the day of the Lord. The contrast is striking. "The day" will shine abroad. The world will be flooded with light. There will also be a heavenly light that shines in a person's heart. Readers have long noted that the morning star precedes the dawn. However, the point here is not the order of events but the imagery of outside and inside. There will be heavenly light everywhere. Until that day the only light is that of prophecy. This light is not the sun or a heavenly star; it is just a lamp. Nonetheless, in this "murky place" this lamp, the prophetic word from heaven, is the only reliable light.

[20–21] It is possible to render the Greek as "no prophecy of scripture belongs to one's own interpretation." The lack of clear antecedent to "one's own" permits reading the text as referring to how people interpret ancient OT prophecies. Consequently, this verse is often read as an attempt to limit heterodox reading of Scripture. However, this reading separates the verse from the verses surrounding it and introduces a sudden and unnecessary change in topic.

The Greek also translates as "no prophecy of scripture happens from one's own interpretation," with the antecedent of "one's own" being the prophet. This makes perfect sense in context. The credibility of the prophecy, as reinforced in the account of the transfiguration and in the affirmation in 1:19, receives further support. In the Mediterranean world, prophets were regularly understood as having to interpret the revelation that came to them. This verse denies that the prophecies contained in Scripture are the result of the interpretive process of the prophets.

The opening denial in 1:21 clarifies the meaning of 1:20. Prophecy is not "carried by the will of a person." This is not a denial that humans are involved; it is, instead, a clarification of their role. Humans do not "carry" the prophecy. Instead, prophecy occurs when "people" are "carried by the Holy Spirit." In the repetition of the term "carry," this account parallels the account of the transfiguration in 1:17–18, where a voice is both "carried" to Jesus "by the majestic glory" and "carried from heaven" so that the eyewitnesses could hear it. Putting all this together, a rather full account of the prophetic event can be constructed. A heavenly voice is carried from heaven to Jesus, to eyewitnesses, and perhaps to all prophets by means of the heavenly glory. These people are themselves carried by the Holy Spirit. When all the carrying is thus ordered, people speak "from God."

The ancient world was filled with debates about prophecies. There was certainly no agreed-upon account. Prophets were accused of all kinds of deceit. Prophecies were often ridiculed. Nonetheless, prophecy had a powerful role throughout the Greco-Roman world. The OT itself is frequented by accounts of false prophets. In agreement with 2 Peter, the common image of false prophets is as people who speak "the deceit of their own minds" (Jer 14:14; see also Jer 23:16; Ezek 13:3). Second Peter itself will move from this defense of prophecy to a prediction of false prophets (2:1) and an attack on them. In any case, the general cast of this defense would probably have given it credence among both Jews and Greeks.

The reading of these verses (1:16–21) offered here proposes a progressive argument about the character of prophecy. Prophecy is described as originating in its entirety from divine powers. Prophecies that are contained in Scripture (and perhaps originate from apostles) are immune from the compromising will of humans that are involved in their hearing, speaking, and inscribing. While on the day of the Lord heavenly light will shine everywhere, including in human hearts, for now the words of prophecy are the only light. The hints about the possibilities of a Christian canon that were offered in 1:15 are further developed here. The apostle Peter in the writing of this letter and in his account of the transfiguration is participating in the canonical roles that traditionally belong to the prophecies of Scripture. The temporary lamp that shines in this murky place comprises the words of both the OT and the writings of the apostles.

Of course, the point of the defense of prophecy is not simply to defend prophecy in general. All of this centers on the status of Jesus as Messiah and the credibility of the prophecy about the second coming. Second Peter does not explicitly articulate the messianic theology that underlies this account. In fact, throughout the letter, the unique status of Jesus is simply assumed. The theological summary in 1:3–11 asserts the status of Jesus Christ without analyzing it. The argument about the second coming in 3:1–13 will say nothing about the role of Jesus. The debate is not over Jesus' status as Messiah but over the very idea of a second coming. Thus what appears to be at stake is not whether Jesus has unique status but whether, for instance, the promise in 1:11 about entry in the "eternal kingdom of our Lord and Savior Jesus Christ" is true.

2 Peter 2:1–22 False Teachers and Their Punishment

2 Peter 2:1–3 The Prediction of False Teachers

This warning against false teachers begins an attack that lasts through the entire chapter and even continues in a somewhat different vein in the arguments against mockers (3:3). At this point 2 Peter begins to follow the imagery and order of Jude. For all the similarities in language and even in specific argument between 2 Peter and Jude, the overall feel of 2 Peter is different. This brief introduction to the intense attack that follows outlines the core argument. False teachers are to be expected: they were predicted by the apostles. They will lead people astray and bring disrepute on the community. Their teaching is full of deceit. God has prepared punishment for them. In some ways, the verses that follow (2:4–22) demonstrate that this pattern is an ancient and expected one.

These verses are full not only of echoes of Jude but also of the particular imagery of 2 Peter. False OT prophets and false Christian teachers parallel the true OT prophets (1:19–21) and apostles (1:16–18). The imagery of people following licentiousness and the accusation of "fabricated words" recalls the denial of the accusation that the apostles follow "cleverly devised myths" (1:16). Finally, the persistent language of destruction and judgment anticipates the promises of judgment (3:7, 10, 12). This reworking of Jude imagery into the rhetoric of 2 Peter will persist throughout this chapter.

There is a curious debate about the relationship between 2:1 and Justin, *Dialogue* 82.1, which reads, "And just as there were false prophets in the time of your holy prophets, so there are now many false teachers among us, of whom our Lord forewarned us to beware." The obvious similarities suggests that one document was copying another or that there is a third document that they both share. This relationship has interesting implications for the date of 2 Peter. Justin's *Dialogue* can be dated with some confidence after 150 C.E. If 2 Peter is copying Justin, then a late date for the origin of 2 Peter is supported. However, it is not possible to have much confidence about the literary relationship between the texts. In fact, it is more likely that Justin is copying 2 Peter than vice versa. Thus no firm conclusions can be drawn.

> 2:1 But there were also false prophets among the people, just as there will also be false teachers among you, who will bring in[a] destructive heresies,[b] even denying the Master who bought them, bringing upon themselves quick destruction. 2 And many will follow their licentiousness,[c] on account of whom the way of truth will be slandered. 3 And in their greed

The Prediction of False Teachers 237

they will exploit[d] you with fabricated[e] words. Against whom[f] the judgment from long ago is not idle,[g] and their destruction is not sleeping.[g]

a. The compound verb *pareisagō* can have the neutral meaning of "introduce" or literally "bring in alongside of." In some contexts, it can convey a sense of deceit or secrecy. Most translations do convey this negative possibility, reading something like "will secretly bring in." There is also a possible echo of the people in Jude 4 who "have slipped in" (*pareisedysan*).

b. The word *hairesis* has a complicated history. Though its basic meaning is "a taking," in common usage it meant "choice." It also had the more specialized meaning of "sect" or "school." It is this last meaning that prepared the way for its Christian use as "heresy." The question here is whether the special Christian meaning is in force or not. Since the word has already acquired this special nuance in Paul (1 Cor 11:19; Gal 5:20), "heresies" is probably the best translation here. The second issue is the force of the genitive in the phrase *haireseis apōleias* (lit., "heresies of destruction"). Although the phrase could, in anticipation of the awaiting destruction, have the sense of "heresies that lead to destruction," it is perhaps best to render it in the more usual form of "destructive heresies." This permits the phrase to attribute other destructive powers to heresies than that of final judgment.

c. The term *aselgeia* denotes libertine behavior or "licentiousness," especially with a sexual dimension.

d. The verb *emporeuomai* means "to travel," "to trade," or "to be a merchant." In certain contexts it can have the negative sense of "to use for gain" or even "to cheat someone financially."

e. While the adjective *plastos* usually means "formed" or "molded," it can have the negative sense of "forged" or "counterfeit." In a similar way, the verb *plassō* normally means "to form or mold." In connection with speech or words, however, it tends to mean "make up," "fabricate," or "invent."

f. Most translations render the relative pronoun *hois* (against whom, whose) as a simple possessive (their).

g. Contrary to the style of most translations, which tend to put the verbs in the past tense, both Greek verbs are in the present. A few Greek manuscripts (Ψ, 𝔐) actually have a future "will not sleep" instead of the present "is not sleeping."

[2:1] There are no supporting examples offered to the assertion that there were many "false prophets" among the people of Israel. Probably such was not necessary. Even the many OT examples that follow in 2:4–22 are not exactly about false prophets. Although the Greek term is rare in the LXX (see, e.g., Jer 6:13; Zech 13:2), the story of Israel is filled with false prophets. The classic definition comes from Deut 18:20: "But any prophet who speaks in the name of other gods, or who presumes to speak in my name a word that I have not commanded the prophet to speak—that prophet shall die." Early Christian literature is also filled with warning about false prophets who will arise in Christian communities (e.g., Matt 24:11, 24; Mark 13:22; 1 John 4:1; Rev 16:13; 19:20; 20:10; *Did.* 16.3).

Given the prevalence of term "false prophets," it is a bit surprising that 2 Peter refers to "false teachers." The next known usage of that term is in the passage from Justin, which is quoted above and is probably dependent on 2 Peter. The brief description of their activity in this passage does not seem to exclude the more common terminology of prophet. Early Christian false prophets could be accused of any of these things. It is possible that early Christian nervousness about the whole category of prophet is reflected here. These people are not called prophets because the term itself is avoided. However, it is also possible that these people were known in these communities as teachers rather than prophets.

The first accusation is that they will bring in "destructive heresies." The language of bringing in emphasizes the foreign status of their teachings. The people themselves, unlike those in Jude 4, are not accused of being outsiders; it is their thinking that is excluded. "Heresy" can refer to sects or groups that think alike, as well as to the pattern of thinking itself. Since it is unlikely that these teachers are introducing multiple sects or groups into the communities, the accusation probably refers to their various teachings. The content of these teachings is never explicitly detailed, although it probably includes the promise of freedom (2:19) and scoffing at the second coming (3:4). The destruction connected with this teaching belongs first of all to the teachers who bring "upon themselves quick destruction." The surety of this destruction is asserted throughout the letter. This destruction is in some ways the most persistent theme in all that follows (2:4, 5, 6, 9, 10, 12, 13, 17, 19; 3:7, 10). However, the destruction connected to these heresies may also include the negative impact on the community and the people in it.

The second accusation is that they deny "the Master who bought them." The language of denying the Master comes from Jude 4, to which 2 Peter adds "who bought them." Readers have long noted the appropriateness of the addition. "Master" (*despotēs*) is an unusual term for Jesus. It normally refers to the master of the house and implies the ownership of slaves. It is often used negatively in parallel with the nearly always negative "tyrant." Rather than reject the term for these negative echoes, 2 Peter reinforces it by pointing out that this Master has bought these people, and they are now his slaves. It is not clear what 2 Peter means by the assertion that they are "denying" this Master who bought them. In Jude the denial seems to have involved rejection of the moral life. Since 2 Peter includes most of the accusations of immorality in Jude, it is likely that rejection of the Master involves refusal to live as the Master commands. However, the debate about the second coming opens the possibility that Jesus' status as Master or Lord is also being questioned.

[2] The prediction that "many will follow their licentiousness" reflects the seriousness of the debate. In some ways, this prediction is a commonplace in early Christianity (see, e.g., Mark 13:22; 2 Thess 2:1–12; 2 Tim 3:13).

Christians constantly warn one another about bad theology, about the people who hold such theology, and about the immorality that results from it. Nonetheless, the very existence of the Letter of 2 Peter suggests that this prediction has come true. It is striking that the warning is not about the ideas or teachings of these false teachers but about their immorality. Though it is the standard belief in the ancient world that bad thinking leads to bad behavior, this focus on licentiousness highlights the centrality of ethics in this conflict. Given the tone of the attack that follows, it may be that licentious behavior is as much the problem as bad teaching.

The result of this immoral living is that "the way of truth" is "slandered." While the phrase "way of truth" occurs in the LXX (Ps 118:30 [119:30 NRSV]; Wis 5:6), early Christianity will often use the term "way" (*hodos*) as a synonym for the Christian life (e.g., Acts 9:2; 19:9, 23; 24:14, 22). Second Peter will use "way" both negatively ("the way of Balaam" in 2:15) and positively ("the straight way" in 2:15; "the way of righteousness" in 2:21). Apparently the way of truth is slandered because outsiders perceive the behavior of the Christians as immoral. This warning anticipates what will become a growing phenomenon in early Christianity. Christians will admonish one another to behave in such a way as to avoid the animosity and rebuke of the non-Christians around them. In 1 Peter the good behavior of Christians could convert non-Christians who observe it (e.g., 2:12, 15; 3:1). The opposite is also the case. For all the disagreements between the worldviews of Christians and non-Christians, they mostly agreed about basic morality. If Christians are living licentiously, then those who observe it will, with some justification, slander "the way of truth."

[3] The third accusation against the false teachers is that "in their greed they will exploit you with fabricated words." The accusation about "fabricated words" obviously plays off the denial that the apostles follow "cleverly devised myths" (1:16). The source of a teacher's ideas was much discussed in the ancient world. In Christian circles the debate will typically take the shape that it has in 2 Peter. Teaching that does not come out of the apostolic tradition is suspect. The credibility and authority of Peter and of all the apostles are crucial here. The apostolic canon is beginning to take shape. Anything that does not agree with it simply comes from human cleverness.

The complaint about teaching for profit is repeated endlessly in the ancient world. This is, in fact, the stock accusation against teachers of all kinds. For the most part, Christianity simply echoes the standard Greco-Roman warnings about money and greed. The stock character of this accusation makes it impossible to know if these teachers were actually receiving money for their teachings.

The passage ends with a nicely framed announcement of judgment and destruction. The idea that judgment is "from long ago" follows a common Christian pattern. Jude 4 makes the same argument. Moreover, readers have long noted that the judgment scene in Matt 25:31–46 has no deliberation to it.

People are divided into sheep and goats according to what they have done. In a sense, the judgment is determined before it starts. In a similar way, the judgment scene in Rev 20:11–15 simply involves the reading of names that have already been written or not written in the book of life. In this account, there is not even the hopeless appeal that there is in Matthew (25:44). Second Peter seems to imagine a similar scenario. The judgment has already been made, and the coming punishment is ready. In the syntax of 2 Peter "judgment" and "destruction" become eerily personified. The present tense of the verbs also adds to threat. Judgment and destruction are actively waiting for their moment.

This prediction of false teachers introduces the intense attack that follows. In some ways these verses (2:1–3) provide a nice theological framework for those attacks. These false teachers are of the same mold as the false prophets who plagued Israel. This connection sets up the following series of scriptural examples of unrighteous people and their punishments. The change in terminology from prophet to teacher probably indicates that these people were seen in the community as teachers, not prophets. The three accusations of introducing "destructive heresies," of "denying the Master who bought them," and of teaching for profit by means of "fabricated words" may actually disclose little about these teachers. At a minimum, these accusations place these teachers within a set of categories that are fundamental to the attack. Whatever their actual theology, the author is convinced that they live and breed immorality and that this brings disrepute on the community.

Hanging over this theological and ethical crisis is a conviction in divine justice. Much of what follows is an account of this justice. Although the coming of eschatological reward and punishment is fundamental to the theology of the letter, it appears that it is exactly at this point that the author disagrees with the false teachers. The author of 2 Peter is convinced that, if there is no second coming and no final judgment, the moral character of the Christian life is abandoned. Yet it is not possible to know if the false teachers actually lived licentious lives or if the freedom advocated by them (2:19) included freedom from moral constraints. The absence of belief in final judgment does not inevitably lead to immorality.

2 Peter 2:4–10a Examples of God's Judgment

The promise of judgment upon the false teachers leads into this series of four scriptural examples of God's judgment. Much of this originates with Jude. In particular, 2 Peter's accounts of the sinning angels (2:4), the burning of Sodom and Gomorrah (2:6), and even the language about the flesh and lordship (2:10a) are drawn from Jude. However, much of this is also distinctive to 2 Peter. Lacking is Jude's opening reference to God's destroying people who were first saved

Examples of God's Judgment

from Egypt and then did not believe. Instead, 2 Peter includes the story of Noah and the flood and the story of Lot. More to the point, the entire mood of these examples is quite different from the mood in Jude. Jude gives examples of sin and disobedience that lead to God's punishment. Its focus is upon the character of sin and the surety of punishment.

Second Peter changes this. While sin and its destiny is certainly part of the argument of these verses, here the focus is upon the character of God, in particular upon God's ability to both save and punish. The story of the terrors of the flood is balanced by the reminder that God saved Noah. The example of the burning of Sodom and Gomorrah leads to an account of the righteous Lot, whom God saves. Accounts of punishment are balanced by accounts of saving. God does both. The assertions in 2:9 summarize nicely the force of this passage: God knows how to save "the pious" and how to punish "the unrighteous." The somewhat awkward grammar of this passage reinforces the centrality of 2:9. The entire passage is a long conditional sentence. The protasis is a confusing series of "if" clauses running from 2:4 to 2:8. The assertions in 2:9 are the apodosis. Thus the logic is striking and to the point. If God saved and punished all these people, this means that God knows how to save and punish.

All of these examples, both the positive and negative, are common in Jewish and Christian tradition. Lists of this kind are especially frequent in Jewish literature (see, e.g., Sir 16; Wis 10). It is, therefore, possible that 2 Peter is drawing his examples not just from Jude but also from this larger tradition, although no extant text is the singular source. It is striking that, apart from faint echoes in the reference to angels, allusions to *1 Enoch* disappear in 2 Peter. Since 2 Peter is drawing from sequences in Jude that contain numerous references to *1 Enoch*, their absence must be intentional.

2:4 For if God did not spare angels when they sinned, but casting them into hell[a] handed them over to chains[b] of darkness, to be kept[c] for judgment; **5** and if God[d] did not spare the ancient world, but guarded Noah, the eighth person,[e] a herald[f] of righteousness, when he brought the flood upon the world of impious people; **6** and if by reducing to ashes the cities of Sodom and Gomorrah, God[d] condemned them to destruction,[g] making them an example of the things that will happen to the impious;[h] **7** and if God[d] saved righteous Lot when[i] he was worn out[j] by the licentious behavior[k] of lawless people,[l] **8** for based on[m] what he saw and heard, the righteous man, as he lived among them day after day,[n] tortured[o] his own righteous soul with lawless[l] works; **9** then the Lord knows how to save the pious from trial[p] and how to keep the unrighteous under punishment[q] until the day of judgment, **10a** especially those who go after the flesh in desire for defilement[r] and despise lordship.

a. The verb *tartaroō* means "to cast into Tartarus." In Greek myths Tartarus was the deepest part of Hades, where the Titans were imprisoned. Its role as a special place for the imprisonment of divine beings may explain its usage here for the destiny of angels.

b. The manuscripts are equally divided between *seirais* (chains) ($\mathfrak{P}^{72}$, P, Ψ, 𝔐) and *seirois* or *sirois* (pits) (ℵ, A, B, C). "Pits of darkness" makes more sense than "chains of darkness," which are hard to envision. Furthermore, it is easy to imagine scribes changing the original "pits" to "chains" in order to cohere with Jude 6. On the other hand, "chains" is certainly the more difficult reading and may have come from the author himself in echoing Jude. It is also easy to imagine scribes changing the curious "chains of darkness" to the less curious "pits of darkness." While this latter scenario seems a bit more likely, either could be original.

c. A number of manuscripts (ℵ, A, Ψ) read *kolazomenous tērein* (lit., "to keep being punished"). This seems to be an obvious emendation that borrows the same phrase from 2:9 and clarifies the purpose function of the circumstantial participle *tēroumenous*.

d. The verb does not have an explicit subject. "God" is supplied from 2:4.

e. The Greek reads rather idiomatically as "the eighth Noah" (*ogdoon Nōe*).

f. The basic meaning of the word *kēryx* is "public messenger." It tends to refer to someone making official announcements. The meaning "preacher" derives from the OT prophetic traditions and from its specialized usage in Christian communities.

g. While several manuscripts ($\mathfrak{P}^{72}$, B, C) omit "to destruction" (*katastrophē*), the weight of textual evidence supports its inclusion. Furthermore, its omission undoes the nice alliteration of *katastrophē katekrinen*.

h. The textual evidence is about equally divided between *mellontōn asebesin* ("the things that will happen to the impious") ($\mathfrak{P}^{72}$, B, P) and *mellontōn asebein* ("those people who are going to act impiously") (ℵ, A, C, Ψ). The latter reading confuses the force of the examples, which are about the surety of punishment.

i. The participle *kataponoumenon* lacks the article and thus could be circumstantial ("when") or attributive ("who") in force.

j. The verb *poneō* means "to work hard," "to be distressed," or even "to be worn out from work." The participle *kataponoumenon* probably means either "to be distressed" by the licentious behavior or "to be worn out" by dealing with it.

k. The somewhat awkward phrase *tēs . . . en aselgeia anastrophēs* means "behavior done with licentiousness."

l. "Lawless" in 2:7 translates *athesmōn*, which is based on *thesmos* ("that which is laid down," "an ordinance," "an institution," or "a law"), while "lawless" in 2:8 translates the more familiar *anomos*.

m. It is not clear how the opening and closing dative phrases should be rendered. Both *blemmati . . . kai akoē* (based on what he saw and heard) and *anomois ergois* (with lawless works) seem to be datives of agency that depend on the main verb. Some translations combine them into something like "by the lawless works that he saw and heard"). The translation above maintains the awkwardness of the Greek, which simply puts one dative at the beginning of the sentence and the other at the end.

n. The temporal reference "day after day" grammatically could connect to "living among them" or "tortured."

Examples of God's Judgment 243

o. Although the subject of the verb "tortured" is clearly "the righteous man," many translations reject the image of Lot torturing his own soul and render the verb as passive ("the righteous man was tortured in his righteous soul" or "his righteous soul was tortured").

p. The word *peirasmos* means "trial" or "test" and in certain contexts, probably not this one, "temptation."

q. The phrase *kolazomenous tērein* means, literally, "to keep being punished." The tense of the participle suggests that God is engaged in ongoing punishment of the impious. Some translators suggest that, since *kolazō* normally refers to eschatological punishment and since the future participle is rare, the phrase could refer to future punishment. However, there are lots of ways of indicating future punishment, and the grammar seems clear enough. God is punishing now.

r. The genitive in the phrase *epithymia miasmou* could also be rendered "defiling desire," although *epithymia* with the genitive normally means desire for something.

[2:4] Although the opening example is, in some ways, derived from the story of the Nephilim in Gen 6:1–4, it comes more immediately from Jude 6, which is in turn dependent on *1 Enoch*. Apart from the existence of these angels, the account in Genesis provides none of the details in this verse. Given the persistent omission of material from *1 Enoch*, it is likely that the punishment aspect of this story comes from Jude. Since the passage will summarize the sins of all these examples as sexual, it is possible that the intercourse between these angels and human women, while not explicitly mentioned, is being recalled.

In any case, this verse paints an intense portrait of divine punishment. Even if the author is following historical order in his series of examples, having angels be the first recipients of God's severity demonstrates that no creature can escape. God will punish even angels. Furthermore, it is not merely that God does not "spare" these angels; God also throws them into hell, puts them in chains, and keeps them thus confined for final punishment. The piling up of these images of punishment compounds the feeling of severity. All of this makes the opening clause rhetorically effective. First of all, it offers warrant to the assertion in 2:3 that the destruction of the false teachers "is not sleeping." Second, it puts the series of examples of God's judgment that follow into the context of enormous severity.

[5] In Genesis the story of the Nephilim (6:1–4) leads immediately to the story of the flood. Thus 2 Peter's narrative of the flood, which is not in Jude, flows naturally from the story of the angels. There is no hint that 2 Peter echoes or even knows the connection between the rebellious angels and the flood that is narrated in *1 Enoch*. Instead, 2 Peter is simply following the sequence in Genesis.

The verse opens with much the same syntax as 2:4, invoking the threat that God does not spare. Here God does not spare the "ancient world." The term "world" typically refers to the inhabitants of the world or the physical world itself. In Genesis the flood destroys all living creatures but does not undo cosmic structures. In any case, "world" couples nicely with the angels in 2:4. God is willing to destroy not only angels but also every creature in the world. The repetition of the phrase "God did not spare" creates an expectation of another litany of punishment. However, before the brief description of the flood comes the reference to Noah. In this way, this verse balances beautifully the two aspects of God's judgment that play off one another throughout this passage.

God "guarded" Noah. The word "guard" is probably chosen in order to convey the sense of God protecting Noah from the water. Noah is called the eighth presumably because, according to tradition (see 1 Pet 3:20), eight people—Noah and his wife, along with their three sons and their wives—were saved in the ark. More curious is the reference to Noah as "herald of righteousness." On the one hand, "righteousness" makes a good contrast to "world of impious people" who perish in the flood. In the OT, on the other hand, Noah is not much of a herald. Later Jewish tradition will depict Noah as trying to persuade his unrighteous neighbors (e.g., *Sib. Or.* 1.129; Josephus, *Ant.* 1.74; *b. Sanh.* 108). Thus it appears that the author is not only personally aware of these later traditions but also expects his readers to know them.

[6] This verse returns to the theme of punishment. The choice of Sodom and Gomorrah as the next example probably comes from Jude 7, although the story of the flood and the story of Sodom and Gomorrah were often linked in Jewish literature. Together they provide the classic descriptions of destruction by water and fire. Apart from the example itself, 2 Peter seems to borrow few details from Jude's account. Jude's references to the surrounding cities, to the sexual nature of the sins, and to fire as the vehicle of punishment are lacking in this verse. In their place is a focus on the fate of cities and their role as examples.

The reference to ashes probably comes from Jewish traditions that claim not only that Sodom and Gomorrah were reduced to ashes but also that the ashes were still there. The ongoing presence of ashes creates an ideal warning. Thus, when 2 Peter claims that God makes Sodom and Gomorrah an example by reducing them to ashes, the example is provided not only by the story but also by the site itself. Few people would actually go and inspect the ashes in person; the tradition that the ashes are there suffices. The story of Sodom and Gomorrah is not simply a demonstration of God's power and willingness to destroy; the story also exemplifies what happens to "impious" people. Almost all Jews and Christians assumed that fire would be the agent of final punishment. Thus the burning of Sodom and Gomorrah prefigures the burning of all impious people. All such people will be reduced to ashes.

[7–8] The contrast with Jude's account of God's willingness to punish is highlighted in these verses. The righteous Lot is offered as an example of the difficulties a righteous person has while living among the impious and as an example of how God saves the righteous from God's own destruction of the

Examples of God's Judgment

impious. The core affirmation of 2:7 is that God saved the righteous Lot. Readers familiar with the story of Lot in Gen 18–19 would know that God did indeed save Lot, but they might not recognize Lot as being especially righteous. He does offer hospitality to strangers, not knowing that they are angels (19:1–3). He does not, however, appear particularly distressed by living in Sodom.

Later Jewish tradition does treat Lot as righteous and includes Lot in Abraham's plea for the righteous in Sodom. The book of Wisdom, for example, declares, "Wisdom rescued a righteous man when the ungodly were perishing; he escaped the fire that descended on the Five Cities" (10:6). However, there is no real development in existing Jewish traditions of the notion that Lot is terribly distressed by the immorality in Sodom. Yet Lot's conflict with the men of Sodom over the angels in his house is certainly evidence of distress and could have provided the beginnings of larger traditions about tension between Lot and the immorality of the city. It seems unlikely that 2 Peter is offering a new reading of the story of Lot. Throughout this section, stories are cited more in the language of reminder than of new information. The rhetoric of these verses assumes familiarity with these accounts. Thus there must have been haggadic developments of the conflict between Lot and Sodom that are no longer extant.

The explanatory aside in 2:8 adds a curious twist. For all the difficulties posed by the grammar of the verse, the point seems straightforward enough. The righteous Lot tortures his own soul. The word *psychē* could also be translated "life," giving the sense that Lot makes his own life miserable. Three phrases are added to this core assertion. First, this is done on the basis of or by means of "what he saw and heard." Second, this is done by means of or with "lawless works." From the context these lawless works are obviously not lawless works that Lot himself does and thereby tortures himself. These are the lawless works that surround him. Third, he does this by or as "he lived among them." Thus the overall image is clear: Lot tortures himself by living among these impious people, by witnessing and hearing their deeds, by surrounding himself with lawlessness. This portrait of Lot is sketched in order to draw a parallel with the experience of the readers of the letter. They too live among impious people. Their lives are also tortured by the lawlessness and immorality around them. Lot remained righteous. The obvious challenge to the readers is to do the same. This challenge comes with a promise that is implied in the story and made explicit in the assertion that follows. God saves righteous people who remain righteous in the midst of immorality.

[9] The apodosis of the conditional sentence that began in 2:4 is finally reached. All of these "if" clauses lead to the conclusion that God knows how to save and how to punish. The contrast with Jude, where punishment is the focus, highlights the balance that is struck in 2 Peter. God is not just the righteous judge who will punish the impious. Nor is God only the Savior who rescues the righteous from the terrors of life and from God's own justice. God is both. The stories of Scripture prove it.

The descriptions of how and whom God saves suggest that eschatological salvation is not the singular focus of this passage. In the language of this verse, God saves from "trials." Both of the examples are trials that occur within the framework of human history. Yet both trials are also inflicted by God. God saves the righteous from being caught up in the punishment that God inflicts on the unrighteous. The assertions in 1 Pet 1:4–5 that believers and their inheritance are both being kept safe by God is not included in 2 Peter. People, first of all, have to resist immorality. Noah and Lot illustrate the claim of 1:4, where the people who are saved are those who have fled from the corruption in the world. The sequences of 1:3–11 are in force here. God calls and bestows gifts. People must confirm that call by living the virtues. When they do, they gain entrance into the kingdom. Though this entrance is obviously eschatological, God's power to save is not confined in 2 Peter to the last day.

For all the centrality of living piously, 2 Peter never describes the precise character of such a life. It is significant that the righteous character of the lives of Noah and Lot are not detailed; they are simply categorized as righteous. Actually, 2 Peter shifts without discernible change in meaning between terms suggesting piety (*seb-*) or impiety and righteousness (*dik-*) or unrighteousness. As close as 2 Peter gets to a description of a pious life is the list of virtues in 1:5–7. Nevertheless, final victory is described as new heavens and a new earth, where "righteousness dwells" (3:13).

The curious assertion that "the Lord knows . . . how to keep the unrighteous under punishment until the day of judgment" has occasioned considerable debate. Given the focus in 3:1–18 on final judgment and the general theological character of early Christianity, punishment should occur primarily at the day of judgment. As noted above, this has led many readers to translate the present tense of this punishing as future. This is not grammatically impossible. However, 2 Peter does not seem to confine God's justice to the last day. The examples of Noah and the flood and of Lot and Sodom suggest that God can save and punish within the sequence of human history. The present tense verbs in 2:3 declare that "judgment . . . is not idle" and "destruction is not sleeping." The rebellious angels are already being held in "chains of darkness" (2:4) as they await final punishment. While 2 Peter never describes the specific terrors of preeschatological punishment, it affirms throughout that God's justice is not confined to the last day.

[10a] This rather abrupt addition anticipates the focused attack on the false teachers in the verses that follow. The argument returns from exploring the character of God to detailing the character of the false teachers. The imagery originates from Jude 7–8. Jude's description of people going after "the flesh of others" in the sense of transgressing sexual boundaries is changed to a charge of general sexual activity. Jude's language of defiling the flesh is changed to "desire for defilement." Thus 2 Peter transforms Jude's account of sexuality that breaks the normal boundaries between humans and angels into a more general attack on sexual behavior.

The precise character of the sexual behavior that is being critiqued is not made explicit. The imagery of going after flesh is not a common phrase for improper sexuality and thus does not disclose much about the issue. The term "flesh" is often used in early Christian literature to convey negative aspects of the human experience. Nevertheless, some memory of the story of Sodom and the sexual attack on the angels is probably assumed in this imagery. Thus people "who go after the flesh" must be people who pursue sex outside the accepted norms. The phrase "desire for defilement" is even more puzzling. It implies that this pursuit of flesh is done with the hope of being defiled. There is nothing in the Genesis story of Sodom or even in later versions of the story that contain such a motive. Since it is difficult to understand such a desire, many translators render the phrase *epithymia miasmou* as "defiling desire." In this reading, defilement would be the unintended consequence, not the goal. However, it is possible that in pointing to defilement as the goal, 2 Peter is disclosing the true character of this pursuit of the flesh. The suggestion would be that these people, whether they know it or not, are in truth desiring the pollution and defilement of the unholy life. The common connection in antiquity between sexuality and holiness is perhaps behind all this.

The second charge is that these people "despise lordship." Since *kyriotēs* could refer to "authority" of any kind, the problem could be that these people disrespect the proper human authorities in the Christian community. However, given the accusation against false prophets that they deny "the Master who bought them" (2:1) and "slander the glorious ones" (2:10b) and the whole debate about the second coming, it is more likely that something about the lordship of Jesus is in question. It is also possible, in light of the focus on God in this passage, that the authority of God is being despised, perhaps in a denial of God's capacity to save and punish. The lack of specificity may even be functional. These people are being accused of disrespecting and denying the authority of both Jesus and God. In any case, this charge leads effectively into the series of charges that follow.

This passage (2:4–10a) makes an argument for God's power and willingness not only to execute judgment but also to do so for both the righteous and the unrighteous. It describes the dual focus of God's judgment as it insists on the reality of that judgment. The force of the argument depends upon the authority of Scripture. As in Jude, each of the stories is cited in brief form, with the assumption that readers know a fuller account. Furthermore, the details of what is cited are assumed to be true. These stories together are treated as proof of the conclusion in 2:9: God knows both how to save and how to punish.

Given the brief scope of the letter and the sketchy character of the arguments, it is not possible to reconstruct the full theological debate of which this letter is a part. The letter provides only one side of an argument and not even the full range of that one side. At a minimum it is clear that there are questions in the community about the second coming and final judgment. The structure of this argument suggests that there are no debates about the authority of Scripture. The debate concerns the peculiarities of the Christian traditions. It is those traditions that are reaffirmed in the letter, beginning with the brief summary in 1:3–11, moving to the affirmation of the credibility of the transfiguration and the reliability of the apostolic witness, and finally focusing on these assertions of God's power to judge, of which this passage forms a crucial part. God's power to judge provides a threatening context for the more specific attacks in 2:10b–22.

2 Peter 2:10b–16 The Immorality of the False Teachers

The indirect attack on the false teachers in 2:1–10a gives way to this series of poignant and direct accusations that begins in 2:10b and continues until 2:22. Most of this is drawn from Jude. However, almost all of the material from Jude is transformed to the extent that the force of the accusations changes. Second Peter does not include Jude's story of Michael and the body of Moses. It also lacks Jude's references to the way of Cain and Korah's rebellion. The story of Balaam is expanded to include the speaking of Balaam's donkey. Furthermore, even when 2 Peter follows Jude closely, the sense of the passage shifts. For the most part, 2 Peter makes the examples more general. They seem less focused on a specific group, and they depend less upon knowledge of the stories. The accusations thereby become more portable, able to be adapted in a variety of settings.

This passage is filled with difficulties. Second Peter's tendency to generalize the examples makes it difficult to ascertain the point. It is often impossible to determine precisely what the accusation is and what the sin might be. If there is an ordering theme in all of this, it is probably contained in the opening imagery of 2:10b. The attack is on people who are willful, who do not submit, who lack proper fear and respect, and who thus slander the apostolic gospel.

> 2:10b Bold people,[a] self-willed, they are not afraid to slander the glorious ones,[b] 11 whereas angels, although greater in strength and power, do not bring against them[c] a slanderous judgment[d] before[e] the Lord. 12 But these people—like irrational[f] animals, instinctive,[g] born[h] for capture and destruction, slandering among things[i] they do not know—will themselves be destroyed in their destruction, 13 suffering injury[j] as the wages for causing injury,[k] considering revelry[l] in the daytime to be a pleasure, spots and blemishes reveling[l] in their deceptions while they feast with you,

The Immorality of the False Teachers

14 having eyes full of an adulteress[m] and unceasing[n] from sin, ensnaring unstable souls,[o] having hearts trained in greed, accursed children. **15** Leaving the straight way, they have wandered away, following the way of Balaam son of Bosor, who loved the wages of unrighteousness[p] **16** but received a rebuke for his transgression; a voiceless beast of burden speaking[q] in a human voice hindered the madness of the prophet.

a. On its own *tolmētai* (bold people) can be positive, referring to people who are courageous and adventurous. When paired with *authadeis* (self-willed), *tolmētai* acquires the sense of being overly bold or reckless.

b. In most contexts, the word *doxa* refers to "opinion," "reputation," or "appearance." Even in this context it could refer to "opinions" in the sense that these people slander the good opinions of the tradition. However, the translation "opinions" fits awkwardly with the contrast to the angels. In Jewish-Christian tradition *doxa*, building on the meaning "reputation" and "appearance," often means "glory." This works best here, although it is not clear who or what the glorious ones are.

c. The antecedent of "them" could be either "the glorious ones" or the "bold people."

d. Second Peter changes *krisin blasphēmias* (a judgment of slander) in Jude 9 to *blasphēmon krisin* (a slanderous judgment). Thus the image in Jude of angels who refrain from judging these people as "slanderous" shifts to angels who refuse to offer judgments that are themselves "slanderous."

e. The major uncials (ℵ, B, C, 𝔐) put "Lord" in the dative case, reading *para kyriō* (before the Lord), while the best papyrus ($\mathfrak{P}^{72}$) declines "Lord" in the genitive case, reading *para kyriou* (from the Lord). The weight of the textual evidence gives slight preference to "before the Lord."

f. The adjective *aloga* could mean either "without speech" or "without reason."

g. The adjective *physika* normally means "natural" or "physical." When paired with *aloga* (irrational), it could mean "instinctive" as opposed to reasoned.

h. Second Peter borrows Jude's style of accumulating negative characteristics almost in catalog fashion, which produces somewhat awkward English syntax.

i. The prepositional phrase *en hois* ("about which" or "among which") could be translated as a somewhat clumsy Koine Greek equivalent of *eis hous* ("slandering things or people they do not understand"). In any case, it is not clear whether *hois* refers to people or things.

j. Since the verb *adikeō* normally means "to do wrong," *adikoumenoi* should mean "suffering wrong." This reading makes little sense since it would impute immorality to God. Somewhat rarely *adikeō* can mean "to injure" without any moral connotations. Thus *adikoumenoi* could mean "suffering injury." The awkwardness of the usage of *adikeō* is probably what led to the textual variants that read *komioumenoi* (acquiring).

k. The noun *adikia* completes the wordplay with *adikoumenoi*. Here *adikia* maintains its usual sense of immorality.

l. While the basic meaning of *tryphē* is "softness" or "delicacy," it has the common usage of "luxuriousness." The repetition of the root in the participle *entryphōntes* gives to both occurrences the sense of revelry, especially of revelry in delicacies and luxuries.

m. While most manuscripts ($\mathfrak{P}^{72}$, B, C, 𝔐) have the striking imagery of eyes full of "an adulteress" (*moichalidos*), some manuscripts (ℵ, A, Ψ) soften the imagery a bit, reading eyes full of "adultery" (*moichalias, moicheias*).

n. The participle *akatapaustous* (unceasing) modifies "eyes."

o. The noun *psychai* in this context probably does not refer to "souls" in the sense of the eternal soul but simply to "persons" or "people."

p. The phrase *misthon adikias* occurred in identical form in 2:13, where it was translated "wages for causing injury" in order to maintain the wordplay with *adikoumenoi*. Though the echo is obviously intentional, in the context of the Balaam story *adikia* probably has its more general meaning of "wrongdoing" or "unrighteousness."

q. The verb *phthengomai* means to "utter a sound." It can be used for the voices of animals or humans.

[10b–11] These verses open with the name-calling pattern familiar from Jude. For the rest of the chapter, 2 Peter will follow this pattern in a somewhat more relaxed syntax than that of Jude. The opening charges seem to summarize the problem. These people are bold to the point of recklessness and are self-willed. Second Peter draws a portrait of teachers who stand in various ways outside the apostolic orders. The assertion in 1:3 that "his divine power has given us everything that leads to life and piety" should lead to an ordering of these gifts to lives of virtue (1:5–8). These people undo this pattern. Instead of being led by the gifts of God, they are "self-willed." Instead of pursuing lives of virtue and love, they are "bold," claim freedom (2:19), but actually are driven by the desires of the flesh (2:2, 10a, 18, 20).

In this freedom they lack appropriate fear. This lack of fear leads to their slandering "the glorious ones." There is much debate about the identity of the glorious ones. Part of that debate includes uncertainty about whom or what these people do not fear. The identity of the glorious ones also depends in part upon the character of the response of the angels in 2:11. The response of the angels has its own difficulties. Since the antecedent of "them" could be the glorious ones or the bold people, it is not clear against whom the angels are not bringing a judgment. It is also not certain whether the judgment is before God or from God. Given this abundance of uncertainties, it is not surprising that there are many different suggestions as to how to read these verses.

Three readings have the most support. The traditional reading was to understand the glorious ones as humans with authority, in the church or out. These bold people were slandering these human authorities. In contrast, the angels did not even slander "them," understood as the bold people, who deserved such judgment. Puzzlement over the imagined behavior of the angels, the context in Jude, and the unlikely use of "glories" to refer to humans, has led most modern readers to reject this interpretation. The second suggestion is to see the "glorious ones" as evil cosmic powers. These bold people have no fear of these powers and feel free to slander them. This arrogance is contrasted with angels, who

The Immorality of the False Teachers 251

are more powerful than these people yet do not bring an accusation "against them," meaning the evil cosmic powers. This accusation could be either one given on God's behalf ("from God") or on their own angelic status ("before God"). The third suggestion is to see the "glorious ones" and the "angels" as the same beings. This has the advantage of reading "glorious ones" in its more normal sense of good cosmic beings. The bold people are not afraid of the good powers because they have no fear of final judgment. They slander these powers perhaps out of indifference or perhaps out of resentment of the ethical orders the angels enforce. In contrast, the angels, who are greater than the bold people, refuse to bring a very justifiable charge "against them," meaning the bold people themselves. They leave judgment to God. If the reading is "from God" instead of "before God," then the angels manifest even more modesty, refusing to pronounce a judgment that God has already given.

While the third reading may create the fewest difficulties, it has proved difficult to decide between the second and third readings. Both are plausible and both are a bit awkward. The second reading requires knowledge of cosmic orders and narratives that are not detailed in the text. The third reading creates the puzzle of why the text calls angels "glorious ones" in one phrase and "angels" in another. In truth, the text displays little interest in providing a clear cosmic grounding for these verses. This is probably because the point of these verses is not to explore certain cosmic narratives but to evoke a contrast in behavior. Whatever it is that the angels are doing, they are manifesting modesty and reserve in evaluating the cosmic and ethical status of others. These bold people, whomever it is that they are attacking, are behaving with arrogance and disrespect. Angels refuse to judge beings they may even have the right to judge. These people feel free to judge beings even greater than they are.

[12] The willingness to slander that was attributed to arrogance and lack of fear in the preceding verses is here attributed to ignorance. This ignorance is compared to the irrationality of animals; because they lack reason, they must act only on instinct. There was much discussion in antiquity about what constitutes the difference between humans and animals (Demosthenes, *Or.* 60.30; Xenophon, *Anab.* 5.7.32).[48] The distinction between reason and instinct was originally Greek but was taken up into Jewish and Christian thought as well. In Jewish thought the focus tended to be more on language or the lack thereof than on reason itself. The Greek word *aloga* that is used in this verse to describe animals can refer to reason or speech. The nuance of "speechlessness" probably anticipates the reference in 2:16 to Balaam's donkey as "voiceless" (*aphōnon*) yet "speaking" (*phthenxamenon*). Of course, these bold false prophets do not lack speech; the problem is that they have too much speech. They happily

---

48. For Aristotle's complex view of animals, see Allan Gotthelf and James G. Lennox, *Philosophical Issues in Aristotle's Biology* (Cambridge: Cambridge University Press, 1987).

slander, but they do so in ignorance. The destiny of animals for capture and destruction probably refers to their common use by humans and not to their eschatological destiny. Humans capture and slaughter animals every day.

The announcement that they "will themselves be destroyed in their destruction" has been interpreted many ways. The problem is that it is not clear (either in the Greek or in the English translation) who might be the antecedent of "their." Among the many proposals, three have gained the most hearing. First, this could be a Hebraic pleonasm in which "destruction" is repeated for emphasis ("they will be destroyed in their own destruction"). However, the syntax of this expression does not really cohere with the usual Hebrew pattern, which would not repeat "their." This reading also weakens the comparisons that form the heart of these verses. Second, if the angels are evil angels who have been condemned by God, "their" could refer to those angels and their destruction. The verse would then be claiming that these people who slander the evil angels will suffer the same punishment that those angels will suffer. They will all be caught in eschatological judgment. This reading has two problems. It depends on the angels being evil. As noted above, it is a bit more likely that they are regular angels. Furthermore, the closest grammatical antecedent to "their" is the animals. The animals are "born for capture and destruction." Thus the phrase "their destruction" most naturally evokes the destruction of animals. This leads to the third reading, which is preferable. Animals are born for destruction. Humans pursue them and slaughter them. These people are like animals. Thus they will share the fate of animals, although they will do so eschatologically.

[13] This verse offers three new images in the attack on the false teachers. The first builds on the imagery of destruction from 2:12. The somewhat unusual meaning of *adikoumenoi* as "suffering harm" results from the wordplay with *adikia*. The wordplay itself stresses the equity that is at the heart of divine justice. Paul's assertion that "you reap whatever you sow" (Gal 6:7) summarizes nicely the theology that undergirds this wordplay. As these people engage in the harm of *adikia* now, so will this same harm be returned to them by God on the day of judgment. Yet as noted above, the suggestion of immorality that the Greek word *adikeō* normally evokes is inappropriate for the righteous judgment of God. Fortunately, there is room in nuances of the Greek term to maintain the equity suggested by the wordplay while avoiding an implication of divine immorality. The choice of the term "wages" (*misthos*), with its sense of established economy, further emphasizes this equity.

The second and third images are connected to one another through the wordplay between *tryphē* (revelry) and *entryphōntes* (reveling). Behind these images lies the language of Jude 12: "These people are dangerous reefs at your love feasts, feasting with you without reverence, shepherding themselves." The uncertainty in the imagery of Jude disappears in 2 Peter. The accusation of reveling in the daytime is common in the ancient world. Greeks and Romans

The Immorality of the False Teachers

particularly frowned on revelry during the day, when people should be working. The term *tryphē*, with its connotations of softness and delicacy, conveys a nice contrast to the responsibilities of daytime labor. The accusation is not only that these false teachers engage in such daytime indulgences but also that they consider such to be a "pleasure."

This daytime revelry is connected ironically with the community's holy feast. These people carry their fondness of revelry into the most holy of gatherings. The language of feasting together (*syneuōchoumenoi*) comes from Jude 12. Second Peter replaces Jude's clarifying "at your love feasts" (*en tais agapais*) with the condemning "in their deceptions" (*en tais apatais*), producing the complex image of people who come to the community's holy feast and bring not only their fondness of revelry but also their deceptive teachings. The elimination of the reference to love feasts probably means only that there was no need to clarify the meaning of "feasting together." This is the Lord's Supper, which at that time included a communal meal. Second Peter also replaces Jude's image of dangerous reefs that could shipwreck members of the community with the more accessible holiness imagery of "spots" and "blemishes." Just as spots and blemishes make a temple sacrifice unacceptable, these false teachers compromise the holiness of the community. This pollution is probably accomplished not just by their deceptive teachings, which are named here, but also by all the qualities and behavior detailed in this chapter.

[14] The beginning of this verse, and perhaps even the whole verse, assumes the context of the community gathering. At this gathering, these teachers have eyes for potential adulteresses. Though the imagery is familiar in Greek, it draws an effective portrait of how improper sexual desires can pollute the community gathering. This eye for adulterous women gives content to the accusation in 2:10a of pursuit of the flesh. Furthermore, the charge of denying lordship (2:10b) fits with this polluting of the Lord's Supper. The ensuing accusation of ensnaring unstable people could refer to the deceptions of their false teaching or to their eye for adultery. Together these opening accusations give a sense of teachers prowling the community with their theological deceptions and their desires of the flesh. These people would undo marriages, the Lord's Suppers, and the entire community.

Given the familiar character of these accusations, it is no surprise that greed is next on the list. Greed is perhaps the most common accusation in the Greco-Roman world against leadership, since it was seen as a unique temptation for people in power. These false teachers were already accused of greed in 2:3, and Balaam will be so accused in the next verse (2:15) of loving the wages of unrighteousness. The stock nature of this accusation makes it difficult to know if these false teachers are particularly greedy or if their success brought the temptations of greed. Whatever the origin of this greed, the use of the athletic image of training underscores the intentionality of the false teachers. These teachers are not simply greedy people; they have also consciously trained their hearts for greed.

The anthropological character of this verse, which is obvious in the Greek, is difficult to reproduce in English. The verse is structured around the words "eyes" and "hearts," both of which are placed at the beginning of their clauses. This emphasis on two central powers of the body also derives from the shift in grammar from the usual opening nominatives to these two accusatives. The point seems to be that these people are outfitted for adultery, sin, and greed. Their personal powers are oriented and trained for such.

The concluding phrase "accursed children" is a bit surprising because it has no clear parallels. This is not a common accusation. There is no particular group known as "accursed children." All of this suggests that the author coined the phrase not in memory of a curse but as a curse itself. The naming is a cursing.

[15–16] The brief reference to Balaam in Jude 11 is considerably expanded in these verses. The story of Balaam was popular in Jewish literature, and various versions of it emerged. Given the brevity of the account in 2 Peter, it is not clear which version or versions of the story may have influenced these verses. Greed provides the obvious link to what precedes. However, there are also connections to the theme of animals' speechlessness and to the question of who in the hierarchy of beings has the authority to rebuke whom.

The opening phrase reinforces the notion that these false teachers are responsible for their unrighteousness. They have left "the straight way." The use of the term "way" is probably not a reference to Christianity as "the Way" (e.g., Acts 9:2; 19:23; 24:14) but to a more common biblical expression (e.g., 1 Sam 12:23; Ps 107:7; Prov 2:16 LXX; Isa 33:15). Apart from the traditional notions of biblical righteousness and God's law, the phrase "the straight way" derives its content from its context. Thus "the straight way" refers to the apostolic life of virtue that is evoked throughout the letter.

In Num 22–24 Balaam is more positive than negative. He resists the request of King Balak to curse Israel. Later canonical accounts depict Balaam in a more negative light and suggest greed as motive (e.g., Deut 23:4–5; Neh 13:2; Philo, *Mos.* 1.264–300). Whatever part of the Balaam tradition is in play, the point in 2 Peter is clear. Some people out of greed engage in false prophecy. These false teachers thereby join a long and infamous tradition. The general cast of the phrase "wages of unrighteousness" does not suggest any specific behavior on the part of the false teachers that might have led to the accusation of greed. Greed can take many forms. Perhaps this is why it is such a common accusation. In any case, 2 Peter offers no specifics about the nature of their greed.

Although in some ways 2:16 reads as a simple elaboration of the Balaam story, each detail in the verse has possible connections to the false teachers. The mention of Balaam's "rebuke for his transgression" probably refers to the behavior of his donkey, who first refuses to pass by the angel and then rebukes Balaam for beating him. However, since all these stories are selected and couched so as to address the false teachers, there may be a reference here to a rebuke given these teachers. The letter itself may be that rebuke. It can hardly be a coincidence that a description of animals in 2:12 as *aloga* ("irrational" or "speechless") is followed almost immediately by the story of a speechless (*aphōnon*) animal that speaks (*phthengomai*). The false teachers come out looking worse than animals. These teachers, in their lack of *logos* ("speech," "reason"), are in some ways like animals. The story of Balaam's donkey shows that animals, which by nature are without speech, can actually speak true prophecies. Animals can speak so as to prevent sins. These false teachers are the opposite. They speak all the time. However, because they have wandered from the way, their speaking promotes sin.

The diversity and richness of the imagery in this attack defies categorization. There is no central thesis or explicit argument to the passage (2:10b–16). It combines a variety of images and arguments without subsuming them to a governing logic. One image does not lead logically to the next. In fact, the passage seems almost intentionally disorganized, moving from image to image and from argument to argument with minimal linkages. The passage includes direct naming, biblical examples, loose analogies, and various descriptions of behavior and attitudes. The result is a hodgepodge of rhetorical forms and argumentative structures.

The passage is also rhetorically effective. It assumes the authority of Scripture. It assumes certain ethical and communal values. It arrogates enormous authority to the speaker of the attack. If those assumptions are granted, then the passage works. It builds a wonderfully condemning portrait of the false teachers. These people in their arrogance have left the straight way and have wandered off into a life of vice. Without the guidance of apostolic tradition, these teachers are ignorant. They are driven by desire and greed. They even enjoy their own luxurious vices. Their lack of reason makes them less than human. In this behavior they join a long list of people who have rebelled. God's righteous judgment awaits them. Beyond their own personal vices and the punishment that awaits them, they damage the community. They entice people to follow them, and they pollute even the most holy of gatherings. They are, as the passage aptly puts it, "accursed children."

2 Peter 2:17–22 The Slavery of the False Teachers

This passage marks a shift in rhetoric. It begins with a continuation of negative naming from Jude but moves to a focused critique of apostasy. Throughout this chapter, 2 Peter has been following the imagery and sequences of Jude. However, this close dependence on Jude comes to an end. The series of images in

Jude 12–16 creates an intense condemnation that builds into Enoch's promise of judgment, all of which is collapsed in 2 Peter into the two images and brief prediction of doom in 2:17. Instead, 2 Peter gives what is probably the fullest account of apostasy in the NT. Most of the imagery in these verses comes not from Jude but from other sources. There are several Jewish proverbs, an echo of a Jesus saying, and imagery from the general fund of ancient ethics. All of this is combined by the author into a unique account of the dangers and pitfalls of heretics and the apostasy that they inspire.

These verses may also give as accurate a glimpse of the behavior of the false teachers as 2 Peter provides. Though the imagery is traditional and common, the danger seems to be real. These verses read less as a theoretical description of potential apostasy and more as an attack on people who have real influence in the community. These teachers are having success in ensnaring these recent converts. The author sees their success as an abandonment of the Christian tradition and a return to the life of sin.

2:17 These people are waterless springs and mists driven by a storm, for whom the gloom of darkness is kept. **18** Speaking[a] inflated emptiness,[b] they ensnare with desires of the flesh, with licentious deeds,[c] people who are only just[d] escaping from those who live in error, **19** promising them freedom, while they themselves are slaves of corruption;[e] for by whatever someone has been overcome[f], to this one becomes enslaved. **20** For if, after escaping the defilements of the world through the knowledge of our Lord and Savior Jesus Christ and becoming entangled again in these things, they are overcome,[f] the last things become worse for them than the first. **21** For it would have been better for them not to have known[g] the way of righteousness[h] than after knowing it to turn back[i] from the holy commandment handed over to them. **22** The image of the true proverb[j] fits[k] with them: "a dog that has returned to its own vomit," and "a pig that is washed in order to wallow in the mud."

  a. The participle *phthengomenoi* (speaking) has the same root (*phthengomai*) as *phthenxamenon*, which is used in 2:16 for the "speaking" of the beast of burden. The speech of "these people" is similar to the noises of animals.

  b. The awkward and striking Greek phrase *hyperonka mataiotētos* (lit., "inflated things of emptiness") has been rendered many ways in English, from an equally striking "bombastic nonsense" to a somewhat more tame "empty, boastful words." The noun *hyperonka*, which comes from Jude 16, evokes both the arrogant character of the speaker and the inflated character of what is said. In context, the force of the phrase is that these arrogant and boastful words turn out to be empty.

  c. The Greek syntax somewhat awkwardly places two nouns in the dative (*epithymiais*, "desires," and *aselgeiais*, "licentious deeds"), with the second in apparent apposition to the first. This awkwardness has led translators to place the conjunction "and"

The Slavery of the False Teachers

in between, noting as they do that Greek often drops the conjunction, or to render the second noun as a modifier ("licentious desires of the flesh"). The translation given here preserves the apposition.

d. It was probably the rareness of the adverb form *oligōs* (just) that led to the textual variant *ontōs* (really) (ℵ, C, P, 𝔐). The adverb *oligōs* both has better manuscript support (𝔓⁷², A, B, Ψ) and makes more sense in the context. While *oligōs* could mean "barely" in the sense of "scarcely," in this context it probably means "just" in the sense of "recently."

e. The basic sense of *phthora* is "destruction," "ruin," or even "decay." In this context it could refer to eschatological destruction or to moral decay. The translation "corruption" conveys a bit of both.

f. The verb *hēttaomai* or *hēssaomai* can mean "to be inferior to," "to yield to," or "to be defeated or overcome by." It is often used for the conquering and enslaving of enemies in battle.

g. The perfect infinitive *epegnōkenai* (to have known) recalls the *epignōsis* (knowledge) that is used in 1:2, 3, 8; 2:20.

h. The noun *dikaiosynē* was translated "justice" in 1:1. However, the more general English term "righteousness" seems to fit better here.

i. Several texts replace the somewhat ambiguous "turn back from" (*hypostrepsai ek*) with "turn back again [*anakampsai*] to the former things."

j. The phrase *to tēs alēthous paroimias* (lit., "the of the true proverb") has been translated many ways. It is often combined with the verb *symbebēken* ("fits with," "agree with," or "happen to") producing something like, "For them the proverb is true." If the phrase is rendered more literally, the question remains as to the substantive content suggested by the article *to*. Some translators transfer the adjective "true" to the article ("the truth of the proverb"). Others supply something from the context, as is done above. The term "image" comes from the images of the dog and the pig.

k. The verb *symbainō* in this context could mean "fits with" or "happen to." The latter produces something like "It has happened to them according to the true proverb" (NRSV). The choice of "fits with" is, in part, an attempt to complete the structure of the proverbs. The images of the dog and pig are not proverbs in themselves but images waiting for proverbial application.

[2:17] Most readers mark a new section at this point not only because of the focus on apostasy but also because of the demonstrative pronoun *houtoi* (these people), which in the style of Jude seems to serve as a rhetorical marker. Nevertheless, the break between 2:16 and 2:17 is minimal. In some ways, 2:12–22 is one rhetorical piece.

Jude's single image of clouds that are waterless and driven by the wind becomes two images in 2 Peter. There is no obvious reason for the change, although readers have suggested a change in geography from Jude's arid Palestine to 2 Peter's rainy Italy (assuming some certainty over place of origin) or even puzzlement over the nonsense of clouds without water. Whatever the cause, the point is clear: springs promise water. Waterless springs do not deliver on that promise. Mists promise a change in weather. Mists driven away by a storm do not produce that change. Thus these images specifically anticipate the broken promise of freedom in 2:19 and evoke in general the danger and seductions of false teachers. Readers have long connected the promise of water with biblical images of water as divine teaching or wisdom (e.g., Prov 13:14; Sir 24:23–31). Thus these images connect to turning back from "the holy commandment" (2:21) and perhaps even to the "pig that is washed" (2:22).

The phrase "for whom the gloom of darkness is kept" is taken word for word from Jude 13. Although the extended prediction of punishment in Jude 12–16 is shortened in 2 Peter, the certainty of punishment for these false teachers remains central to the argument of the letter. In fact, it is this certainty of divine punishment for those who "turn back from the holy commandment" that makes these teachers so dangerous. The problem is not simply that these teachers are enticing people to follow them but, more important, that following these teachers earns divine destruction.

[18] At this point the description of the false teachers becomes more straightforward. The opening accusation comes in part from Jude but with a new twist. These people speak (*phthengomai*) as animals speak. The account of what they say ("inflated emptiness") suggests words blown up beyond their true size and actually empty on the inside. This imagery recalls the waterless springs and evaporating mists that look good on the outside but produce nothing. All of this creates a rather classic accusation against the teaching of these teachers. It looks good, sounds wonderful, but in fact is nothing.

The problem is that these teachers are effective. The description of their success returns to the familiar charge of immorality. First of all, they do not simply teach; they "ensnare." The verb *deleazō*, with its connotations of hunting and of capturing with bait, draws on the animal imagery that runs throughout the passage. These people capture other people as hunters capture animals. Their means, their bait, is immorality itself. Though the term "desires" is not always negative in Greek ethics (people need desires in order to live), when modified by "flesh" and paired with "licentious deeds," it takes on its common Jewish and Christian negative role. These desires of the flesh prevent a person from doing what the person wants. The claim that they ensnare by means of "licentious deeds" depends upon the common notion that people, to some extent, enjoy immorality.

The people they ensnare are described as having "just" escaped from the company of those "who live in error." The suggestion that recent converts are more susceptible to this heresy is understandable and comes without explanation. The imagery here and in what follows recalls the description of the new life in 1:3–11, where readers are described as "having escaped [*apophygontes*] from the corruption that is in the world because of desire" (1:4). That account focuses on the life of virtue that emerges from God's own virtue (1:3). The

The Slavery of the False Teachers 259

life of virtue contrasts with the life of the false teachers described here, which is lived in "error," driven by the "passions," and accompanied by "licentious deeds." The peculiar syntax of this verse, wherein these recent converts have just escaped not from the life of passions but from the company of people who live in error, suggests that the problem is not simply about virtue and vice but also about whose company someone keeps. Thus the danger of the false teachers may lie less in their teaching and more in their behavior. They seem insufficiently immersed in the Christian community. The conflict between old loyalties to old friends and new loyalties to new Christian friends is a perennial issue in early Christianity. In a way, these false teachers are accused of being insufficiently sectarian. They retain too much of their pre-Christian lives.

[19] Apart from skepticism about the second coming, this claim that they promise freedom is the letter's most specific description of the teaching of the false teachers. Since this is not a stock charge in early Christianity, almost all commentators conclude that the teaching of these false teachers includes something peculiar about freedom. The question that has troubled readers is not whether these people champion freedom but from what do they promise freedom. Some gnostics believed in freedom from cosmic powers, but there is no hint of such a concern in 2 Peter. In the Greco-Roman world the word freedom (*eleutheria*) most often referred to social or political freedom, but again there is no hint of such in the letter. A bit more likely is the suggestion that they are promising freedom from corruption. This suggestion comes from the accusation in this verse that these people who promise freedom are actually "slaves of corruption." However, the accusation that these people are slaves of corruption is probably another way of asserting the eternal punishment that awaits them.

This leaves two possibilities. First, the context of the passage suggests that this freedom is from the demands of Christian morality. In 2:21 these teachers or their followers are described as turning back from "from the holy commandment handed over to them." They ensnare people by means of "desires of the flesh" and "licentious deeds." The Christian life is depicted in 1:3–11 as a life of classic virtue. All of this indicates a problem with morality. It is not clear what these teachers actually teach about morality. It is only clear that the author of 2 Peter believes that the freedom they promise leads to immorality. Certainly many people found the ethical norms of much of early Christianity to be excessively narrow. Early Christians will have long debates over ethical norms.[49] Second Peter appears to participate in this, even though we cannot reconstruct much about the contours of this debate from the few hints in the letter. Second, most readers connect this problem with immorality and ridicule

---

49. For a survey of those debates, see Francine Cardman, "Early Christian Ethics," in *The Oxford Handbook of Early Christian Studies* (ed. Susan Ashbrook Harvey and David Hunter; Oxford: Oxford University Press, 2008), 932–56.

of the second coming. Since the discussion about the second coming in 3:1–13 includes warnings about behavior, these teachers could be denying final judgment. This denial of final judgment gives permission for immorality. These teachers are thereby announcing that since there is no final accounting to God, people can live immoral lives. Most readers of 2 Peter make this connection. However, there are problems with this reading. Whatever these teachers might teach, they apparently consider themselves to be members of the community and are considered such by others. It would be extremely unusual for early Christians to promote unrighteousness in this way. Furthermore, theological ideas can be connected in many ways. Skepticism of final judgment does not in itself lead to immorality. Ethics has many other possible grounds apart from fear of punishment. In any case, it appears that these teachers are proclaiming freedom from certain ethical norms. However, this does not mean that they think they are teaching immorality.

This promised freedom is contrasted to slavery. The obvious irony is that these people are slaves themselves but promise freedom for others. Their slavery to "corruption" (or perhaps "decay") signals both the metaphorical character of this slavery and the ethical context. This accusation of moral slavery is reinforced by a saying that appears to be a known proverb. Though the saying does not occur in this form in extant literature, the idea is familiar enough. The closest parallels are found in Paul. Almost exactly the same point is made in Rom 6:16: "Do you not know that if you present yourselves to anyone as obedient slaves, you are slaves of the one whom you obey, either of sin, which leads to death, or of obedience, which leads to righteousness?" In Rom 8:21 Paul speaks of creation as in "bondage to decay" (*apo tēs douleias tēs phthoras*). All of this evidences the pervasiveness of these ideas. Whether the powers are cosmic or moral, obedience to them is slavery.

[20] This account of apostasy probably refers to the teachers and not the followers, although the generalizing tone could fit with both. Even if it serves as a description of the apostasy of the false teachers, it also serves as a warning to their followers and would-be followers. The description has extensive echoes of 1:3–4. The escaping from "the corruption that is in the world because of desire" in 1:4 has become in 2:20 an escape from "the defilements of the world." If there is anything at stake in this slight shift in terminology, it is probably contained in the cultic echoes of the term "defilements." The sense of the being in or out of cultic holiness fits with the communal focus of these verses. In any case, the similarities are more important than the differences. Knowledge of Jesus Christ enables escape from corruption and defilement. As in 1:3–11, the power of that knowledge seems less concerned with cosmic transformation, a realignment of powers, and more with ethics. The "defilements" of the world are not conceived here as ritual purity but as immorality. This means that entanglement is not just a return to the company of people who live in error but is also participation in

their moral error. In these verses is an ongoing conviction that the company a person keeps determines, or at least nearly so, the person's ethics.

The final phrase is an almost exact replication of the Jesus saying in Matt 12:45 and Luke 11:26. The only difference is the change from the singular "of that person" in the Jesus saying to the plural "for them." The Jesus saying involves the person who sweeps out the single unclean spirit, which returns to the house with seven more. The Shepherd of Hermas (*Sim.* 9.17.5–18.2) uses this saying almost exactly as 2 Peter does. The saying that Jesus applied to a person's relationship to unclean spirits is apparently taken up in Christian tradition to address apostasy. It is not explicitly stated that a person gets only one chance at the Christian life, although this verse and the next two give little attention to second chances. In the Jesus saying it is clear why the last state is worse than the first since eight unclean spirits are more powerful than one. Here it is less clear why things become worse. The core argument seems to be simply that people are slaves to whatever they obey. This slavery is not only in itself bad; it also leads to judgment. The next verse gives a further hint.

[21] This genre of saying is common in Jewish and Christian literature. In Christian literature the most famous come from the series of three "better-than" sayings in Mark 9:42–48. In the Markan sayings and in this one, a mixed experience is contrasted with a purely negative one. Though in Mark the mixed experience is couched as superior to the purely negative, this verse ironically makes the purely negative superior to the mixed. The force of this irony comes from the seriousness of apostasy. It is striking that the imagery in this saying is classically Jewish. There is nothing peculiarly Christian in the terminology. This suggests that the saying may derive from Jewish tradition, although it is not present in extant literature.

The opening assertion is intentionally counterintuitive. It should be and is a good thing to know "the way of righteousness." However, it is only a good thing if a person persists in it. Second Peter uses forms of *epignōsis* (knowledge) almost as a summary of the Christian faith. The object of this knowledge in 2 Peter is usually God or Jesus Christ or both. Thus the phrase "way of righteousness" is a bit unexpected although both terms are common to 2 Peter. In 2:2 the licentiousness of the false teachers results in the slandering of "the way of truth." The term *dikaiosynē* (righteousness, justice) is used, in its familiar way, to summarize the character of God (1:1) and the character of Noah (2:5). In 3:13 the final victory of God's promises results in new heavens and a new earth, where "righteousness dwells." The entire phrase "the way of righteousness" is certainly common in Jewish literature. Jesus' reference in Matt 21:32 to John the Baptist's coming "in the way of righteousness" is a typical use of the phrase. The phrase summarizes the nature of life in obedience to the torah. It also recalls the ethical demands that are central to 2 Peter.

Given the terminology of this first example, the Jewish character of the second is not surprising. Apostasy is described as turning back "from the holy commandment handed over to them." The language of holy commandment comes from Jewish theology of the torah. Although the term would need no explanation in most Jewish contexts, it is not clear precisely what it means in 2 Peter. The frequent suggestion that the commandment is Christian proclamation that Jesus is Lord results in an awkward and unusual use of the term commandment. It is more likely that the term evokes not the act of belief in the lordship of Jesus but obedience to the ethical demands of the Christian life. Thus the "holy commandment" would demand and produce "the way of righteousness." The details of how the holy commandment was handed over are not given because they do not need to be. This imagery of handing over the commandment fits with the role of eyewitnesses in 1:16–18 and the Petrine authorship of the letter itself. Second Peter assumes the coherence of its theology with apostolic tradition.

The counterintuitive claim of this verse, wherein not ever knowing the way of righteousness is better than apostasy, suggests that there was a unique fear of apostasy in these communities. This condemnation of apostasy is highlighted by use of the language of holiness. Jews, Greeks, Romans, and Christians all understood the need to protect the holy. Pollution of holy space was considered to be a serious crime. Yet in early Christian literature, holiness does not refer primarily to space but to ethics. It is not the cella of the temple that is holy but the righteous deed.

[22] The final proverbs are syntactically incomplete. The opening of the verse calls upon the readers to complete the proverb. There are two ways to complete the images. The participles could be turned to indicatives so that it reads "a dog returns to its own vomit" and "a pig is washed in order to wallow in the mud." Or if the comparison is completed, it would be something like "people who turn back from the holy commandment are like a dog returning to its vomit and a washed pig wallowing in the mud."

The first image is probably derived directly from Prov 26:11: "Like a dog that returns to its vomit is a fool who reverts to his folly." For the most part, ancient Mediterranean people saw the dog as a disgusting animal (see, e.g., Horace, *Ep.* 1.2.26; P.Oxy. 840.33–34). Few behaviors were more repulsive than a dog's tendency to eat its own vomit. The repulsiveness of the image is key to its force in 2 Peter. Apostasy is not only the profaning of the holy; it is also disgusting. There is no obvious source for the pig imagery. There is the common Greek image of the pig that washes in the mud (e.g., Sextus Empiricus, *Pyr.* 1.14.56). There are also several references in Jewish literature to pigs going to the bath and then washing in the mud (*Syriac Ahiqar* 8.18). Nothing is a precise parallel. It may be that the proverbial image of the pig washing in mud is adjusted in 2 Peter for the sequences of apostasy. First, there is a cleansing. Second, there is a wallowing in mud.

Both images make the same point. The animal is cleansed, either by vomiting or washing. Once cleansed, it returns to the very thing that made it filthy. The comparison with apostates is obvious. They have escaped the defilements of the world through the knowledge of our Lord and Savior Jesus Christ (1:3–4) but now have returned to their former licentiousness. They are once again entangled in the very things that polluted them. It is not stated why the situation of apostates is worse than that of people who never became Christian. Perhaps they have no hope. Perhaps God reserves special punishment for them.

The passage (2:17–22) has two sections. The first deals with the dangers of false teachers on the rest of the community. These teachers are depicted as being effective in the community but only in the sense that they entice people to follow them. Their key characteristic is that they make promises but cannot deliver on them. They are like springs with no water and clouds with no rain. More literally, they promise freedom but deliver slavery. The second section focuses on the seriousness of apostasy. An apostate Christian is declared to be worse off than a non-Christian, although it is not said why. The aggressiveness of the attack on these apostates suggests that apostasy was seen as a peculiarly heinous sin. The concluding images of a dog eating its vomit and a pig washing in filth nicely summarize the mood of the attack.

The passage as a whole presents a portrait of people outside the way of righteousness who call others to follow. They are effective teachers in that they gather followers. Since they stand outside of the way of truth and righteousness, they are also destructive teachers. Second Peter never clearly articulates their precise heresy. It is unlikely that they are calling people to abandon the Christian faith and return to former values. These people seem to consider themselves Christian. Whatever they are teaching, the letter asserts that the gloom of God's darkness hovers over them and their followers. To be them and to follow them is to fall under God's judgment. This assurance anticipates the discussion in the next chapter.

2 Peter 3:1–13 The Promise of His Coming

2 Peter 3:1–7 The Coming of Mockers

In some ways 3:1–13 is a single sustained argument about final judgment, punctuated by various shifts in tone and topic. Given these shifts, it is not surprising that readers have divided the section many ways. Despite the considerable debate about the proper division of 3:1–13, there is actually little at stake in how the section is divided since the entire passage is interconnected. The division offered here reflects the common observation that 3:1–7 focuses mostly on the mockers and 3:8–16 on the faithful.

The passage first predicts the coming of mockers who will mock at "the promise of his coming" and includes in this prediction a summary of their argument against the second coming. The rest of the passage is a theological response. The core of the response is fairly straightforward. God creates and sustains the world and thus has absolute power over it. This is a traditional Jewish and Christian idea. However, while the basic theology is typical of early Christianity, the details are a bit surprising. Readers have long noted that the theological imagery is more Jewish than Christian. This has led to speculation that the author is drawing on an unknown Jewish apocalyptic source. It has even been suggested that this is the same source that underlies *1 Clement* 23.3 and *2 Clement* 11.2, although the parallels are a bit too meager for a definite conclusion. It is more likely that the author is drawing upon an unknown Jewish source that has somewhat unusual roles for water and fire. The passage also has clear echoes of Jude.

For all the possible sources underlying the passage, the author has produced a coherent rhetorical piece. It is also one of the most interesting discussions of final judgment in the NT.

> 3:1 This is now, beloved, the second letter I am writing to you, in which I am awakening[a] your pure thinking with a reminder 2 to remember the words spoken beforehand by the holy prophets and the commandment of the Lord and Savior through your apostles, 3 knowing[b] this first of all, that in the last days mockers[c] will come with mockery,[c] walking according to their own passions 4 and saying, "Where is the promise of his coming?[d] For from the time the fathers fell asleep,[e] all things remain as they were from the beginning of creation."[f] 5 For this escapes their notice willingly,[g] that there were heavens from of old[h] and an earth formed[i] out of water and through water by the word of God, 6 through which[j] the world of that time being flooded with water was destroyed. 7 And by the same word the present heavens and earth have been stored up for fire and are being kept for the day of judgment and destruction of impious people.

a. The expression "I am awakening . . . with a reminder" occurs in almost exactly the same form in 1:13. The verb *diegeirō* means to "awaken," "rouse," or even "disturb."

b. The present circumstantial participle *ginōskontes* (knowing) carries an imperatival sense from the context.

c. The nouns *empaiktai* and *empaigmonē* come from the verb *paizō*, which means "to play like a child [*pais*]." They could be translated "scoffers" and "scoffing," "deceivers" and "deception," or with the more common sense of "mockers" and "mockery."

The Coming of Mockers

d. The noun *parousia* can mean either "presence" or "coming."

e. The verb *koimaō* ("fall asleep," "put to sleep") is a common metaphor for death and need not imply a time of sleep before final judgment.

f. The noun *ktisis* can mean "the act of creating" or "that which is created."

g. This phrase can be translated either as "It escapes their notice when they will this" or "This escapes their notice willingly," depending on whether the pronoun *touto* is taken as the object of the participle *thelontas* (willing) or the subject of the verb *lanthanei* (escapes). Both are plausible grammatically. Since the usage of *thelō* in the sense of willing something to be true is a bit rare, it best to read *touto* as the subject of the verb.

h. The adverb *ekpalai* (from of old) could modify the entire sentence, and both "heavens" and "earth" could be the subject of the verb "formed." If so, the sentence would be rendered "Long ago there were heavens and an earth formed out of water." Admittedly, there is little at stake in choosing between these two readings. The one offered above simply follows the natural order of the Greek more closely.

i. The compound verb *synistēmi* can mean "combine," "unite," "form," "hold together," or even "exist." The active voice often has a passive meaning.

j. The relative pronoun in the prepositional phrase "through which" is plural. There are two plausible options for the antecedents. The reference is to two sources of water mentioned in the phrase "out of water and through water." This would be a reference to the waters of chaos that are held above the firmament and to the waters that form the earth itself. The Genesis account of the flood refers to these two sources of water (7:11). However, since 2 Peter will focus on the creative and destructive power of water and word, "which" probably refers to these.

[3:1] The announcement that this is the second letter that "Peter" has written to this community raises the question of the identity of the first. The description of the letters as reminders of the words of the prophets and the commandment of the Lord and Savior does not offer much help. This description not only does not identify any particular letter; it also does not serve as a particularly apt summary of 2 Peter, although 2 Pet 1:15 uses similar language. Four suggestions have attracted attention. First, if 2 Peter is composed of more than one letter, then this reference in 3:1 may look back on chapters 1 and 2. Since few readers still divide 2 Peter, this proposal no longer has many followers. Second, since 2 Peter clearly draws on Jude, the first letter could be Jude. However, since Jude claims to be written by Jude and 2 Peter by Peter, it is unlikely that Jude is the first letter written by "Peter." Furthermore, Jude is a source for 2 Peter, not a parallel letter. Third, the first letter could be 1 Peter. This suggestion has proved to be more interesting than the first two. In some ways 1 Peter is an obvious candidate since it is by far the best-known early Christian letter that claims to be written by Peter. The *Letter of Peter to Philip* that was found at Nag Hammadi apparently had little circulation. Fourth, some readers argue that 1 Peter makes a poor fit since it seems to have been written to different communities with different issues, and by a different author. Therefore, the first letter is probably an unknown and lost letter that carried Peter's name. This is possible. Still, the best guess is 1 Peter.[50] If 1 Peter is the intended referent, then it is likely that the author of 2 Peter is simply borrowing on the credibility of 1 Peter. There is no need for the communities or the issues to be the same. All that is necessary is for 1 Peter to have apostolic authority in the communities of 2 Peter.

The claim that the letter serves as a reminder recalls 1:15. The language of reminder coheres with the apostolic allegiances of the letter. The author presents the theology of 2 Peter as traditional and apostolic and not as something new. As 3:2 will point out, the words and commandments of 2 Peter come from apostles and prophets. Yet these apostolic words need reliable people to preserve and think them. The imagery of "pure thinking" suggests people who have not given in to the false teachers, who still possess the apostolic teaching, and who only need be reminded of it. This pure thinking forms an interesting contrast to the mockery and life of passion in 3:3.

[2] At first glance this rewriting of Jude 17 seems simply to affirm the apostolic roots of the traditions in 2 Peter. And it certainly does that. However, it also raises a number of puzzles. It is not clear who the "prophets" and "your apostles" are supposed to be. Nor is it clear what the words are that the prophets spoke nor what the commandment is that came through "your" apostles.

"Prophets" can be either Christian prophets or the prophets of ancient Israel. Since the references to prophets and apostles in 1:16–21 assume that "prophets" are the ancient prophets of Israel and "apostles" are the original followers of Jesus, most readers see the same references in this verse. Furthermore, this fits. The "prophets" are the classic OT prophets. "The words" they spoke cannot and probably should not be specified. It is the overall prophetic authority that matters. Each citation, as it occurs, will participate in that.

It is more difficult to decide the precise referent of "your apostles" and "the commandment" that comes through them. As in 2:21, "commandment" probably does not refer to a particular commandment or even to the general proclamation of the lordship of Jesus but to the call for obedience to the ethical demands of the Christian life. Thus the "commandment" produces the life of righteousness (2:21; 3:13). The term "apostle" in early Christianity can refer to the original Twelve, the early college of apostles, or anyone sent by a Christian community to spread the gospel. The unusual phrase "your apostles" suggests that these apostles might be the founding apostles of these communities, who first proclaimed the gospel to these Christians. However, most readers find the expression "your apostles" an awkward way to refer to the founding apostles of the community. Furthermore, the naming of Peter as an apostle in 1:1 and

---

50. See G. H. Boobyer, "The Indebtedness of 2 Peter to 1 Peter," in *New Testament Essays: Studies in Memory of T. W. Manson* (ed. A. J. B. Higgins; Manchester: University of Manchester Press, 1959), 34–53, for a discussion of options and for 1 Peter as being the source.

the reference to eyewitnesses in 1:16 indicates that "your apostles" refers to the original apostles sent forth by Jesus. In any case, however these terms are parsed, the point remains rather much the same. This letter is a reminder of the apostolic teaching that the readers already know.

[3] This verse announces the focus of the passage by way of an apostolic prophecy. Given the sequences of the opening verses, this announcement of the coming of mockers in 3:3 must have some relationship with the words of the prophets in 3:2. At a minimum this prediction of the mockers is another instance of prophecy. However, it is not clear whether the prediction is intended as coming from the OT prophets or from the apostolic authority of Peter. Since 2 Peter combines the authority of these groups, it is probably unnecessary to draw a clean distinction. The phrase "last days" is traditional, as is the accusation of "walking according to their own passions," but the prediction of mockers in those last days is not. This prediction is drawn directly from Jude 18, where "mockers" seems to be another word for the "impious." However, in 2 Peter the mockers are not simply impious or immoral people; they also engage in mockery.

[4] The content of the mockery that is summarized here contains two accusations, both of which challenge the notion of a final cosmic judgment. Ironically, the mockers who are predicted to come in "the last days" deny the very idea of last days. Both accusations are stated in brief form without explanation. Thus it is not surprising that there are questions about their content.

The first comment is couched as a question: "Where is the promise of his coming?" Both the form and content of this question are reminiscent of the frequent questions about God's absence in the OT. In fact, the psalmist is taunted by enemies with the similar question: "Where is your God?" (42:10; cf. 79:10; Joel 2:17; Mal 2:17). Such taunts and questions frequent any religion that is built upon unfulfilled promises. The taunt does not specify whose coming has been promised. It could be either God or Jesus. Most readers think that, while the syntactical links to the OT suggest that it is the God of Israel whose coming is delayed, in the context of 2 Peter the question more likely refers to the return of Jesus. There is actually little at stake in whether God or Jesus is the specific referent, since in the theology of 2 Peter and early Christianity, both God and Jesus will be involved in the coming of the kingdom.

The second comment provides evidence for the appropriateness of the opening question. The mockers point to the obvious fact that in spite of all these promises, the world continues as it always has. Some readers have suggested that "our fathers" refers to the generation of the first followers of Jesus. They are dying out before the promises to them have been fulfilled. However, "fathers" is the usual term in Jewish and Christian circles for the OT patriarchs. Such a usage makes perfect sense. The reference to "from the beginning of creation" suggests that the data is about the eternal character of the created order. In this context, a reference to patriarchs makes more sense than to the first Christians.

In any case, the peculiar character of the Christian promises involves not just a new divine manifestation but also the reconfiguration of cosmic order. Thus it is a good counterargument to this promise to point to the ongoing, uninterrupted structure of creation.

The presence of similar arguments and phraseology in *1 Clement* 23.3 and *2 Clement* 11.2 has led to a discussion of whether 2 Peter might be quoting a source that is also quoted in these documents. The images of this verse are part of larger theological discussions in both Judaism and Christianity. It is possible that 2 Peter is quoting a Jewish text where the reference was to God's coming within the confines of history to fulfill a particular historical promise. However, there is no way to be certain. In any case, in 2 Peter these promises are eschatological.

As the debates throughout Christian history show, the simple pointing to the unfulfilled character of the promises, to the stability of creation, and to the absence of divine justice or judgment calls into question the reliability of the fundamental Christian promises. The mockers have a good case.

[5] The initial counterargument is directed toward the ignorance of the mockers. This verse claims that these mockers, in their mockery, display an ignorance of basic theological history. As noted above, it is not clear in the Greek whether this ignorance is intentional or not; but it is, in any case, ignorance. In order to counter the mockers' argument about the persistence of creation, the author points to the creation account in Genesis. Apart from the basic observation that the heavens and earth are created and thus are not eternal, the verse points to water and to the word of God as both having unique power over created order. The reference to "word" as the immediate agent of creation is taken directly from Gen 1. Moreover, this unique role of the word of God becomes the standard narrative in Jewish accounts of creation (see, e.g., Pss 33:6; 148:5; Herm. *Vis.* 1.3.4). Less obvious is the role given to water. The imagery of the earth being created "out of water and through water" probably refers, first of all, to the waters of chaos that are separated in Gen 1:6–7 and now reside above the firmament. However, the dual phrases may also include a reference to water as the, or one of the, constituent elements of creation. There is probably no reference here to Greek philosophical discussions of the cosmic elements. It is more likely that 2 Peter is simply reading the Genesis account, with its complex references to water. In any case, the references to water and word put into question the mockers' claim that the world has been and always will be stable and persistent. Creation is not eternal. It is fragile, dependent on the vagaries of the cosmic waters and the word of God.

[6] This reference to the flood serves as proof of creation's fragility. The water out of which and through which it was formed can be and actually has been its means of destruction. Although several narratives of the cosmic destruction through water emerged in Jewish literature (*1 En.* 10.1–11.2; 83.3–9; *Sib.*

Or. 1.125–280), all are variations or extrapolations from the Genesis flood story. Furthermore, 2 Pet 2:5 has already referred to the Genesis flood and its destruction of "the ancient world." The context in 2:5 was God's punishment of the impious and protection of the righteous. Here it is concerning the fate of creation itself. In Gen 7:11 there seems to be two sources of water. "The fountains of the great deep" and "the windows of the heavens" combine their water in order to create the Noachian flood. This dual reference probably refers to the waters of chaos that are in the heavens and waters of the earth contained in the great seas. It is possible that 2 Peter's dual reference to creation out of and through water echoes these two sources. And as noted above, it is also possible that "through which" refers to these two kinds of water.

The phrase "the world of that time," when compared to the phrase "the present heavens and earth" in the next verse, suggests that the preflood world was completely destroyed. This is not clear in Genesis, but it does intensify the argument in 2 Peter. The world has been destroyed once by the very powers that created it. And, as the next verse insists, it will be destroyed again.

[7] The preceding verses point to both the power of water and the power of the word of God. Though water is described as one of the constituent elements of creation and the means through which the world "of that time" was destroyed, it is "the word" that is described as the real agent of creation. This distinction is not only faithful to traditional Jewish theology; it also anticipates the character of final judgment. Given God's promises to Noah, water cannot be used again in order to destroy the earth. However, in the creation account given here, water is not key. The word of God is the primary force. Thus it will be this "same word" that will structure the destruction of the present world.

The imagery of being "stored up" for judgment is fairly common in Jewish thought. Similar language occurs in 1 Pet 1:4, where rewards are kept in heaven. However, the closest imagery comes from 2 Peter itself, wherein angels are kept for judgment (2:4), the unrighteous are kept for judgment (2:9), and the gloom of judgment is kept for the impious (2:17). All of this suggests a theologically awkward time between death and judgment in which people and the powers of judgment are kept for the final day. Second Peter imagines a considerable time between death and final judgment, but this period does not indicate any uncertainty in coming judgment. Everything and everyone is faithfully kept in place for the final day.

The use of fire as the means of cosmic destruction occurs in Iranian, Jewish, Greek, and Christian thought.[51] Although Iranian ideas may have had some influence on Jewish imagery, it probably is the story of Sodom and Gomorrah

---

51. See, e.g., Diogenes Laertius, *Hist. phil.* 7.134; Justin, *1 Apol.* 20. For further texts, see John J. Collins, *The Sibylline Oracles of Egyptian Judaism* (SBLDS 13; Missoula, Mont.: Scholars Press, 1974), esp. 104–6.

that inspires Jewish thinking on fire and judgment. Jewish imagery on final judgment is diverse and fluid; it never settles on one scenario. However, fire is one of the most common forces of destruction in these accounts (e.g., Deut 32:22; Isa 30:30; 66:15–16; Mal 4:1). The NT does not have many narratives of final judgment. However, fire is by far the most common tool of destruction and judgment in the NT. Hell is the place of fire, and fire is God's manner of punishment (e.g., Matt 5:22; 18:8–9; 25:41; Mark 9:48; Luke 12:49; 17:29; Rev 20:9–15). In Heb 12:29 God is actually called "a consuming fire." Given the prevalence of this use of the image of fire, it is no surprise that 2 Peter names fire as the means through which God will destroy the present heavens and earth.

There are numerous Greek traditions about the destruction of the cosmos, the most famous being the Platonic alternating cycles of destruction by water and fire and the Stoic periodic conflagration (Plato, *Tim.* 22C–E; Lucretius, *De rerum nat.* 5). The Stoics imagined that the cosmos would at some point return to fire, which was its founding element. The existing world would be burned in this fire and then be regenerated into a new order. The account in 2 Peter seems to echo these Greek narratives. In fact, the sequence in 3:5–6 in which the heavens are formed out of and through water and then are destroyed by this same water recalls this Greek cosmology of the power of the cosmic elements. Many early Christian readers would probably have heard the reference to fire in this verse as a reference to the cosmic elements as much as to the Sodom and Gomorrah trajectory in which God destroys by means of fire. Nevertheless, the judgment narrative in 2 Peter remains more Jewish than Greek. The universe is not destroyed because its founding elements turn on it but because the word of God so orders.

Much is left unsaid here. There is no hint, for instance, of how the word of God keeps the present heavens and earth for its eventual judgment. There will be hints as to why this keeping is occurring in the following verses. At this point, the main theme is that the existence of the universe is fragile. Furthermore, its continuance depends on the active decision of God to let it do so.

This passage (3:1–7) addresses two issues, both of which are central to the theological argument of the letter. This early community finds itself in a difficult situation that seems to challenge the good promises of the gospel. Not only are they being persecuted; they are also beset by mockers within their own community. Thus the first issue is the simple presence of such people. This passage insists that such people are not a sign of the failure of the gospel to persuade but are an expected part of the gospel story. They are actually predicted by "the holy prophets." If they are a sign, they are a sign of the nearness of judgment. They will come "in the last days."

The second issue is that these mockers attack a fundamental aspect of the gospel. This attack occasions the bulk of the argument of this passage and the passage that follows. The universe, by all appearances, seems to be eternal. This is a challenge to the theological coherence of 2 Peter for its theology depends on the capacity of God to judge. Unless God can judge, righteousness and justice cannot prevail. Yet there is no suggestion in the processes of history that justice will ever flourish, and the stability of creation suggests that a scene of final judgment is unlikely. The mockers have a good case.

Second Peter responds by calling upon both Greek and Jewish cosmic narratives. The Greek references point to the physics of creation. The very elements of which the universe is composed are capable of destroying it. The universe is created out of waters that can destroy it. It is not clear whether readers would hear Platonic cosmologies in this argument. Second Peter points explicitly not to Plato but to the Noachian flood. In a way, it offers a Greek philosophical reading of the flood narrative. The endless rain of the Noah story becomes a cosmic element that ceases to give life and produces death instead. The prevalence of fire as the means of cosmic destruction in Greek narratives suggests that most readers would hear these Greek cosmologies in 2 Peter's reference to fire. The elements of which the universe is composed are dangerous and unreliable. Nothing guarantees the eternity of the current balance of forces.

In spite of these Greek echoes, Jewish narratives play a more fundamental role in 2 Peter's argument. The force of argument about water ultimately depends on the evidence of the flood. The flood story proves the fragility of the universe. However, it does so not because the physics of the universe is unstable but because God is both a righteous and powerful God. Faced with injustice and unrighteousness, God is willing and capable of destroying the world. The fact that God uses the world's own elements against itself seems more a convenience than a physical necessity. The word of God is the controlling force in all of this. The centrality of the word of God in the status of creation would surprise no one in antiquity since both Greek and Jewish accounts of creation refer to the force of the divine word. In 2 Peter this word is portrayed not only as still active but also as driven by morality. The fate of the universe lies not in its physics but in its righteousness.

In the following passage, the story of Jesus will be inserted into this Greek and Jewish narrative. God will judge by way of Jesus' second coming. It is intriguing that 2 Peter's account of this coming of Jesus will raise questions about God's willingness to judge. God's justice and God's mercy apparently fit together somewhat awkwardly.

2 Peter 3:8–13 God's Patience

As noted above, this section of 2 Peter has a continuous argument that runs from 3:1 to 3:16. There are, in the sequence of this argument, numerous rhetorical and topical shifts. Consequently, this section has been divided many different ways.

Some readers, noting that an indirect imperative is addressed to the readers in 3:11 and a direct imperative in 3:14, divide this passage into two sections, with 3:8–10 addressing the problem of the delay of the coming of Jesus and 3:11–16 addressing the behavior of the readers. This certainly makes sense. The division offered here resists any separation between doctrinal questions and ethical ones or between indicatives and imperatives. It relies more on rhetorical clues than on topical ones. Three times in this chapter the letter addresses the readers directly, calling them "beloved" (3:1, 8, 14). Each of these addresses also marks a slight shift in both topical focus and rhetorical style. Although the entire chapter concerns the issues of final judgment, each direct address seems to open a distinct approach to the question. The divisions used here reflect these shifts.

The issue is no longer that of the eternity of creation but the timing of the day of the Lord. In this argument it is assumed that the readers perceive a delay, a slowness, in the coming of the Lord. The letter responds to this perceived slowness, first, with an argument about theological time and the character of God, and second, with an admonition to the readers concerning how they should live in light of this theology. Along the way, the letter makes some of the most interesting comments about the character of God's judgment in the NT.

3:8 Do not let this one thing escape your notice,[a] beloved, that with the Lord one day is like a thousand years, and a thousand years is like one day. **9** The Lord is not slow[b] about the promise as some reckon slowness,[b] but is patient[c] toward you, not wishing anyone to be destroyed but for all to come into repentance. **10** But the day of the Lord will come like a thief; in it the heavens will pass away with a rushing noise,[d] and the elements[e] will be destroyed[f] by burning,[g] and the earth and the works in it will be found.[h] **11** Since all these things will be destroyed[f] in this way, what sort of people[i] must you become in holy behavior and piety, **12** waiting for and hastening[j] the coming of the day of God,[k] because of which the heavens being set on fire will be destroyed[f] and the elements burning will melt? **13** But we, according to the promise, wait for new heavens and a new earth, in which righteousness dwells.

a. While *lanthanō*, used here and in 3:5, comes from *lēthē*, which means "forgetfulness" or "the act of forgetting," the active form of the verb has the sense of "escape notice" or "be unnoticed." Thus there is no sense in the verb itself, either here or in 3:5, that people are forgetting or might forget what they once knew.

b. The verb *bradynō* comes from *bradys*, which means "slow." In reference to time, the verb can mean to be "late" or "tardy." Given the lack of accent in ancient uncials, it is not clear whether the form *bradynei* is present or future tense. Since the framing of the argument suggests that the day of the Lord is already a bit late, the present tense is more likely. The verb "slow" and the noun "slowness" in this verse both come from the same Greek root.

God's Patience

c. The compound verb *makrothymeō* has the sense of being "patient," "long-suffering," and "slow to anger."

d. The adverb *rhoizēdon* comes from *rhoizos*, which means "whistling" as of an arrow or a flute, "hissing" like a snake, or the "rush" or "roar" of any loud noise. Here it could refer to the roar of God's voice at judgment or the roar of the flames of judgment.

e. While the singular *stoicheion* refers to anything in a row or series, such as the letters of the alphabet, the plural *stoicheia* was often used to refer to cosmic elements. For its meaning here, see below.

f. The verb *lyō* has a wide variety of meanings and in different contexts can be rendered "loose," "undo," "dissolve," "destroy," "annul," "release," or even "accomplish."

g. The passive circumstantial participle *kausoumena* (which is also used in 3:12) probably has the causative force of "by burning."

h. The textual problems with the last word of the verse are probably unsolvable. The best textual support (א, B, K) is for *heurethēsetai*, "will be found"; but this reading is so peculiar as to have inspired some later texts to add a negative: "will not be found." Thus the earth and its works will not be found because they are burned up with the elements. Various Greek texts have various readings. Perhaps the most interesting is the papyrus ($\mathfrak{P}^{72}$) that adds *lyomena*, "will be found dissolved." However, all of the variants seem to be attempts to avoid the problematic "will be found."

i. The adjective *potapos* usually means "what sort of" or "what kind of" in the interrogative sense, although it can have exclamatory force. Both usages are a bit awkward in this verse. However, whether a question mark or an exclamation point goes at the end of 3:12 does not really change the meaning. Either way, these verses function as exhortation. There is no word for "people" in the Greek. It is added simply to make sense in English.

j. The usual meaning of *speudō* is to "urge" or "hasten." Some readers, not liking the theological implications of that translation, suggest the less common meaning of "to be eager" or "zealous." However, in that usage the verb is followed by a dative object or an accusative with an infinitive; neither is present here.

k. Although a few manuscripts (C, P) read "Lord," by far the majority ($\mathfrak{P}^{72}$, א, A, B, 𝔐) read "God."

[3:8] The opening address forms a contrast to the charge in 3:5, where the mockers are accused of intentionally failing to notice the composition of the heavens and the earth. This failure of the mockers leads in this verse to a call to the readers not to mimic their error: "Do not let this one thing escape your notice." This one thing will be a quotation from the Psalter. This quote introduces a quite different argument into this narrative of final judgment. In the ongoing address to the readers, the letter in 3:10–11 will return to the question of the composition of the heavens and the earth. However, before it does that, it makes a claim about theological time and the character of God.

The heart of this verse is a quote from Ps 90:4 (89:4 LXX). In the context of Ps 90, the assertion "For a thousand years in your sight are like yesterday when it is past" is part of a series of affirmations about the eternity, power, and wrath of God. The form in which 2 Peter cites the verse ("with the Lord one day is like a thousand years, and a thousand years is like one day") is typical of how the verse is taken up in Jewish and Christian literature. The verse gives warrant to a theological formula about God and time: a thousand years of historical time is equivalent to one day of theological time. In both Jewish and Christian literature, this theological formula often becomes a literal mathematical equation that is used to calculate the mysteries of time.[52] For example, the *Epistle of Barnabas* combines this equation with the six days of creation in order to calculate the end of the world: "Therefore, children, in six days, that is, in six thousand years, everything shall come to an end" (15.4). The formula is used to calculate not only the end of world but also other mysteries, such as the length of the messianic kingdom and sequences of creation. Some readers of 2 Peter detect such calculation here, suggesting, for instance, that 2 Peter may be claiming that the day of judgment itself will last a thousand years.

Most readers of 2 Peter see such mathematical calculations as extraneous to the argument of this passage. Psalm 90:4 was also used in Jewish literature simply to note the gap between human time and divine time as a way of reminding people that they cannot calculate the ultimate mysteries of God's time. This seems to be the point in 2 Peter. The text is not offering a calculation formula for the day of judgment. It is doing precisely the opposite: it is denying any attempt to calculate the end.

[9] Given the centrality of eschatological promises in 2 Peter, anticipation of the end is inevitable. Though 2 Peter has asserted that God can and will effect cosmic judgment (3:5–7) and that humans cannot know the timing of that judgment (3:8), the question of what governs the timing of judgment remains. At this point 2 Peter points to the character of God.

The claim that "the Lord is not slow about the promise" recalls numerous OT references to the fulfillment of divine promises, the judgment of the wicked, and the delay in both. The accusation of the mockers in 3:4 ("Where is the promise of his coming?") echoes these OT discussions. In Jewish literature the most influential text is Hab 2:3, which asserts, "For there is still a vision for the appointed time; it speaks of the end, and does not lie. If it seems to tarry, wait for it; it will surely come, it will not delay." The Aquila version of the LXX uses the same Greek word, *bradynei*, for "delay." Readers of 2 Peter have typically pointed to Sir 35:19 (35:22 NRSV), since it contains both *bradynō* and *makrothymeō*. However, it is significant that, while Sirach agrees with 2 Peter in insisting that the Lord will not be slow, it disagrees with 2 Peter in insisting that the Lord will also not be patient. In this affirmation, it is Sirach, not

---

52. Daniel von Allmen, "L'apocalyptique juive et le retard de la parousie en II Pierre 3:1–13," *RTP* 16 (1966): 255–74.

2 Peter, that is out of line with most of the OT and most Jewish and Christian literature.

Second Peter's claim that the Lord "is patient" echoes the common OT claim that God is patient and thus delays judgment. The formative text is Exod 34:6–7, in which God announces, immediately after Moses cuts the two stone tablets, both that the Lord is "merciful and gracious, slow to anger [LXX; *makrothymos*]" and that this same Lord does not clear the guilty but visits "the iniquity of the parents upon the children." This combination sets the agenda for OT discussions of judgment (e.g., Neh 9:17; Pss 86:15; 103:8; Joel 2:13; Jonah 4:2). God is patient, and God will judge. Second Peter's second claim, that God's patience gives room for repentance, is also the common OT notion (e.g., Joel 2:13; Jonah 4:2). Paul in Rom 2:4 gives the classic argument: "Or do you despise the riches of his kindness and forbearance and patience [*makrothymia*]? Do you not realize that God's kindness is meant to lead you to repentance?"

The one possible deviation from the most common OT scenarios of judgment would lie in 2 Peter's claim that the Lord does not wish for "anyone to be destroyed but for all to come into repentance." There were diverse opinions in the OT, Jewish thought, and early Christian thought about who will and will not be saved and about what God's intentions are for final judgment. As Exod 34:6 declares, God is both merciful and just. Furthermore, God is God of all, and in different moments God has chosen both Israel and the followers of Jesus Christ. The combinations that ensue from all this defy categorization. The NT ranges from the focus on mercy in Rom 11:32 ("For God has imprisoned all in disobedience so that he may be merciful to all") to the extensive descriptions of wrath in the book of Revelation.

Some readers suggest that 2 Peter is not declaring that the Lord wants "all" people to repent but only for all of "you," the Christian recipients of the letter. In this reading "all" is limited by the "you" to whom the Lord is patient. This reading is possible, but there is no semantic need for the "all" to be defined by "you." Furthermore, the weight of the assertion that the Lord "is patient toward you" is not upon the identity of "you" but upon the patience of the Lord. The claim that the Lord wants "all to come into repentance" stands fine on its own. This universalist-sounding moment is a standard part of the tradition. God is merciful, and God is the God of all. This universalist trajectory is typically combined with assertions of God's justice and God's intention to judge the righteous and the unrighteous. Most Jewish and Christian literature does not try to harmonize God's mercy with God's justice, and neither does 2 Peter.

The rabbis famously wondered whether the degree of Israel's repentance influenced the timing of the day of judgment (see, e.g., *b. Sanh.* 97b–98a). Second Peter will suggest in 3:12 that these Christians might be capable of hastening the day of judgment. This verse (3:9) transforms the apparent delay in "his coming" from a sign of something negative about God to something positive. God is not slow; God is patient. In 3:12, the delay will become not simply a challenge to one's theology but also to one's behavior. These readers can hasten the day.

[10] The seeming delay in the day of the Lord and God's patience and desire for repentance do not mean that the day of the Lord is not coming. Not only will it come; it will also come "like a thief." This imagery for the day of the Lord coming as a thief is probably derived from Jesus' parable about the lord of the house not knowing when the thief was coming (Matt 24:43–44). In the context of Matthew, the point of the parable is that the "Son of Man is coming at an unexpected hour" (24:44). Luke has the same parable with the same conclusion (12:39–40). The image is taken up in a variety of ways by Christian literature (1 Thess 5:2; Rev 3:3; 16:15; *Did.* 16.1), but the closest parallel to 2 Peter is 1 Thess 5:2. The only difference is that in 1 Thessalonians the day comes like a thief "in the night." The similarity in wording has suggested to many readers that 2 Peter must have taken its imagery from 1 Thessalonians. Yet there is no way to determine that. In any case, the point is that the timing of the day of the Lord cannot be calculated. There are no signs or secrets that can be combined into a computation of the date of the day of the Lord. In fact, it will come when it is least expected.

It is the standard expectation in Jewish and Christian literature that the day of the Lord will produce a reconfiguration of the cosmos. This verse begins the narrative of the destruction of the heavens and the earth that was announced in 3:7. The imagery recalls that of the Jesus sayings that predict the passing of heaven and earth while the law or the words of Jesus endure (Matt 5:18; 24:35; Mark 13:31; Luke 16:17; 21:33). In concord with this Jesus tradition, the first event of the day of the Lord is this passing of the heavens and the earth with an accompanying roar.

The second event is that the elements (*stoicheia*) will be burned up and destroyed. It is not clear what the elements are. There are three more-or-less reasonable suggestions. First, *stoicheia* could mean what it does in Greek philosophical cosmologies. The term is used to refer to the four constitutive elements of the universe: earth, air, fire, and water.[53] In discussions of cosmology, this is the most common meaning of the term, and it would certainly be how most Greek readers would have understood the reference. Having fire destroy fire, along with the other elements, recalls the use of water in 3:5–6, where the first heavens and earth are composed "out of" and "through" water and then are destroyed by this same water. If this is the case, then 2 Peter would be arguing that even the foundational elements of the universe would be destroyed. They

---

53. Gerhard Delling, "στοιχεῖον," *TDNT* 7:672–82.

could not, as in Stoic circles, be the stuff from which the next heaven and earth were built. The new heaven and earth would need to rely entirely on the word of God. The second suggestion is that the elements refer to the fallen angels mentioned in 2:4. These angels would become rebellious heavenly powers that rule the present cosmos and control the lives of people. The term *stoicheia* is used that way in Gal 4:3 and Col 2:8, 20 (where the force of those powers have been broken by Christ).

The best suggestion is the third, in part because it keeps the term more closely attached to standard Jewish and Christian cosmologies. Jesus' apocalyptic speech in Mark 13 combines Isa 13:10 and 34:4 into a cosmic judgment narrative that becomes the canonical account. "But in those days, after that suffering, the sun will be darkened, and the moon will not give its light, and the stars will be falling from heaven, and the powers in the heavens will be shaken" (Mark 13:24–25). If this is the proper context, then 2 Peter is making the relatively straightforward claim that God's judgment affects everything. There is no argument about the structure or hierarchy of creation beyond the assertion that it is all subject to the power of God. It even becomes possible to combine the assertions of all three suggestions. Not only the sun and the moon, not only the ruling cosmic angels, not only the constitutive elements of the universe, but everything that can be named will melt before the arrival of the Lord.

The final assertion of the verse, that "the earth and the works in it will be found," has long puzzled readers. However, the puzzlement has come more from the awkwardness of the expression than from its meaning. Given the other claims about the day of the Lord in 2 Peter, this concluding phrase must mean that "the earth and the works in it" will be made manifest before God's judgment. Thus the expression "will be found" (*heurethēsetai*) is equivalent to the more common "will be made manifest" (*phanerōthēsetai*; cf. Mark 4:22; Luke 8:17; 1 Cor 3:13; 14:25; Eph 5:13). The choice of "will be found" instead of "will be made manifest" may be an attempt to emphasize the role of God, since the phrase "will be found" implies that it is God who does the finding. Second Peter uses the same verb (*heuriskō*) in much the same way in 3:14, but without the syntactical awkwardness. Thus the letter shows a certain fondness for the image that on the day of judgment the Lord will find out about all righteousness and unrighteousness.

The precise sequence of events on the day of the Lord that is imagined in 2 Peter is difficult if not impossible to reconstruct. It is not clear what the reader is to imagine by these references to the heavens passing away with a rushing noise or the elements being destroyed by fire. But that is not the point. This verse, much like the others in this chapter, is not arguing for a specific cosmology or specific apocalyptic sequence; rather, it is using classic Jewish and Christian judgment imagery to assert the surety of judgment and the patience of this God who will judge.

[11–12] Many readers treat these verses as the beginning of a new section that focuses on direct exhortations to the original recipients of the letter. These verses build on the preceding account of cosmic judgment for purposes of ethical admonishment. In some ways these verses add little to the cosmic imagery. The images in these two verses mostly repeat those of 3:10. There is no attempt to clarify or complete the cosmic narrative of judgment day. The point of all this is not in the details but in the very fact that the whole universe is subject to God's judgment. The opening phrase, "since all these things will be destroyed in this way," shows that the focus in these verses lies in the consequences of judgment, not in its details. It is, however, interesting that the usual and nearly ubiquitous expression "day of the Lord" (3:10) is replaced with "day of God." It is hard to know what is at stake in this. It may mean that the Lord in "day of the Lord" and the "his" in "his coming" (3:4) refer to God and not Jesus. However, the "coming" in 1:16 is clearly that of Jesus. It may be part of the growing emphasis in this entire chapter on the power and activity of God. Yet this may even be a change in wording for stylistic reasons, with nothing meaningful being signaled.

In any case, the point of rehearsing these images of the day of the Lord is to encourage righteous behavior. The language of "waiting for" (*prosdokaō*), used here and in 3:13–14, expresses the standard Jewish and Christian attitude of watchfulness and expectation toward the day of the Lord (e.g., Matt 11:3; Luke 7:19–20; *1 Clem.* 23.5). More striking is the suggestion that the recipients can hasten or quicken the arrival of the day. Many modern readers have resisted the implications of this text because it seems to be an affront to divine sovereignty. Nevertheless, this is what the text says. Although it is typically God who hastens the day (Isa 60:22; Sir 36:10), the rabbis wondered about the role of human repentance and righteousness in the timing and character of God's judgment (*b. Sanh.* 97b–98a; *y. Taʻan.* 1.1). Furthermore, Acts 3:19–20; *2 Clement* 12.6; and Hermas, *Similitude* 10.4.4, all suggest that human behavior can influence the timing of the day of the Lord. Thus such a notion is part of the Jewish and Christian tradition even if it is not the norm. The assertion here is fairly straightforward. Christians can hasten the day of the Lord by living righteous lives.

[13] The announcement of new heavens and a new earth recalls Isa 65:17 and 66:22. The coming of a new heaven and earth is common in Judaism (e.g., *1 En.* 45.4–5; 72.1; 91.16; *4 Ezra* 7.75) and is detailed in Rev 21–22. However, most of the NT seems to envision a rebirth or renewal of creation rather than an entirely new heaven and earth (e.g., Matt 19:28; Rom 8:19–23). Nonetheless, 2 Peter is clear. Everything is going to be destroyed, and there will be an entirely new heaven(s) and earth. This affirmation illustrates again that 2 Peter is not trying to ascribe different fates to different aspects of the created universe. The references to the elements burning and the heavens being destroyed does not

mean that everything else survives. The elements and the heavens are examples of the larger destruction.

In the coming of new heavens and new earth, the promise of God is finally fulfilled. The accusation of the mockers in 3:4, "Where is the promise of his coming?" will then be answered. Rather than adopting the skepticism of these mockers, the readers are called to wait for these new heavens and earth "according to the promise." The precise content of the promise is detailed neither here nor in 3:4. Given the argument of the mockers in 3:5 that "all things remain as they were from the beginning of creation" and the cosmological arguments that follow, the promise must include a reconfiguration of the created order. Yet the purpose of that reconfiguration is not simply to demonstrate the power of God. Its purpose is to realize righteousness. Thus what people are waiting for is not only a new creation but also a creation "in which righteousness dwells." Furthermore, the coming of the world in which righteousness dwells authorizes the constant call to righteousness in the letter. Perhaps 3:11 summarizes the argument nicely: given that all these things will be destroyed and that a new creation will come in which righteousness dwells, "you" should live "in holy behavior and piety."

In some ways this passage (3:8–13) reads as a gathering of traditional Jewish and Christian apocalyptic imagery. There is nothing in here, either in terminology or argument, that does not emerge from earlier texts. Nevertheless, together these traditional pieces produce an intriguing and distinctive account. While 3:5–7 asserts that creation in its very existence is subject to the word of the creator God, these verses explain the reason for the apparent delay in the coming of the day of the Lord and suggest an ethical and theological response to that delay.

The passage asserts that God is withholding the day of judgment because there is too much unrighteousness. God wants everyone to be saved, and if God came now, too many people would perish. God's mercy causes a hesitation in God's justice. The letter further asserts that humans can actually hasten the coming of the day of the Lord by living righteous lives. If there is more righteousness, then God's arrival will not be as destructive. Although nearly all Jewish and Christian theologies of judgment claim that the proper way to wait for the day of the Lord is by living as righteously as possible, here the edge is somewhat different. People live righteously not only in order to avoid punishment and receive reward but also to call forth the day itself. Admittedly, this is strikingly different from most Jewish and Christian judgment scenarios, both ancient and modern, wherein God will come to judge when things are at their worst. In most accounts, the prevalence of evil and injustice is a sign that the day is near. In 2 Peter, the opposite is the case. The more justice and righteousness there are, the closer the day is.

2 Peter 3:14–18 Final Exhortation and Doxology

The conclusion of the letter includes a series of summary exhortations in the style of most ancient letters. These exhortations repeat imagery from elsewhere in the letter and add little to the theological or thematic content of the letter. Nevertheless, concluding exhortations in ancient letters often have a sorting function in that they identify the main arguments. This seems to be the case here. Unlike most letters, including those in the NT, 2 Peter lacks the usual epistolary greetings and blessing, having instead a rather classic doxology. In the midst of this, the letter provides a brief and puzzling reference to the Letters of Paul. Altogether these pieces compose an appropriate and effective conclusion.

3:14 Therefore, beloved, since you are waiting for these things, be eager to be found without spot or blemish[a] by him at peace[b] 15 and consider the patience of our Lord as salvation, just as our beloved brother Paul wrote to you according to the wisdom that was given him, 16 speaking about these things as he does in all his letters, in which some things are hard to understand,[c] which the unlearned[d] and unstable twist[e] as they do the rest of the writings[f] to their own destruction. 17 So you, beloved, knowing this beforehand,[g] be on guard lest[h] being led away by the error of lawless people[i] you fall away from your own stability.[j] 18 But grow in the grace[k] and knowledge of our Lord and Savior Jesus Christ. To him be glory both now and to the day[l] of eternity. Amen.[m]

    a. The two adjectives *aspiloi* (spotless) and *amōmētoi* (lit., "blameless") are used in 2:13 to describe the false teachers at the community feast. Both terms are used for animals that have been judged to be adequate for sacrifice.

    b. It is not clear how the dative pronoun *autō* (by him) and the prepositional phrase *en eirēnē* (in peace) relate to the rest of the sentence and to each other. Since personal agency is usually expressed in Greek by means of *hypo* with the genitive, some readers suggest that *autō* is a dative of reference and render the sentence "to be found without spot or blemish in his sight." The final prepositional phrase "at peace" can be connected with *autō* so that the verse is translated "to be found at peace with him." However, the simplest way to read the verse is to render *autō* as agency ("by him") and to connect "in peace" independently with the verb.

    c. The term *dysnoētos* is rare in ancient Greek. This is its only occurrence in the NT. The prefix *dys* either reverses the positive meaning of a word or increases its negative meaning. The adjective *noētos* means "perceptible" or "thinkable." Thus *dysnoētos* means something like "hard to understand (or think or perceive)."

    d. The common translation of *amatheis* as "ignorant" is misleading. The word means "uninstructed" or "unlearned."

Final Exhortation and Doxology

e. The verb *strebloō* normally means "to twist" or "to stretch tight," as with cables, the strings of an instrument, or a body on a rack. However, when used about words, the twisting has the sense of distortion.

f. The term *graphai* means "writings." In a Greek context, the term can refer to any writing, drawing, or even a single letter of the alphabet. In the NT *graphai* normally refers to any text in the full collection of OT Scripture (e.g., Matt 21:42; Luke 4:21; Acts 8:32; Rom 4:3; 1 Tim 5:18). Thus the term would include all the texts in the traditional Jewish categories of Torah, Prophets, and Writings. However, in this verse *graphai* includes at least the Letters of Paul and thus almost certainly other early Christian writings. In the first century, Jewish canon discussions are not completely finalized and Christian discussions are just beginning. Thus it is not clear precisely what *graphai* includes and does not include.

g. The obvious object of *proginōskontes* (knowing beforehand) is the capacity of the unlearned and unstable in 3:16 to twist the writings. However, the summation function of letter closings suggests that echoes of all the attacks on false teachers and mockers might be included here.

h. Translators have typically rendered the negative purpose clause (*hina mē*) by changing the participle *proginōskontes* to an indicative and by placing a negative with both verbs. The somewhat awkward "lest" follows the feel of the Greek syntax more closely.

i. The same substantive adjective *athesmōn* (lawless people) was used in 2:7 to refer to the Sodomites.

j. The noun *stērigmos* (stability) comes from the same root as the adjective *astēriktoi* that is used in 2:14 and 3:16 for "unstable people" (cf. also 1:12).

k. The Greek could be rendered with the genitive of "our Lord and Savior Jesus Christ" attached to both "grace" and "knowledge" or as attached only to "knowledge" ("Grow in grace and in the knowledge of our Lord . . . ").

l. The usual phrasing of NT doxologies *eis tous aiōnas* is replaced by this reference to the "day of eternity" (*eis hēmeran aiōnos*). There is no other reference to the idea of the eternal day in 2 Peter, although the image does occur in the OT (Ps 90:4; cf. Isa 60:19–20).

m. As with most concluding doxologies in the NT, this one has numerous variants. The most interesting is the absence of "amen" in several texts (B).

[3:14] This verse signals the transition to the conclusion of the letter by means of a gathering reference to the preceding argument. The passage will continue this conclusion-style rhetoric by offering brief summaries of earlier arguments. Furthermore, in the typical rhetoric of conclusions, the author assumes the persuasiveness of the letter. The reader is rhetorically convinced. This verse asserts that the readers are "waiting for these things," clearly referring to the coming judgment and the new heavens and earth. The argument of the mockers and their skepticism about final judgment is regarded as being rejected by the readers. They await judgment and the new heavens and earth "where righteousness dwells" (3:13).

Since righteous judgment is coming, the readers must themselves become righteous. The imagery of 3:11 of "holy behavior and piety" gives way to classic sacrificial language. Although Christianity will develop a peculiar context for sacrificial imagery due to the centrality of the crucifixion and the notion that Jesus was a sacrifice (e.g., Heb 9:14; 1 Pet 1:19), the imagery itself and the use of such sacrificial language to refer to morality and ethics would not be strange to anyone in antiquity. The border between cult and personal ethics was porous. As is usually the case in 2 Peter, the letter does not make explicit how a person could be found "without spot or blemish." Yet the list of virtues in 1:5–7 and the attacks in chapter 2 give a basic idea of what righteousness might be and might not be.

The final note of being found "at peace" could mean at peace with God or at peace with one another. Both make perfect sense in the context. In the moment of judgment, it would be nice to be at peace with God. Nevertheless, given the potential tensions in the community that are narrated in the letter, it is perhaps more likely that this is a final call to peace with one another.

[15–16] The call to "consider the patience of our Lord as salvation" depends upon the argument of 3:5–13. God "is patient toward you, not wishing anyone to be destroyed but for all to come into repentance" (3:9). Thus these opening verses (3:14–15a) reiterate the striking argument about the Parousia. God does not initiate final judgment because God wants everyone to be saved. Hence instead of worrying about the timing of the Parousia, people should focus on the righteousness of their own lives. The proper response to a sense of delay in the coming of the kingdom is to live so as to be found "without spot or blemish" when that day does arrive.

The calling upon "our beloved brother Paul" for theological support is a bit unexpected. There are, of course, numerous echoes of Paul's letters in 2 Peter, but until now there has been no expression of direct dependence. Furthermore, there is no place in Paul's known letters that explicitly rehearses the judgment arguments of 2 Peter. The reference to Paul is made more pointed by the assertion that Paul "wrote to you." The usual reading of such a phrase would be that Paul had written a letter directly to this community. Yet Paul's Letters soon escaped their initial destination and became an essential part of the authoritative literature of early Christianity. Thus Paul's writing "to you" could mean that "you," as part of the general Christian population, have read Paul's Letters. Neither reading provides any specific Pauline passage that might be evoked here. This reference to Paul's having written "to you" along with the mention in 3:16 of "all his letters," to which both the readers and the mockers have access, creates the image of a community in which at least some of Paul's Letters are being read and are regarded as having some kind of authority.

Readers have attempted to use these somewhat awkward references to Paul and his Letters to reconstruct more precisely the setting and date of the letter. The naming of Paul as "our beloved brother" instead of "apostle" has provoked lots of speculation. Some commentators suggest that, given the later

Final Exhortation and Doxology

pervasiveness of the title "apostle," the use of "brother" means this letter must be early, perhaps written by Peter himself. Others suggest the opposite, that Peter would not have called Paul "beloved brother" because there was conflict between them. Others point to the pronoun "our," arguing that "our" refers not to the author and the readers but to the college of apostles. There is little persuasiveness in any of this. "Brother" or "beloved brother" are common Christian designations (2 Cor 2:13; Eph 6:21; Phil 2:25; Col 4:7, 9; 1 Pet 5:12) that simply include people in the Christian community. Nothing about dating or authorship can be learned from its presence here. Commentators have also argued that the status of Paul's Letters suggests a certain moment in Christian history. It is argued that 2 Peter can probably be dated in the early stages of the Pauline collection. However, the precise sequences of the collection and usages of Paul's Letters throughout the early Christian world are beyond reconstruction. Furthermore, the references to Paul's Letters in these verses are too general to offer many specifics. For instance, it is not clear how many or which Pauline Letters might be known to the readers.

More interesting are the references to the authority, difficulty, and danger in the Pauline Letters. Second Peter appears to include Paul's Letters among "the writings." The accusation that "the unlearned and unstable twist [Paul's letters] as they do the rest of the writings" has been read by some commentators as maintaining a distinction between Paul's Letters and the official writings. However, this is a rather forced reading of the text. As noted above, it is not possible to identify a precise list of what qualifies as writings and what does not. The writings (including Paul's Letters) are the texts that are not only being read in the community but also have authority. It is not necessary and is probably misleading to import later discussions of the canon or inspiration into 2 Peter. What is clear is that Paul's Letters are regarded as having authority and thus are potentially dangerous. In this regard the assertion that Paul wrote "according to the wisdom that was given him" is somewhat curious because of the indirect phraseology. It must be assumed that it was God who gave Paul wisdom. Wisdom is a standard gift from God (e.g., Eph 1:17; Col 1:9; Jas 1:5) and is the proper virtue for the writing of authoritative texts. There may also be echoes of Paul's frequent reference to "the grace given to me" (Rom 12:3; 15:15; 1 Cor 3:10; Gal 2:9). In any case, the claim is somewhat muted compared to a text like 2 Tim 3:16, which asserts more positively that "all scripture [*graphē*] is inspired by God [*theopneustos*]." The indirect feel of 2 Peter may reflect the dangers that Paul's Letters pose.

Paul's Letters are dangerous because some things in them are "hard to understand," and these difficulties permit the "unlearned and unstable" to "twist" the meaning of the text. It certainly is rather easy for any reader of Paul's Letters to imagine early Christians having difficulty with "some things" in the letters. Almost all readers would agree that in Paul's Letters "some things are hard to understand." Unfortunately, attempts to be more specific have been unpersuasive. Most commentators assume that the "unlearned" and "unstable" include the false teachers in 2:1–22, the mockers in 3:3–4, and the people who listen to them. In 2:14 the false teachers are accused of "ensnaring unstable [*astēriktous*] souls." There is no hint in any of these negative descriptions of these people that they were using readings or misreadings of Pauline texts. Thus it is not clear what parts of Paul are being read or how Paul is being twisted. Commentators have occasionally pointed to later gnostic readings of Paul that advocated antinomianism or realized eschatology. To some extent both readings fit with the characterizations of the false teachers and mockers. The assertion that these twisted readings of Paul lead "to their own destruction" also fits with antinomian tendencies and with denials of judgment. Nevertheless, as is the case throughout the letter, it is not possible to reconstruct the theological or historical context with much confidence. It is best to confine our readings to the explicit claims of the text. Unstable and unlearned people misread Paul. This poses a danger to themselves and to the community.

[17–18] The final closing of most NT Letters includes some combination of a final exhortation, a blessing upon the readers, and a doxology. All of these elements are not always present, and what is present can be ordered in different ways. There is no standard form. Second Peter includes all three elements but does so in a rather abbreviated style. The placement of "you" at the beginning of the sentence, when coupled with the familiar "beloved," signals a rhetorical transition.

As is typical in these closings, there is little new in the warning in 3:17. The point is to summarize and evoke previous argument, not to introduce new ideas. So there is no puzzle about what any of this means. The readers have been warned about the danger of false teachers and mockers. They should now be on guard for the dangers of these people. The character of the attack on these false teachers in 2 Peter suggests that these people were having success in gaining followers in the community. These are people in the community with recognized standing. Thus the letter has not made them go away. The readers must continue to be on guard. The terms used to describe these people ("lawless") and the dangers they pose fit nicely with the earlier imagery in the letter. The final warning of what happens, if being "led away" by these people they "fall away" from their "stability," creates an effective contrast to "unstable" people in 2:14 and 3:16. The readers are presently stable. The false teachers and mockers threaten that stability. Hence the readers must be on guard.

The usual NT blessing in which "grace" is evoked on the readers is here replaced by the imperative to "grow in grace." However, the language of growing in grace and knowledge is familiar in the NT (e.g., 2 Cor 10:15; Eph 4:15; 1 Pet 2:2). The reference here recalls the exhortations in 1:3–11. The Christian life requires growth. The terms "grace" and "knowledge" are common in such

Final Exhortation and Doxology 285

exhortations and blessings. There is no need to specify what this knowledge might be or how grace might be configured. The purpose of these terms is to connect in the most general possible way to the larger imagery of the Christian life.

Although the imagery of the final doxology is standard (apart from the reference to "the day of eternity"), it is unusual in the NT to address a doxology to Christ and not to God. The only other clear instance is Rev 1:5–6. This reference to Christ is all the more striking in a letter that has so few references to Christ. On the other hand, the call to grow in the grace and knowledge of Christ leads naturally to a doxology to Christ.

This conclusion effectively summarizes the rhetoric and mood of the letter. The opening call to the virtues and powers of the Christian life in 1:3–11 is nicely evoked in the call to be found spotless and at peace in 3:14 and in the imperative to grow in grace and knowledge in 3:18. The dangers of the false teachers and mockers (2:1–3:7) are evoked in the misreading of Paul's Letters by the "unlearned and unstable" in 3:16 and in the dangers of being "led away" by these unstable people in 3:17. The promises and threats of judgment (1:11; 2:1–3:13) are recalled in the challenge to "be found without spot or blemish by him" (3:14). Even the promise of "the eternal kingdom of our Lord and Savior Jesus Christ" (1:11) is reinforced in the concluding doxology. The conclusion also effectively rehearses the mood of the letter, moving from challenge, to danger, to promise. In a way, the letter, after all its debate and attack, returns to the sense of surety and celebration with which it began.

INDEX OF ANCIENT SOURCES

OLD TESTAMENT

Genesis
1	268
1:6–7	268
4:1–16	186
6	116
6:1–4	179, 243
6:1–6	112–13
6:4	116
7:11	265, 269
18:12	92
18–19	245

Exodus
12:11	41
15:24	191
16:2–12	191
19:3–8	62
19:5	66
19:6	66
24:3–8	27
29:1	203
34:6	275

Leviticus
1:3	203
1:10	203
17–26	44
17:7	47
19:2	44
19:15	190, 192
19:18	44

Numbers
14:11–12	179
14:27–29	191
16:1–2	186
16:1–50	186
16:11	191
22–24	186, 254

Deuteronomy
9:29	142
10:17	190, 192
18:20	237
21:23	80
23:4–5	186, 254
32:5	79
32:22	270

1 Samuel
12:23	254

1 Chronicles
22:5	60
28:10	60

Nehemiah
9:6	203
9:17	275
13:2	186, 254

Psalms
1:1	195
1:3	188
2:7	232, 233
15:2	203
22:13	150
22:21	150
23:1–4	144
28:9	144
33:6	268
34	23, 99
34:8	57
34:13–17	96
34:16	97
42:10	267
55:22	147, 150
56:13	203
65:5	203
66:9	203
79:9	203
79:10	267
83:18	203
86:10	203
86:15	275
89:26	45
90:4	273, 274, 281
103:8	275
106	179
107:7	254
110:1	114
116:8	203
118	58, 61, 63, 64, 67
118:2	61
118:22	64
119:30	239
121:3–8	203
148:5	268

Proverbs
1:22	195
2:16	254
3:34	147
9:7–8	195
11:31	139
13:14	258
24:23	192
25:14	188
26:11	262
28:21	192

Isaiah
8:12–13	104
8:14	65

Isaiah (continued)

10:11–12	138
11:2	136
13:10	277
17:10	203
28:16	60, 61, 63, 64
30:30	270
33:15	254
34:4	277
40:6–8	52, 53
40:7	50
40:8	51
40:11	144
42:1	233
43:3	203
43:20	66
43:20–21	66
43:21	66
50:9	103
53	84
53:4	85
53:5	85
53:5–6	85
53:7	103
53:9b	84
53:11–12	85
57:20	188
60:19–20	281
60:22	278
65:17	278
66:15–16	270
66:22	278

Jeremiah

2:15	150
6:13	237
8:19	47
10:15	47
14:14	235
23:16	235
32:29	138

Ezekiel

9:1	138
9:5	138
9:6	138
13:3	235
34:2–3	187

Daniel

4:1	25, 169
4:13	179
4:17	179
4:23	179
6:25	169
6:27	51
7:8	191
7:20	191

Hosea

1:6	67
1:9	67
2:1	67
2:25	67

Joel

2:13	275
2:17	267

Amos

5:21–24	95

Jonah

4:2	275

Habakkuk

2:3	274

Zechariah

3:1–5	199
3:2	184, 185, 199
3:3–5	200
13:2	237

Malachi

1:6	45
2:9	192
2:17	267
4:1	270

NEW TESTAMENT

Matthew

3:10	200
5:3–7:27	103
5:10	104
5:11	135
5:18	276
5:20	223
5:22	200, 270
5:23–24	95
5:38–42	98
5:44	21, 76, 99, 128
5:48	44
6:25	147
6:25–34	149
7:15–20	42
7:16–20	188
10:1–4	161
10:6	144
11:3	278
12:45	261
13:35	48
13:55	161, 169
15:14	222
16:27	191
17:5	233
18:3	223
18:8–9	270
18:9	200
19:28	278
20:25	145
21:32	261
21:42	61, 64, 281
22:34–40	44
23:16	222
24:11	237
24:24	237
24:35	276
24:42	150
24:43–44	276
25:31	191
25:31–46	123, 239
25:34	48
25:41	200, 270
25:44	240

Mark

1:30	155
3:16–19	161
4:2	277
6:3	161, 169
8:38	137
9:1	232
9:42–48	261
9:48	270
10:23	223
10:42	145
12:10	61
12:10–11	64
12:28–31	44
13:5–6	194
13:21–22	194
13:22	237, 238

Index of Ancient Sources

13:24–25	277	2:9	26	8:21	260
13:31	276	2:14–20	14	8:34	114
13:35	150	2:32–36	14	9:5	215
13:37	150	2:34	114	9:25–26	67
14:62	114	2:39	14	9:32–33	14, 63
Luke		2:40	79	9:33	61, 65
1:33	223	3:19–20	278	11:32	275
1:47	203	4:11	61	12:1	62
3:9	188	5:30	80	12:2	14, 43
4:21	281	8:32	281	12:3	283
6:16	161, 169	9:2	239, 254	12:6	14, 129
6:22	135	10:34	14	12:6–8	129, 130
6:29–30	98	10:39	80	12:9–21	79
6:32	81	11:26	137	12:14–17	96
7:19–20	278	12:12	156	12:16	98
8:17	277	12:25	156	12:16–17	14
10:25–28	44	13:29	80	13:1–7	14
11:26	261	14:15	47	13:11	79
11:50	48	15:14	213	13:12	56
12:22–32	149	15:22	154, 162	15:5	98
12:35	41	15:23	169	15:8	223
12:39–40	276	15:27	154, 162	15:15	225, 283
12:49	270	15:32	162	16:16	156
13:9	188	15:37	156	16:22	154
16:17	276	15:39	156	16:25–27	201
17:29	270	17:31	123	16:27	202, 203
18:17	223	19:9	239	**1 Corinthians**	
20:17	61, 64	19:23	239, 254	1:8	223
20:21	192	20:17	143	2:7–16	185
21:33	276	20:17–35	141	2:14–15	193, 195
22:25	145	20:29–30	194	3:10	283
23:42	223	23:26	169	3:10–14	198
24:21	46	24:14	239, 254	3:11	198
24:34	226	24:22	239	3:13	277
John		26:28	137	4:17	154, 156
1:1	215	**Romans**		6:3	183
3:5	223	1:1	215	6:20	131
9:40–41	222	1:21	47	7:22–23	170
10:1–18	144	2:4	275	9:7	187
13:36	226	2:19	222	9:9	155, 162
17:3	203	3:24–25	47	10:11	127
17:11	203	4:3	281	10:31	131
17:24	48	4:16	223	11:19	237
20:28	215	5:3	82	11:20–29	95
21:16	187	5:3–5	217	12:4–11	129
21:18–19	226	5:8	80	12:7–11	130
Acts		6:16	260	13	76
1:10–11	114	6:17	50	13:13	200
		8:19–23	278	15:1	225

Index of Ancient Sources

1 Corinthians (*continued*)
15:3	80
15:5	226
15:24	114
15:53–54	226
15:58	46
16:20	156
16:21	154

2 Corinthians
1:3	30
1:3–7	152
1:19	155
2:5–8	201
2:13	283
5:1–4	226
5:3–4	226
8:16–19	154
10:3–5	120
10:15	284
13:12	156

Galatians
2:8	8
2:9	283
3:13	80
4:3	277
5:19–21	121
5:20	237
5:22–23	217
6:7	252
6:11	154

Ephesians
1:3	14, 30
1:4	48, 203
1:17	283
1:18	14
1:20–22	14
1:21	114
2:2–3	14
2:20	198
2:20–22	14
3:5	14
3:20–21	201
4:2–3	79
4:11	187
4:15	284
4:17	47
4:22	56
4:25	56

5:13	277
5:21–6:9	77
5:27	203
6:8	46
6:9	46
6:11–17	120
6:21	283
6:21–22	154

Philippians
2:2	98
2:12–13	32
2:15	79
2:22	156
2:25	283
4:2	98
4:20	201

Colossians
1:9	283
1:13	223
1:22	203
2:8	277
2:10	114
2:11	226
2:20	277
3:5–8	121
3:8	56
3:9–10	226
3:12–17	79
3:18–4:1	77
3:24	46
4:1	46
4:7	283
4:7–9	154
4:9	283
4:10	156
4:18	154

1 Thessalonians
1:1	155
1:3	200
2:14	152
3:13	203
4:13–18	124
5:2	276
5:6	147, 150
5:8	150
5:11	198
5:26	156

2 Thessalonians
1:1	155
1:7	191
1:12	215
2:1–12	238
3:3	203
3:17	154

1 Timothy
1:1	203
1:2	156
1:15	201
1:17	203
1:18	156
2:3	203
2:8–15	77
2:9–11	91
3:1–7	141, 217
3:8–13	141
4:1–3	194
4:10	203
5:1–6:2	77
5:17–19	141, 143
5:18	281
6:1	79
6:20	134, 175, 200

Titus
1:1	215
1:4	156
1:5	143
1:5–6	141
1:7–9	141
1:16	176
2:1–10	77
2:9	79
2:13	215
2:14	46
3:1–2	77

Philemon
24	156

Hebrews
1:2	49
1:8–9	215
1:13	114
2:7	183, 232
2:9	232
5:12	58
9:12	47
9:14	282

Index of Ancient Sources

9:24	110	1:16	21, 62	2:21	20, 27, 64, 70, 99, 111, 134, 135, 153
11:1	35	1:16–17	27, 76		
12:1	56	1:17	14, 22, 32, 57, 58, 81, 93, 101, 123, 139, 147	2:21–24	125
12:23	112			2:21–25	72, 73, 110, 111, 146
12:29	270				
13:5	79	1:18	9, 54, 86	2:22	112
13:20–21	201	1:18–19	20, 27, 34	2:22–23	11, 17, 98
		1:18–21	30	2:23	11, 20, 22, 93, 99, 123
James		1:19	17		
1:5	283	1:21	14, 22	2:25	10, 17
1:21	56	1:22	22, 34, 44, 56, 57, 128	3:1	22, 70, 136
2:1–9	192			3:1–2	11, 20, 63, 105
2:10	223	1:22–25	50–54	3:1–6	70, 86
3:1	46	1:23	30	3:1–7	78, 87–95
3:2	223	1:23–25	55, 65	3:4	17
4:6–10	147	1:25	22	3:6	9, 11
5:20	127	2:1–2	45	3:7	70
		2:1–3	55–58	3:8–9	14
1 Peter		2:2	18, 30, 56	3:8–12	95–101
1:1	7, 143, 153	2:2–23	96	3:9	11, 18, 153
1:1–2	17, 25–27	2:3	46, 60	3:10–12	57
1:2	42, 47	2:4–6	14	3:13	83
1:3	14, 18, 20, 22, 52, 56	2:4–10	55, 58–67	3:13–16	117
1:3–5	14, 20	2:6–8	14	3:13–17	96, 101–7, 110
1:3–7	151	2:9	21, 43	3:13–18	11, 18
1:3–12	17, 28–39, 41	2:9–10	30	3:14	135
1:3–4:11	18	2:10	9, 21	3:15	11, 90
1:4	17, 22, 54, 100, 140	2:11	10, 20, 76, 89	3:15–16	136
1		2:11–12	56, 67–70, 126	3:16	11, 20, 63, 70, 90, 93, 136
1:4–5	125, 131	2:11–17	94		
1:5	22, 23	2:11–3:7	78, 96, 98	3:17	136
1:5–6	83	2:11–4:6	89	3:17–18	83
1:6	99, 134	2:11–4:11	62, 68, 134	3:18	17
1:6–7	11, 18, 132, 135, 140, 144	2:12	9, 11, 20, 90, 93, 105–6, 131, 136	3:18–22	107–16
				3:19	123, 124
1:7	22, 86, 131, 133	2:13	55	3:20	22, 112
1:8	17	2:13–17	14, 70–77	3:21	18, 105
1:9	22	2:14	17, 83	3:22	14, 72, 117, 135
1:10	17, 22	2:15	20, 105	4:1	83, 97
1:10–12	14	2:15–3:7	10	4:1–3	131
1:11	8, 48, 144	2:17	20, 34, 81, 128	4:1–4	11, 18
1:12	54	2:18	88	4:1–6	56, 117–25, 127, 139
1:13	59	2:18–20	70		
1:13–21	39–49	2:18–23	18	4:2–4	9, 11, 12, 20, 69
1:14	9, 14, 20, 27, 51, 62, 74, 86	2:18–24	119, 120	4:3	9, 42, 86, 128
		2:18–25	77–87	4:3–4	41, 135
1:14–17	104	2:18–3:7	59, 68	4:4	11, 136
1:15	18, 51, 66	2:19	105, 112	4:5	22
1:15–16	32, 90	2:19–20	135	4:6	17
1:15–17	90	2:20	99, 136	4:7	132

Index of Ancient Sources

1 Peter (continued)		1:16–18	144, 214, 236, 262	3:12	236
4:7–11	126–31	1:16–21	225, 228–35, 266	3:13	224, 246, 261, 266, 281
4:8	34	1:16–3:13	211	3:14–18	211, 280–85
4:10–11	14	1:19	223	3:18	215
4:11	17, 18, 68, 131	1:19–21	215, 236	**2 John**	
4:12	18, 76, 84, 86, 134, 137, 151	2:1	235, 247	1	143
4:12–19	11, 18, 22, 56, 117, 131–40, 143	2:1–3	236–40	13	155
4:12–5:11	18, 131, 134	2:1–18	207	**3 John**	
4:13	32, 33, 83, 144	2:1–22	284	1	143
4:14	11, 13, 103, 144	2:1–3:7	285		
4:15	11	2:2	250, 261	**Jude**	
4:16	11, 13, 131	2:3	246, 253	1	191
4:17	23, 33, 127	2:4	116, 269	1–2	169–72
4:17–18	22	2:4–10a	240–48	3	162, 165, 175, 198
4:19	123	2:4–22	236, 237	3–4	166, 172–76
5:1	26, 33, 131	2:5	261	4	163, 166, 174, 175, 179, 180, 181, 183, 186, 191
5:1–4	10	2:9	269		
5:1–5	140–47	2:10a	250, 253		
5:2	10	2:10b	247		
5:2–3	17	2:10b–16	248–55	4–13	207
5:4	26, 131, 151	2:14	284	4–16	175
5:5	149	2:15	239	5	191
5:5b	17	2:17	269	5–7	177–81, 183
5:6–11	17, 141, 147–53	2:17–22	255–63	5–11	175
5:8–10	11, 18	2:18	250	5–16	177
5:9	33	2:19	240, 250	6	116, 171, 176, 180, 243
5:10	22, 43, 131	2:20	215, 250		
5:12	8, 39	2:21	239, 266	7	163, 180
5:12–14	17, 153–57	3:1	213, 272	7–8	246
5:13	27	3:1–3	207	8	163, 176
		3:1–7	263–71	8–13	181–89
2 Peter		3:1–13	235, 260, 263	10	195
1:1	261, 267	3:1–16	271	11	180
1:1–2	213–16	3:1–18	246	12	252–53
1:3	215, 250	3:3	49, 194, 236	12–16	256, 258
1:3–4	260	3:3–4	231, 284	13	171
1:3–11	211, 216–24, 225–26, 227, 228, 235, 246, 258, 259, 284, 285	3:4	232, 274, 278, 279	14–15	174
		3:5	273, 279	14–16	189–92
		3:5–6	276	14b–15	165
		3:5–7	274, 279	16	163
1:5	215	3:5–13	282	16–18	207
1:5–8	250	3:7	236, 276	17	162, 165, 175, 198, 200, 266
1:6	215	3:8–13	271–79		
1:8	215	3:8–16	264	17–19	192–96
1:11	285	3:9	212	17–23	163, 174
1:12–15	216, 224–28	3:10	236	18	49
1:16	215, 239, 267, 278	3:11	281	19	163, 198
		3:11–16	272	20–22	194

Index of Ancient Sources

20–23	166, 174, 196–201	12:35	143	*2 Enoch*		
				7.1–3	112, 117	
21	171	*4 Ezra* (**2 Esdras**)		*Jubilees*		
24	171, 174	3.14	49	7.21	112	
24–25	191, 201–4	7.75	278	10.1–9	112	
		12.9	49			

Revelation

1:4	204	4 Maccabees	84	*Sibylline Oracles*	
1:5–6	285			1.125–280	269
1:6	131	**PSEUDEPIGRAPHA**		1.129	244
1:8	204				
3:3	276	*2 Baruch*		*Testament of Moses*	
3:10	203	78.2	25	5.5	192
3:17	222			7.9	191
4:8	204	*1 Enoch*			
11:17	204	1.2	190	**JEWISH LITERATURE**	
13:8	48	1.8	191		
14:8	156	1.9	166, 189, 190, 192, 198	**JOSEPHUS**	
16:3	237			*Antiquities*	
16:15	276	2.1–5.4	188	1.74	244
17:5	156	6	116	1.73	117
18:2	156	6–7	116		
18:10	156	8–9	116	**QUMRAN**	
18:21	156	10	116	CD 1.14	195
19:20	237	10.1–11.2	268		
20:9–15	270	10.12	116	**RABBINIC**	
20:10	237	12.4–6	109, 116	*b. Sanh.*	
20:11–15	240	13.1–2	116	108	244
20:15	200	13.1–3	116	97b–98a	275, 278
21–22	278	13.1–10	109		
		14.5	116	*y. Ta'an.*	
APOCRYPHA		15.1–16.3	116	1.1	278
Tobit		18.12–14	109	*Num. Rab.*	
14:5	60	18.13–16	188	18.3	186
		21	117		
Wisdom of Solomon		21.3–6	188	*Syriac Ahiqar*	
5:6	239	45.4–5	278	8.18	262
6:17–20	217	46.6	188		
10	241	54	116	*Targum of Pseudo-Jonathan*	
10:6	245	56.1–2	116	Num 16:1–2	186
14:25–27	121	60.8	189		
		63.6	188	*Testament of Levi*	
Sirach		67.2	113	3.3	117
7:1–22	121	67.4	117		
16	241	67.7	117	**GRECO-ROMAN LITERATURE**	
24:23–31	258	72.1	278		
35:19	274	80.2–8	188		
36:10	278	83.3–9	268	**ARISTOTLE**	
		88.1	116, 188		
1 Maccabees		91.16	278	*Pol.*	
11:23	143	93.3	189	1.5.8	90

DEMOSTHENES

Or.
60.30 — 251

DIO CASSIUS

Roman History
52.36 — 47

DIO CHRYSOSTOM

Or.
39.2 — 73

DIOGENES LAERTIUS

Hist. phil.
7.134 — 269

EPICTETUS

Ench.
40 — 91

HORACE

Epodes
1.2.26 — 262

LUCRETIUS

De rerum natura
5 — 270

PAPYRUS OXYRYNCHUS

840.33–34 — 262

PHILO

Leg.
1.64 — 217

On the Life of Moses
1.118 — 191
1.264–300 — 186, 254

Sacr.
27 — 217

PLATO

Apol. — 84

Tim.
22C–E — 270

PLINY THE YOUNGER

Pan.
70.7 — 73
83.7 — 91

SEXTUS EMPIRICUS

Pyr.
1.14.56 — 262

SOPHOCLES

Ajax
293 — 90

TACITUS

Ann.
15.44 — 12

XENOPHON

Anab.
5.7.32 — 251

Oec.
9.14 — 73

EARLY CHRISTIAN WRITINGS

1 Clement
7.6 — 14
9.3–4 — 14
21.7 — 14
23.3 — 264, 268
49.5 — 14

2 Clement
11.2 — 264, 268
12.6 — 278
16.4 — 127

Acts of Peter — 8
Acts of Peter and Andrew — 8
Acts of Peter and Paul — 8

Acts of Thomas
31 — 162
39 — 162

Apocalypse of Peter — 8

Apostolic Constitutions
7.46 — 161

Barnabas
2.2–3 — 217
5.5 — 48
6.4 — 64
15.4 — 274
19.4 — 192

CLEMENT OF ALEXANDRIA
— 184

Strom.
7.11 — 155

DIDACHE
4.3 — 192
16.1 — 276
16.3 — 237

EPIPHANIUS

Pan.
31.7 — 195

EUSEBIUS

Historia Ecclesiastica
1.13.11 — 162
3.3.1–4 — 207
3.25.3 — 207
3.39.15–16 — 227
4.5.3 — 162

GOSPEL OF PETER — 8

GOSPEL OF THOMAS — 162
95 — 98

HERMAS

Mandates
6.1.1 — 217
8.9 — 217

Similitudes
9.17.5–18.2 — 261
10.4.4 — 278

Index of Ancient Sources

Visions
1.3.4   268
3.8.7   217

HIPPOLYTUS

Trad. Ap.
21   56

IRENAEUS

Haer.
1.6.1ff.   195
3.1.1   227

3.3.2–3   156

LETTER OF PETER TO PHILIP
8

MARTYRDOM OF POLYCARP
21   201

ORIGEN

Comm. Jo.
5.3   207

De Princ.   184

POLYCARP

Phil.
1.3   14
8.1   14

SLAVONIC ACTS OF PETER   8

INDEX OF SUBJECTS

Abraham, 9, 88, 92, 245
abuse, 2, 9, 11, 13, 19–22, 27, 31, 38, 56, 67, 70, 73, 77–79, 82–85, 95–97, 99–100, 103–7, 117, 123–26, 131, 133, 135–38, 140, 144–45, 147, 149–53, 183, 190
affection, 50, 52–53, 56, 217–18, 220–21
alien, 10–11, 19, 21, 25, 41, 46, 67–70, 78, 96, 139
angels, 22, 28–29, 38, 43, 54, 108–9, 112–17, 135, 163, 171, 177–81, 183–85, 190–91, 199, 202, 209, 232, 240–52, 254, 269, 277
antinomian, 163–64, 170, 184, 186, 191, 284
apocalyptic, 36, 48, 116, 162, 164–65, 210, 264, 277, 279
apology, 37, 83, 105
apostasy, 255–57, 260–63
apostles, 7, 25–26, 143, 162, 165–66, 171–72, 192–94, 196, 198, 211, 214–16, 220, 227–28, 231, 233, 235–36, 239, 264, 266–67, 282–83

babes, 30, 45, 54, 56–58
Balaam, 165, 181, 186–88, 239, 248–51, 253–55
baptism, 18, 43, 53–54, 56, 108, 110, 113–15, 222
baptismal homily, 18, 43, 53, 56
beatitude, 103–4, 135–36
beloved, 18, 68, 76, 131–32, 134, 166, 172–73, 192–200, 202–4, 229, 233, 264, 272, 280, 282–84
blessing, 17, 19–20, 25–28, 30–36, 38–39, 49, 68, 82, 95–97, 99–101, 104, 107, 130, 134–36, 151, 153–54, 169, 171–73, 191, 198, 201, 213, 215–16, 218, 223–24, 280, 284–85
blood, 20, 25, 27, 34, 40–41, 47–49, 52, 186

Cain, 163, 165, 181, 186–88, 201, 248
called (calling), 20–22, 26–27, 40, 43–45, 49, 52, 59, 62, 66, 69, 72, 77, 79, 83–84, 87, 89, 93–94, 97, 99, 101, 118, 120–21, 125, 128, 131, 137, 139, 142, 146, 148, 151–52, 169, 171–72, 174, 179, 198, 211, 217, 219–20, 222–23, 279
"Christian" name, 12–13, 136–37
collegia, 12–13, 122, 125
commandment, 44, 256, 258–59, 262, 264–66
community, 2, 9–10, 13, 19, 21, 32, 45–46, 53, 56, 60, 71, 75–76, 89, 96–98, 115, 126, 128–31, 140–41, 143–46, 148–49, 155–56, 164, 172, 174, 177, 181, 187, 189, 192–93, 195–96, 198–99, 201, 209, 221, 228, 236, 238, 240, 247, 253, 255–56, 260, 263, 266, 270, 280, 282–84
conflict, 2–3, 73, 77, 96, 99, 111, 118, 120–21
crucifixion, 37, 85, 109, 111–12, 115, 144, 282

day of the Lord, 74, 212, 217, 223, 229–30, 234–35, 272, 277–79
day, 230, 234, 276, 278–79
day of eternity, 280–81, 285
day of God, 272, 278
day of judgment, 46, 117, 193, 241, 246, 252, 264, 274–76, 279
day of visitation, 68, 70, 74, 106
final day, 41, 138, 269
great day, 116, 177, 180
last day, 46, 48, 70, 106, 146, 149, 193, 246, 264, 267, 270
devil, 147–52, 181–82, 184–85
disobedience, 65–66, 109, 113, 176, 187, 241, 275
Domitian, 12–14
doxology, 18, 126, 130–31, 165, 201–204, 211, 280–81, 284–85

Egypt, 48, 163–65, 177, 241
elders, 10, 140–47
elect (election), 7, 9, 25–27, 33–34, 36, 38, 66, 93, 138–39, 153–56, 191, 198–99, 217, 222
emperors, 12–14, 70–76, 128
  See also individual names of emperors
Enoch, 109, 112, 116–17, 165, 179, 189–90, 208, 256
Epicureanism, 210
ethics, 20–22, 32, 34, 39, 44, 46, 49–51, 53, 56, 68, 78, 86, 93–95, 104, 119–20, 126, 128, 176, 211, 220, 239, 256, 258, 260–62, 282
evil (evildoer), 11, 21, 55–56, 68, 71, 73, 75, 95, 97, 99–100, 103, 114–16, 132, 136, 150, 155, 179, 183, 250–52, 279
example (as a paradigm), 2, 83–84, 92, 99, 105, 112, 117, 120, 141, 145–46, 177–81, 183–84, 187, 210, 226, 237, 240–44, 246, 248, 255, 262

faith, 22, 28–29, 31–36, 38, 68, 83–84, 86, 93, 100–101, 117, 125, 129, 135, 137, 143, 148, 150, 152, 162, 165–66, 172–74, 196–98, 200, 213–18, 220–21, 261, 263
faithful, 17, 22, 31, 41, 123, 132, 139–40, 153, 155, 221, 264
false teachers, 209–11, 236, 238–40, 243, 246, 248, 252–56, 258–61, 263, 266, 280–81, 284–85
Father, God as, 22, 28, 30, 40, 42, 44–46, 53–55, 57–58, 62, 169, 171, 198, 229, 232
fear, 12, 87–88, 90, 93–94, 102, 104–5, 107, 197, 200, 250–51, 262
fear, of God, 22, 32, 40, 46, 49, 57, 71, 75–76, 81, 87, 90, 96, 102, 104–5, 197, 200, 248, 250–51
feasts, 118, 121–22, 163–64, 182, 187, 248, 252–53, 280
flesh, 10, 50, 54, 68–70, 108–9, 111, 114, 118–21, 124–25, 177–78, 180–81, 183, 186, 197, 200, 211, 226, 240–41, 246–47, 250, 253, 256–59
flood, 112–16, 241, 243–44, 246, 264–65, 268–69, 271
  See also water
foreknowledge of God, 25–27, 48

free (freedom), 65–66, 71, 73–75, 86, 119–20, 176, 209–10, 238, 240, 250, 256, 258–60, 263

Gentile life (former life), 11, 42–43, 56, 117–25
Gentiles, 8–12, 21–22, 26, 46, 68–73, 77, 85, 89–90, 95–96, 99, 105–6, 117–25, 128, 134, 145, 152, 162, 165
gifts (spiritual), 129–32, 171, 195, 218–19, 222–23, 246, 250
glorious ones, 163, 180–83, 185, 247–51
glory, 22, 26, 28–29, 31, 33–35, 38, 40, 49–50, 53–54, 67, 106–7, 111, 117, 125–26, 131–33, 135–37, 140–42, 144, 146–47, 151–53, 155, 171, 191, 201–4, 217–19, 229, 232–35, 249, 280
gnostics, 1, 163–64, 195, 231, 259, 284
good behavior (doing good), 11, 20–22, 62, 68, 70–71, 73–75, 77–79, 82–84, 88, 90, 93–97, 100–7, 117–19, 131–36, 139–40, 143, 219, 221, 239
gospel (good news), 26, 28, 29–30, 38, 46, 54, 65–66, 81, 95, 105, 112, 118, 123–25, 132, 138–39, 155, 215–16, 219, 221–22, 226–28, 248, 266, 270
grace, 22, 25–26, 29–30, 36–37, 39–41, 46, 49, 51, 77–79, 81–82, 84, 88–89, 94, 99, 106, 126, 129–30, 138, 141, 148, 151, 153–55, 157, 173–76, 178, 181, 213, 215, 280–81, 283–85
grief, 33, 35, 79, 81–82

heresy, 236–40, 258, 263
heretic, 2, 175, 186–87, 200, 256
holiness, 9, 19, 21–23, 27, 39–55, 62, 65–66, 76, 90, 104–5, 122, 139–40, 157, 204, 247, 253, 260, 262
holy, 18, 20–23, 32, 39–55, 59–63, 66–67, 69, 74, 76, 87–88, 90, 92–93, 104, 113, 131, 138, 140, 147, 149, 156, 189–90, 197–98, 200, 229, 233, 236, 253, 255–56, 258–59, 262, 264, 270, 272, 279, 281
Holy Spirit, 29, 91–92, 197–98, 229, 232, 234–35
honor, 10, 19, 21, 23, 29, 33–35, 59, 61, 63–64, 71, 75–76, 78–79, 81, 87–95, 98–99, 106, 128, 142–43, 146, 213–16, 218, 229, 232, 234

Index of Subjects

hope, 11, 20, 22, 28, 30–32, 34–35, 38, 40–42, 46, 49, 54, 76, 88, 92–93, 96, 100, 102, 105, 117, 124, 196, 198, 200
hospitality, 126, 129, 131, 245
household, 10, 46, 59, 62, 71, 73, 77–78, 80–81, 86–87, 89, 94–95, 127, 129–31, 140, 218, 221
humble, 97–98, 140–41, 147–49
humility, 98, 105, 140–41, 145–47, 149–50
husbands, 10, 19, 65, 70, 72, 77–78, 87–95

idolatry, 20, 122, 125, 128
impious, 132, 139, 163, 165–66, 171–204, 208–9, 223, 241–46, 264, 267, 269
inheritance, 20, 22, 29, 31–35, 38, 41–42, 46, 54, 66, 125, 131, 139–40, 246
injustice. *See* justice
intruders, 163–64, 177, 180–83, 198

James, 161–65, 169–70, 172
Judas (Jude), 161–62, 169
judgment, 22–23, 27, 34, 40, 45–46, 58, 65, 70, 76, 101, 107, 113, 116–19, 122–27, 131–40, 147, 164–66, 173–77, 180–82, 184, 186, 189–93, 197–200, 203, 210, 212, 216, 232, 236–37, 239–52, 255–56, 260–61, 263–65, 267–79, 281–82, 284–85
justice, 44, 46, 63, 71–73, 82, 84, 92, 101, 107, 125, 138–39, 198, 210, 212–15, 240, 246, 252, 257, 261, 268, 271, 275, 279

keeping (kept), 20, 29, 31, 34, 42, 46, 49, 54, 55, 59, 66, 100, 116, 125, 140, 169, 171–74, 176–78, 180, 182, 187, 198, 202, 241, 246, 254, 258, 264, 269–70
kiss of love, 152–57
knowledge, 35, 43, 47, 213–22, 256–57, 260–61, 263, 280–81, 284–85
Korah, 163, 165, 182, 186–88, 191, 201, 248

lords, 70, 72, 75, 77
Lot, 241–46
love, 21–22, 29, 34–35, 42, 44, 50, 52–54, 56, 65, 68, 71, 76, 81, 97–98, 100, 126–29, 131, 166, 169, 171–75, 197–202, 217, 220–21, 249–50

master, 10, 77–81, 86, 173, 185, 238, 247

Master (Jesus), 163, 173, 176, 181, 183, 209, 236, 238, 240
meals. *See* feasts
mercy, 28, 30, 38, 46, 59, 67, 70, 76, 166, 169, 171–72, 174, 196–201, 204, 212, 271, 275, 279
Michael, 181–82, 184–85, 199, 248
milk, 30, 45, 52, 54–58, 60
mockers, 193–95, 209–10, 217, 228, 236, 264, 267–68, 270–71, 273–74, 279, 281–82, 284–85
Mother, God as, 45, 52, 54–55, 57–58, 62
myth, 116, 229–31, 236, 239, 242

name-calling (naming), 172–75, 186, 250
Nephilim, 116, 243
Nero, 12
new birth, 30, 32, 41, 54–55
See also rebirth
new life, 20, 34, 42, 44, 53–54, 75, 258
Noah, 108, 112–13, 241–42, 244, 246, 261, 269, 271

obedience, 22, 25, 27, 40, 42, 44, 47–48, 50–51, 53–54, 57, 74, 88, 92, 104, 113, 215, 260–62, 266
oracles, 1, 37, 126–27, 130
outsiders, 3, 25–26, 31–32, 62, 67, 69, 72–74, 76, 84, 87, 89, 96–97, 106, 126, 128, 131, 136–38, 140, 143, 147, 149, 164, 176, 238–39
overseer, 10, 79, 86, 133, 146

Parousia, 121, 148, 210, 212, 228–33, 235, 238, 240, 247–48, 259–60, 264–65, 271, 282
passions, 20, 40, 42–44, 54, 56, 69, 93, 121, 139, 183, 210–11, 219–22, 259, 264, 266–67
Paul, apostle, 1–2, 8, 16, 25–26, 63–67, 76, 81–82, 85, 98, 129, 141, 152–57, 162, 169–70, 194–95, 201, 215, 223, 226, 237, 252, 260, 275, 280–85
persecution, 2, 8–9, 11–14, 16–18, 20, 27, 73, 84, 93, 95, 106, 118, 138–43, 146, 148–50, 152, 157, 221
Pliny, 12, 14, 26
prayer, 30, 88–89, 94–95, 97, 99, 110, 116–17, 126, 128, 150, 169, 172, 197–200, 202, 204, 213, 216

priests (priesthood), 21, 45, 49, 58–62, 66–67, 109, 186, 202–3
promise, 22, 27, 31, 38, 45, 92–94, 103, 107, 114, 117, 125, 127, 136, 147, 151–52, 166, 171, 176, 189, 209–10, 212, 216–20, 222–23, 232, 235–36, 238, 240, 245, 256–61, 263–64, 267–70, 272, 274, 279, 285
prophecy, 1, 30, 36–37, 136, 165, 189–96, 228–35, 254, 267
prophets, 1, 23, 28–31, 36–38, 44–45, 48, 54, 104, 138, 155, 190, 196, 211, 217, 223, 228–30, 232–38, 240, 242, 247, 249, 251, 264–67, 270, 281
punishment, 12, 65, 70, 73, 116–17, 122–23, 138, 165, 171–72, 177–81, 186, 197–98, 209–10, 236, 240–46, 252, 255, 258–60, 263, 269–70, 279

rebirth, 29–31, 38, 42, 52–54, 56, 59, 278
 See also new birth
rejoice (rejoicing), 29, 32–35, 133, 135, 202–3
resurrection, 20, 26–28, 30–31, 34–35, 38, 41, 65, 76, 108–9, 111–115, 125, 226
righteous, 20, 84–87, 89, 92, 97, 100, 103, 108, 110–11, 132, 138–39, 147, 164, 188, 203, 212, 222–24, 241, 243–47, 252, 255, 262, 269, 271, 275, 278–79, 281
righteousness, 44–45, 79–80, 85, 100–105, 107, 119, 136, 139, 188, 212, 214–15, 222, 224, 239, 241, 244, 246, 254, 257, 260–63, 266, 271–72, 277–79, 281–82

salvation, 22, 27, 29, 32, 34–38, 41, 43, 46, 49, 55, 57–58, 60–61, 65, 67, 69, 83–84, 86, 92–95, 120, 122, 125, 134, 151, 166, 173–74, 198–201, 203, 216, 223–24, 228, 246, 280, 282
Sarah, 9, 88, 92–93
Savior, 202–3, 213–14, 215, 217, 235, 245, 256, 263–65, 280–81, 285
Scripture, 23, 36, 38, 44–45, 53–54, 59–60, 63, 65, 171, 177, 229, 233–35, 246–48, 255, 281, 283
 See also writings
second coming. *See* Parousia
serve, 127, 129–30, 147, 149
shame, 59, 63–64, 75, 98–99, 102, 105–7, 132, 137, 141, 145, 182, 188–89

shepherd, 79, 85, 86, 141–47, 163, 182, 187–88, 192, 196, 252
silence (silent), 71–74, 84, 87, 90–92, 105, 136
Silvanus, 8, 15–16, 153–55, 157
Simeon, 213–14
Simon, 208, 213–14, 216
sin, 69, 78–79, 80, 82, 84–85, 108, 110–11, 114–15, 118–20, 126, 128–29, 131, 178, 180–81, 186, 190, 200, 203–4, 217, 222, 241, 243–44, 248–49, 254–56, 260, 263
slave (slaves, slavery), 46, 70–71, 73–75, 77–78, 80–81, 86, 94–96, 98–99, 127, 143, 146–47, 149, 170, 173, 209, 211, 213, 215, 238, 255–57, 263
Sodom and Gomorrah, 163, 165, 177–78, 180, 201, 209, 240–41, 244–47, 269–70
sojourner, 9–11, 19, 21, 25–26, 67–70
spirit, 30, 87–88, 91–92, 108–9, 111, 119, 195, 261
Spirit (of God, of Christ), 20, 25, 27, 29, 37–38, 50, 109, 111–12, 118, 123–25, 133, 136, 140, 144, 163, 185, 193–96, 198–99
 See also Holy Spirit
stoicism, 121, 193, 270, 277
stone, 55, 58–67, 275
submission, 19, 34, 70–95, 102–3, 146–49, 191, 195, 248
suffering, 8, 11, 13, 18–23, 26–35, 37–39, 42, 44, 48, 54, 62–64, 67, 69, 73, 77–87, 89–90, 92, 95–96, 98–122, 126–27, 131–40, 141–42, 144, 147–53, 155, 180, 221, 248–49, 252, 277

temple, 12, 48, 62–63, 65, 67, 111, 138, 253, 262
temptation, 20, 23, 33, 38, 134, 137–38, 140, 148, 150, 199, 203–4, 243, 253
 See also test; trial
test, 20, 23, 29, 33, 38, 132–34, 137–38, 140, 243
 See also temptation; trial
testament, 210–11, 213, 224–28
Trajan, 12, 14, 26
transfiguration, 144, 214, 216, 225, 228–29, 231–35, 248
trial, 23, 29, 33, 99, 138, 241, 243, 246
 See also temptation; test

Index of Subjects

trust, 32, 35, 40–42, 49, 53–54, 59, 63–66, 85, 87, 92–93, 99, 105, 125, 139, 148

vice, 12, 21–22, 56, 58, 82, 86, 98, 120–22, 125, 136, 183, 186, 212, 220, 255, 259

violence, 12–13, 32, 63, 69, 90, 93–96, 103, 116, 142, 174

virtue, 21–22, 34, 42–43, 56, 59–60, 66, 70, 78, 84–86, 90–91, 96–98, 100–101, 120–21, 125–26, 128–31, 133, 150, 152, 197, 211–12, 216–24, 246, 250, 254, 258–59, 282–83, 285

watchers, 116, 179

water, 108, 110, 113–15, 117, 163, 182, 187–88, 201, 209, 244, 256–58, 263–65, 268–71, 276

witness, 8, 62, 69, 72–74, 90–91, 95, 105, 141–42, 144, 210, 214, 216, 228–29, 231–35, 248, 262, 267

wives, 10, 19, 65, 70, 77–78, 80, 87–95, 105, 113, 116, 136, 140, 146, 155, 244

Word (of God), 19, 22, 38, 50–54, 55–58, 59, 65–66, 77, 87, 89, 95, 130, 138, 172, 264–65, 268–71, 277, 279

writings, 63, 235, 280–81, 283
See also Scripture

young persons, 140, 142, 146–47

www.ingramcontent.com/pod-product-compliance
Lightning Source LLC
Chambersburg PA
CBHW032028290426
44110CB00012B/711